SYMBOLISM

An International Annual of Critical Aesthetics

SYMBOLISM

An International Annual of Critical Aesthetics

Volume 6

Rüdiger Ahrens
Klaus Stierstorfer
Editors

2006

AMS PRESS
NEW YORK

SYMBOLISM

Volume 6

ISSN 1528-3623
Set ISBN-10: 0-404-63560-1
Set ISBN-13: 978-0-404-63560-2
Volume 6 ISBN-10: 0-404-63566-0
Volume 6 ISBN-13: 978-0-404-63566-4

AMS PRESS, INC.
Brooklyn Navy Yard, 63 Flushing Avenue–Unit #221
Brooklyn, NY 11205-1005, USA

MANUFACTURED IN THE UNITED STATES OF AMERICA

CONTENTS

GENERAL SECTION

BOOK REVIEWS

Foreword

After five volumes of *Symbolism*, filled with intense discussions of signifying practices and textuality, and opening various trajectories in the study of symbolic functions in a large number of fields, the focus of the sixth volume in a sense returns to the underlying fundamentals of these studies. Its inquiry into recent developments in the discussion on representation and mimesis clearly projects the wider framework within which negotiations on various forms of symbolism are embedded and with which they generally share the ups and downs in critical thought. Symbolic practices are forms of representation where signifier and signified enter into a very specific relationship, even if that relationship is by no means less volatile and unstable than it has come to be seen in the context of representation in general.

The return to issues of representation at this point is, however, not only well-placed within the sequence of this journal's issues. It also reflects a growing sense of rediscovery and a new feeling of urgency in recent approaches to representation after decades of comatose stasis, when the entire concept of representation had apparently succumbed to the onslaught of criticism levelled against it mainly from postmodernist positions. Arguably, it had all been the modernists' fault, if this simplification be permitted, and the plot line runs from a persistent over-anxiety in the representative functions of language and art, as for example in the early Wittgenstein on the linguistic or philosophical side or in the search for an "objective correlative" in T. S. Eliot's poetics, which had resulted in an ever more rigid disciplining of language in science and art towards ideally functional situations of representation. The drawback was obvious, as these (self-)disciplinary strategies might improve what later critics would see as an illusion of representation, but they seriously reduced the flexibility and versatility of language as it was harnessed into the precisions of the representative function. What had led to the well-known prominence of silences in Wittgenstein's *Tractatus Logico-Philosophicus* and, by the same token, it could be argued, to the reductive use of language in late modernist writers such as Samuel Beckett, then seemed to explode into the language games of Wittgenstein's later work and the unfettered exuberance of sheer narrativity or voluble experimentation in postmodern writing. The gamut of voices and styles now prevalent all shared in a general disregard of the exigencies of representation. On the side of the theorists, representation was criticized on all fronts, most powerfully perhaps in the work of Michel Foucault, and even turned on its head in a postmodernist volte-face, when Jean Baudrillard coined the concept of the simulacrum as a type of representation without referent, as a representation which actually produces a reality-effect out of itself and constitutes a referent which did not previously exist: the signifier precedes the signified which consequently becomes, literally speaking, *in*significant.

A tradition of understanding fundamental aspects of human signification and the constitution of meaning had thus come to an end were it not for a small number of voices, Wolfgang Iser's prominent among them, who could not share in postmodernism's sweeping condemnation of representation. As so often happens with postmodernist positions, the critics of postmodernist views on representation in turn began to unmask the postmodernist's view on—one should say: representations of—representation as mono-dimensional and reductionist, while arguing for a more complex and variegated understanding of the practices and concepts of representation all along. These early critics of postmodernism are now gradually gathering into a chorus of voices, and the focus of this sixth volume of *Symbolism* can give a convincing impression of how substantial this reorientation has already become.

Foreword

Under the experienced aegis of Robert Weimann as guest editor, this issue's focus sets out to chart a departure, as Weiman so felicitously puts it, "toward a post-poststructuralist theory of representation." Far from constituting a reactionary return to well-worn concepts of mimesis and representation, Weimann and his contributors assemble a survey of the rich heritage of respresentational approaches while incorporating and ultimately benefiting from postmodernist critique in recreating a newly vibrant and highly flexible field where representational concepts can develop new significances and uses in twenty-first-century critical debates, taking in quixotic structures of making rather than finding (Gordon), juxtaposing the lightness in the quality of the sketch with the heavily symbolic (Baker), reconsidering representation as defying unity and plenitude (Weimann), reading James Joyce's *Ulysses* as deconstructing affirmative practices of representation (Wicht), and exploring new facets of representation in opera (Pfeiffer), while Douglas Bruster suggests in his reading of Antonioni's film *Blow-Up* that the present state of affairs is neither "after" nor "outside" representation, as it remains the quality of a fundamental, very human need.

As usual, the general section following the focus will take readers further afield, from early Scottish poetry explored by Ian Ross with a topographic focus on Iona, and Hildegard Hammerschmidt-Hummel's new investigations into the contexts of Shakespeare's life and literary career, to Ralph Pordzik's revisiting of Orientalism, Liu Dan's building of bridges between American and Chinese poetry, to Sandra Gottfreund's analysis of representations of Africa in Rider Haggard and Joseph Conrad, while Nic Panagopoulos provides another approach to Joseph Conrad's life and work in its early reception. Maria Alfaro, finally, takes a look at Charles Palliser's subversion of Victorian realism in his first novel, *The Quincunx*, and Ruth Y. Y. Hung examines the precarious conditions of representing lives in Chinese memoirs written in English.

The editors would like to take this opportunity to thank first of all Robert Weimann and Douglas Bruster as guest editors of this issue's focus, and then all contributors for deciding to join in this project and for their excellent cooperation. On the publisher's side, thanks are due to Gabriel Hornstein for his expert advice and routine in seeing this volume through the press, and, at the University of Würzburg, Bertram Richter has been of invaluable help in preparing the typescript. The editors hope that these combined efforts will stimulate new insight and discussions on representation and symbolism among this volume's readers.

Rüdiger Ahrens and Klaus Stierstorfer

SYMBOLISM

SPECIAL SECTION

REPRESENTATION

Corresponding Editors:

DOUGLAS BRUSTER
University of Texas at Austin

ROBERT WEIMANN
University of California, Irvine

INTRODUCTION

REPRESENTATION AND MIMESIS: TOWARDS A NEW THEORY

Robert Weimann

In his profound critique of representation, Michel Foucault views its "decline"[1] almost as a moment of liberation, as when language, recapturing its freedom and movement, is about to triumph once more. At long last, the immense power of representation to order and command language appears to be nearing exhaustion; the time has come, or so it seems, when a troublesome incompatibility of representational language and human kind explodes and, "since language is here once more, man will return to that serene non-existence in which he was formerly maintained by the imperious unity of Discourse."[2] This is not the place critically to examine the inverted teleology behind this grandiose panorama of the rise and fall of representation. But if Foucault's project cannot convince us of the *end*, it is certainly very persuasive on the *ends* of representation. Nowhere else do we find so fierce a sense of its vulnerability and, especially, its limitations vis-à-vis the shadowy realm of birth and death, violence and desire, work and sexuality. Failing to encompass this underside of our unspeakable existence, representation cannot but conceal its own inefficacy in face of the hardness of things, the irreducible and the inexpressible—in short, the non-representable dimension of existence. In the words of Foucault, it is "the

---

[1] Michel Foucault, *The Order of Things. An Archaeology of the Human Sciences.* (New York: Random House, 1973) 209.

[2] Foucault, *Order* 1973, 386.

obscure but stubborn spirit of a people who talk, the violence
and endless effort of life, the hidden energy of needs"[3] that will
not and cannot be articulated through representation.

Perhaps the best way to revisit the circumstantial ends and
means of representational practice is to situate it on a plane
broader and more vibrant than either the discursive parameters
of verbal signs and meanings or the epistemological standards
of insight and cognition (or, for that matter, the political
economy of *aliquid stat pro aliquo*). While all of these systems
of reference can be of great and, even, crucial importance, any
single one of them, when pursued exclusively on its own
ground, fails to yield a compelling perspective on
representation in the full range of its forms and functions. Even
more important, none of these different points of reference can
adequately come to terms with either the limitations,
formulated by Foucault, or the transformative powers as both
inseparable from the mimetic underside of representation.
Mimesis, as Walter Benjamin noted, may generally be defined
as the "formidable compulsion ... to become and behave like
something else."[4] The mimetic substratum of most
representational practices goes hand in hand with a move of
going outside of ourselves. This move, in Theodor W.
Adorno's phrase, constitutes a "nonconceptual affinity between
what is individually brought forth [in the text or art work] and
its Other." Such affinity, whether or not it embraces
resemblance, accommodates both separation and participation

[3] Foucault, *Order* 1973, 209.
[4] Walter Benjamin, "On the Mimetic Faculty," *Reflections*, ed. Peter
Demetz, trans. E. Jephcott (New York: Harcourt, 1979) 333. Benjamin's
phrase refers to the "gewaltigen Zwang, ähnlich zu werden und sich zu
verhalten," which might also be rendered as the "compulsion in likeness
to (re)act." He adds that humans "perhaps have no higher purpose (keine
höhere Funktion) that has not crucially been conditioned (mitbedingt) by
mimetic faculties" ("Über das mimetische Vermögen"; see Walter
Benjamin, *Schriften*, ed. Th. W. Adorno and Gretel Adorno, vol. I
(Frankfurt a. M.: Suhrkamp, 1955) 507. My translation.

(*getrennt und doch nicht durchaus getrennt*[5] from its Other). Since in mimetic practices both aspects are ultimately indivisable, alterity and likeness bring forth a terrific ambiguity, an uncanny doubleness in cultural utterances: "the power to represent the world, yet that same power is a power to falsify, mask, and pose."[6]

A New Mimesis

A brief survey of recent developments in theory may suggest that some such larger perspective on the nexus of mimesis and representation is overdue. The more recent history of mimeticism follows Benjamin and Adorno in that it makes it abundantly clear that the nexus in question does not primarily derive from, let alone culminate in, imitation. Instead, in recent decades the question of mimesis was reformulated in terms of diverse and different emphases, which altogether pointed beyond centuries-old classical horizons. The traditional notion of the concept as some form of *imitatio vitae* was by and large guided by an attempt, as in S.H. Butcher's words, to integrate Aristotelian mimesis in some modern theory of the arts, and of poetry in particular, as "a representation of the universal."[7] In conjunction with the "curative and tranquilizing influence" and the unifying impact of *katharsis*, mimesis (especially in its theatrical environment) was seen to serve as "a harmless and

---

[5] Theodor W. Adorno, *Ästhetische Theorie* (Frankfurt am M.: Suhrkamp, 1970) 86f. My translation. As Taussig puts it, "mimesis plays this trick of dancing between the very same and the very different" (129; cf. note 6).

[6] Michael Taussig, *Mimesis and Alterity. A Particular History of the Senses* (New York: Routledge, 1993) 42f. According to Wulf/Gebauer (see note 12), this ambivalence goes back to the earliest strategies of human control and resemblance/imitation (372).

[7] S.H. Butcher, *Aristotle's Theory of Poetry and Fine Art, with a Critical Text and Translation of the Poetics* (London: 1907) 266. Revealingly, a footnote on p. 268 adds, "if this is not what Aristotle meant, it is at least the natural outcome of his doctrine."

pleasurable outlet for instincts which demand satisfaction."[8] It
is precisely against traditional positions such as these that over
the last half century challenging counterproposals have led to
radically revisionist readings of mimesis.

Best known among these revisionist projects is perhaps
René Girard's, which shifts the very grounds on which to
revisit mimesis. Rejecting its classical and neoclassical
readings, Girard proceeded on the premises that these have
"always excluded one essential human behavior from the types
subject to imitation—namely, desire and, more fundamentally
still, appropriation. If one individual imitates another when the
latter appropriates some object, the result cannot fail to be
rivalry or conflict."[9] Such emphasis on the acquisitive aspect of
mimesis as a source of conflict may well be stimulating when it
helps criticism to look beyond any purely formal standards
derived from rhetoric and aesthetics. Girard's project is to
reopen the question of mimesis in other than its purely
representational and figurative terms. Such an approach makes
it possible for Girard to claim that mimesis precedes the
interest in sign systems, that it "exceeds the problematic of
signification in all directions," and that there is "a conflictual
mimesis before anything definable as human, in animal life
itself."[10]

---

[8] Butcher, *Aristotle's Theory* 1907, 246, 254.

[9] This is a concise (and incomplete) summary taken from René Girard, *'To
Double Business Bound': Essays on Literature, Mimesis and
Anthropology* (Baltimore: Johns Hopkins U P: 1978) vii. Girard has
pursued the fuller context of imitation, desire, and mediation from his
early *Deceit, Desire, and the Novel*, trans. Yvonne Freccero (Baltimore:
Johns Hopkins U P, 1965), with its emphasis on "triangular desire" (1-
52), to *Violence and the Sacred* (Baltimore: Johns Hopkins U P, 1977)
where mimetic desire in ritual leads up to a "conflictual mimesis"
(148)—"not through words" but through the example of a model
conveying "the supreme desirability of the object" (146) to be
appropriated.

[10] René Girard, "Interview," *diacritics*, 8, No.1 (Spring 1978): 34.

To offer these conclusions for discussion is not to overlook a number of problems in Girard's position, as when he proceeds from what he calls "the disconcerting simplicity and elementariness of that starting point" to show how the escalation of mimetic rivalry "beyond the point of no return" ultimately results "in a new and infinitely more complex form of society." In the course of this trajectory, the "murderous exasperation of mimetic rivalry" is said to trigger a mechanism of symbolicity and to become reunitive "as the very intensity of the escalation substitutes one single scapegoat for many disputed objects."[11] Thus offering us a historical (rather than purely anthropological) narrative, he takes a changeful social and cultural situation as the premises on which to address a rich spectrum of forces (social, tribal, reproductive, cultural, etc.). Can these be accounted for in terms of an approach that is designed to show "that the fundamental institutions of mankind, funeral rites, the incest taboos, the collective hunt, the domestication of animals, become structurally and genetically intelligible as products of unanimous victimage?"[12] For a consistently monistic construct like this, the burden of explanation is as immense as the chosen code must be closed to other, no less rudimentary, aims and modes of appropriation. Thus the most elementary objects of appropriation, the domesticated animal, the slain deer, the primitive tool, all drop out of the picture to make room for a radically reduced space, within which the function of mimesis is closed to the challenge of survival, the needs for collective safety, preservation, and reproduction. But ultimately it is some such larger challenge of

---

[11] Girard, Interview 1978, 33.

[12] Girard, Interview 1978, 35. For a persuasive critique of Girard's approach, see Gunter Gebauer/Christoph Wulf, *Mimesis. Kultur-Kunst-Gesellschaft* (Reinbek bei Hamburg: Rowolt, 1992) 327-34, 356-69. This study, with its emphasis on social *Praxis* (35 et passim), is probably the most comprehensive, well informed, and balanced study of the subject that we have. There is an English translation, *Mimesis: Culture, Art, Society*, trans. Don Rensen (Berkeley: U of California P, 1995).

appropriation, I submit, which in its own turn provides a more deeply existential space within which mimesis serves purposes in aid of both social cohesion and conflict.

As distinct from the highly conjectural anthropological directions in Girard's definition of mimesis, a second revisionist departure was marked by the appearance of *Mimesis des articulations* (1975). The volume may well be taken as a deconstructionist manifesto in which a number of distinguished French critics (Sylviane Agacinsky, Jacques Derrida, Sarah Kofman, Philippe Lacoue-Labarthe, Jean-Luc Nancy, and Bernard Pautrat) collectively sign as authors. In the present context, the volume deserves considerable interest because in it cultural uses of language, images, and products are approached first and foremost through mimetic practice, including that in the (highly self-reflexive) collection itself, composed "selon la loi d'une *désarticulation* générale."[13]

The texts of the essays collected are indeed being made to serve some sort of paraphrase or mimesis of the Platonic fears, the Kantian compensation, E.T.A. Hoffmann's bad conscience, Wittgenstein's *Urzeichen*, and Brecht's estrangement of mimesis. As Derrida in his deconstruction of Kant's emphatic distinction between the useful arts and the fine arts can show with great conviction, the notion of genius as semidivine source of incomparable productivity is at odds with the material matrix of mimesis itself as "une flexion de la physis, le rapport à soi de la nature."[14] In other words, the self-productive artful genius is shown as a metaphysical construct à la theology, which at least by implication obliterates the pre-Socratic materiality of "physis" (Heidegger's word). Kant's alternative

---

[13] Sylviane Agacinsky, et al., *Mimesis des articulations* (Paris : Aubier-Flammarion, 1975) blurb. As Mihai Spariosu notes, the "audio-visual conundrum" in the book's title (ambiguously arranged, so as to permit *désarticulation* as alternative reading) carries "the double claim that the title only mimes (simulates) the title" (*Literature, Mimesis and Play. Essays in Literary Theory* [Tübingen: Niemeyer, 1982] 53).

[14] Agacinsky, *Mimesis* 1975, 59.

to the neoclassical concept of *imitatio vitae* leads him ultimately into a theological foundation of "l'opposition hiérarchique de l'art libre et de l'art mercenaire."[15]

However, in his deconstruction of the Kantian aesthetics, Derrida does not content himself with tracing the impasse in the attempt to shift the mimetic relationship from that between two products to that between two modes of production—one of nature divine, the other of natural genius. As he further pursues the tie between mimesis and *oikonomia*,[16] he comes to define Plato's concept as a "double inscription of mimesis" but one that connotes "the free unfolding—refolding of physis."[17] Positing such duplication outside any system of truth, Derrida can affirm, through the mime's unprescribed refolding of physis, what he calls "the differential structure of mimicry or mimesis," a structure "without reference, or rather a reference without a referent."[18] This comes as a paraphrase of Mallarmé's *Mimique* and, as in Derrida's reading of Artaud, presupposes not only the absence in the performer of any phonocentric presence but an alternative to representation itself. Accordingly, the theater of cruelty is said to be no representation. What it demands, as an "autopresentation of pure visibility," is that "theater or life must cease to 'represent' another language." In foregrounding the play of mimesis in its freedom from "any conformity, resemblance, or adequation between a presence and a representation," Derrida redefined the "differential structure of mimicry or mimesis" as re-sembling "somewhere the being of something that 'is'."[19] In doing so, he himself re-iterates and extends Heidegger's profound challenge

---

[15] Agacinsky, *Mimesis* 1975, 68.

[16] Agacinsky, *Mimesis* 1975, 58: "Il s'agit d'exhiber de lien de système entre le deux."

[17] Here I use an apt phrase from R. Klein's translation of "Economimesis," *diacritics*, 11 (1986): 6.

[18] Jacques Derrida, *Disseminations*, trans. Barbara Johnson (Chicago: U of Chicago P, 1981) 207.

[19] Jacques Derrida, *Writing and Difference*, trans. Alan Bass (Chicago: U of Chicago P, 1978) 238.

of the modern metaphysical tradition which, having forsaken *physis* and being, had replaced it by logocentric representations of their absence.

Ironically, Heidegger's critique of modernity serves as a major point of reference for an altogether different, third approach to mimesis, which can best be exemplified in the work of Hans-Georg Gadamer. Taking one of his cues from classics philology, Gadamer resituates the concept in historically sustained hermeneutical coordinates. For him, the philological or, more strictly, etymological component is important because it helps to reconceive certain wider, potentially hidden pre-Socratic connotations of mimesis, which by implication defy the classical version as a containment of untamed *physis*. In reference to Hermann Koller, the etymological context of both noun and verb indicate that they "originally have their home only in the cultic sphere, in the orgiastic cult": Both *mimos* and *mimeisthai* suggest a "close link between mimesis and the dance."[20] While the nature of the evidence is too selective to be definitive, it seems difficult, if not impossible, in this light to confine the early uses of the word to purely verbal or poetic contexts.

In view of its widely discussed conclusions (Gadamer's response being just one of many), Koller's intervention remains significant in that it draws attention to cultural purposes and practices that almost certainly must be seen as either anterior to or coeval with early forms of representation. Thus, the archaeology of mimesis, which presents us with (post-)ritual functions and a semantic field pointing beyond purely verbal forms of staged delivery, suggests that the early understanding of *mimos* preceded the differentiation of pre-Socratic *technai*.[21]

---

[20] Hermann Koller, *Die Mimesis in der Antike. Nachahmung, Darstellung, Ausdruck* (Bern: Francke, 1954) 12, 75, 119.

[21] See Göran Sörbom, *Mimesis and Art. Studies in the Origins and Early Development of an Aesthetic Vocabulary* (Uppsala: Svenska, 1966) 41ff. Among at least 63 fifth-century uses of words derived from *mimesthai*, less than 20 have aesthetic connotations.

It was a *topos* which only about the time of Aristotle's treatment was transformed into a specifically aesthetic term well beyond its practical and political applications. The result of such transformation resembled the poetic use of *kartharsis*, which by the time of Aristotle was just about to shed its strictly medicinal associations. As distinct from Plato's apprehensive response to their "mixed" and uncontrolled locations, Aristotle attempts to harness and domesticate mimetic practices by directing them towards knowledge and pleasure. In conformity with these aims, the more wholesome, sympathetic, and tranquilizing effects of *katharsis* are encouraged.

In our context, the suggested proximity between mimesis and the dance is of considerable consequence. In Gadamer's own revisionary approach, where Koller's emphasis on dance and the performative is unambiguously acknowledged,[22] it helps shift the gravitational center of mimetic and other types of artful action away from imitation to communicative practices centering by and large on play (*Spiel*) and (re)presentation (*Darstellung*). These, as one might expect from this philosopher, are seen as formative forces at work in a hermeneutic engaging the basic nature of understanding. Moving from a mirrored type of understanding of history or tradition to a performative element in the process of its reception and participation, Gadamer's project culminates in what an astute observer calls a hermeneutic "with mimesis as a form of structured praxis."[23]

Such performative approach to mimesis and play seeks to dissociate these from what subjective meaning they obtained in

---

[22] The reference (and implicit expression of indebtedness) to Koller coincides with Gadamer's pivotal statement that both mimesis and *Darstellung* emanate from the ludic practice of *Spiel* and dance: "von dem Spiel ausgegangen" (108) or "abgeleitet wurde" (110). Such "Ausgehen vom Spielbegriff" (111)—translatable as "proceed" or "derive from a concept of play"—is crucial in Hans-Georg Gadamer's *Wahrheit und Methode*, second ed. (Tübingen: J.C.B. Mohr, 1965).

[23] William Schweiker, *Mimetic Reflections. A Study in Hermeneutics, Theology, and Ethics* (New York: Fordham UP, 1990) 35, 44.

their treatment by Kant, Schiller, and in more recent modern aesthetics and anthropology. Postulating "the primacy of play over the consciousness of the player,"[24] Gadamer's project is critically informed by an awareness of the need to contain *Fremdheit* or alienation. Such self-estrangement is viewed as an unwelcome result of a consciousness suffering from a profusion of boundless subjectivity. Following Heidegger in his critique of the latter, Gadamer as a matter of course proceeds to reject an understanding of a given text, a given practice or event as a (necessarily subjective) copy of what it says or is or does. Rather, the hermeneutical challenge, the difficulty inherent in *Verstehen*, implicates a dynamic figuration marked by dialogic action in aid of *Verständigung*. In other words, to understand a text is to undersign the larger social text of its previous exegesis; it presupposes a willingness to negotiate with other readings.

Here, the concept of figuration, marked by play and presentation, is significant. As distinct from reflections in a mirror, the dynamic moment of *Spiel* is that of an open participatory action or movement that defies closure. As he puts it in *Wahrheit und Methode*, play connotes

> the to-and-fro of a movement unattached to any goal at which it ends. This is in perfect correspondence with the original meaning of the word *ludus* (Spiel) as dance ... The movement which is play aims at no ending but renews itself in permanent iteration. Such to-and-fro-movement is obviously so central for defining the essence of play that the question can be neglected who or what actually delivers the movement ... Play is the consummation of the movement as such.[25]

---

[24]   Gadamer, *Wahrheit* 1965, 100; cf. 97, 106, and 101f.: "alles Spielen ist ein Gespieltwerden."

[25]   Gadamer, *Wahrheit* 1965, 99. Here and throughout my translation.

While Gadamer insists on the nonteleological openness of play, he does retain a memory of classical *Nachahmung* or imitation. There results a certain tension between mimesis *qua* play and what mimesis there is in "Darstellung" as an element in *re*presentation. As, characteristically, he underlines instability and yet the inevitability of emphasis and selection, he resists the notion of both total mediation and an absolute subject. Thus, while there is no pure and no purely imitative aspect of *re*production,[26] the semantic value of the "re" in "representation" is qualified accordingly.[27] At the same time, Gadamer's own hermeneutic postulate of a *Horizontver-schmelzung*, an approximation toward the merging of horizons between texts and their readings, seeks to secure a practical mode, historically conditioned, of assimilation and application (*Anwendung*[28]).

Representation: A Divided Project

At this juncture, this brief overview leads up to the point where more fully the issue of representation comes into the picture. So the question must finally be raised, what do these revisions of neo-Aristotelian mimesis contribute to a fresh departure toward a post-poststructuralist theory of repre-sentation? To ask this question is not to offer any ready-made solutions to the knotty issues involved; to retrieve mimesis from the ashes of classicism and metaphysics does not by itself amount to any salvaging operation for representation. Rather, the assumption is that the new mimesis set forth by Girard, Derrida, Lacoue-Labarthe, Koller, Gadamer, Taussig, Gebauer/Wulf, and others can stimulate a critical mass of provocative thought that, in a first move, will prepare the

---

[26] Gadamer, *Wahrheit* 1965, 109: "weil [Nachahmung und Darstellung, i.e., Mimesis] nicht bloß Wiederholung, sondern ,Hervorhebung' sind."
[27] Schweiker seeks to reduce the difficulty by translating Gadamer's "Darstellung" as "presentation" (82, n. 5). See below note 44.
[28] Gadamer, *Wahrheit* 1965, see esp. 288-95.

ground for more clearly (and more widely) defining the neglected space between representation and related practices in aid of appropriation, alienation, identification, "othering," and so forth. In a further move, the problem has to be faced as to what this approach can and what it cannot do to advance our understanding of the uses of difference, division, and reconciliation in and through representational practices.

More modestly, let us begin by reconsidering what these greatly diverging revisionist approaches have in common; in particular, what mediating body of shared ideas may potentially advance the nexus of mimesis and representation. At first sight, these approaches are all marked by the rejection of only one position, that of univocal, subject-centered, and self-contained, uses of imitation and unmediated meaning. But upon closer inspection they together also depart from the resurging interest in mimesis that in the early-twentieth century was inspired by new developments in phonography, photography, and of course film. In that period, fascination with the camera eye appeared especially promising where its "optical unconscious" (Walter Benjamin) was in collision with an alleged objectivity and authenticity or where, as in the context of a new mass culture, modern technologies of reproduction constituted a pattern of "copy swallowing up contact."[29] But these past pleasures of copying, the triumphs of replication, the shocks of resemblance, the thrills of likeness cannot today hope to establish a new space of concurrence between mimesis and representation. On the contrary, what the more recent revisionism appears to advance is, rather, a reversal of the pattern, one that I am tempted to call "contact consumes copy." Or, perhaps, to use a more pertinent terminology, the pattern is one of "practice dispelling reflection."

---

[29] According to Taussig, the "capacity of mimetic machines to pump out contact-sensuousity" intriguingly testifies to "the two-layered character" of a mimetic process whereby photography, in Benjamin's phrase, materially reveals the "physiognomic aspects of visual worlds" (*Mimesis and Alterity* 1993, 24).

In view of the forbidding difficulties in our time to distinguish the copy from the copied, the new departures have more and more come to be preoccupied with the staging of mimesis, its performance and delivery. If anywhere there has emerged a new cultural space for a rapprochement between mimesis and representation, it is on this terrain. Although thoroughly relevant as background, the phenomenal rise in the humanities of performance and related concepts of the performative must not detain us here.[30] Enough when we recall that its rise has effected a veritable paradigm change in that performative approaches have reached out to inform a broad spectrum of disciplinary reorientations, especially in anthropology, epistemology, linguistics, and theater studies. These reorientations appear entirely opportune at a time when the theory of representation as both imaginary *Vorstellung* and practical *Darstellung* are especially exposed to the growing distrust of any foundational claims on the part of a knowledge-centered order of things. In their rejection of this order, Dewey, Heidegger, and Wittgenstein were in agreement that the entire notion of knowledge as accurate representation located in, and available through, the mirroring capacities of the mind or the *Subjekt* needed to be abandoned. Hence, there was no point in "viewing knowledge as an assemblage of representations."[31]

---

[30] Among an abundance of recent studies of performance, I have found most helpful, at least on theater, Marvin Carlson, *Performance. A Critical Introduction;* Elin Diamond, ed., *Performance and Cultural Politics;* Patrice Pavis, ed., *The Intercultural Performance Reader.* Significantly, all these studies, coming on the crest of a new paradigm, appeared in New York: Routledge, 1996.

[31] Richard Rorty's phrase; see his *Philosophy and the Mirror of Nature* (Princeton: Princeton U P, 1979) 136. Rorty's project takes to the extreme and partially oversimplifies positions much more subtly developed by Wittgenstein and Heidegger. See, e.g., on the former David Schalkwyk's reading of Wittgenstein in his eye-opening study of *Literature and the Touch of the Real* (Newark: U of Delaware P, 2004): Wittgenstein's challenge of "the gap classically posited between language and the world" leads to the preposition "that aspects of the

But if representations in their turn could derive their strength and usefulness from neither the grounds nor the results of a given order of cognition, the time had come to search for and locate the resilience of representational practice elsewhere.

At this juncture, the focus on play and performance was more than welcome. For one thing, this focus foregrounded a mimetic tradition which now was fraught with strength and complexity enough to mobilize a hitherto fairly static concept of representation. Unburdened, with the help of semiotics, of any unmediated load of "meaning," this new concept of representational practice now appeared capable of discarding the traditional ménage of reference and cognition in favor of a new alliance among intransitive forms of figuration and performance. Since the referential range of these practices was obliterated or at least curtailed, it appeared possible to shift the performative thrust to locations of immanence, of self-reflexivity or to the medium itself. Here was part of the reason that turned J. L. Austin's speech act theory into a highly influential conceptual platform on which the performative was repositioned within the uses of language itself.

These few notes must suffice to convey a sense of the context in which the mimetic and performative components of representation could provide sufficient stimulus to distinguished critics and theoreticians to revisit representational action. In this connection, theoretical work associated with Paul Ricoeur and Wolfgang Iser is perhaps most noteworthy in that their approach, rather than disputing the challenging thrust of the poststructuralist critique, proceeded by preempting any purely logocentric definition of representation with the help of such nonlogocentric concepts as "performance," "play," and "staging."

---

extralinguistic world are available to be appropriated as rules of representation for the way in which words are used" (127). Elsewhere, Schalkwyk pointedly notes that "Representation is not a purging of the world from the sign ... but the essential contamination of the sign by the world" (71).

If, as Paul Ricoeur suggests, there is a way "to extricate representation from the impasse to which it has been relegated" by returning "it to its field of play,"[32] then this return may indeed provide tools of aperture vis-à-vis the closure of representation, opening its language and function in the service not only of play but also in reference to acts of production, delivery, and appropriation. In this direction, Ricoeur reassociates poiesis (and "all artificial fabrication and production") with the surplus energy which, out of "the opaque depths of living, acting, and suffering," transcends logocentrism in representation and liberates "meaning" from its reading as re-presented presence. Mimesis as a mode of imaginary production, including the figuration or *Darstellung* of and in a literary work, is a concrete process; in its course, a prefigured world with the help of a textual or narrative configuration moves to a state of transfiguration.[33]

While Ricoeur reopens representation through notions of "play" and figuration as contiguous with *fingere*, feigning, polysemy, and mobility, Wolfgang Iser takes the study of the performative up to the point where "playing" and "staging" enter into "the recipient's performance." Along these lines, "representation," in its problematic bridging of the difference between internal images and external relations, is taken to presuppose "active imaginings" through "the recipient's ideational performative activity."[34] But this activity "resembles

---

[32] Paul Ricoeur, "Mimesis and Representation," *Annals of Scholarship*, 2 (1981): 15. Mimesis, in Ricoeur's reading, is "less shut in, less locked up"(*ibid.*), it offers plenty of polysemy and mobility"(31) for a "sortie" out of the impasse.

[33] Ricoeur, Mimesis 1981, 28; see pp.17-18, where in this "concrete process" the moment of poiesis is underlined more strongly when it is said that "the textual configuration conjoins" the latter two types of figuration.

[34] Wolfgang Iser, *Prospecting. From Reader Response to Literary Anthropology* (Baltimore: Johns Hopkins U P, 1989) 243. In a later, more comprehensive study, Iser proceeds to compare Ricoeur's emphasis on process with E.H. Gombrich's position ("making comes

that of an actor, who in order to perform his role must use his thoughts, his feelings, and even his body as an analogue for representing something that he is not." Hence, representation in seeking "to bridge difference" and make accessible the inaccessible, is transformed "into a performative act" of staging "oneself as someone else."[35]

Even while both Ricoeur and Iser circumscribe the space in which the nexus of mimesis and representation can further be developed, they are cautious enough not to enlarge on the area of difference between them. However, since this area helps condition the point of connection, i.e., the nexus, in the first place, we must be indebted to any pointer in this direction. To recall the ritual background of mimesis is not that helpful, except of course that it may permit us to say, in the words of Philippe Lacoue-Labarthe, that "mimesis in general" can claim to be "anterior in some way or other, to representation."[36] Let us in this context recall Adorno who in his own archaeology of mimesis attempted to specify a *Doppelbewegung*, a bifold movement even in its prehistory: "Mimesis in the arts is pre-spiritual (*das Vorgeistige*), it counters the intellect (*Geist*) and yet kindles it."[37] Thus, in Adorno's view there is no static opposition between the mimetic in its sensuous or material forms and the rational; ever since mimesis had surrendered its

---

before matching") which, in the order of mimesis, may also be said to enhance the performative by putting imitation last. Gombrich's German phrase ("daß das Bilden vor dem Nachbilden kommt") is perhaps even more illuminating; cit. Wolfgang Iser, *Das Fiktive und das Imaginäre. Perspektiven literarischer Anthropologie* (Frankfurt a. M.: Suhrkamp, 1991) 489.

[35] Iser, *Prospecting* 1989, 244. cf. the entire chapter "Representation: A Performative Act"; *ibid.*, 236-49.

[36] Philippe Lacoue-Labarthe, "Mimesis and Truth," *diacritics*, 8 No.1 (Spring 1978): 17. Note that this partially at least paraphrases Girard's position.

[37] Adorno: "Mimesis ist in der Kunst das Vorgeistige, dem Geist Konträre und wiederum das, woran er entflammt" (*Ästhetische Theorie* 1970, 180).

magic purposes and practices it became complicit with rationality. But the continued existence of the nonrational in the midst of conceptual and cognitive functions, in a word, the resilience of *Doppelbewegung* in modern mimetic practices is a way "to react against the bad irrationality of the rational world as an administered one."[38] The resulting ambivalence, the Protean moment of duplicity in mimesis has many forms and functions reaching from Nietzsche's "Apollinian" and "Dyonisian" elements to Elin Diamond's "impossibly double" design[39]—a doubleness that is different from and yet recalls an analogue in representation, to which I shall return in a moment.

Adorno's view of mimesis as harboring a prerational or pre-intellectual element may easily be linked to what Taussig, in more generous reference to contemporary mass media, has called "a veritable rebirth ... of the mimetic faculty." Following Benjamin's suggestion, Taussig projects this "rebirth" not so much against as within the technology of modern popular representations. As he phrases it, Benjamin, almost preoccupied with "the surfacing of 'the primitive' within modernity as a direct result of modernity," can view "the curious and striking recharging of the mimetic faculty caused by the invention of mimetically capacious machines such as the camera" in a highly complex context, in which mimesis is coupled with "alterity" toward a new sort of "primitivism." It is a context which in Benjamin's view is "a lot more performative

---

[38] Adorno, *Ästhetische Theorie* 1970, 86; again my translation. Cf. 72, 148 f., 178, 424, 429.

[39] For Diamond's dictum, see the citation in the opening paragraph of my essay below. Nietzsche's distinction is made in *The Birth of Tragedy* where, ironically, Adorno's view of mimesis as the *Vorgeistige* finds an analogue in the celebration of "a more profound wisdom" which was destroyed by the "dialectics of knowledge" with its classical preference for "words and concepts." See Friedrich Nietzsche, *Sämtliche Werke*, eds. Giorgio Colli and Mazzino Montinari (Berlin: Dt. Taschenbuch Verlag/de Gruyter, 1988) I, 101, 109-10. My translation.

and physical, a lot more realist yet fanciful, than implied in the way 'othering' is alluded to in discussions today."[40]

While incidentally this presents us with a hint at mimesis in twentieth-century entertainments, Taussig's distinction is curiously forgetful about what has happened to Benjamin's fervent hopes for cultural democracy in the media. For him to underline the physical and material in modern popular representations is to overlook the potential displacement of the gulf between what performs and what is represented through performance. In the course of these mediated shows the difference between the agencies and the objects of representation is next to obliterated; the independent strength of performance is sapped or glamorously contained by the institution of stardom. Often enough, the elimination of doubleness inside representations goes hand in hand with a superficially benign or downright commercial bridging of the very real difference between the world of social circumstances and the image of their artful rendering.

However, as Iser notes in a different context, "the source of performance is different from what is to be represented."[41] This indeed, is fully evident where in the theater the agent of performance delivers a dramatic text composed in his/her absence, under circumstances that may radically differ from the site and institution of its staging. But in literary representations, despite the invisibility of performing agencies, there is a comparable gap. The depth of this gap increases to the degree that the act of representation needs to fall back on what the perceptive and imaginative faculties can yield. Such performing practice, as Iser has shown, was not anticipated in Aristotle's concept of mimesis; it is only when a cosmological and, by analogy, moral and political frame of reference ceases to be given that a forceful performative is given free rein. It is only after a generally acceptable, preconceived order of "nature"

---

[40] Taussig, *Mimesis and Alterity* 1993, xix, 20, xiv.
[41] Wolfgang Iser, *The Fictive and the Imaginary. Charting Literary Anthropology* (Baltimore: Johns Hopkins U P, 1933) 281.

surrenders that individual uses of perception, play, and performance are called for to counterbalance what certitude, security, and conviction had informed classical mimesis or classically modern forms of representation. As I have shown, increasing inroads into political and cultural consensus force representational practice through enhanced performance to cope with the absence of any unquestioned system of equivalences between worldly circumstances and cultural practices. [42]

To understand these triangular relations (mimesis— performance / play—representation) in their contingency, as a movable, unfolding set of cultural responses helps reveal the "nexus" in question as an entirely contingent point of interconnection. As an illustration, let us for a moment recall the uses of performance in the late-twentieth-century theater where the classical and the classically modern relationship of making and matching tends to be reversed: Mimetically consistent uses of matching (imitation/resemblance) radically give way to a new initiative in performance (the making). The pendulum swings in a direction entirely opposite to what we have in, say, the nineteenth-century theater. In fact, the act of representing dramatic characters can so be intercepted by performance that, instead of obtaining the image of imaginary persons, we find the mimetic process itself delivered. What, in the drama of Müller, Handke, and Beckett can result is not character but, rather, a staged image of what performance it takes to undo the representation of character.

In the language of modern fiction there is a comparable pattern of a different type of performance practice asserting itself at the cost of representational closure and equivalence. Here, performative practice emerges within representation as an independent rather than merely subservient force. Its

---

[42] Iser uses the concept of a cultural *Fraglosigkeit* (unquestionability) whose loss finally demands that "Mimesis durch den Repräsentationsvorgang selbst fundiert wird." Cf. *Das Fiktive und das Imaginäre* 1933, 490.

impact—as this volume suggests—can distinctly be traced in the composition of narrative between Flaubert and Joyce. The decline in anything like a social consensus goes hand in hand with a growing refusal to continue to take for granted a naturally or socially acceptable frame of reference. The absence of valid referentiality is countered, partially even intercepted, by *écriture*, by an artful type of performative practice in writing. Such performative needs to assert its distance from, even its irreconcilability to, the matter of representation. The gap between what performs and what is represented, between cultured writing and its raw *sujet*, can easily be turned into an "abyss." The depth of this "abyss" in representation (to use George Hartley's phrase[43]) has generally been ignored or at least underestimated.

The best way to engage this gap in representation may well be a recourse to the German terminology usually used as equivalent to "representation" or to the related French term *représentation*. Revealingly, in the language of this equivalent two concepts come together: *Darstellung* (usually translated by either "presentation" or "[re-]presentation" [44]) and *Vorstellung*. While the latter is a purely imaginary act of reconstituting in the mind what is being represented in terms of character,

---

[43] George Hartley, *The Abyss of Representation. Marxism and the Postmodern Sublime* (Durham and London: Duke U P, 2003). The focus is on a "gap" in the language of theory, "a chasm, separating the concept from its representation" (85) in the writings of Kant, Hegel, Marx, Althusser, and Fredric Jameson.

[44] As for instance, Schweiker, *Mimetic Reflections* 1990, 47, 82, et passim; Hartley, *Abyss of Representation* 2003, esp. 4, 55-64, 301; see also the editorial note 4 to Lacoue-Labarthe, "Mimesis and Truth," 13. However, none of these suggested eqivalents appear quite adequate. For an exploration of subtle differences in the two vocabularies, see Martha B. Helfer, *The Retreat of Representation: The Concept of 'Darstellung' in German Critical Discourse* (Albany, NY, 1996) and Dieter Schlenstedt's article "Darstellung" in *Ästhetische Grundbegriffe—Ein Historisches Wörterbuch*, ed. Karl-Heinz Barck, et al. (Stuttgart: Metzler, 2000) I, 831-75; esp. 846-49.

image, idea, and meaning, the former denotes the act or process of rendering. In view of these two different aspects of representation, Hartley provides what is perhaps the subtlest and most stringent distinction between them that we have in English:

> Vorstellung places an object before us and is thus related to the proposition ... Darstellung stages the unfolding of the proposition and is thus an exposition, a projecting forward and an exposing of the positing process. While Darstellung is an exhibition, a staging of the act of display, Vorstellung is an inhibition, an internalization of the presupposed object. Darstellung enacts drama; Vorstellung presents a picture. [45]

While *Vorstellung* can be rendered by "conception," "picture," "idea," but also by any other imaginary type of mental response to the text, *Darstellung* has more material connotations, potentially implicating craftsmanship (such as "shaping," "forming," "figuring," and "composing") as well as showmanship (such as "exposition," "exhibition," and "staging").

As this distinction suggests, both these different connotations testify to the absence of any unified or unifying absolute in "representation." Positively speaking, there is space within one representation for entirely different aims and purposes. For instance, there is on the one hand the matter of what is to be represented for its insight, information, moral, or political purpose; on the other hand, we have what *fingere*, what counterfeiting, what shaping, making, fashioning go into the representation through artful performance and craftsmanship. The two aspects are not the same, even when each is subsumed under the other; in fact and both are

---

[45] Hartley, *Abyss of Representation* 2003, 61.

interactive in the process between producing and consuming, i.e. re-producing representations.

The relationship between them, however, is not a stable one; rather, as I have hinted, it is marked by considerable contingency. This holds good especially for the achieved degree of resemblance. In the first place, similitude is extremely variable between what is staged or shaped and what is perceived; *Vorstellung* is a response to rather than a copy of *Darstellung*. Even more important is the (dis)similarity between the meaning of representation and its potential subject or referent. It is of course true that the gap between what is represented on the imaginary level of *Vorstellung* and what is representing on the more material level of *Darstellung* can be narrowed to a point almost of nonexistence, but it can also be turned into a veritable chasm. Again, the theater provides a most telling illustration: In the audience's perception, the distance between the purely imaginary dimension of the performed role and the performing actor with his/her audible, visible delivery can practically be eliminated when the performer completely identifies with, and is "lost" in, the character to be represented. But the continuity between the two, the closure in representation, can also be broken up; as on the modern stage, in Brecht's well-known *Verfremdung*, the gap between the semantics in the dramatic text of the role and the ways and values of its performance is deliberately displayed for critical inspection. In each case, today's representational practice is free to pursue totally diverging aims and purposes, ranging from empathy to "alienation" in representation, each with its own degree of (dis)continuity.

Still, the space for rupture and/or closure in representation, even when turned into a historically contingent site of impact, is more complex than can be suggested by the duality inherent in dramatic representations of character. In the first place, the socio-semiotic study of symbolic relations between what is represented and what is performing in modern culture needs to come to terms with a wide spectrum of fleeting transitions in the space of difference and indifference between the two extremes of rupture and closure. At the same time, the variability in the use of this space conjugates both the physical and the imaginary and of course their coordination. Thus, the act of presentation or *Darstellung* cannot be a purely material, nonsymbolic act of rendering when—at every moment—its moment-to-moment progress already turns the language of the body into a symbolic mode of sensuously conveyed signification. The same can be said about the acoustic signifiers of spoken and the visual signifiers of written or printed language. Together, in the changeful degrees of their promiscuousness or separation, the material and the imaginary provide us with what can arguably be viewed as the crucial axis, the most consequential and pregnant correlation among the diverse formations of Western representation.[46]

However, in view of the given interpenetrations, these proposed divisions must remain in several ways provisional. The oversimplification becomes more obvious as soon as we return to the question of *Darstellung* (presentation/rendering) as a practice within different types of discourse, dramatic, political, historical, ethnological, and philosophical. The latter type of discourse appears especially illuminating because, if we follow George Hartley, it provides the context in which the concept of *Darstellung* first emerged and flourished. This period in the history of philosophy coincides with the thought of Kant, Coleridge, and Hegel. Between them, until about the time of the Schlegels, there dominated in representational theory what Winfried Menninghaus calls a preoccupation with the *Vollzugscharakter* of representation, that is, an emphasis on doing and design, on execution and delivery. Whereas during this period the concern, in mimetic practices, with faithful reproduction and resemblance receded into the background, the presentational, delivery-oriented angle resonated with

---

[46] I have studied and historicized this correlation in my *Author's Pen and Actor's Voice. Playing and Writing in Shakespeare's Theater* (Cambridge: Cambridge U P, 2000).

traditional meaning in *darstellen* which is "to signify a direct and physical positing somewhere."[47] Such setting up of something, such shaping and placing of the unshaped helped explore, assimilate, and localize an unlocalized habitation and a name. It was a task that from afar recalled the ancient issue of nonacquisitive appropriation. In grappling with this task presentation and representation would never operate as two opposites. In what may possibly have been a hidden piece of romantic irony, Friedrich Schlegel punctured the notion of any fixed dualism, when he noted: "Humans will and must *darstellen* (render/perform/present) precisely what they cannot *vorstellen* (conceive/imagine/represent). "[48] No matter whither the drift of the irony (if it was irony), pride of place is given to the doing and the delivering; the writing of the poem, the rendering of the image, the painting of the picture came first, its represented meaning second.

The romantic poets (whose first point of reference was of course the artist as creator) coupled insight with blindness when it came to viewing the intrinsic divisions inside representation in conjunction with its political and juridical correlatives. Here it was Thomas Hobbes who had first projected a comprehensive sense of interconnection among diverse types of representational practice. Disregarding for his purpose the area of difference among these, Hobbes associated the act of representation with "any representer of speech and action as well in tribunals, as theaters." As set out in chapter 16 of *Leviathan*, the concept of a "Representer" was closely linked to that of a "Representative"; as such it embraced activities associated with "a *Lieutenant*, a *Vicar*, an *Attorney*, a *Deputy*, a

---

[47] Winfried Menninghaus, "'Darstellung.' Friedrich Gottlieb Klopstocks Eröffnung eines neuen Paradigmas," *Was heisst "Darstellen"?*, ed. Christiaan L. Hart Nibbrig (Frankfurt a. M.: Suhrkamp, 1994) 209. My translation.

[48] "Darstellen will und soll der Mensch grade das was er nicht vorstellen kann." Cit. *Menninghaus*, Darstellung 1994, 210; the source is *Kritische Friedrich-Schlegel-Ausgabe,* ed. Ernst Behler, vol. 18, 341.

Procurator, an *Actor*, and the like."[49] In this assortment, representational practices were intimately conjoined with the execution of power but also, or even more so, with the need for validating and substantiating the credentials of power in an emerging civil formation of society. Significantly, Hobbes approached representation and representativeness in terms of issues of authority and authorization as indispensable premises on which to verify the legitimacy of representational *qua* representative action.

Representation: Proxy and Portrait

It seems difficult to believe but it has taken almost three centuries before representational practice has again come to be considered in the full diversity of its functions. Not fortuitously, it was in the 1930s and early 1940s when American critics like Kenneth Burke drew attention to what a more recent critic calls "the structural similarities of the two forms of representation."[50] Still, for a full and comprehensive study we had to wait until 1967 when Hanna Fenichel Pitkin published *The Concept of Representation*.[51]

In view of the close links between representation and authority (or power[52]) it may not come as a surprise that we owe one of the most trenchant forays into representation *qua*

---

[49] Thomas Hobbes, *Leviathan*, ed. C.B. Macpherson (Harmondsworth: Penguin, 1969) 217-18.

[50] W. J. T. Mitchell, "Representation," *Critical Terms for Literary Study*, ed. Frank Lentricchia and Thomas McLaughlin (Chicago: Chicago U P, 1990) 12.

[51] Hanna Fenichel Pitkin, *The Concept of Representation* (Berkeley: U of California P, 1967) is a conceptually rich and complex study even though its primary focus is on political representation. As a pioneering project, her study had to confront (and overcome) the perception that "theories of representation are something of a morass" (cit. *ibid.* 6).

[52] I have discussed at some length the ambivalence of these links in my *Authority and Representation in Early Modern Discourse* (Baltimore: Johns Hopkins U P, 1996).

representativeness to Gayatri Chakravorty Spivak's reading of
Marx's *The Eighteenth Brumaire of Louis Bonaparte*. Studying
therein the use of sociopolitical "representation" (the German
word in Marx is *Vertreten*), Spivak combines and integrates the
sense of "standing for" (proxy) with "portrait" as an act of
portraiture bringing forth the picture of an individual or a group
or class of people.[53] There is no simple equation but a
"complicity between the two." What and who is representative
of a social group or class cannot be ascertained without any
represented image or picture of it. The politics behind the
delegation of power and authority to a representive may all be
wrong and harmful if the general interest is not made available
and circulated in terms of a picture or image. As Hartley
paraphrases the issue, "when a class cannot form a picture of
itself as a class (re-present as *darstellen)*, it turns to others to
speak for its interests (re-present as *vertreten)*."[54] This reading
is no doubt congenial to what Marx had in mind when
accounting for small French peasantry and their questionable
political preference for Louis Bonaparte.

However, to view the relationship between "proxy" and
"portrait" as marked by "complicity" is, in its vagueness, not
good enough. Let me suggest that what semantic continuity we
have between "proxy" and "portrait" can best be explored by
their mutual affiliation to the exercise of power in the political
and the cultural field respectively. While the representative
action of "proxy" may yield an immediate access to power
resulting from an act of standing-in-for groups or classes of
people, imaginary representations can—at least under certain
conditions—only hope to seek culturally mediated forms of
powerful impact or influence. Under exceptional circumstances
(let us think of Harriet Beecher Stowe or Nikolay Gavrilovič

---

[53] Gayatri Chakravorty Spivak, "Can the Subaltern Speak?" *Marxism and
the Interpretation of Culture*, ed. Cary Nelson and Lawrence Grossberg
(Urbana: U of Illinois P, 1988) 271-318.

[54] Hartley, *Abyss of Representation* 2003, 247-48. This paraphrases
Spivak.

Černyshevsky) purely imaginary representations can serve as a powerful force in the world of politics. So although there are a good many borderline cases, especially in reformist or political writings such as Luther's, Calvin's, Marx's, or Lenin's, the respective relationship between the two forms of representation can (although still an oversimplification) best be summed up in terms of two different modes of authority. What authority is exerted by political representation calls for a legitimation in terms of ends and means; what imaginary writings entail is at best an intellectual, aesthetic, or moral authority subject not so much to public political legitimation but personal or interpersonal authorization.

While, then, some such distinction between "proxy" and "portrait" allows for an intriguing link between political and aesthetic forms of representation, Spivak's design simply does not approach the issue in terms of a theory of representation. In particular, it does not go far enough toward establishing a perspective on what, in drama or literature, can serve as a correlative to either the politics of "standing-in-for" or, for that matter, the political economy of *aliquid stat pro aliquo*. The question that needs to be raised is therefore: how does the representational, reproductive function of "portrait" relate to a culturally specific form of "proxy"? In other words, what potentially is the equivalent in the arts of "standing for," or "serving as delegate of," given formations of people, their power, and interests. While this introduction cannot hope to submit anything like a satisfying answer,[55] there is only room in conclusion to draw attention to two or three forays in this direction.

The first is Susan Wells's study of *The Dialectics of Representations,* which posits as one of its major premises a

---

[55] I have attempted to grapple with this question in an article (which has substantially been revised and used in my essay to this volume): "Text, Author-function and Appropriation in Modern Narrative: Toward a Sociology of Representation," *Critical Inquiry*, 14 (Spring 1988): 431-447.

"deep relationship of interdependence between reading and reference." Distinguishing throughout her study between "the typical register" and "the indeterminate register" of a text, she pointedly offers an "interpenetration of opposites" in the sense "that the deepest indeterminacy marks the most referential moment of the text."[56]

The seeming paradox, which privileges the act of reception as historically most variable and contingent, needs to be borne in mind when it is proposed that the act of representation have a "typical" dimension. While it may seem difficult for most of us to accept a concept outrageously abused in a certain type of political propaganda masking as criticism, it appears only fair to note that Wells dismisses the Russian nineteenth-century and Soviet concepts as well as Hippolyte Taine's sociological version of "typicality" without much fuss. Instead, the "referential power" behind the typical register is viewed on two, not necessarily continuous, levels: "The text labors over the world and transforms it by representing it; the reader transforms the text by interpreting it" (17). But once the typical register applies to both an audience response and a piece of writing, the inevitable question is, how can this register *pre*clude its grounding in a flat version of "reflection" and yet *in*clude that literary practice of sociopolitical delegation and authorization which makes an activity representative?

According to Wells, an answer can be found in the representation of such worldly forces and constellations as inform "relations of sovereigns and subjects, of public life and private intimacy." What in these representations is at issue are "the relations of parts to wholes, of individuals to groups, of the hidden to the manifest" (62). Rejecting in these relations any "objectivity" à la Lukács,[57] Wells seeks to expand the scope

---

[56] Susan Wells, *The Dialectics of Representation* (Baltimore: Johns Hopkins U P, 1985) 17. Further page references in the text.

[57] See Wells's long note on the treatment of Lukács's "typicality" (179-81) which, even through it does not include his late work on mimesis, is very likely the best concise overview that we have.

and spectrum of representational practices not only in her undogmatic stance that these be "concerned with the connections and distances between the text and the world" (103) but, more revealingly, by viewing relations of reference and reading, typicality and indeterminacy as being informed by "a dialectic of concealment and disclosure" (167). But while her desire to undo the flatness of typicality must be granted, the concept of the typical provides a problematic clue for the links and gaps between the representative and the representational. Altogether, despite a good deal of valuable thought and interpretation in Wells's project, the liabilities of "reflection" persist in the teeth of important qualifications. What this project finally teaches us is that a preoccupation with a purely epistemological and partially hermeneutic approach cannot very well come to terms with the links and gaps between literary and other forms of representation, no matter how much insight such approach otherwise provides.

If *The Dialectic of Representation* remains strongly indebted to a Hegelian Marxism of the traditional kind, poststructuralism, in the midst of its radical critique of representation, provides us with a number of surprising departures, which so far have received very little attention. As we have seen, there is first of all a certain readiness not only to reconsider nonclassical versions of mimesis but, in Lacoue-Labarthe's case, to raise the question, whether such mimesis would "not require a rethinking of representation." Such "rethinking" would lead us to question "the dualism of the present and the represented" and point to a "conception of representation in which the *re-* of repetition would govern—and dispel ... any sense of 'objective' exhibition, derived of secondary externalization."[58]

These tentative suggestions are in response to the same author's question, "Is there no representation other than the external or spectacular?" The most brilliant answer to this question comes from Louis Marin's book-length study *De la*

---

[58] Lacoue-Labarthe, Mimesis and Truth 1978, 18.

représentation (1994); it seems impossible to ignore this work even though it uses a poststructuralist terminology only in terms of pragmatic insight and inversion. Taking his cue (and initial quotation) from Pierre Charpentrat, Marin notes about representational practice in painting:

> "Figures bear absence and presence, pleasure and displeasure." What does it mean to represent, then, if not to convey an absent object into presence, to bar it into present as absent, to *master* its loss, its death by and in representation, and, by the same token, to *dominate* the displeasure or the anguish of its absence in the pleasure of a presence that takes its place, and in that deferred appropriation—"reality excludes absence and displeasure"—through transitive reference and recognition, to enact the reflexive movement that is constitutive of the subject itself ... [59]

Here representations are seen in terms of living responses and their needs. Production and reception are marked by attempts to *master* what is borne "into presence as absent," to *dominate* (italics in the original) the sense of absence to appropriate "representative and transitive images" as well as the strangeness, "the uncanniness" (*ibid.*) of artful resemblance, including trompe-l'oeil, in representations. In this view, the negative connotations of "absence" and, together with it, the fearsome suspicion and resentment of metaphysics are taken care of in a more relaxed spirit. Paintings can have a referent, and the "exact visibility of the referent is conjugated with its absence" (*ibid.*). This is not an intrinsic but an extrinsic view of representation, which is seen as inseparable from its worldly effect and affect. Hence (even though, admittedly, the French

---

[59] Louis Marin, *On Representation* (Stanford: Stanford U P, 2001) 311; cf. esp. §21 "The Frame of Representation": "to represent means to present oneself representing something" (352).

original is somewhat ambiguous here) an image can be "representative"—just as "the representative screen is a window" (*ibid.*) through which real spectators in the pleasure of their presence contemplate an imaginary, absent figuration.

Finally, while Louis Marin with considerable blandness and/or discretion keeps the extrinsic sense of (public or political) representation in the background, it may come as a surprise that it is Jacques Derrida to whom we owe the most explicit treatment of *représentation* as designating a mandate served by "representatives, delegates, ambassadors, emissaries."[60] The reference is to a paper entitled "*Envoi*" read at a Strasbourg/Strassburg congress of French-speaking philosophical societies. While the venue of the congress with its bilingual connotations is of considerable import to Derrida's position (speaking in "a city which, while it does not, as it once very symbolically did, lie outside of France" [296]), the forum of philosophical societies itself is even more important. Repeatedly formulated as his point of departure, *On dirait alors que nous sommes en représentation* (here translated as "One might say that we represent something") hails the congress not only with a sense of massive presence; it pronounces an office, a delegation of some consequence. As the excellent translator says in a note, *en représentation* in its most pertinent meaning here "conveys the responsibilities of a class or office to be seen as standing for something."[61]

To paraphrase Marin's phrase, Derrida under the burden of his personal presence represents a mandate that, by his own speech and physicality, is very much present at the congress. As one of the more eminent philosophers, he is sent to represent his philosophical constituency; he is and carries an *envoi* which as *envoyé* he in his address delivers to the

---

[60] Jacques Derrida, "Sending: On Representation," trans. Peter and Mary Ann Caws, *Social Research*, 49 (1982): 294-326; cit. 296. Further page references in the text.

[61] The note is signed by Peter Caws only. The French as cited here is reproduced in the English translation.

assembly "under some form or degree of legitimacy" (296). Speaking in a "frontier city" site "of passage and translation," Derrida proceeds to examine "the relation between *repraesentatio* and the positing or placing (Stellen) in *Vorstellung* or *Darstellung*" (297). Such "linguistic duality, or duel" leads him to a prolonged encounter with Heidegger's German, which helps the better to engage that multiplicity in the uses of "representation," the crossroads of "two codes, the political and the aesthetic"(297).

In view of these two codes and their multiple meanings "the authority of representation constrains us, imposing itself on our thought through a whole dense, enigmatic, and heavily stratified history" (304). But the constraint is complemented as well as compensated by an "ability to master" or to "dominate" (Marin's terms) an absence, a capacity for summoning it by, as Derrida says, "a power-of-bringing-back-to-presence" (307).

At this point, the *re-* of representation must be conjoined with Heidegger's sense of "this positionality, this power-of-placing, disposing, putting, that is to be read in *Stellen*" (306), which of course is to place or to dispose before oneself. Thus, the repetition or duplication (the *re-* in representation) and the positioning or *Stellen* come together somewhat like *Vorstellen* and *Darstellen*, and "this duplicity is at work in the term representation" (308).

The site of both this duplication and duplicity is the subject constituting itself in the act of making representation happen. The irony is that it is precisely at this juncture that Derrida locates the nexus between philosophical/poetic and political representations:

> The subject is what can or believes it can offer itself representations, disposing them and disposing of them. When I say offer itself representations, I could just as easily say, scarcely changing context, offer itself representatives (political ones for instance) or

even, and I will come to this, offer itself to itself in
representation or as a representative (309).

While this nexus is thinkable "in relation with a certain
highly determined concept of freedom—marked within the
Stellen of Vorstellen," it also and at the same time embraces the
re- in representation. Is it, then, the conjuncture itself of this
doubleness or "duplicity" which allows for "the continuum of
the semantic coherence between representation as an idea in the
mind ... and on the other hand aesthetic, political
representations." The essay at its most crucial culminates in a
question mark—a question not pointing (as many would
expect) in the direction of any deconstructive conclusion. On
the contrary, there is great caution, almost an impatience with
such deconstruction.[63] The final move, the ultimate alternative
to representation (which "commits us perhaps to thinking
altogether differently") is "the law" as something that
"manages to do no more than transgress the figure of all
possible representation" (326).

Still, the question remains, and it is a question which—
harboring plenty of "reseach opportunities"—may
appropriately be posited, that is, offered as a *position* in
concluding this introduction. In Derrida's words, "How is man,
having become a representative in the sense of *Vorstellend*,

---

[63] In response to Heidegger's move away from "the space of representation
and of the calculable," Derrida notes "that a criticism or a deconstruction
of representation would remain feeble, vain, and irrelevant if it were to
induce a criticism of calculable objectivity, of criticism, of science, of
technique, or of political representation. The worst regressions can put
themselves at the service of this antirepresentative prejudices" (311).

also and at the same time a representative in the sense of *Repräsentant*, in other words, not only someone who has representations, who represents himself, but also someone who himself represents something or someone? Not only someone who sends himself or gives himself objects but who is sent (*est l'envoyé de*) by something else or by the other?" (316).

QUIXOTISM, FETISHISM, AND THE PLACE OF REPRESENTATION

Scott Paul Gordon

ABSTRACT

The story of Quixote typically functions as a cautionary tale about representations that transgress their proper place: most quixote tales, which end with the quixote's distorted vision cured and the quixote returned to the reality the rest (supposedly) share in common, celebrate the moment when representations cease to usurp reality's priority in the process of perception. Quixote stories embody an Enlightenment dream of removing the barriers that impede proper perception to reveal the "truth" that these barriers had obscured. Critics treat Ann Radcliffe's *Mysteries of Udolpho* (1794) as a conventional "quixote cured" narrative, obsessed with distinguishing the "real" from its distortions and positing unmediated vision as an attainable ideal: its heroine, Emily, learns to distinguish reality from her powerful and pervasive imaginative distortions of it. But *Udolpho* exposes that any way of construing the world enacts a quixotic structure of making rather than finding: the novel ridicules Emily's superstition but does not establish as its alternative a clear-sighted perception of the "real," of objects as they "really are." Instead, *Udolpho* moves readers from one filter that produces the "given" to another (borrowed, albeit anachronistically, from James Thomson's *Seasons*). Despite the critical desire to make *Udolpho* confess its commitment to the "real," Radcliffe's text stages the replacement of one habit, superstition, with another, Thomsonism. The text thus legitimizes not merely the perceptions themselves but the *process* by which subjects and the representations they have consumed make the objects that captivate them.

The story of Quixote has long functioned as a cautionary tale about representations that transgress their proper place. The quixote, as Susan Staves writes, is one "whose consciousness is formed by the reading of some particular kind of literature, and who then goes forth into the world, assuming the world's reality will match the literary reality he knows,"[1] and most quixote tales expose the danger of allowing representations ("literary reality") to mediate one's world. Less than thirty-five years after the first volume of Cervantes's *El ingenioso hidalgo Don Quixote de le Mancha* (1605) had been "Englished" as *The history of the valorous and wittie knight-errant Don Quixote of the Mancha* (1612), English writers began to describe as "*Quixotes*" any individuals whose perceptions diverged from the larger community's. The quixote story helped writers explain (or explain away) such divergent perceptions, which occur, these stories imply, when an individual allows an internalized but unacknowledged generic lens—a set of representations—to filter the "real." John Cleveland's *Character of London-Diurnall* (1645) ridiculed the parliamentary forces that opposed Charles I as "*Quixotes* of this Age [who] fight with the Wind-mills of their owne heads; quell Monsters of their owne creation, make plots, and then discover them." The odd *Midsummer-Moon, Or Lunacy-Rampant* (1648) complained that Francis Cheynell's attempts to reform Oxford reveal that "he's *Don Quixoted*" and "takes the Colledge for an Enchanted Castle, the fellows for Giants, W. W. Ink—and L. L. for three distressed damsels."[2] These passages wield the word "quixote" as a term of abuse that, like "enthusiast" or "paranoiac," positions *others'* perceptions as faulty, excessive, or invalid (one never describes one's own perceptions as quixotic); applying the term "quixote," as Cleveland's comment shows, separates those whose perceptions "discover" objects that are really out there from

---

[1] Susan Staves, "Don Quixote in Eighteenth-Century England," *Comparative Literature* 24 (1972): 193-215, 193.

[2] John Cleveland, *The Character of a London Diurnall* (London, 1647) 3; *Midsummer Moon: or, Lunacy Rampant* in *J. Cleaveland Revived: Poems, Orations, Epistles, and Other of His Genuine Incomparable Pieces* (London, 1660) 173. For Cheynell, see Nicholas Tyacke, "Religious Controversy During the Seventeenth Century: The Case of Oxford" in *Aspects of English Protestantism, c. 1530-1700* (Manchester: Manchester U P, 2001) 262-319.

those who illegitimately "make" the objects they (mis)take to be given.[3] The representations stored in the quixote's mind replace the real that (traditional quixote stories insist) accurate perception must simply register. These accounts use the figure of Quixote to warn against representations that exceed their properly subordinate role as an imitation or reflection of a priorexisting reality. Three centuries ago the quixote embodied the charge often lodged against our postmodern world, in which, it is said, subjects "now inhabit a real of purely fictive or illusory appearances" and cannot differentiate "between truth and the various true-seeming images."[4]

Most quixote tales end with the quixote's distorted vision cured and the quixote returned to the reality the rest (supposedly) share in common. Such cures celebrate the moment when representations cease to usurp reality's priority in the process of perception. John Richetti notes that while some eighteenth-century novels, such as Sterne's *Tristram Shandy* (1759-69), imply that "reality is largely the construction of particular minds," more typically novels that use the "example of Cervantes' *Don Quixote* ... feature the deflation or

[3] Nelson Goodman's *Ways of Worldmaking* (Indianapolis: Hackett, 1978) emphasizes this distinction between acts of finding and of making. See also Richard Rorty, *The Consequences of Pragmatism* (Minneapolis: U of Minnesota P, 1982) xxx, xxxix.

[4] Christopher Norris, *Uncritical Theory: Postmodernism, Intellectuals, and the Gulf War* (Amherst: U of Massachusetts P, 1992) 14-15. Jean Baudrillard has explored these notions in *For a Critique of the Political Economy of the Sign*, trans. Charles Levin (St. Louis: Telos P, 1981) and *Simulations*, trans. Paul Foss, Paul Patton, and Phillip Beitchman (New York: Semiotext[e], 1983). Don DeLillo's account in *White Noise* (New York: Viking, 1985) of the most photographed barn in America ("Once you've seen the signs about the barn, it becomes impossible to see the barn": 12) has led many critics to propose that "the distinction between the real and fictional cannot be sustained" (Frank Lentricchia, "Don DeLillo," *Raritan* 8 [1989]: 1-29, 6) and to explore "representations which are ... lived as real" (John Frow, "The Last Things Before the Last: Notes on *White Noise*" in *Introducing Don DeLillo*, ed. Frank Lentricchia [Durham: Duke U P, 1991] 175-91, 180).

cancellation of eccentric individual perspectives by social
norms or by the brute factual force of the physical world."[5] This
normative procedure is evident, for instance, in Richard
Graves's *Spiritual Quixote* (1773), where Mr. Wildgoose's
"romantic and irregular undertaking," his quest for "primitive
Christianity," begins after he reads too many seventeenth-
century Puritan tracts. The novel ends with Wildgoose "cured"
and "reclaim[ed] ... from his erroneous opinions," confessing
that he "find[s] my head much clearer than it has been for some
months" and that "many things appear to me in a very different
light from what they have lately done." His friend Dr. Greville
rejoices that Wildgoose can now "see things in their proper
light" and that "the mist was dispelled from his mind," phrases
so crucial to the text's project that Greville repeats them ten
chapters later when he notes that Wildgoose had "been for
some time under the influence of a deluded imagination: but ...
the mists, which had clouded his reason, seemed now to be
dispelled." Wildgoose himself, in the novel's last chapter,
testifies that "it had pleased God lately to open his eyes" and
that "a weight of gloom had ... been removed from his mind."[6]
Wildgoose and his Panzo-like companion, Jerry, return to the
very community from which, Graves's text suggests, their
mistake of substituting representations for reality had alienated
them.

Graves's language reveals how effortlessly quixote stories
embody an Enlightenment dream. The language of "clouded ...
reason," of "mists ... dispelled," of "open[ing] ... eyes,"
reproduces the key elements of the Enlightenment belief that if
one could only remove the barriers that impede proper
perception, we would be able to see the "truth" that these
barriers had previously obscured. The disintegration of these

---

5   John Richetti, "Introduction" in *The Cambridge Companion to the
    Eighteenth-Century Novel*, ed. John Richetti (Cambridge: Cambridge U
    P, 1996) 1-8, 5.
6   Richard Graves, *The Spiritual Quixote*, ed. Clarence Tracy (Oxford:
    Oxford U P, 1967) 435-36, 448.

barriers, typically conceived of as religious, philosophical, and scientific authorities, was the primary aim of what Hans-Georg Gadamer has called the "emancipatory Enlightenment." The "heritage of the Enlightenment," Gadamer contends, has always contended that "a progressive process of clarification" can "set man, the actor and agent, free": "undertak[ing] to free us of outer and inner social forces and compulsions simply by making us aware of them," the "customary Enlightenment formula" requires us to "see through pretexts or unmask pretensions," a "demagicification of the world" designed to leave subjects perceptually acute and free. Modern science, whose claims to objectivity have enticed other disciplines to adopt its model as theirs, "stands or falls," Gadamer summarizes, with this "principle of being unbiased and prejudiceless." Above all, Enlightenment discourse promises that if individuals would struggle to "see through prejudices or tear away the pretenses that hide reality" a day will arrive when (in Graves's terms) all the "mists" will have disappeared and individuals will be able to "see things in their proper light."[7]

This central Enlightenment metaphor promises that illumination can dispel the dark shadows that previously obscured our perceptions of things. Enlightenment writers, according to Peter Hulme and Ludmilla Jordanova, believed that "[t]o look well and carefully, sufficient light is required, and looking in this way was deemed the only route to secure knowledge." In Enlightenment thought, as Frederick Beiser says, reason gains "sovereignty" and becomes "the highest authority, the final court of appeal, so that it takes precedence over *every* other source or standard of truth, such as inspiration, tradition, or the Bible." But the implication that the impediment to accurate vision is the lack of light on the objects one tries to understand obscures the *internal* barriers that impede one from accurately knowing objects and that prevent reason from

---

[7] Hans-Georg Gadamer, *Philosophical Hermeneutics*, ed. and trans. David E. Linge (Berkeley: U of California P, 1976) 32-33, 51.

functioning properly.[8] Francis Bacon famously calls these
barriers "idols," a term developed from the Latin "idola" that
refers not to false gods but to phantoms or delusive images.
The *Advancement of Learning* (1605) calls them "false
appearances" while *Valerius Terminus* (1603) prefers "idols"
and "fictions."[9] Each variant identifies the same phenomenon:
the internalized fictions that prevent minds from gaining real
knowledge of nature. Bacon's *Novum Organum* (1620) lists
four types of Idols, each emanating from a different source. The
"Idols of the Tribe," rooted in "human nature itself," lead men
to "measure … things" according to the "measure of the
individual": we "suppose the existence of more order and
regularity in the world" than exists; we stubbornly preserve our
opinions by neglecting contrary evidence and embracing "all
things" that "support and agree with it;" we are so captivated
by the familiar that our mind "feigns and supposes all other
things to be somehow, though it cannot see how, similar to
those few things by which it is surrounded." The "Idols of the
Cave," Bacon's second category, arise from each individual's
"peculiar constitution" and vary depending on one's education,
conversations, reading, accepted authorities, or occupation.
"Every one," Bacon notes ruefully, "has a cave or den of his
own, which refracts and discolours the light of nature." The
"Idols of the Marketplace," the "most troublesome of all"
according to Bacon, have "crept into the understanding through
the alliances of words and names"; the "ill and unfit choice of
words wonderfully obstructs the understanding." Finally, the
"Idols of the Theater" are "impressed and received into the
mind from the play-books of philosophical systems," a

---

[8] "Introduction" to *The Enlightenment and its Shadows*, eds. Peter Hulme
and Ludmilla Jordanova (London: Routledge, 1990) 1-15, 3-4; Frederick
C. Beiser, *The Sovereignty of Reason: The Defense of Rationality in the
Early English Enlightenment* (Princeton: Princeton U P, 1996) 3.

[9] Francis Bacon, *The Works of Francis Bacon*, ed. James Spedding,
Robert Leslie Ellis, and Douglas Denon Heath, 14 vols. (London:
Longman, 1857-74) 3: 219, 397. Subsequent references will be
parenthetical.

problem, as Bacon wrote in his *Natural and Experimental History for the Foundation of Philosophy* (1622), particularly dire in his own culture that "confined" the "sciences ... to certain and prescribed authors" who are "imposed on the old and instilled in the young" (4.54-62, 5.132). Each of these Idols, Bacon warns, prevents the understanding from encountering things themselves.

Individuals believe that their perceptions deliver to them things themselves. They are unaware that these Idols mediate their perceptions, and as a consequence they misrecognize a confused mixture—"things" blending with their own imagination—as the "nature of things" themselves. The mind, Bacon warns, "in forming its notions mixes up its own nature with the nature of things" (4.27). Bacon fears that the mind's captivity to these Idols ensures that this mixture occurs not intermittently but persistently. As he argues in *De dignitate et augmentis scientiarum* (1623, an expanded Latin translation of his own *Advancement*):

> False Appearances or Idols ... do not deceive in particulars, as others do, by clouding and snaring the judgment; but by a corrupt and ill-ordered predisposition of the mind, which as it were perverts and infects all the anticipations of the intellect. For the mind of man (dimmed and clouded as it is by the covering of the body), far from being a smooth, clear, and equal glass (wherein the beams of things reflect according to their true incidence), is rather like an enchanted glass, full of superstition and imposture (4.431).

These Idols, Bacon suggests, shape (in his view, "pervert") *all* perception, "predisposi[ng]" the mind to see "things" improperly. By insisting that it is not the "judgment" that Idols infect, Bacon rejects the possibility that the mind *first* encounters "things" themselves and *then* wrongly evaluates them. The errors of the understanding do not result from a failed second step in a two-step process. On the contrary, Idols ensure that the very objects that the mind receives—to observe, judge, analyze, assess—are *already* reshaped by cultural or personal forms.

Quixotes embody the idolatrous mind that "in forming its notions mixes up its own nature with the nature of things," but critics have ignored the resemblance between these two cultural fantasies with one major exception: Several early-twentieth-century critics argued that Bacon actually *authored Quixote.* Disputing the ascription of the first English translation (indeed, the first complete translation into any language) of Cervantes's *El ingenioso hidalgo Don Quixote* to Thomas Shelton, who was named as its translator only in 1700, these critics claim that it was Cervantes who clumsily translated into Spanish an English manuscript by Bacon. As Parker Woodward declared confidently in a 1916 issue of *Baconiana*:

> That Shakespeare the actor was only a mask for Bacon, the dramatic author, is, to those who will look carefully into the evidence, about as well proved as any fact three hundred years old can be proved ... We may say as much about Cervantes, the actual or more probably only nominal author of "Don Quixote."

Woodward exposes the "many half concealed intimations that Bacon was the real author," whose embedded ciphers (now decoded) had "set another problem for solution by inductive reasoning." Even for a reader trained in *Baconiana*'s hermeneutics, which convert any verbal phenomenon into a sign of Bacon's presence, such an ascription may seem unlikely: while composing *Quixote*, these same critics insist, Bacon was also writing Shakespeare's plays and the many "nouvelles which he put forth under the vizards of Lyly, Greene and Nashe."[10] All recent Bacon biographies ignore the claim that Bacon authored *Quixote* (indeed ignore Cervantes altogether), and I will neither defend it here nor posit direct influence between the two men. I will argue, however, that Cervantes's prose romance and Bacon's scientific writings share an obsession with distinguishing the "real" from its distortions. Both posit unmediated vision as an attainable ideal. And both focus on figures whose perceptions have been shaped by the representations they have consumed but who, unaware that their perceptions are mediated, naively believe they perceive the "real" itself.

Bacon reiterated his theory of Idols in each of his scientific works. The description in *De augmentis* of the mind as "an enchanted glass, full of superstition and imposture" had, in the *Advancement*, concluded with the phrase "if it be not delivered and reduced" (3.395)—and the promise of "deliver[y]" runs through all Bacon's work. Bacon does warn that some Idols "are hard to eradicate" and others "cannot be eradicated at all" (4.27), and James Bono is right to note that for Bacon "the real weaknesses of human knowledge are nearly intractable" and "cannot simply be bracketed by, for example, attempting to remove the biases and distortions that individuals bring to sense perception." But Bacon believes that instruments and experiment *can* solve this problem by, as Donna Haraway writes, "factor[ing] out human agency from the product."[11] This

---

[10] Parker Woodward, "Don Quixote," *Baconiana* 56 (1916): 173-186, 173, 179. See also Edwin Durning-Lawrence, "Did Bacon Write 'Don Quixote'?" *Baconiana* 47 (1914): 169-70; S. A. E. Hickson, "Review of Bacon-Shakespeare-Cervantes," *Baconiana* 64 (1923): 50-61 and *Baconiana* 65 (1923): 136-44; Horace Nickson, "The Authorship of 'Don Quixote,'" *Baconiana* 78 (1931): 271-85; R. Langdon-Down, "Observations on Shelton's *Don Quixote*," *Baconiana* 143 (1952): 58-67. See also Nieves Mathews, *Francis Bacon: The History of Character Assassination* (New Haven: Yale U P, 1996) 388.

[11] James Bono, *The Word of God and the Languages of Man: Interpreting Nature in Early Modern Science and Medicine. Volume 1: Ficino to Descartes* (Madison: U of Wisconsin P, 1995) 226-27; Donna Haraway,

solution's validity is, for my purposes here, less important than the consistency of his promise that the mind can be corrected so it no longer functions like "an uneven mirror [that] distorts the rays of objects according to its own figure and section" (4:27). Proper "interpretation of nature" depends, as *Novum Organum* insists, on individuals having first "performed these expiations and purgings of the mind" (4:70). If men would "discard, or at least set apart for a while, these volatile and preposterous philosophies" that have "led experience captive," if they could achieve "minds washed clean from opinions," men could then "study" the "works of God" in "purity and integrity" (5.132). Bacon's model, then, insists that only the mind that is empty, "washed clean," can encounter the "works of God" without impediment. "True philosophy," his *Advancement of Learning* opines, "echoes most faithfully the voices of the world itself, and is written as it were at the world's own dictation; being nothing else than the image and reflexion thereof, to which it adds nothing of its own, but only iterates and gives it back" (4.327).

Bacon's demand that the mind must "[add] nothing of its own" suggests that in proper perception "things" control the process by depositing their "true" image in the mind (as if through a "smooth, clear, and equal glass"). Locke's *Essay Concerning Human Understanding* (1690) theorized similarly that objects "obtrude their particular *Ideas* upon our minds, whether we will or no" and insisted that "the mind can no more refuse" these impressions "than a mirror can refuse, alter, or obliterate the Images or *Ideas*, which, the Objects set before it, do therein produce," and the assumption of perception's passivity persists through the eighteenth century: Edmund Burke's *Philosophical Enquiry into the Origin of Our Ideas of the Sublime and the Beautiful* (1757) describes how different types of objects produce different responses in passive

---

"Modest Witness: Feminist Diffractions in Science Studies" in *The Disunity of Science: Boundaries, Contexts, and Power*, ed. Peter Galison and David J. Stump (Stanford: Stanford U P, 1996) 428-441, 431.

spectators. Rebuking those who "attribute the cause of feelings which merely arise from the mechanical structure of our bodies, or from the natural frame and constitution of our minds, to certain conclusions of the reasoning faculty on the objects presented to us," Burke positions observers at the mercy of external objects, whose particular features necessarily produce the sensations that differentiate "sublime" or "beautiful" experiences.[12] Some claim that Burke's aesthetic theory marks a "transitional moment when speculation withdrew from the search for sublimity in the object and began to be centered in the emotions of the subject," but Burke's account preserves the focus on the object by proposing that its particular structure generates the perceiver's subsequent response. As Frances Ferguson notes, Burke's account "relies on the absolute reality of objects and upon the immutable reality of differences among them," and Thomas Weiskel's description of Burke's model reveals how thoroughly objects remain in control: objects "'occasion' sensations, and sensations quite automatically produce reflections, which may in turn be recognized by consciousness." This automatic or mechanical account of aesthetic experience depicts proper minds as passive, "mak[ing] no conscious or voluntary contribution" to perception.[13] An idolatrous mind, on the other hand, imposes on things its own images, and it is this illicit activity that Bacon consistently attacks. We "impress the stamp of our own image on the creatures and works of God, instead of carefully examining and recognising in them the stamp of the Creator himself" (5.132), Bacon complained: "God Forbid that we

---

[12] John Locke, *Essay Concerning Human Understanding*, ed. Peter Nidditch (Oxford: Clarendon, 1975) 118; Edmund Burke, *A Philosophical Enquiry into the Origin of Our Ideas of the Sublime and Beautiful*, ed. J. T. Boulton (London: Routledge, 1958) 45.

[13] Francis Ferguson, *Solitude and the Sublime: Romanticism and the Aesthetics of Individuation* (New York: Routledge, 1992) 40; Thomas Wieskel, *The Romantic Sublime: Studies in the Structure and Psychology of Transcendence* (Baltimore: Johns Hopkins U P, 1976) 14.

should give out a dream of our own imagination for a pattern of the world" (1.145).

It is crucial for Bacon to create minds that can see things "in themselves" because, as Bono argues, Bacon felt that "God's marks and traces *are* his creatures and works." Bacon thus departed from a Paracelsian tradition that, seeing in things "signatures" or "symbols," required interpreters to convert observed things into the larger network of which they are part. For Bacon it is necessary that the mind *not* redescribe through a hermenuetic exercise the "thing" itself into "complex webs of signification whose nodes, through resemblance, reverberate sympathetically, if occultly." These hermeneutical operations reveal only the Idols that hold minds captive. Bacon contrasts what the mind "suppose[s]" with what it would "find" did not such suppositions or predispositions distort its perceptions, accepting as "real" those things which "do not exist." For Bacon, then, *only* a mind purged or "cleansed" can encounter the "thing" itself (and the knowledge of God this enables). This belief functions, in part, to minimize the significance of the interpreter of nature. Unlike the Paracelsian "enterprise" at the center of which "were not facts, but rather the individual investigator's mind and imagination" whose "actual role as producer of this knowledge was at the forefront of *scientia*," the Baconian "regime of 'facts' ... efface[s] the role of the individual scientist," who must disappear so things can speak for themselves.[14] Only then can one gain knowledge about the reality that preexists observers and their theories.

One product of seventeenth-century empiricist ideology was the notion of *pure facts*, which wait to be discovered: The "facts" seen through the new scientific instruments "were not of one's own making," as Stephen Shapin and Simon Schaffer demonstrate, but "were, in the empiricist language-game, discovered rather than invented." Lorraine Daston concurs, arguing that during the seventeenth century " 'fact' shed its associations with 'doing' and 'making' ... and migrated toward

---

[14]   Bono, *Word of God* 1995, 245.

'datum,' that which is given rather than made." Despite their shared etymology, " 'fact' and 'manufacture' were nearly antonyms by the late eighteenth century," and in the sciences "that which is made edged closer to that which is made up, to fabrication or invention in the pejorative sense." "The solidity and permanence of matters of fact," Shapin and Schaffer continue,

> reside in the absence of human agency in their coming to be. Human agents make theories and interpretations, and human agents may therefore unmake them. But matters of fact are regarded as the very "mirror of nature."[15]

Bacon makes his "regime of 'facts,'" as we have seen, depend on a mind cleansed of all fictions, all opinions, all representations. "The expurgation of the intellect," the *Great Instauration*'s "Plan" insists, "qualif[ies] it for dealing with truth" (4.27). Don Quixote embodies an *un*purged mind. Bacon likens a proper intellect capable of discovering the "nature of things" to "a fair sheet of paper with no writing on it" (4.26-27), but Quixote's mind cannot find the "nature of things" because it *already* has "writing on it." The romances he has consumed have inscribed Quixote's mind, and his perceptual problems—taking windmills for giants, flocks of sheep for threatening armies—confirm Bacon's theory that these internalized representations control not only our response to what we see but what we see itself.

This dream of policing representations—of dispelling internalized fictions so that the "thing itself" can impress itself

---

[15] Steven Shapin and Simon Schaffer, *Leviathan and the Air-Pump: Hobbes, Boyle, and the Experimental Life* (Princeton: Princeton U P, 1985) 67, 23; Lorraine Daston, "Introduction: The Coming into Being of Scientific Objects" in *Biographies of Scientific Objects* (Chicago: U of Chicago P, 2000)1-14, 4; see also Daston, "Baconian Facts, Academic Civility, and the Prehistory of Objectivity" in *Rethinking Objectivity*, ed. Allan Megill (Durham: Duke U P, 1994) 37-64.

without mediation upon a receptive mind—pervades the many
eighteenth-century quixote stories, like Graves's *Spiritual
Quixote*, that reaffirm the opposition between fact and
interpretation so dear to Bacon. This opposition takes many
forms—questions of fact versus questions of meaning,
objective versus subjective, primary versus secondary
qualities—but in all forms it separates (to privilege) what John
Dewey called "objects already empirically given or presented,
existentially vouched for" from subsequent "conceptions" or
"representations" of such objects.[16] The many quixote stories
that stage this binary opposition define the "real" as that which
is left, so to speak, after subjects' illusory projections have
been dispelled. The active contribution Quixote's imagination
makes is precisely what marks him as an *il*legitimate perceiver,
since in proper perception the subject contributes nothing.
Inverting proper perception, quixote stories—as typically
used—demonstrate the dangers of "changing 'reality' into
appearance, of introducing 'relativities' into things as they are
in themselves—in short, of infecting real things with
subjectivity."[17]

Not all eighteenth-century texts, however, deploy quixote
figures to affirm the necessity of purging the mind of
representations so it can directly encounter reality itself. Some
use quixote stories, on the contrary, to show that *all* perception
involves internalized representations, preconceptions, or
"prepossessions"; in so doing these texts anticipate philosophers such as Nelson Goodman, who argue that

> habit, context, explicit instruction, interests, and
> suggestions of all kinds can blind or activate our
> perception, conceal or reveal a mountain or a

---

[16] John Dewey, "What Pragmatism Means by Practical" (1908) in *John Dewey: The Middle Works, 1899-1924*, ed. Jo Ann Boydston, 14 vols. (Carbondale: Southern Illinois U P, 1976-1983) 4: 98-115, 102.

[17] John Dewey, "The Need for a Recovery of Philosophy" (1917) in *John Dewey: The Middle Works* 10: 3-48, 25.

molehill. Far from merely recording what is before us, perception participates in making what we perceive; and for perception there are processes and stages of preparation.[18]

Critical writing on eighteenth-century fiction has overlooked this unconventional use of quixote stories, perhaps because critics, themselves embracing the opposition between fact and interpretation so central to typical quixote stories, have assumed that every quixote story reaffirms this opposition. This assumption is evident, for instance, in Wendy Motooka's *The Age of Reasons*, a recent study of eighteenth-century quixotes. Motooka suggests that

> the senses of English quixotes are always reliable. Their unusual views cannot be dismissed as the raving results of faulty perception. Rather, English quixotes are characterized by their uncommon ways of *interpreting* the findings of common sense.

It is a "consistent fact," she repeats, "that eighteenth-century English quixotes ... never err in their senses (they never mistake burlap for silk, or garlicky breath for Arabian perfume); they err only in their judgments about the empirical evidence before them."[19] Motooka distinguishes between "judgment" and "perception," between "interpret[ation]" and "the findings of common sense"; moreover, she describes these activities as if they follow a two-step process: all perceive an object alike and then some interpret it wrongly. But, as Bacon recognized, quixote figures can problematize precisely these distinctions on which Motooka relies: Quixote stories can

---

[18] Nelson Goodman, *Of Mind and Other Matters* (Cambridge: Harvard U P, 1984) 25.

[19] Wendy Motooka, *The Age of Reasons: Quixotism, Sentimentalism and Political Economy in Eighteenth-Century Britain* (London: Routledge, 1998) 6, 92.

suggest the collapse of these two stages into each other by
exposing the subject's role in constructing the very objects that
powerfully affect him or her as "givens."

The peculiar structure of Sophia Lee's rich and bizarre *The
Recess, or a Tale of Other Times* (1783-85), for instance,
exposes the representations that "prepare" or haunt all
perception, including each reader's. *The Recess*—which tells
the "secret history" of Matilda and Ellinor, two twin daughters
of Mary, Queen of Scots, whose lives conventional histories
have failed to record[20]—demonstrates that genres we have
consumed persistently mediate what we take to be the "real."
The Recess's critics have recognized its interest in genres,
contending that the novel depicts

> history ... turned into romance, or even a soap opera
> ... For Lee, history is 100 percent personal: it is
> made in the bedroom, the nursery, the court banquet,
> rather than in the study, on the battlefield, or in the
> countinghouse.[21]

But *The Recess* does not turn history into romance; its
narrators do (Essex fails in Ireland, Ellinor claims, because he
"sacrifice[s] every consideration to the recovery of one adored

---

[20] This paragraph condenses an argument I make at greater length in
"Quixotic Perception in Sophia Lee's *The Recess*" in *Eighteenth-Century
Women* 4 (2004).

[21] David Richter, *The Progress of Romance: Literary Historiography and
the Gothic Novel* (Columbus: Ohio State U P, 1996) 72; for the critical
consensus on this point, see also J. M. S. Tompkins, *The Popular Novel
in England, 1770-1800* (London: Constable, 1932) 227-28; Kate
Ferguson Ellis, *The Contested Castle: Gothic Novels and the Subversion
of Domestic Ideology* (Urbana: U of Illinois P, 1989) 69; Jane Spencer,
The Rise of the Woman Novelist: From Aphra Behn to Jane Austen
(Oxford: Blackwell, 1986) 195; Jayne Elizabeth Lewis, " 'Ev'ry Lost
Relation': Historical Fictions and Sentimental Incidents in Sophia Lee's
The Recess," *Eighteenth-Century Fiction* 7 (1995): 165-84, 182.

individual," herself).[22] The text hints that these narrators are quixotes who systematically filter experience through internalized representations of which they are unaware. Quixote stories typically encourage readers to differentiate themselves from such figures either by the comfortable clarity of retrospective narration (in which a cured narrator disowns past perceptions) or overtly ridiculous quixotes (which enable readers easily to distinguish real from representation), but *The Recess*'s innovative narrative structure denies readers these positions: It confines readers in a series of potentially deluded consciousnesses as securely as its heroines are confined in a series of prisons. Depositing readers in lengthy first-person narratives without allowing a view from outside to disrupt their trust, *The Recess*'s readers experience a quixote's filter. Matilda's romance redescription of Elizabethan politics (the text's first four hundred pages) seems a credible secret history until another character unexpectedly reveals its blindnesses and misconstructions. These subsequent narrators, moreover, are as unreliable as those whose tales they critique as quixotic. No narrative stands outside, above, or beyond the charge of quixotism. Repeatedly staging the conflict between interpretive modes, pitting one productive filter against another, Lee's text leaves readers hesitating between unresolved alternatives: they can credit either an interpretation shaped by the ghost of romance narratives or an alternative based on "interest," largely assembled themselves, whose structural similarity to quixotic narratives undermines its validity. By keeping both these possibilities in play, *The Recess* asks its readers (perhaps unlike its characters) to recognize what they typically cannot see: their own behaviors enact scripts of which they are largely unaware. Intensely aware of the residue one's reading deposits in one's mind, *The Recess* explores how the ghosts of representations, invisible to the subject, mediate what seems like immediate

---

[22] Sophia Lee, *The Recess; or, A Tale of Other Times*, ed. April Alliston (Lexington: U P of Kentucky, 2000) 226.

experience, an exploration of what we today call the discursive nature of experience.

The Recess's structure cannot, of course, force readers to wonder about their own quixotism. The familiarity of typical quixote stories, indeed, may "prepare" readers to use them to differentiate an *us* (who perceive the world unmediatedly) from a *them* (who improperly allow representations to mediate the world). *The Recess*'s risky strategy, that is, appropriates a cultural story typically used to keep representations in their properly subordinate place to insist instead that representations always stand between a subject and the "real." *The Recess* shows that quixote tales can be used to suggest that we are *all* quixotes, our own perceptions, no matter how free of presuppositions they may seem, shaped by internalized representations. Ann Radcliffe's *Mysteries of Udolpho* (1794) registers, perhaps contradictorily, these competing uses of the quixote story. *Udolpho* aims, on the one hand, to cure its heroine, Emily St. Aubert, of quixotic superstitions so that she sees only the "real" objects before her eyes. But Radcliffe's novel abandons quixote tales' traditional task of policing representation when it shows that Bacon's epistemological two-step—the mind must be a "receptive wax tablet" before it can legitimately be an " 'active' interpreter of what nature has there imprinted"[23]—misrepresents a process in which the mind actively endows nature with the capacity to imprint it. In *Udolpho* the "given" emerges from an interpretive situation: A representation, an interpretation, a filter, participates in producing those "givens" that exert real effects upon us. Most importantly, *Udolpho* explores this quixotism without attempting to cure it. The text hopes to produce, not to cure, quixotes.

Udolpho's critics write as if Radcliffe's novel belongs in the genre of "quixote cured": its heroine, Emily, "learn[s] to separate reality from illusion" and finds that only "by paying close attention to actualities of the external world can [she]

---

[23] Rorty, *Consequences of Pragmatism* 1982, 4.

hope to check her fantasies." Such critics focus on *Udolpho*'s mystery plot in which Emily struggles to make sense of ambiguous signs: flickering lights, unidentifiable music, gliding human figures, sheets that rise unexpectedly off beds. By exposing the natural cause or mundane object beneath Emily's fantasies, the text routinely ridicules her tendency to use supernatural explanations to make sense of these objects or events. Many critics, indeed, see Montoni himself, the novel's villain, as the product of Emily's imaginative distortions. Montoni's "sublime," according to Patricia Meyer Spacks, is largely Emily's projection, and by its conclusion the text strips him of the "add-ons" (his "phallic power") bestowed by Emily's imagination. Kim Ian Michasiw claims that Emily compensates for "the inadequacy of her senses" by positing a force that controls the varied things that happen to her: "the name of her god is male power or, in Italian, Montoni." Emily "sees as if enchanted," Michasiw demonstrates, "and all her visions lead her towards Montoni," a "petty *condottieri* captain" who "becomes a figure imbued with supernal power, a transformation effected almost entirely by Emily and her aunt." Agreeing that "the illusion" of Montoni "is more potent than the reality," Kenneth Graham declares that the "potentially-explosive force of obscure purposes who smoulders in the shadows of his castle" is "almost wholly the creation of Emily," who "creates of [Montoni] a figure of Burkean sublimity that both attracts and repels her."[24] These accounts

---

[24] Barbara M. Benedict, *Framing Feeling: Sentiment and Style in English Prose Fiction, 1745-1800* (New York: AMS, 1994) 175, 181, 194; Patricia Meyer Spacks, *Desire and Truth: Functions of Plot in Eighteenth-Century English Novels* (Chicago: U of Chicago P, 1994) 165, 167-68; Kim Ian Michasiw, "Ann Radcliffe and the Terrors of Power," *Eighteenth-Century Fiction* 6 (1994): 327-46, 332; Kenneth W. Graham, "Emily's Demon Lover: The Gothic Revolution and *The Mysteries of Udolpho*" in Kenneth W. Graham, ed. *Gothic Fictions: Prohibition/Transgression* (New York: AMS, 1989) 163-171, 167-68. See also Elizabeth Napier, *The Failure of the Gothic: Problems of Disjunction in an Eighteenth-Century Literary Forms* (Oxford:

assimilate Emily to a conventional quixote, whose penchant for
passing the "real" through a set of aesthetic representations
transforms a petty bandit into a sublime god—much as
Quixote's internalized romances turn windmills into giants.
Treating this technique of the "explained supernatural" as the
key to *Udolpho*'s meaning positions the text as a conventional
quixote story in which a deluded and inexperienced young girl
learns to stop creating objects that don't exist.

Emily herself scorns others' superstition, calling Annette a
"ridiculous girl" who "indulge[s] … fancies" and believes
"silly tales"[25]: she repeatedly "smiles" (231, 247, 391) at her
"simple" servant's "superstitious weakness" (392). But, the text
notes ironically, although Emily "could smile at" superstition
"when apparent in other persons," she "sometimes felt its
influence herself " (247). Emily comes to even ridicule herself,
"smil[ing]" at the recollection of how "she had suffered herself
to be led away by superstition" (490). The fact that her
"determin[ations]" to "resist its contagion" (490) often fail
merely affords her further chances to display shame that
mundane occurrences "had given her so much superstitious
terror" (635). That superstition persists in mediating Emily's
experience so late in the novel hints that she never surmounts
her superstitious quixotism, a fact recognized in the many
readings arguing that Emily does not grow or learn.[26] But
Emily's learning curve seems less important than the novel's
consistent ridicule of the quixotism of superstition. In this
effort it enlists not only Count de Villefort, whose daughter
Blanche, like Emily, credits "superstitious tales" until "the

---

Clarendon, 1987) 107 and David Punter, *The Literature of Terror: A History of Gothic Fictions from 1765 to the Present Day* (London: Longman, 1980) 68.

[25] Ann Radcliffe, *The Mysteries of Udolpho*, ed. Bonamy Dobrée and Terry Castle (Oxford: Oxford U P, 1998) 237-39. Subsequent references will be parenthetical.

[26] See Coral Ann Howells, *Love, Mystery and Misery: Feeling in Gothic Fiction* (London: Athlone, 1978) 48, and David S. Durant, "Ann Radcliffe and the Conservative Gothic," *SEL* 22 (1982): 519-30, 525.

ridicule in her father's glance" makes her blush (550), but also Montoni himself, who rebukes Emily with the very language with which she had rebuked Annette. When Emily reveals that she "had seen an apparition," Montoni demands that she "conquer" such "idle whims" and "release [her]self from the slavery of these fears" (243-44). After Udolpho's other inhabitants join Emily in the fear that "the north side of the castle [is] haunted," Montoni "employ[s] ridicule and then argument to convince them they had nothing to apprehend from supernatural agency" (543). At these moments, *Udolpho* counters quixotism with a chastened empiricism in which subjects respond without distortion to the "given" world of objects.

Udolpho exposes at other moments, however, that *any* way of construing the world enacts a quixotic structure of making rather than finding. If the novel ridicules Emily's superstition, it does not establish as its alternative a clear-sighted perception of the "real," of objects as they "really are." Instead, *Udolpho* moves readers from one filter that produces the "given" to another, from one "description," to use Richard Rorty's term, to another.[27] The "description" it advocates might be called "Thomsonism," in that the novel adopts it from James Thomson's *The Seasons* (1730). Thomson's *Seasons* popularized a way of seeing that finds God's presence in all his works. It is a Newtonian world that escapes mechanism by insisting that we read nature's order and regularity (indeed, its beauty) as signs of God's immanent presence. Speaking both of the natural cycle of seasons and *The Seasons* itself, Thomson's concluding "Hymn" begins with these lines: "These, as they change, ALMIGHTY FATHER, these, / Are but the *varied* GOD. The rolling Year / Is full of Thee."[28] The speaker of Thomson's "Summer," having wondered how "to sing of HIM,

[27] Richard Rorty, *Contingency, Irony, and Solidarity* (Cambridge: Cambridge U P, 1989) 39.

[28] James Thomson, "A Hymn" in *The Seasons*, ed. James Sambrook (Oxford: Clarendon, 1981) 254 (lines 1-2).

/ Who, LIGHT HIMSELF, in uncreated Light / Invested deep,
dwells awfully retir'd / From mortal Eye," solves this problem
by reading *through* nature to the invisible God. Like Robert
Boyle, who, says Thomson, the "great Creator sought" "Amid
the dark recesses of his works," Thomson learns to read
"Nature's Volume broad-display'd, / And to peruse its all-
instructing Page, / Or, haply catching Inspiration thence, /
Some easy Passage, raptur'd, to translate."[29] Thomson teaches
his readers to "translate" nature into God, to make an "easy
Passage" from one to the other. This rhetorical strategy works
by assimilating *all* phenomenon, whether a beautiful flower, a
sublime mountain, or a lightening bolt that destroys the
happiness of a young couple; indeed, it is built to explain the
otherwise inexplicable. *Udolpho* tries to interpellate its readers
into this Thomsonian "way of seeing," one quixotism, one way
to produce objects taken as "given," to replace another. Emily
St. Aubert, her father, and the narrator are the novel's primary
practitioners of Thomsonism. Nature's appearances frequently
prompt St. Aubert's "thoughts" to "ascend to the Great
Creator," and Emily's mind, too, often "arose" from "the
consideration of His works" to "the adoration of the Deity":
"wherever [Emily] turned her view," the text notes, "the
sublimity of God, and the majesty of His presence appeared"
(36, 47-48). However, improbably (*Udolpho* is set in 1584)
Emily and her father have internalized Thomson: Skilled
hermeneuts, they perform what Stanley Fish calls, in another
context, a "continual exercise in translation, a seeing through
the literal contexts of things (objects, events, persons) to the
significance they acquire in the light of a larger perspective."[30]
This exercise demands that *all* "appearances" tell the *same*
story. A prior narrative, that is, does produce what they see: If

[29] James Thomson, "Summer" in *The Seasons* 1981, 68-69, 130 (lines 175-
78, 192-95, 1553-55).
[30] Stanley Fish, *Self-Consuming Artifacts: The Experience of Seventeenth-
Century Literature* (Berkeley: U of California P, 1972) 25.

Emily cannot find "the Deity" in "His works," she must look harder.

Udolpho's exhaustive (and exhausting) natural descriptions—the novel reads like a "how to" manual of Thomsonism—reveals the need to teach that which, the novel implies, ought to occur naturally. But the text itself may be unaware of the quixotism of its Thomsonian "way of seeing": the discourse of quixotism exposes, above all, the tendency to consider the beliefs we hold (pragmatists would say that our beliefs "hold us") as accurate reflections of the "real" itself, as found rather than made. Quixotes must be blind to their own imaginative projection, must *misrecognize* the power they bestow *on* objects as inherently *in* objects, if the objects thus created are to become "real" enough to exert pressure back on the subject. Slavoj Zizek illustrates the process of misrecognition with an example of a monarch and his subjects:

> We, the subjects, think that we treat the king as a king because he is in himself a king, but in reality a king is a king because we treat him like one. And this fact that the charismatic *power* of a king is an *effect* of the symbolic ritual performed by his subjects *must remain hidden*: as subjects, we are necessarily victims of the illusion that the king is already in himself a king.[31]

Zizek's contention that the king's "power" is the "effect" of subjects' activity does not diminish this power's "reality" to subjects trapped in "illusion." The act of believing in an object empowers it, as Karl Marx argued in his doctoral dissertation (1841): "*all gods*, the pagan as well as the Christian ones," he proposed, "possessed a real existence. Did not the ancient Moloch reign? Was not the Delphic Apollo a real power in the life of the Greeks?" (Marx glosses "real power" as "something

---

[31] Slavoj Zizek, *The Sublime Object of Ideology* (London: Verso, 1989) 146. My italics.

that works on me.")[32] John Dryden's image in *Absalom and Achitophel* (1681) of rebellious Jews who "wondered why, so long, they had obey'd / An Idoll Monarch which their hands had made" describes similarly an object created by subjects that exercises "real power" over them.[33] Such objects gain power only to the extent that perception is quixotic, blind to its own activity: "if we come to 'know too much,'" Zizek argues, "this reality would dissolve itself."[34] The moment quixotes recognize their imagination's role in creating an object, it loses its power, as the cures with which typical quixote tales recognize. In this sense, the novel's success at leading readers to adopt Thomsonism depends on it masking its quixotism. The fact that *Udolpho*'s narrator shares its characters' Thomsonism, depicting individuals' passivity before natural scenery ("the stilly murmur of the brook below and of the woods around" "soothed" Emily's "spirits ... to a state of gentle melancholy" [416]), helps endow the objects thus produced with a strong "reality effect."

These formulations that depict natural objects acting upon Emily invoke the mechanical, Burkean model described above, in which a body's sensibility causes it to respond to natural objects precisely in the way it recoils from heat or salivates in response to certain foods. Uvedale Price's writings on the picturesque, a discourse important to *Udolpho*'s natural descriptions, explicitly invoke Burke: Price's *Dialogue on the Distinct Characters of the Picturesque and the Beautiful* (1801) contends that our response to the picturesque, like our response to beauty or sublimity, arises from certain "qualities" that "exist in" objects. "Each object," Price elaborates, is "composed of qualities" that produce in us specific responses

---

[32] Karl Marx, "Difference Between the Democritean and Epicurean Philosophy of Nature" in Karl Marx and Frederick Engels, *Collected Works*, 47 vols. (New York: International, 1975) 1: 25-105, 104-05.

[33] John Dryden, *Absalom and Achitophel* in *The Works of John Dryden*, 20 vols., ed. H. T. Swedenberg, Jr., et al. (Berkeley: U of California P, 1969-2000) 2: 7 (lines 63-64).

[34] Zizek, *Sublime Object* 1989, 20-21.

"independently of our being ... accustomed to them."[35] If Burke contends that beauty "was composed of smooth round atoms which were sensed as pleasure, and sublimity of hooked and implicated atoms which acted as pain," then Price insists, as Andrew Ballantyne shows, that the picturesque "work[s] in the same way."[36] When *Udolpho* implies that individuals respond mechanically to nature's prompts and depicts natural objects' power as a "matter of fact," it masks the quixotism of its Thomsonism.

The discourse of the picturesque, however, fractured over whether responses to scenery were as mechanical as Burke and Price claimed. Writers differed over how the objects that powerfully affect us gain their power. Richard Payne Knight, whose *Landscape: A Didactic Poem in Three Books. Addressed to Uvedale Price* (1794) had provoked Price's *Dialogue*, countered Price's theories again in his *Analytical Inquiry into the Principles of Taste* (1805) by insisting that our pleasure in beauty, sublimity, and the picturesque results not "solely from the eye, but must involve the intervention of the mind."[37] Aesthetic responses arise from a learned "association of ideas," Knight contends, which has become "so spontaneous and rapid" that "it *seems to be* a mechanical operation of the mind." Painters have *taught us* to respond to particular types of landscape, our responses occurring not because of an object's "intrinsic" qualities but because we have consumed a series of visual representations, and such "trains of thought will continue to haunt us in spite of all we can do to free ourselves from them."[38] A natural scene that we register as "picturesque," that

---

[35] Uvedale Price, *Sir Uvedale Price on the Picturesque, with an Essay on the Origin of Taste*, ed. Sir Thomas Dick Lauder (Edinburgh: Caldwell, 1842) 483-88.

[36] Andrew Ballantyne, *Architecture, Landscape, and Liberty: Richard Payne Knight and the Picturesque* (Cambridge: Cambridge U P, 1997) 83.

[37] Ballantyne, *Architecture* 1997, 143.

[38] Richard Payne Knight, *An Analytical Inquiry into the Principles of Taste*, 4th ed. (London, 1808) 136.

is, has been *made* picturesque "through the medium of the imagination."[39] An identical process, Knight notes, gives the "most trivial of objects" sentimental value. Such accounts position Thomsonism less as an "accurate" description of the "real" itself—imagined as immediately available, the "given" that exists before subjects attempt to know it—than as the means to produce a "given" that affects subjects in desirable ways. At moments, it is true, *Udolpho* shows that characters find in nature powerful objects that affect them, but at other times it suggests that they make these objects powerful by means of their imagination.

Udolpho often depicts its Thomsonism, the process of discovering "the Deity" in "His Works," as an operation subjects must perform (unknowingly) *on* the real, not something that the real does *to* properly configured subjects. Take, for instance, the natural scenery it describes with so much energy. The text encourages readers to judge characters, as critics have noted, "by their responses to natural scenery,"[40] by repeatedly contrasting sensible with insensible responses. When Emily and her aunt travel through the Alps to Udolpho itself, the Countess "only shuddered as she looked down precipices near whose edge the chairmen trotted lightly and swiftly," but Emily's experience differs. Filtered through Burke's aesthetics (the "solitary grandeur of the objects that immediately surrounded her ... received a higher character of sublimity from the reposing beauty of the Italian landscape below"), the landscape captivates her: "with [Emily's] fears were mingled such various emotions of delight, such admiration, astonishment, and awe, as she had never experienced" (166). The novel repetitively stages such scenes. As the Villeforts travel across the Pyrennes, the text contrasts

---

[39] Richard Payne Knight, "Review of *The Life of Sir Joshua Reynolds* by James Northcote," *Edinburgh Review* 23 (1814): 292, quoted in Ballantyne, *Architecture* 1997, 146.
[40] Daniel Cottom, *The Civilized Imagination: A Study of Ann Radcliffe, Jane Austen, and Sir Walter Scott* (Cambridge: Cambridge U P, 1985) 35.

Blanche's delighted response to their castle with her mother's, who

> reflecting, with regret, upon the gay parties she had left at Paris, surveyed, with disgust, what she thought the gloomy woods and solitary wildness of the scene; and, shrinking from the prospect of being shut up in an old castle, was prepared to meet every object with displeasure. (468)

The text systematically undermines the Countess's perceptions both by inserting qualifiers ("she thought") that imply that the woods and forest seem "gloomy" and "solitary," and the castle merely "old," *only* in her mind, and by noting that she was "prepared" to be displeased.

The mechanistic epistemology described above would contend that while some persons, due to insensible bodies or acquired prejudice, fail to register the impressions given off by the scenery "itself," others' bodily sensibility registers properly the impressions of the "real."[41] But *Udolpho* does not contrast the Countess's *mis*construction of the landscape due to her prepossessions with Blanche's delight prompted by accurate perception of the objects themselves. By noting that Blanche, who "had once or twice obtained" access to "reliques of romantic fiction" while in her convent, "fancied herself approaching a castle, such as is often celebrated in early story, where the knights look out from the battlements on some champion below" (468), *Udolpho* suggests that her delight is no less "prepared." This landscape affects subjects differently not because of empirical bodily differences but because of internalized representations. By invoking the narratives imbedded in Blanche's head, the text suggests that her

---

[41] I have explored the mechanical nature of sensibility in eighteenth-century discourse in my *The Power of the Passive Self in English Literature, 1640-1770* (Cambridge: Cambridge U P, 2002), 163-71, 201-04.

privileged perceptions—hearing the "melancholy dashing of oars" or the "low murmur of the waves"—depend on the representations through which she perceives: only her "preparation" by "romantic fiction" enables the scenery to affect her and to produce her "pensive mood."

The rigor with which Emily perceives through aesthetic categories provokes the suspicion, similarly, that the landscape can affect her because she has endowed it with such power. The landscape's sublimity moves her and its beauty soothes her because Burke's aesthetics and Thomson's poetry have taught her to be moved and soothed. Emily, of course, could not have read Burke or Thomson, her way of seeing being one of Radcliffe's many anachronisms. But perhaps it is precisely this anachronism that makes visible the lens through which she sees. Emily resembles the eighteenth-century landscape writers who, as John Barrell writes, so internalized paintings by Claude Lorrain and Salvador Rosa that they "would have seen ... a landscape as if it were already composed into the accepted structure." "The contemplation of landscape," says Barrell, "was not ... a passive activity; it involved reconstructing the landscape in the imagination, according to principles of composition" that were "learned so thoroughly that in the later eighteenth century it became impossible for anyone with an aesthetic interest in landscape to look at the countryside without applying them, *whether or not he knew he was doing so or not.*" In denying that this process involves an observer's "deliberate distortion of what he really saw into what he really did not see," Barrell collapses what he calls the "unimaginable antithesis" between an initial common sense perception ("what he really saw") and a subsequent interpretation ("deliberate distortion"). Rather, Barrell insists, observers were "so saturated in Claude's way of seeing and composing landscape" that they "could see it ... in no other way."[42] Perception *is* interpretation; more crucially, to perceive an object or

---

[42] John Barrell, *The Idea of Landscape and the Sense of Place, 1730-1840* (Cambridge: Cambridge U P, 1972) 6, 16.

landscape is to endow it with powers that enable it to act upon you.

The landscape functions, in effect, like a fetish. Terry Castle has suggested that *Udolpho* leaves the supernatural not so much "explained" as "displaced," "rerouted ... into the realm of the everyday": the text reveals that "spectral images of those one loves," rather than "old-fashioned ghosts," haunt us.[43] But the novel seems more interested in our investments in inanimate objects than in our relations with human (spectral or otherwise) others. The landscapes through which Emily travels comfort her more than any person with whom she comes into contact after her parents' deaths. *Udolpho* is obsessed about our obsession with objects. From its promise in its opening pages to explore our "attachment to objects," *Udolpho* teems with objects that resemble fetishes: the chestnut tree over which St. Aubert mourns; the books, pictures, chairs, and trees that the errant Valancourt embraces because memories of Emily seem to inhere in them (this return to fetishism marks his return to virtue [594]); the "plane tree" that Emily and Valancourt sacramentalize, endowing it with power to make them remember their shared history and thus to knit them together. If, as critics suggest, the novel depicts Emily as both poet and artist, this plane tree is her supreme fiction, a representation valued not because it corresponds to a prior-existing "real" but for what it does to subjects in the present. These objects, like classic fetishes, exert pressure from the moment of their creation back on the subjects who create them.

The figure of the fetishist, like the figure of the quixote, emerged in seventeenth-century discourse to police the boundary between the "real" and imaginative distortions of that "real." Theories of the fetish, as William Pietz's influential articles have shown, grew out of cross-cultural encounters

---

[43] Terry Castle, "The Spectralization of the Other in *The Mysteries of Udolpho*" (1987) in *The Female Thermometer: Eighteenth-Century Culture and the Invention of the Uncanny* (New York: Oxford U P, 1995) 120-39, 123-24.

between African and seventeenth-century European traders, whose accounts of African cultures describe fetishism as "the definitive mistake of the pre-enlightened mind": by "superstitiously attribut[ing] intentional desire and purpose to material entities in the natural world," African fetishists mingle their own imaginations with "given" objects. Seventeenth-century writers liken the process that produces a fetish to that which leads Catholics to see blood instead of wine: Thomas Astley's *New General Collection of Voyages and Travels* (1746) contends that both African natives and "*Romish* Church and Priests" believe that "the supreme Deity, for the Benefit of his Creatures" has endowed certain "material Objects" ("*Fetishes*") "with certain Virtues and Powers."[44] This figure of the fetishist was widespread. In the same year as Astley's *Collection*, an issue of Eliza Haywood's *Female Spectator* (1744-46) ridiculed politicians by likening them to South Seas natives who "idolize, and in a Manner worship, what has no other Merit than *themselves have given it.*"[45] These accounts insist that a fetish's "Power" arises not from an object's inherent "Merit" or "Virtue" but rather from the natives' imaginations, which improperly transform simple objects into divine things.

African fetishists, like European quixotes, are unable to see what lies in front of their faces, "real" things in all their objective ordinariness. The "scandal" of fetishistic thought involves such competing accounts of objects: the "essential problem" of the fetish, Pietz shows, is "the problem of the

---

[44] William Pietz, "Fetishism and Materialism: The Limits of Theory in Marx" in *Fetishism and Cultural Discourse*, ed. Emily Apter and William Pietz (Ithaca: Cornell U P, 1993) 119-51, 138-39; Pietz, "The problem of the fetish, II: The origin of the fetish," *Res* 13 (1987): 23-45, 41-42; and Pietz, "The problem of the fetish, IIIa: Bosman's Guinea and the enlightenment theory of fetishism," *Res* 16 (1988): 105-23,106; Astley quoted in Pietz, The problem of the fetish, II 1987, 40. See also Pietz, "The problem of the fetish, I," *Res* 6 (1985): 5-17.

[45] Eliza Haywood, *The Female Spectator*, ed. Kathryn R. King and Alexander Pettit, 2 vols. (London: Pickering and Chatto, 2001) 2: 364.

social and personal value of material objects."[46] Writers deploy the discourse of fetishism (or of quixotism) to denounce the subject's role in creating the very object he takes to be "given," contending that individuals misrecognize as essential to an object qualities or values with which they themselves have endowed it. Marx (who annotated de Brosses's *Du culte des dieux fétiches* [1760], which coined the word "fetish") suggests in *Capital* (1867) that it is not only in the "mist-enveloped regions of the religious world" that "productions of the human brain appear as independent beings endowed with life" but also "in the world of commodities," where "the social character of men's appears ... as an objective character stamped on the product of that labor." Enveloped in this "mist," "the social relation between men ... assumes, in their eyes, the fantastic form of a relation between things." Marx intends his "scientific discovery" to "*dissipate the mist* through which the social character of labor appears to us to be an objective character of the products themselves," a phrase that allies Marx's aim with the Enlightenment project to reduce objects that have been "overvalued" (Sigmund Freud's term) to their proper value or size. An object takes one real and many distorted forms, each of these generated by a deluded, mistaken, irrational, superstitious, or traumatized subject (for Freud, subjects "endow" or "appoint" objects to play powerful roles in their erotic life).[47] Were it not for such factors that lead subjects to misconstrue objects, we would all see the identical "real." Indeed, the ultimate product of the discourse on fetishism (like

---

[46]   Pietz, The problem of the fetish, II 1987, 35.
[47]   Karl Marx, *Capital: A Critique of Political Economy*, trans. Samuel Moore and Edward Aveling, 3 vols. (New York: International, 1967) 1: 72-74; Sigmund Freud, *Three Essays on the Theory of Sexuality* (New York: Basic Books, 1962) 20 and "Fetishism" in *The Standard Edition of the Complete Psychological Works of Sigmund Freud*, ed. James Strachey, 24 vols. (London: Hogarth P, 1953-74) 21: 149-59.

traditional quixote tales, as I've argued above) *is* the "real" as
something that *preexists* our encounter with it.[48]

These writers invoke fetishists (or quixotes) to insist on their
cure, but *Udolpho*'s representation of fetishistic behavior is
striking in that the novel surrounds the perceptions it *most*
wants to privilege with phrases that expose the perceiver as
actively making, rather than passively finding, the real.[49]
Udolpho refrains from explaining differential responses to
scenery, as we have seen, by invoking a "real" that puts
properly sensible observers through certain paces: instead, the
prior consumption of texts controls the impressions one
(mis)recognizes as immediate. Similarly, from its opening
pages, when St. Aubert discovers the "improvements" his
brother-in-law Quesnel will visit upon his boyhood home,
Udolpho exposes the omnipresence of fetishism without trying
to cure it. Its exploration of the "social and personal value of
material objects" never depicts this phenomenon as a problem.
Quesnel, who values only "œconomical prudence" and
"pecuniary advantage" (195), plans to cut down a beloved
chestnut tree that St. Aubert loves both because of his personal
history ("How often, in my youth, have I climbed among its
broad branches, and sat embowered amidst a world of leaves"
[13]) and transcendent taste (the replacement trees belong "on
the banks of the Brenta," not "near a heavy gothic mansion"
[13-14]). St. Aubert loses this battle because Quesnel's power
(he owns the tree) ensures that his *economic* evaluation of this
object triumphs over St. Aubert's *sentimental* evaluation of it.
Or so it seems: By insisting that Quesnel is blind when it comes

---

[48] To borrow Baudrillard's words, traditional quixote stories "provide …
the guarantee of the real, the lived, the concrete … of an objective
reality": *Political Economy* 1981, 137.

[49] James Watt has claimed that "instead of presenting her as a female
Quixote … Radcliffe in effect authorizes Emily's experience"
(*Contesting the Gothic: Fiction, Genre and Cultural Conflict, 1764-
1832* [Cambridge: Cambridge U P, 1999] 105): my argument here, on
the contrary, contends that Emily is *both* a female quixote *and* the novel
"authorizes" her "experience."

to taste, *Udolpho* itself awards St. Aubert the victory he cannot achieve within the novel. What is crucial here is that the novel stages a competition between two vocabularies (economic vs. sentimental) to demean a rationalism that would strip from objects the auras illusorily bestowed on them by romantic and quixotic minds like St. Aubert's. Indeed, *Udolpho* portrays such rationalism as itself quixotic:[50] Quesnel's ability to register only what can be calculated not only lacks "taste" but fails to recognize the chestnut tree's particularity. Admitting that his "feelings" must look "as old-fashioned as the taste that would spare that venerable tree," St. Aubert contends that Quesnel can "neither comprehend, nor allow for his feelings" (13). Quesnel epitomizes (anachronistically) the eighteenth-century spirit of "improvement" (14) that implies, as Frances Ferguson writes, "the relative interchangeability" of human beings. Only by accepting the "generic equivalence of one person's ownership and another's, of one person's technical knowledge and another's, and of one person's connection on one place or another" could improvers justify the actions that "produce[d] the satisfactions of visible productivity." Some, like William Gilpin's *Remarks on Forest Scenery* (1791) and *Observations … Made in the Year 1772* (1792), counter this collapse of the particular into the general by stressing the "individuality and specificity of natural objects," by exposing the histories—"the accidents that a tree has sustained through time"—that differentiate one object from another.[51] Like Gilpin, St. Aubert insists on the "individuality" of his tree, a position *Udolpho* endorses. The novel worries, in effect, about the *un*superstitious mind.

---

[50] David S. Durant argues that readers "are asked to eschew the rational faculty" ("Aesthetic Heroism in *The Mysteries of Udolpho*," *The Eighteenth Century: Theory and Interpretation* 22 [1981]: 175-88, 186). For an alternate claim that *Udolpho* idealizes the "rational and scientific voice of [Emily's] absent father," see Ian Duncan, *Modern Romance and the Transformations of the Novel: The Gothic, Scott, Dickens* (Cambridge: Cambridge U P, 1992) 42.

[51] Ferguson, *Solitude and the Sublime* (1992), 133-35.

Immediately after the text endorses St. Aubert's perceptions of objects and rejects the rationalist Quesnel's, St. Aubert exclaims that he is

> not yet wholly insensible of that high enthusiasm, which wakes the poet's dream: I can linger, with solemn steps, under the deep shades, send forward a transforming eye into the distant obscurity, and listen with thrilling delight to the mystic murmuring of the woods. (15)

When Emily first "listen[s] in deep silence to the lonely murmur of the woods," the text describes her, too, as "wrapt in high enthusiasm" (37). By the late-eighteenth-century, writers had begun to free the word "enthusiasm" from the pejorative connotations it possessed in seventeenth-century writing, which used it to demean those who while religiously inspired claimed to hear or see things unavailable to ordinary senses.[52] By 1744 Joseph Warton deployed the term to describe those who prefer "Nature's simple charms" to "coldly correct" art or "smoaky cities," but Warton's enthusiasts possess no special perceptual gift; they simply prefer natural to cultivated or civilized forms.[53] When *Udolpho* describes Emily and her father's "high enthusiasm," alluding to their state of absorption or even loss of self-awareness, it draws on the earlier sense of inspiration and thus provokes the questions that always dog that word: Is

---

[52] See Clement Hawes, *Mania and Literary Style: The Rhetoric of Enthusiasm from the Ranters to Christopher Smart* (Cambridge: Cambridge UP, 1996); Shaun Irlam, *Elations: The Poetics of Enthusiasm in Eighteenth-Century Britain* (Stanford: Stanford U P, 1999); Lawrence E. Klein and Anthony J. La Vopa, eds., *Enthusiasm and Enlightenment in Europe, 1650-1850* (San Marino: Huntington Library, 1998).

[53] Joseph Warton, "The Enthusiast: Or The Lover of Nature" in *Eighteenth-Century Poetry: An Annotated Anthology*, ed. David Fairer and Christine Gerrard (Oxford: Blackwell, 1999) 359-64 (lines 88, 144, 169).

she inspired by something outside herself or projecting herself on external nature?

Quixote tales, as we have seen, typically insist that to know the "real" subjects must resist "enthusiasm," purge their heads of "dreams," and discipline the "eye" from "transforming" (so it can passively register) the real. But here these phrases ("high enthusiasm," the "poet's dream") do not undercut St. Aubert's perceptions. One *should* hear the woods murmur. These passages link the capacity to hear the "mystic murmuring of the woods" not only to "high enthusiasm" and a "dream" but to a "transforming eye," an eye, that is, that *makes* rather than *finds* what it perceives: They simultaneously expose and authorize the subject's active role in producing objects or phenomenon he takes to be "given." Rather than suggesting, as Wordsworth did, that in hearing the woods murmur he "see[s] into the life of things" or discovers "knowledge, to the human eye / Invisible,"[54] *Udolpho's* phrasing insists that St. Aubert's "transforming eye" *produces* this "knowledge." Such supplementary phrases unmoor the way of seeing that Radcliffe privileges from a correspondence, or subordinate relationship, to the "real." Emily and Blanche can be moved and comforted by the landscape because they have fetishistically appointed it to play that role: St. Aubert's "transforming eye" suggests that one *needs* to be a quixote to hear the waves or the trees murmur. *Udolpho*, then, at once authorizes certain perceptions *and* betrays the representations that have shaped them. The text thus legitimizes not merely the perceptions themselves but the *process* by which subjects and the representations they have consumed make the objects that captivate them. Despite the critical desire to make *Udolpho* confess its commitment to the "real," Radcliffe's text stages the replacement of one habit, superstition, with another, Thomsonism. *Udolpho* frees us from

---

[54] William Wordsworth, "Tintern Abbey" (line 50) and *The Prelude* (Book 2, lines 423-24) in *William Wordsworth (The Oxford Authors)*, ed. Stephen Gill (Oxford: Oxford U P, 1984) 133, 403.

one "picture which held us captive" not to land us in the "real" itself but so another "picture" can captivate us.[55]

---

[55] See Ludwig Wittgenstein, *Philosophical Investigations* (New York: Macmillan, 1953) 35-36: "A *picture* held us captive. And we could not get outside it, for it lay in our language and language seemed to repeat it to us inexorably." See also Rorty, *Consequences of Pragmatism* 1982, 32.

ANIMATED LOOKS:
THE ROMANTIC LITERARY SKETCH
AND THE UNFINISHED PROJECT OF
MODERN TRANSPARENCY

Samuel Baker

ABSTRACT

If the formal quality of sketchiness has long fascinated modern artists and writers, that may be because sketches evoke a certain transparency, or immediacy of artistic experience, that can seem antithetical to the more intensely mediated modes of representation which characterize modernity. British Romantic writing gave a central role to figures of the sketch in a manner that could counteract both the gravity of symbol-heavy aesthetics and the rigidity of the representational order of politics emerging out of the Age of Revolution. Mary Shelley's tale "The Swiss Peasant" effectively emblematizes how sketch figures (such as her title character, first introduced as the model for a drawing) can lend animation even to otherwise quite generic narratives. Such literary sketches import a palpably political sense of mutability into a representative tradition associated by critics such as David Lloyd with a self-consciously state-centered practice of literary culture. .

Lingering under the spell of photographic media, and newly enraptured by digital technologies for visual representation, we sometimes seem on the verge of forgetting the sketch. Actually or figuratively, we now capture a person, a place, or a moment in a snapshot, a freeze-frame, a slide, or a file in formats designed to rule out, at whatever resolution, any trace of sketchiness. Beyond the confines of schools and museums, we perhaps most often hear *sketch*, in its primary sense of "a hasty or undetailed drawing or painting,"[1] in the phrase "composite sketch," which denotes a representation drawn from the memories of victims and eyewitnesses, of a criminal who has evaded security cameras. By thus turning the sketch out toward the margins of society, we have reversed the situation that obtained in the nineteenth-century media landscape. Before the popular dissemination of photographic equipment, the sketch was a central vehicle for polite representation, whether visual or verbal, domestic or public, intimate, biographical, historical, or touristic. In recent years, art historians and literary critics have reconstructed how the discourse and practice of sketch drawing fundamentally informed the sensorial disposition of that epoch.[2] As drawing became in the Romantic period a more common accomplishment, sketching became a preeminent art of feeling, and the word "sketch" became, by extension, a generic term for improvisatory, gestural works, whatever their medium: for works, be they pictorial, literary, or dramatic, whose incompleteness or formal impurity only heightens their felt immediacy. The term came into broad use to denote representations that bring their audience into the moment of creation, minimizing the sense of mediation to the point where artist, work, subject, and proper audience seem one body.

To be sure, in some measure because this sketch mode held such potential, it was restricted to particular practitioners, select

---

[1] "Sketch," *American Heritage Dictionary of the English Language*, 3rd ed. (Boston: Houghton Mifflin, 1992).

[2] Ann Bermingham details the rise of the sketch aesthetic in *Learning to Draw: Studies in the Cultural History of a Polite and Useful Art* (New Haven: Yale UP, 2000), now the definitive treatment of how "the discourse and practice of drawing interpellated a draftsman" in early modern England. Kim Sloan's *'A Noble Art': Amateur Artists and Drawing Masters, c.1600-1800* (London: British Museum Press, 2000) also offers an excellent overview of this process. Richard Sha's *The Visual and Verbal Sketch in British Romanticism* (Philadelphia: U of Pennsylvania P, 1998) focuses on the sketch form itself, and includes a thorough survey of its literary uses. In what follows I indicate citations to Sha's book parenthetically.

audiences, and ritualized moments of creation and consumption. To some extent, these restrictions were anchored in the traditional subordination of sketch to finished product, but the lack of a public for even those works in their day underlines the general rule that only a connoisseur would seek out more typically preliminary or occasional sketches, absent some personal connection to the artist or subject.[3] Still, the rage for drawing in the era democratized connoisseurship, engendered a taste for sketches, and encouraged their public circulation, whether in books or exhibitions. Sketching may have seemed a fundamentally private pursuit, a way of producing occasional mementoes and keepsakes to share with intimates. But as Richard Sha shows in his valuable analysis of *The Visual and Verbal Sketch in British Romanticism*, the very identification of sketching with private life lent it power as a mode of public rhetoric. Sha goes so far as to say that "the alleged privacy of the Romantic sketch is usually staged" (Sha 25); and while this claim of his applies in the first place to sketches designed to have a public life, it suggests how public agendas could inhere even in the more ephemeral sketches that littered the everyday life of the Romantic-period gentry.

When applied directly to Romantic writing, the label "sketch" indicated a work of purportedly extemporaneous origin or ephemeral quality, and also signaled a certain intangible sublimity. In poetry, for instance, William Blake's early volume of *Poetical Sketches* and William Wordsworth's apprentice travelogue *Descriptive Sketches* both use the term to disavow their authors' preparations and thereby hint at their intuitive brilliance. When writers appropriated the sketch mode in this fashion, they employed an aesthetic gambit, opening up new possibilities for descriptive evocation, but also subtly deprecating the picture that their writing conveyed, pleading in advance that its shortcomings be forgiven. Such rhetorical

---

[3] On the "paradox of Constable's preparatory oil sketch ... that appears to do almost no preparatory work" (p. 129), see Ann Bermingham, *Landscape and Ideology* (Berkeley: U of California P, 1986) 126-36.

humility seems the burden of the "biographical sketch" title affixed to the author profiles that stand at the head of many eighteenth- and nineteenth-century volumes: a title that subordinates these introductions both to some idea of a fuller, stand-alone biography and to the more fully realized works of their subjects, the authors whom readers would go on to encounter face-to-face in the main body of the text. Yet if Romantic writers considered sketches to be works in a minor mode, in which everyday contingencies and ambiguities subsisted, they also exploited the permission that the "sketch" label granted them to be thus unrefined. They found the faintness and fuzziness allowed to sketches an almost divinatory resource when they sought to trace the residues of an evanescent past, to envision emergent forms of life, or to catch quotidian details too subtle to be registered otherwise.

Much as a tourist might limn an old cottage, hoping to fashion a future memento of yesteryear, local color writers like Washington Irving's "Geoffrey Crayon" recorded their experiences in works with titles like that of his *Sketch Book.* Much as an architect might submit plans in outline, political writers of the day, often reflecting on the revolutionary theorist Condorcet's influential *Esquisse,* offered "outlines of an historical view of the progress of the human mind" that likewise gestured towards future, utopian horizons.[4] Even the biographical sketch, long a marginal genre, became a central vehicle when Samuel Taylor Coleridge published his *Biographical Sketches of My Literary Life and Opinions*— a.k.a. the *Biographia Literaria.* Since the sketch mode minimized the felt separation between artist, subject, and audience, it could serve well for exploring brief, private

---

[4]   The Marquis de Condorcet's *Esquisse d'un tableau historique des progress de l'esprit humain* was first published in English as *Outlines of an historical view of the progress of the human mind: being a posthumous work of the late M. de Condorcet* (London: J. Johnson, 1795), by a radical bookseller with whom William Wordsworth was then closely associated.

moments, for encapsulating a given structure of feeling, or for communicating that structure to a broad public. By risking the chaos of contingency, the art of the sketch achieved new communicative intimacy. Sketching meant compressing space, time, and social relations into a minimal series of marks that nevertheless could potentially hold maximal significance. Thus by the end of the period in question, when Baudelaire extolled the "perfect" sketches produced by the well-nigh anonymous "painter of modern life," he would link the sketch's power to trace life's details with its ability to characterize public manners generally, and moreover with the power of lithographic reproduction to circulate the artist's vision to the masses.[5] In retrospect, one can see that if the lithograph as Baudelaire celebrated it was clearly an avatar of the photograph, it in turn had its forerunners in the visual and verbal sketches of British Romanticism, which likewise lent themselves to capturing everyday scenes felt to represent broadly a whole way of life.

Insofar as they seemed simultaneously intimate and public, such Romantic sketches could seem to conjure the social whole from the individual part without obvious recourse to some intermediary, all-encompassing symbolic system. In this way, the rhetoric of immediacy that the sketch mode facilitated made it particularly useful for capturing representative subjects. In its felt immediacy, the sketch seemed singularly mimetic, rather than semiotic; predicated on prior iconic similitude rather than on a mediating apparatus of symbols. Hence immediate representations in the sketch mode could seem to work outside of those more convention-driven circuits of representation into which "representation" as such is still sometimes collapsed, and could thereby give access to some seemingly basic truth. Again, it may help here to see sketching as a rough, imprecise

[5] These were Constantin Guys's drawings, engraved for publication in newspapers. Charles Baudelaire, "The Painter of Modern Life" [1863], in *The Painter of Modern Life*, Jonathan Mayne, trans. and ed. (New York: Da Capo, 1964) 1-40.

art that nevertheless anticipated photography when it conjoined a naturalistic visual rhetoric with strong claims for the general significance of specific scenes. (And of course photography itself has undergone a long process of refinement that is in some ways continuous with the refinement of drawing technique.) Mimetic sketch representations seemed vital, expressive, natural, Romantic: Perhaps they even *were* these things. Whatever their status along such lines, they often encouraged the naïve belief that they might briefly *touch* their audience with an intimate appeal that bypassed political and aesthetic convention altogether.

To say this is to associate sketching with the ethos of transparency whose importance to the Romantic-period nexus of sentimentalism and egotism is well known.[6] But it is also to highlight how Romantic writers, when they took recourse to the sketch mode, positioned themselves in regard to an ethical tension between purportedly transparent or immediate representation on the one hand and representation mediated by symbol systems on the other, a tension crucial to the social history of modernity, over and beyond its political and aesthetic history. If the privilege the Romantics afforded the sketch persists in the special relation that the "composite sketch" of today bears to our sense of fear, or (to take a less marginal example) in how sketch comedy regulates our ironic attitudes, this persistence suggests that the representational strategy our sketch artists inherited from their Romantic forerunners retains a singular effectiveness. The media and the status of sketch representations may have changed since the Romantic period, but the sketch mode, however residually, still seems to grant artists a special access to feelings organizing everyday life; the gestural art of the sketch captures emotive structures that otherwise would lie hidden in plain sight. Both then and now, sketches profess to abjure more conventional or symbol-laden

---

[6] See for instance Jean Starobinski's classic study *Jean-Jacques Rousseau: Transparency and Obstruction*, Arthur Goldhammer, trans. (1971; Chicago: U of Chicago P, 1988).

representation as itself an obstacle to divining public feelings, or, to use a Romantic term, the general will.

Recognizing how sketches evade—or refuse more intrinsically symbolic modes of representation—we find ourselves on the ground of arguments about the history of representation that have recently been made by David Lloyd and Paul Thomas. In their collaborative book *Culture and the State*, Lloyd and Thomas argue that it was only with the later Wordsworth and other Romantic reactionaries (and only *contra* the teachings of Jean-Jacques Rousseau) that the representation of the whole by its parts emerged as the intrinsic logic common to modern culture and the modern state, to modern aesthetics and politics alike.[7] In the view of Lloyd and Thomas, if we want to achieve critical distance on the modernity we inhabit, a modernity suffused by a representational logic of symbolic proxies ultimately anchored in the state form, we must take fuller measure of the alternative epistemology of transparency opposed to that logic by Rousseau, and for that matter by Wordsworth in his early career—not least in his poetic "sketches." In the balance of this essay, I seek to revise Lloyd and Thomas's story about Romantic-period social form by adducing to their small gallery of Romantic texts more literary works in the sketch mode. Romantic literary sketches reveal much about how writers in the era adjudicated between the rhetoric of transparency and the rhetoric of symbolic representation (what Lloyd and Thomas call "representation" *tout court*). By foregrounding transparency, such sketches mark what were felt at the time to be the limits of representational symbolization (if not of representation itself in the broader sense). For such limits inhere even in literary sketches that otherwise seem quite clearly focused on how proxy representation became a dominant modality of power relations. If the Romantic period saw a substitutive logic of representation assert its dominance, it also saw the art of the

---

[7] David Lloyd and Paul Thomas, *Culture and the State* (New York: Routledge, 1998).

sketch mark off a zone of immediacy in which the hegemony of
that logic could be seen to falter.

My central exhibit here will be Mary Shelley's 1831 tale
"The Swiss Peasant," a character study that highlights the story
of its own sketching, and in so doing claims to represent an
emblematic denizen of Switzerland with aesthetic immediacy.
Following out some of the threads of politics and aesthetics
woven into Shelley's text, I will further investigate the sketch
mode in light of Lloyd and Thomas's arguments by comparing
Shelley's sketch motifs to those of her older contemporary,
Wordsworth. Shelley's tale delineates how its eponymous
subject and her husband represent their state, and in so doing it
exemplifies how the political and aesthetic valences of
representational form intersect in the period. But "The Swiss
Peasant," like related sketches by Wordsworth, uses the open
nature of the sketch to supplement an emergent aesthetic
ideology of the social body with a notion of how one might
consider that body animated, granting life and agency to those
represented by affording them the independent energy
attributed to the sketch itself.

In the *Keepsake* annual for 1830, Mary Shelley, identified as
"The Author of Frankenstein," published a story that sketched a
representative portrait, in a representative landscape: the figure
of "The Swiss Peasant."[8] Shelley's main subject is a lively

---

8   Mary Shelley ["The Author of Frankenstein"], "The Swiss Peasant: A
     Tale," *The Keepsake for MDCCCXXXI*, ed. Frederic Mansel Reynolds
     (London: Hurst, Chance, and Co. [1830]) 121-46; reprinted in Charles E.
     Robinson, *Mary Shelley: Collected Tales and Stories* (Baltimore: Johns
     Hopkins UP, 1976) 136-52. Henceforth cited parenthetically by page
     number in the Robinson edition. First published anonymously in 1818
     and attributed by many critics at the time to Percy Shelley, *Frankenstein*
     had been republished under Mary Shelley's name in 1823, and would in
     1831 appear in a new edition. Laurie Langbauer convincingly reads "The
     Swiss Peasant" as a parable of political aporia in "Swayed by Contraries:
     Mary Shelley and the Everyday," in Audrey A. Fisch, Anne K. Mellor
     and Esther H. Schor, eds., *The Other Mary Shelley: Beyond
     Frankenstein* (New York: Oxford UP, 1995) 185-203; see also Gregory

peasant woman, Fanny Chaumont by name. Fanny's tale
emerges when Shelley's narrator (given a male identity) and his
friend "Ashburn," traveling together through the sublime
landscapes of Switzerland's ecclesiastical territory, fix on the
Swiss woman almost at random, first as a model to be
sketched, then as a native informant. The "romantic tale" Fanny
tells turns out to be of a piece with the political history of
Switzerland's revolutionary-era turmoil (137). In the meantime,
it is a love story, which Shelley's narrator presents as "a
lesson" on "the strange pranks love can play with us" by
"blending in one harmonious concord the harsh base [sic], and
melodious tenor of two differently stringed instruments" (138).
We discover in the course of the story that Fanny's husband
Louis rivals, or complements, her as a representative "Swiss
Peasant." By the story's end, it has become clear that the
romance of Fanny and Louis conveys an implicit, if very much
generic, argument illustrating the public ramifications of
domestic intimacies. On another level, Shelley uses Fanny's
tale to wed the sketch mode, the art of immediate feeling
associated with Fanny, with a more definitively symbolic mode
of representation associated in turn with her husband. This
second, symbolic mode tracks coins, soldiers, and other things
strongly stamped by the state—things that are connected in the
semantic web of the story by the heavily freighted name
"Louis" and that stand as interchangeable proxies for the
national and universal qualities of wisdom, constancy, and duty
whose essence Shelley seeks to capture. Another kind of union
effected by Shelley's story is the mixing of the verbal with the
visual it accomplishes as an exercise in ekphrasis. The story
spins the tale of an illustration included with its original
publication, both elaborating on the caption for the engraving

---

O'Dea's sensitive treatment of Shelley's stories "'Perhaps a Tale You'll
Make it': Mary Shelley's Tales for *The Keepsake*," in Syndy M. Conger,
Frederick S. Frank, and Gregory O'Dea, eds., *Iconoclastic Departures:
Mary Shelley after Frankenstein* (Madison: Farleigh Dickinson UP,
1997) 62-78, especially 72-75.

of "The Swiss Peasant" printed with it and explaining how such a picture could come to be.[9]

At the outset of the story, Shelley emphasizes the sketchy side of her aesthetic. She does so, in part, through the frames in which she sets Fanny's tale; the failings and false starts that Shelley's narrator initially shares with the reader do much to establish the story's brief for a risky sketchiness, even as they suggest how the story will also recuperate the conservative solidity that Louis comes to personify. The first such framing sketch is put in place by Shelley's narrator's opening meditation on perceptual limitations, both emotional and physical. "Why," he asks rhetorically, "does the imagination for ever [sic] paint the impossible in glittering tints?" Having once "apostrophized the coy nymph" of solitude, the narrator is finally alone; but now, experiencing an excess of solitude, he "abjure[s]" it, even

> in [its] fitting temple—in Switzerland—among cloud piercing mountains, by the resounding waves of the isle-surrounding lake. I am beside the waters of Uri—where Tell lived—in Brunnen, where the Swiss patriots swore to die for freedom. It rains— magic word to destroy the spell to which these words give rise—the clouds envelop the hills—the white mists veil the ravines—there is a roar and a splash in my ears—and now, and then, the vapours break and scatter themselves, and I see something dark between, which is the hoar side of a dark precipice, but which might as well be the turf stack or old wall

---

9 On the illustration to Shelley's story see O'Dea, "Perhaps a Tale You'll Make It"; on the relationship between text, image, and production values in the *Keepsake* more generally, especially with regard to the publication's cultivation of women writers and editors as well as readers, see Kathryn Ledbetter, "'White Vellum and Gilt Edges': Imaging the *Keepsake,*" *Studies in the Literary Imagination* 30:1 (Spring 1997): 35-49.

that bounded Cumberland's view as he wrote "The Wheel of Fortune." (136)

The Swiss landscape captured here is a "temple" of solitude because its physical ambiguities are well fitted to the suspended mental state of reverie. Here experience is perfectly immediate to the perceiver, and perfectly fragmentary. Fancy overwhelms the imagination, which cannot shape a proper representation of what is seen because it is paralyzed by a surfeit of indeterminate cues. On Shelley's page, traces of sensation flash by in short phrases: shards of linguistic material that might—if properly assembled—"spell" political history or figure national vistas, but that will not quite cohere as such so long as the reverie lasts. Instead, the evocation of the sounds of waters suggests that meaning here emerges out of an aleatory process that bypasses human signification. This formal analogy between the narrator's mode of perception and the sketch mode of representation actually turns out to be a linguistic homology, if we recall that "sketch" derives from the Italian *schizzare*, "to splash." In this context, when the narrator ends by evoking, as the ultimate screen for his imaginings, a precipice plane that might just as well be a wall of stone or turf, he brings to mind Leonardo's well-known draughtsman's exercise of splashing water on a wall and then quickly tracing in paint whatever figures the randomly splashed shapes suggest.

Thus even before Shelley's narrator outlines his portrait of Fanny, he prepares the ground for it by evoking, in the rainy Swiss landscape, the vagueness out of which such sketches must emerge. Still, the inchoate atmosphere of this initial backdrop records nothing of the vitality by way of which a sketch gives definition to what it communicates. Instead, the narrator portrays a soul drowning in description; the very immediacy of the sketch mode here places it in uncomfortable proximity to solipsism. Significantly, it is not another character, but rather another text that intervenes to dispel this fog of description and catalyze the narrator's will to "beguile" the "weary hours" by composing a narrative. Shelley's narrator, he says, is inspired to write by what he calls "the sole book that I possess": Byron's sublime tale of sensory deprivation "The Prisoner of Chillon." It is Byron's example, and that of Byron's hero, which lead the narrator to represent Fanny to his reader: to escape the bonds of ennui and transcribe, he says, "a true tale," one "lately narrated to me by its very heroine, the incidents of which haunt my memory, adorned as they were, by her animated looks and soft silvery accent." Tracing out this line of thought, Shelley's narrator again proleptically anticipates the mixed representational character of Fanny's tale, resorting to an intertextual plane to adumbrate the dialectic between drawn sketch and stamped symbol that structures the story that follows. It is the printed text of Byron's poem that inspires Shelley's narrator's recollection of Fanny's "silvery accent," a characterization suggesting the metallic blur of a sketcher's pencil. Likewise, it is Byron's vivid memorialization of a state prisoner legendary for wearing a path in the stone of his dungeon floor that prompts the narrator to "follow" albeit "with unequal steps," "cheat[ing] the minutes in this dim spot" by giving new life to Fanny's "animated looks" (a figure that evokes the vitality with which a sketch seems to surge towards completion in the eye of the beholder).

So when the strength of Byron's characterization of his prisoner of solitude echoes in the fancy of Shelley's narrator, it gives rise to a companion sketch of a Swiss figure who, although an everyday woman rather than a historically significant man, proves no less representative of the Swiss state than Byron's hero (136-37). Then, after the narrator has harnessed Byron's strength to draw the Swiss peasant Fanny into existence in the story's initial frame, a second interior frame finds him deploying a figure reminiscent of Percy Shelley to prompt further his imagination. For having announced he intends to relate Fanny Chaumont's tale, the narrator introduces it more particularly by describing his recent travels with the aforementioned Ashburn, a character whose affinities with Percy Shelley go far beyond his name's evocation of "The Ode to the West Wind." The narrator relates how, as they journeyed through the sublime Swiss landscape, he and Ashburn came upon

> a view which so awoke the pictorial propensities of my friend, that he stopped the coupée (though we were assured that we should never reach our inn by nightfall, and that the road was dangerous in the dark), took out his portfolio, and began to sketch. As he drew I continued to speak in support of an argument we had entered upon before. I had been complaining of the commonplace and ennui of life. Ashburn insisted that our existence was only too full of variety and change—tragic variety and wondrous incredible change.—"Even," said the painter, "as sky, and earth, and water seem for ever the same to the vulgar eye, and yet to the gifted one assume a thousand various guises and hues—now robed in purple—now shrouded in black—now resplendent with living gold—and anon sinking into sober and unobtrusive gray, so do our mortal lives change and vary. No living being among us but could tell a tale of soul-subduing joys and heart-consuming woes, worthy, had they their poet, of the imagination of Shakespeare or Goethe. The peasant will offer all the acts of a drama in the apparently dull routine of his humble life."
>
> "This is pure romance," I replied; "put it to the test. Let us take, for example, yonder woman descending the mountain-path."
>
> "What a figure!" cried Ashburn; "oh that she would stay thus but one quarter of an hour!—she has come down to bathe her child—her upturned face—her dark hair—her picturesque costume—the little

plump fellow bestriding her—the rude scenery
around—
"And the romantic tale she has to tell."
"I would wager a louis that hers has been no
common fate. She steps a goddess—her attitude—
her looks, are all filled with majesty."
I laughed at his enthusiasm, and accepted his bet.
We hurried to join our fair peasantess, and thus
formed acquaintance with Fanny Chaumont. A
sudden storm, as we were engaged conversing with
her, came, driven down from the tempest-bearing
hills, and she gave us a cordial invitation to her
cottage. (137)

With a degree of condensation that verges on the parodic,
this interior narrative frame locates in Ashburn the mimetic
sensibility of Percy Shelley—recognizable from his elemental
figurative palette ("sky, and earth, and water"), his fascination
with mutability, and his insistence on the universality of
beauty—and identifies this Shelleyan sensibility with
Ashburn's activity of sketching. At the same time, the narrator
introduces the problematic of transparency by calling for proof
of Ashburn's "romantic" concept that each everyday person has
a public interest legible to the gifted onlooker. It is this very
problematization that brings Fanny herself into the foreground,
singled out as a subject random enough to provide a
representative test of this notion for which Ashburn evinces
such "enthusiasm." Meanwhile, the wager here—a "louis"—
strikingly asserts a general linguistic equivalency among
Fanny's life story, the man with whom, we learn, her fate is
entwined, and the coin of the French ancien régime. Here
again, as in the story's initial frame, Mary Shelley supplements
a figure of sketch vivacity with figures of personification and
material symbolization. This pattern continues, now moving
across the threshold between the second frame and Fanny's
proper tale, as Fanny invites the travelers out of a sudden storm

and into the fixed refuge of her home, where they can hear her story at leisure. This hospitable gesture finds Fanny echoing (or, rather, anticipating) the narrator's framing move; both storytellers take advantage of a stormy mountain atmosphere, shelter, and a biographical tale to overcome solitude by recollecting for others "common[] incident[s]" from her past (136). Yet Fanny's story begins with a shock to the presumed safety of its circle of auditors; she informs her guests, once they are all safely sheltered together, that the founding event of her life was an avalanche's erasing her family in their cottage.

This literal blurring of Fanny's origins emblematizes the sketchy evanescence that turns out to be the hallmark of her character. Orphaned by nature, the young Fanny, we are told, also by nature could not be placed in the order of language, given her allure as "one of those lovely children only to be seen in Switzerland, whose beauty is heartfelt but indescribable" (138). Without losing this overdetermined sublimity, Fanny is to some degree recuperated into the symbolic order when a noble family adopts her and gives her "a bourgeois education" (140). Despite being thus wrested out of what might have been considered her proper station in life, Fanny grows to womanhood innocent of any moral or intellectual failings. Nevertheless, the conflict that drives her tale derives from her confused status, for Fanny draws suitors from both the aristocratic and peasant classes. These suitors—Henry de Marville, heir of the family into which Fanny is adopted, and Louis Chaumont, an ambitious peasant of yeoman stock—vie with each other not just for her hand, but also as representatives of their respective classes in the wars following the French Revolution. Fanny's own representative status, as it emerges, derives from her ability to hold open the possibility of a future Switzerland that might incorporate both classes without privileging either.

The story resolves this conflict not by elevating one class or the other, but by subsuming both to the power of Fanny's femininity. To this end, Shelley constructs a somewhat convoluted plot. When Fanny and Louis build on their shared status as members of an educated peasant vanguard to become confidants, Henry grows jealous of his peasant rival and engineers Louis's banishment from their region. Louis returns at the head of an insurrection; but at the moment of Louis's triumph, Fanny prevails upon him to spare Henry and the rest of the de Marville family, claiming that she has married the young aristocrat. Years later, Louis, returning from the wars, happens upon Fanny again. She reveals her subterfuge, marries him, and bears the child whom she carries on her back when the narrator and Ashburn encounter her. The narrator describes the reconciliation of Fanny and Louis as less a case of good fortune than a matter of purification and idealization at the altar of womanhood. Whereas Louis, in his years at war, had "alloy[ed]" "rage and hate" with "love" (151), he rediscovers Fanny after "[h]er image, side by side with all that is good in our nature, had dwelt in his heart; which thus became a shrine at which he sacrificed every evil passion" (152). As the narrator concludes Fanny's story, she is shown to be indeed the "goddess" Ashburn perceives, condescending as she does, at the last, to reward an acolyte who has sufficiently propitiated her.

By unfolding the epic dimensions of Fanny's experience, the narrator's recounting of her story purports to confirm the claim Ashburn makes as he sketches: the claim that the commonest soul bears immanent within it the public "drama" of "majesty," and reveals that drama transparently to the true artist. Just as in the story the epic emerges from the interstices of the everyday, Ashburn's sketch captures at random the grandeur of the feelings that materially organize contemporaneous society. It is true that while Fanny personifies the vital mimetic capacity of the sketch, she also becomes, for Ashburn as for Louis, an idol, which is to say, an icon invested with worth and power as a matter of belief. A definite symbol of nothing but the immediate iconicity she embodies, Fanny at least to some degree serves as a fetish for the wishful power of fiction to materialize our desires in the delimited, minor sphere of our choice. But still, while Fanny's mutability may make her an apt screen on which to project desire, it also makes her an apt representative for categories of persons held to be in flux. Her status as a sketch converges with her status as a woman; and if she takes on the lineaments of the "angel of the household" increasingly touted by fiction of the period, she also has the practical, improvisatory character of an everyday worker, and intimates, through her reasoned engagement with historical progress, the revolutionary prospect of female citizenship. Along similar lines, Fanny's mutability makes her an apt representative of the Swiss people, coming once again to exercise some degree of self-determination after decades of oppression.

In light of the active quality that Fanny's character thus exhibits, the yearnings and estrangements that frame her story and constitute its plot add to the fetishism of feminine beauty undeniably present here as a persistent wish for general movements of spirit, movements that will express themselves through the cipher of identity as they organize new, unlooked for forms of life. The sense of a desire for such organized novelty, indeed, takes us back to the "something incongruous" that the narrator notes "in the pair" of peasants, who only seem "more strangely matched" once he has heard their story. In the final analysis, it is this very incongruity of Fanny and Louis, both at once proxies of broader movements and dynamic prime movers, that holds open the promise of change. It is this fundamentally contingent quality of their story—its sketchiest aspect—that as Shelley's narrator puts it, "lost me my Louis, but proved Fanny at once to be a fitting heroine for romance."

A similar romance of the synthetic imagination seems to underwrite how Shelley's tale enlists the spirits of both Lord Byron and Percy Shelley, citing the former's strong sense of agency and the latter's idealistic sensibility as touchstones for its own sui generis world-making. At the same time, by putting forward a sketch whose subject both is and is not a symbolic proxy of her time and place, and which teases with its indeterminacy while flaunting its conventionality, Shelley perhaps above all revises and extends the literary practice of Wordsworth. Ashburn's sketching, the activity that sets the story in motion, self-consciously adapts Wordsworth's celebration of the rustic encounter while transporting it from rural Britain to the Switzerland praised so fulsomely in Wordsworth's political poetry.[10] Meanwhile, Shelley's tale adapts the story of a woman left by a soldier love that Wordsworth tells in "The Ruined Cottage," a narrative poem that would have been familiar to Shelley in its published form as an episode related early in *The Excursion* (a poem excoriated by Byron). Finally, the conventionality of Shelley's sentimental tale, however thematized within the story, or befitted to its *Keepsake* setting, follows Wordsworthian precedent in hewing to the constrictions of generic forms. This final point raises the question of the status of the sketch mode for Wordsworth. Can the sketch be said to work for Wordsworth, as it does at least to some degree for Shelley, to grant his subjects a degree of autonomy from his conception of them—a degree of animation?

To bring this question about the status of Wordsworth's sketches, and about the Romantic sketch in general, into focus from another, illuminating angle, I want to turn now to consider Wordsworth's role in the story Lloyd and Thomas tell in their recent critique of the ideology of modern representation. In their account of the modern attenuation of the arts of transparency, Wordsworth figures most importantly for how he comes to impress his works with a strong stamp of state ideology. Lloyd and Thomas stress how in *The Excursion*, and elsewhere in later works, Wordsworth explicitly celebrates—

---

[10] On this point and those that follow about Shelley's relation to Wordsworth see Robinson's note to the story, *Mary Shelley*, p.382, as well as O'Dea, "Perhaps a Tale You'll Make it,'" p. 73, and Laurie Langbauer's "Swayed by Contraries: Mary Shelley and the Everyday," p. 193-94.

and seeks to enact—what they identify as the process of "forming citizens for the modern state."[11] In so doing, he models what they consider "the function that culture plays for the state" in nineteenth-century Britain, and moreover in modern nation-states generally. Lloyd and Thomas take their overall cue here from Matthew Arnold's remark, in *Culture and Anarchy*, that "the idea of culture suggests the state." Writing in critical dialogue with Raymond Williams's *Culture and Society*, they describe how nineteenth-century British political and literary thinkers conceptualized culture in terms of its ability to produce proper subjects for liberal capitalism and institutionalized this function for culture through educational organization. Their central contention is "that the discourse of culture, precisely insofar as it intersects with a simultaneously emergent theory of the state," establishes "the discursive parameters within which, to borrow from Benedict Anderson's important formulation, the citizen can be imagined" (CSt 62). This account of cultural function as the colonization of everyday life at the behest of state organization helps explain a major strand of Romantic commentary on those topics. For instance, the state culture form that Lloyd and Thomas describe certainly does seem congruent with that which Wordsworth invokes when he claims in *The Excursion* that Britain's "indivisible sovereignty" entails the obligation to teach culture to those from whom it would reap allegiance. It likewise captures an important dimension of the pedagogical work we have seen Shelley undertake with "The Swiss Peasant," insofar as her protagonists stand as proxies representative of a model national culture.

For Lloyd and Thomas, representation is the key term that links political and aesthetic ideology. This is now a fairly familiar idea.[12] But Lloyd and Thomas claim not just that a

---

[11] Lloyd and Thomas, *Culture and the State*, 1. Henceforth cited parenthetically as CSt.

[12] On "representation" across aesthetics and politics, see Gayatri Spivak, "Can the Subaltern Speak?" in *Marxism and the Interpretation of*

historical connection exists between the work of aesthetic representation and the establishment of representational structures in politics, but that the logic of representation in those spheres is historically identical (CSt 81, 156-57). If the ethical work of subject formation through acculturation underwrites the modern state, Lloyd and Thomas argue, it can do so because culture and state alike are previously underwritten by the substitutive form of representation itself. According to this analysis, resisting the state entails enlisting with working-class activists who remain suspicious of the promise of ameliorization through political representation. Such activists make their goal not gaining education or the franchise, but overcoming capitalist relations of production by decolonizing themselves of state culture. (However counterintuitively, Lloyd and Thomas cite Chartism as a prime example of a radical activist movement—not beholden to a rhetoric of representation—thereby weighing in on a scholarly dispute over the matter).[13] Meanwhile, resisting state culture, for Lloyd and Thomas, entails resisting aesthetic representation, and instead seeking out a Rousseauvian experience of social immediacy. Lloyd and Thomas read Rousseau's ideal of transparency as an alternative before the fact to the representational state; his polemics against theatrical entertainments and his praise of public festivals (especially in the first *Discourse*) stand for them as a critique of its emergence. Significantly, of course, this alternative state of

---

Culture, Cary Nelson and Lawrence Grossberg, eds. (Urbana: U of Illinois P, 1988) 271-313, and James Chandler, *England in 1819: The Politics of Literary Culture and the Case of Romantic Historicism* (Chicago: U of Chicago P, 1998) 155-202.

[13] "Chartists," they write, citing Joan Wallach Scott and Eileen Yeo, "far from being fixated on the franchise as a nostrum or a panacea (as for instance Gareth Stedman Jones would have it), constantly stressed that economic and social reforms were expected to follow from the inception of popular government" (95). On these issues see also Margot C. Finn, *After Chartism: Class and Nation in English Radical Politics, 1848-1874* (New York: Cambridge U P, 1993).

transparency was widely associated with Switzerland, whose republican heritage seems to underwrite the teachings of the "Citizen of Geneva." Thus the very Swiss setting of Shelley's tale underscores how it carries forward a project of transparency that may elsewhere be in eclipse.

For a positive program, Lloyd and Thomas look to foster the quality of immediacy that Rousseau champions. In their view, the ethical virtue of social immediacy for which Rousseau offers a brief not only characterized the prepolitical communities that were disappearing in Rousseau's day, but also could characterize the unmediated culture of a future radical democracy. (Lloyd and Thomas step carefully here around the association of such Rousseauvian idealism with Fascism.) Wordsworth, for Lloyd and Thomas, shows a capacity to capture Rousseauvian immediacy but turns self-consciously to a proto-Arnoldian commitment to the mediatory work of ethical culture. In their early incarnations, on this account, Wordsworth's *Lyrical Ballads* feature dialogic moments when the voice of the people speaks without mediation. Here, then, we have the countertradition of speaking sketches that runs through "The Swiss Peasant" as well, bearing forward into modernity the residual, or still emergent, project of transparency.

"Sketches," here, becomes quite literal; Lloyd and Thomas take, as their central example of such persistent immediacy, the speech of the title character that concludes Wordsworth's poem "Old Man Travelling; Animal Tranquility and Decay, A Sketch." Wordsworth here undercuts the poem's initial view of the old man as "by nature led / to peace so perfect," directly quoting him to reveal that he is instead bound up in a state of war:

> Sir! I am going many miles to take
> A last leave of my son, a mariner,
> Who from a sea-fight has been brought to Falmouth,
> And there is dying in an hospital.

That Wordsworth dropped these lines in his 1815 revision of his poem and whittled the title down to "Animal Tranquility and Decay," demonstrates for Lloyd and Thomas how he generally sought to rewrite the feelings of the people into a narrative of ethical acculturation, a narrative that refuses them integrity outside of their place in the system of state culture (CSt 72-75). Although Lloyd and Thomas do not say exactly this, one might well apply their categories to this speech as follows: The old man's testimony affords a shocking glimpse of the immediate character of everyday experience in a mass society mobilized by war. Wordsworth's "Sketch" serves as an immediate window into a reality sutured up by the patriotic bromides of his later, more "complete" efforts. Noting the use of the word "sketch" in the poem's original subtitle, Lloyd and Thomas make something like this point in the context of a critique of aesthetic norms:

> The poem is also self-confessedly a sketch, at once provisional and immediate, open and unfinished, experiential and experimental. If it has been declared a sketch that fails to produce a masterpiece ... examination of the grounds for what seems, now, so self-evident an aesthetic judgment will illustrate how bound up with political representation our norms of verisimilitude are. (CSt 74)

Along these lines, one might conceive of the difference between Wordsworth's 1798 "Old Man Travelling" and his 1815 "Animal Tranquilty and Decay," or for that matter that year's *The Excursion*, as the difference between a sketch, with all of its immediacy and potentiality, and a detailed, finished print, stamped with a certain finality into the page. The material difference here is also a difference in the authority that the composer of the picture claims for its representativity. Yet whereas Wordsworth's "sketch," advancing no claim for its subject as a proxy for a wider society, captures significant feelings and the very voice of its subject, with great tact, his later works substitute cant and false sentiment even while they seek definitive status as national representations.

Still, even those later works have their redeeming aspects, and the main revision that I propose to the way that Lloyd and Thomas read such texts as Wordsworth's is to argue that a sense of immediacy surfaces in these texts more often than such critics would allow. The fact that the sketch persists to this day as a minor but powerful aesthetic form presents a major problem for their argument about aesthetic norms. Meanwhile, we can track, as I have been trying to do here interlinearily, the ongoing vitality of the project of transparency. We can note how even a arguably conservative work of generic fiction, such as Shelley's tale of "The Swiss Peasant," centers on a Wordsworthian speaking sketch that asserts its right to represent itself; and we can read onward with an eye for the generative ambiguities in more contemporary cultural artifacts. Shelley and the other Romantics, including Wordsworth, may have contributed to the colonization of culture by the state, but they were also witnesses, however compromised and insensitive, to a moment of decolonization in Switzerland; and they captured energies at work in that transformation that we would do well to bring forward into an age when the character of information threatens to be ever more firmly stamped into place, while many liberatory gestures of human self-definition remain to be highlighted.

DOUBLY ENCODED REPRESENTATIONS IN MODERN DRAMA AND FICTION: RUPTURING COORDINATES OF (RE)SEMBLANCE AND MEANING

Robert Weimann

ABSTRACT

As a point of departure, the present essay undertakes to challenge what may well be today's most persisting objection to representation. According to its poststructuralist critique, representation bridges difference, removes rupture, constitutes closure. But while under certain circumstances this may indeed be one of its functions, representation in modern drama and fiction cannot very well be reduced to healing the breach between language and the world. Far from constituting a space for unity, homogeneity, and indifference, the late nineteenth- and twentieth-century modes of representation can themselves be shown to defy unity and plenitude. Being itself divisively encoded, modern representational writing draws on areas of considerable instability in which picture and perception, signs and meanings diverge. In particular, both literary genres bring forth sites of collision on which coordinates between mimesis and meaning, between what is shown or said and what is meant, are ruptured. The traditional conjuncture of world-picturing/world-appropriating functions and empathy in text-appropriating practices gives way to a new relationship of literary production and reception, wherein the image of what is represented is largely suspended in, or intercepted by, the artful practice of what is performed or performing.

There are at least two art forms or genres in Western culture whose comparative understanding can profit from reinstating a nexus between representation and mimesis. One is the theater, the other is the novel or prose fiction in a wider sense. Once mimesis, as the introduction to this volume has suggested, can be conceived beyond its neo-Aristotelian domestication, we are faced with an "other" or different type of mimesis that, as Elin Diamond has recently noted, is "impossibly double." It is double in that it is "simultaneously the stake and shifting sands: order and potential disorder, reason and madness." It is a mimesis that, on the one hand, "speaks to our desire for universality, coherence, unity, tradition, and, on the other hand, it unravels that unity through improvisations, embodied rhythm, power instantiations of subjectivity, and … outright mimicry."[1]

Representation and Mimetic Practice in the Theater

In the history of the theater, representation may be said to achieve a particularly wide spectrum of composite forms and functions, largely because it is bound to, and must be achieved through, diverse types of mimetic practice. On the one hand, there is the text of the author, which through plot and dialogue projects the dramatic representation of an imaginary world. No matter whether or not this verbally constructed world aims at any *imitatio vitae*, it does engage, address or, defy images—or at least fragments of a behavioral order—that, in Hamlet's phrase, tend to "hold the mirror up" to motivations and circumstances. While on this compositional level mimesis "intrinsically" informs the language of drama, it is being complemented by a second, partially nonverbal level of staged mimetic practice. Such practice inspires and consummates through performance the dramatic text in the process of its theatrical transaction.

---

[1] Elin Diamond, *Unmaking Mimesis: Essays on Feminism and Theater*. (London: Routledge 1997), p. v. In preclassical and non-Aristotelian types of mimesis I have noted a similar conjunction of enchantment and disenchantment, celebration and parody, the fantastic and the ordinary; see the first two chapters of my *Shakespeare and the Popular Tradition in the Theater* (Baltimore: Johns Hopkins U P, 1978) 2-48.

Thus, whatever is represented in the imaginary world of the text is mediated and thereby, one might say, intercepted through visible, audible, physically present bodies in pursuit of a different sort of signification. Structurally as well as culturally, the composition of dramatic fictions and their delivery by living bodies and voices are not at all identical; the difference between them is that between two potentially discontinuous modes of cultural production and socially informed codification. In theatrical productions, they can of course be perfectly complementary; in so far as together they are impelled by both imaginary and material versions of mimesis, each of these mimetic practices is to double business bound.

Such doubleness involves mode and matter. Even while performers re-present what is contained in verbally constructed fables, their performance retains an existential underside—a surplus that cannot quite be contained in and by any writing, any text, or any purely verbal articulation. No matter how hard actors try and subsume their own delivery under the regime of an imaginary world of dramatic illusion, the immediacy of their impact on spectators either exceeds or does not exhaust itself in a faithful rendering of what the text represents. What over and beyond their scriptural pretext obtains is a hybrid result, in which the represented fiction of an imaginary world is engaged on an elementary level by real labor, professional skill, and an irreducible investment of physically finite energy and experience.

Hence, a dramatically performed representation, in drawing on and mobilizing two different sources and directions of mimetic practice, is "impossibly double." Even where, in the theater of traditional closure and illusion, the gulf between the represener (the real actor) and the represented (the imaginary character) appears to be suspended under the spell of dramatic action, it is irreducibly there, hidden under the illusion of the moment. As far as such concurrence of role and actor appears unified as well as unifying, it can at best narrow the gap between them, never entirely annihilate it.

Since a dramatic representation produced in the theater is an event that can be structured by but never reduced to a verbal text, semioticians have for years sought to study performance as a signifying practice in relation to the conditions of its production and reception. Jean Alter, for instance, has attempted to define "an inherent duality of theatrical activity" by distinguishing between its two basic functions. As he notes,

> the very essence of theater lies in a permanent tension between its referential function, which relies on signs to produce meaning, and what I have called the performant function, which ... satisfies the emotional need to witness special achievements: physical, aesthetic, technical, and so on.[2]

The point that Alter neglects to make is that there is a remarkable amount of historical contingency in the changing patterns of how, in their "duality," represented meaning and skillful delivery relate over the centuries. To illustrate their changeful relations, it is possible in the early modern period to trace a gradually unfolding shift from a traditional emphasis on dancing, tumbling, tight-rope walking showmanship to textually prescribed dramatic representations. In England in particular, the exuberance of a performer like Dick Tarlton or Will Kempe, who knows his own identity as that of a common player, gives way to the predominance of the excellent actor representing textually prescribed roles. In the history of the theater there is not only a dual need for game/showmanship *and* knowledge/meaning; relations between performance and writing are themselves embedded in sociocultural circum-

---

[2] In Michael Issacharoff and Robin F. Jones, eds., *Performing Texts.* (Philadelphia: U of Pennsylvania P, 1988) 32; cf. Alter's pathbreaking study, *A Sociosemiotic Theory of Theater.* (Philadelphia: U of Pennsylvania P, 1990).

stances and as such participate in patterns of historical conflict and change, which in their turn affect what doubleness there is in the forms and functions of representation.

As distinct from the eighteenth- and nineteenth-century theater, the late-twentieth-century stage sets out to limit the undisputed dominance of verbally prescribed representations. In the Romantic period, at the height of literacy as an authorizing force, mimesis in the actor's practice was as a rule reduced to a state of absolute subservience. As such it was viewed instrumentally, as a mere tool. As Charles Lamb noted, the actor is "only a medium, and often a highly artificial one"[3]—in short, an ultimately inadequate vessel to carry what in Romantic parlance was poetry in its deepest earnest. Shakespeare, in Wordsworth's phrase, "stooped to accomodate himself " to the theater and the people; and Coleridge was prepared to add, "as far as he can be said to have written for any stage but that of the universal mind."[4]

As against these positions and their late-nineteenth-century variations, performance practice has in the course of the twentieth century radically been revalued. Since the 1980s it "has been honored with dismantling textual authority" as well as "the conventions of role-playing."[5] In fact, performance has come to be praised precisely because it "clogs the smooth machinery of reproductive representation."[6] In other words, what meaning used to be associated with the represented world in dramatic fables has either been sidestepped or has altogether been displaced by a material practice associated with mimetic or other types of performance. In our time, mimesis and

[3] Charles Lamb, "On the Tragedies of Shakespeare, Considered With Reference to their Fitness for Stage Representation." *English Critical Essays: Nineteenth Century.* (London, 1934) 96.

[4] *Coleridge's Shakespearean Criticism*, ed. T. M. Raysor. 2 vols. (London: 1930) I, 4.

[5] *Performance and Cultural Politics*, ed. Elin Diamond (London: Routledge, 1996) 3.

[6] Peggy Phelan, *Unmarked. The Politics of Performance.* (London: Routledge, 1993) 148.

meaning have drifted asunder with particular force; performers, even when they continue to speak a dramatic text, tend often enough to play against the script rather than play with it.

At this point, the modern avant-garde theater has established a new paradigm which in this essay may serve as both a foil and a parallel to changing uses of representation in modern fiction. While the difference between the two genre is obvious enough, the question deserves to be asked: What is it that representations in the two different cultural media have in common? As an answer, let me draw attention to a sociocultural constellation in which the increasing role of performance and performativity is intriguingly interlocked with a groundswell of uncertainty in the order of what is to be represented. From a feminist angle, Peggy Phelan has pointed to "the loss and grief attendant upon the recognition of the chasm between presence and re-representation."[7] Let me suggest that such sense of loss is part of a more widely held apprehension that representation, as far as it is inseparable from the achievement of meaning through both semblance and resemblance, can no longer deliver as of old. If this is so, the site of intersection between "making" and "matching" (E.H. Gombrich's terms) no longer yields a meeting ground on which the performative force of the maker is content to picture something that can hope to "match" by image, symbol, or simile a situation outside the picturing process.

While the difficult balance and the sense of mutuality between relations of performing practice and representation give way, the performance tends to become self-reflexive. There is no better illustration of this than the phenomenal rise of performance art in recent years. "For performance art itself however, the referent is always the agonizingly relevant body of the performer ... In performance, the body is metonymic of self, ... of voice, of 'presence.' "[8] For the body to perform intransitively may be "agonizingly relevant"; but what

---

[7]   Phelan, *Unmarked* 1993, 163.
[8]   Phelan, *Unmarked* 1993, 150.

relevance obtains may well be coupled with a sense of relief when bodies, in their boundless (and unbonded) sovereignty feel potentially free to dismiss representation and to shed the burden of having to project similitude as potentially meaningful.

However, such dismissal is neither identical with nor limited to the rejection of neoclassical standards of mimesis. To associate (re)semblance with "meaning" as either a purely referential and reproductive or, for that matter, a transcendental signified is one thing. But it is an altogether different matter to conceive of meaning as doubly encoded, that is to say, as a divided site of production that attests to an ongoing contest, even a divisive process among different ways of conception and codification. As Gunter Gebauer and Christoph Wulf have shown, the contestatory quality of different codes at work constitutes the historical moment of mimesis as a literary projection—a moment marked by "a permanent pre-occupation with the problem of codification."[9]

As distinct from either a referential or a metaphysical bracketing of mimesis and meaning, the present conjunctural approach to representation is such that it defies some of the most persistent poststructuralist charges against representation, in particular its definition as a site of unity, homogeneity, and indifference. It seems implausible to reduce the function of representation to closure or to the removal of difference (as between language and the world, images and their referents) when the mimetic potential in representation itself is conceived as being constitutive of a clash between different codes and media of cultural articulation.

These are no doubt large questions, in fact too large in this context to be pursued further on a purely theoretical plane. Instead, let me propose to illustrate some of the divisive sites and forces within modern dramatic representation. In what follows my special focus is on the representation of such self-

---

[9]   Gunter Gebauer and Christoph Wulf, *Mimesis: Kultur—Kunst— Gesellschaft* (Reinbek bei Hamburg: Rowohlt, 1992) 30. My translation.

reflexive mimetic practices that propel doubly encoded forms and functions.

The Performer's Code: A Divided Scene for (Post)Modern Representations

Some of the major innovations in the early twentieth-century theater can be seen to anticipate the more radical breach in the closure and the unifying function of representation. As early as in the theater of Bertolt Brecht and, even more distinctly, in that of Antonin Artaud we find a new, in many ways unprecedented, degree of discontinuity between performative action and representational text. Brecht was among the first to herald an ongoing "battle" between theater and dramatic text. Recognizing "the great struggle for supremacy between words, music, and production," he was prepared for "radically separating the elements"[10] of theater. In a process of deliberate differentiation, Brecht effectively redesigned the uses of performance, especially in relation to what representational text was traditionally sanctioned by the late-nineteenth-century theater with its unchallenged standards of empathy. Although the Brechtian actor remained under strict directorial control, the performer's position was transformed from one naturalizing and affirming the text of representation to an agency reviewing, distancing, and "alienating" this text. Instead of serving as a congenial site of mediation between a traditionally sanctioned script and its reception by the audience, mimetic practice was redesigned to differentiate and dissociate what meaning the text of the play sought to represent. The so-called V-effect, that is, the Brechtian strategy of *Verfremdung*, was designed not only to disturb the impact of traditional dramatic representations; it was, positively, to reveal therein the strange and unwonted, to expose social division and conflict beneath the show of competing passions,

---

[10] *Brecht on Theater: The Development of an Aesthetic*, ed. and trans. by John Willett. (London: Methuen, 1978 repr.) 22, 37.

to unmask false pretensions and illusions of harmony and unity and to show up hidden workings of ideology and exploitation. Along these lines, new areas of difference and disparity were exposed (and practically welcomed on stage) between the actor's mimesis and the play's meaning as was inscribed in the text.

As opposed to Brecht's theater of social *gestus* and commitment, the Nietzschean tradition of a theater of release from textualized representations of knowledge and meaning went several steps further in seeking to emancipate performance from the confines of a literary type of representation. Here, the most provocative point of departure was that of Antonin Artaud's when he called for a renouvellement of the theater as "an independent and autonomous art."

This theater must, in order to revive or simply to live, realize what differentiates it from text, pure speech, literature, and all other fixed and written means. We can easily continue to conceive of a theater based upon the authority of the text, and of a text more and more wordy, diffuse, and boring, to which the aesthetics of the stage would be the subject. "But this conception of theater … is, if not the absolute negation of theater … certainly its perversion."[11]

For Artaud, the language of dramatic representation is not like a key that helps unlock the secrets of life; it is rather like a veil that covers or blurs a deeper level of mimetic action. Hence, to "break through language in order to touch life is to create or to recreate the theater" (13). Taking his cue from the Balinese theater that "has revealed to us a physical and non-verbal theater, in which the theater is contained within the limits of everything that can happen on a stage, independently of written text," Artaud challenges the Western theater's "alliance with the text," which he views as a "subordination of theater to speech" (68).

---

[11]   Atonin Artaud, *The Theater and Its Double*, trans. M. C. Richards (New York: Grove Press, 1958) 106. All further page references in the text.

Le Théâtre et son double appeared in 1938. In our own time and context, Artaud's point of departure appears neither dated nor that of an isolated avant-garde intellectual. Nor does his heritage serve as an indifferent position vis-à-vis the production of classical dramatic texts on our own stage. We only need to remember how Peter Brook, distinguished director of Shakespeare's plays in our time, talks about the twentieth-century "acting revolution through Brecht" and how, through using Artaud "as a springboard," Brook sought "to recover, by other means, the variety of Shakespeare's expression" in "the search for theatrical language as flexible and penetrating as the Elizabethans."[12] As Patrice Pavis suggests, Peter Brook's work is influential and significant for its "hermeneutic refusal" in staging the classical text of representation. For Brook, the text is "received as a series of meanings which contradict and answer one another and which decline to annihilate themselves in a final global meaning." Since the play's representation, far from being a closed, unified whole, is seen as an open conglomerate of dramatic significations, the director's response is seen as "a refusal to interpret."[13]

Along these lines, Peter Brook's strategy was to privilege mimetic practice at its most brilliant and, leaving meaning alone, see what happens. Thus, he cautiously anticipated what has since become a veritable distrust of textual authority in representation. This distrust, for instance, has inspired the theatrical project of Robert Wilson in America where, as Christopher Innes noted, "the active factor is the disjunction between words and staging," including a mode of staging marked by "casting against concept" and the shaping of a "visual action that had no illustrative relation to the

---

[12] Peter Brook, *The Shifting Point, 1949-1987* (New York: TCG, 1987) 43, 58. This confronts the danger of a "deadly theater"; see Peter Brook, *The Empty Space* (New York: Atheneum, 1969) 10.
[13] Patrice Davis, *Theater at the Crossroads of Culture*, trans. Loren Kruger (London: Routledge, 1992) 60.

speeches."[14] In other words, the text ceases to be privileged as a primary force in theatrical representation. An overwhelmingly strong reluctance to connect word and action, language and mimesis, culminates in an oblique relationship of the visual and the aural, which positively discourages spectators to perceive any achieved representation of "meaning." It is the yawning gulf between a visually enthralling mimetic practice and what meaning is or is not represented that provides the site for a new dramaturgy informed by pictorial indifference to any verbal representations.

Wilson's theater is of course in close touch with the work of at least one of the two leading German language dramatists in the late-twentieth century, Peter Handke and the late Heiner Müller. Significantly, the disaffection from the text of representation is "writ large" in Müller's *Hamlet-Maschine,* first produced by Wilson himself. This radical adaptation of Shakespeare's best known drama is profoundly concerned with vanishing locations of meaning in the classical text of the play, even with the imagined or performed loss of its "script." Significantly, the main character's opening speech in scene four includes the shedding of "mask and costume," whereupon the performer of Hamlet (*Hamletdarsteller*) deliberately seeks to cancel, in no uncertain terms, any textualized representation of dramatic character:

> I'm not Hamlet. I don't take any part any more. My words have nothing to tell me ... My drama doesn't happen anymore ... Nor am I further interested in it ... the script has been lost.[15]

---

[14] Christopher Innes, *Avant Garde Theater, 1892-1992* (London: Routledge, 1992) 204-05.

[15] Heiner Müller, *Revolutionsstücke,* ed. Uwe Wittstock. (Stuttgart: 1995) 42-44. My own translation; cf. *Hamletmachine and Other Texts for the Stage,* trans. and ed. Carl Weber (New York: PAJ, 1986) 53; all further page references in the text.

Once the performer's "words" have become meaningless, at least in terms of the classical stage-play called *Hamlet*, the speech is no longer viewed as that of the main character; rather, it is made to relate to "the actor playing Hamlet." As the premises of representation as well as characterization are dispensed with, the dramatist is content to render a thoroughly contemporary image of mimetic practice: the twentieth-century performer performing the business of performance.

Similarly, in Müller's *Gundling*, which is also a play about Lessing, the dramatic representation of the eighteenth-century German dramatist is forestalled through strongly foregrounding the business of mimesis. As a represented character, Lessing never properly enters; what we have is an actor preparing for his performance of the role of Lessing. On stage he receives his make-up in the form of Lessing's mask. But the mask of the classical dramatist is used to preclude rather than implement plenitude in the mirror of characterization. Thus, the material figure of the performer displaces the imaginary figuration of the performed. In the concluding scene "Lessing" is more than half buried under a heap of sand on which stage personnel, "disguised as theater audience," empty buckets of sand. At this moment, waiters—serving as stagehands—enter carrying onto the stage "busts of poets and thinkers." Now

> Lessing searches in the sand, unburying one hand, one arm. Waiters, their heads covered with safety hard hats, topple upon him a Lessing-bust covering head and shoulders. Lessing, on his knees now, attempts to free himself from the bust, without success. A muffled scream is heard from under [the bust]. Waiters, stage personnel (theater audience) applaud.[16]

---

[16] My own translation. For the original German version, see Heiner Müller, *Leben Gundlings Friedrich von Preußen Lessings Schlaf Traum Schrei: Ein Greuelmärchen* (Frankfurt M., 1982) 43.

The stupor of the poet-performer, first under the mask of his role, then under the weight of his own bust, constitutes a pregnant theatrical metaphor of failure on the part of the classical dramatist in authorizing a modern text of his own imaginative rendering. Both the character and the characterization of Lessing are disowned; they are halfway, as it were, suspended in the mimesis of an outrageous effort to undo the performer's move toward impersonating the character and to arrest what meaning the latter might be supposed to associate. Even as "Lessing" heaves under the incubus not of an inscribed role but an exorbitant stage business, the performance is applauded. The script is marked by a different and more radical type of "hermeneutic refusal," one that successfully thwarts not just the plenitude but the delivery of a dramatic *persona*. Thus, the representation of the poet, himself a source of classically canonized texts for the stage, never gets properly started. As "Lessing" suffocatingly struggles to rid himself of the (for him) meaningless signs of his own authorship, the imposing uses of both mask and bust foreground the outward accoutrements of mimesis as finally incompatible with a dramatic impersonation of a classical character and his meaning in the world today.

There is a similar articulation of profound discontent with the project of representation in Peter Handke's *Offending the Audience*. What is truly provocative in the play is the rebellion of actors, levelled not simply at spectators as such but, rather, at their expectation to have delivered on stage the centuries-old text of representation itself. Directly addressing the audience, they say:

> You see no picture of something. Nor do you see the suggestion of a picture. You see no picture puzzle. Nor do you see an empty picture. The emptiness of this stage is no picture of another emptiness. The emptiness of this stage signifies nothing. This stage is empty because objects would be in our way. It is

empty because we don't need objects. This stage
represents nothing. It represents no other emptiness.
This stage is empty. You don't see any other objects
that pretend to be other objects ... The time on stage
is no different from the time off stage ... We are no
pictures of something. We are no representatives.
We have no pseudonyms. Our heartbeat does not
pretend to be another's heartbeat. Our bloodcurdling
screams don't pretend to be another's bloodcurdling
screams. We don't step out of our roles. We have no
roles. We are ourselves.[17]

Here, again, is a playfully staged dramatic text that
paradoxically seeks to render nothing except the protracted
challenge resulting from the performer's refusal to represent.
What, positively speaking, is asserted is the self-sufficiency of
mimetic practice, the undaunted claim of its apparent
autonomy, its authority to do without holding the mirror up to
the nature of any imaginary action outside itself. What meaning
remains derives from the shocking refusal to signify; what
representation in its residual stage can do is to represent
mimetic practice in its refusal to represent.

The play responds to that deep crisis in the representational
function of dramatic discourse that, on a level unsurpassed by
either Müller or Handke, is inflected in the work of Samuel
Beckett. In view of the size and significance of his contribution
to a post-representational stage, we must content ourselves with
the barest of illustrations. Addressing the dramatic uses of
language at the very point where they invoke the virtually
nonrepresentable experience of dying, sleeping, waking, and
"making an exit," Beckett seeks to reveal and cope with, in
Hamm's words, the moment when we "play and lose and have

[17] Peter Handke, *Kaspar and Other Plays,* trans. Michael Roloff (New
York: Farrar, 1969) 44. The German text is: Peter Handke, *Die
Theaterstücke* (Frankfurt M.: Suhrkamp, 1992) 18.

done with losing."[18] In the context of our argument, we have
done with losing and cease to be baffled by the loss of the
mirror when the illusion of plenitude is finally punctured and
loss itself is arrested as a series of dramatic moments in the
playing of what games are feasible still. These, then, constitute
those superb "moments for nothing, now as always," when
"time was never and time is over, reckoning closed and story
ended" (83). Since, in the theater of our lives, "play" and
"story" alone continue to render us capable of making an entry
or "making an exit" (81) still, the uses of dramatic language are
closely circumscribed by the final game that Beckett's
characters are made to play. Unless of course Beckett (Handke
recently followed suit[19]) prefers to put on stage an *Act Without
Words*, meaning-full uses of language can be unrelentingly
interrogated, as in the closing scene of *Endgame*. Here are
Clov's words:

> Then one day, suddenly, it ends, it changes, I don't
> understand, it dies, or it's me, I don't understand,
> that either. I ask the words that remain—sleeping,
> waking, morning, evening. They have nothing to say.
> (81)

Endgame consummates itself when the statement of finality
ceases to be comprehensible. What Clov does not understand is
how the ending is supposed to represent meaning. At this point
the most elementary "words," the idiom of ordinary existence,
"have nothing to say."

The moment for nothing becomes unrepresentable. It is only
in the absence of meaning that Hamm's concluding words do
make sense:

---

[18] *Endgame. A Play in One Act*, trans. from the French by the author (New
York: Grove Press, 1958) 8. Further page references in the text.
[19] Peter Handke's play without words, *Die Stunde in der wir nichts
voneinander wussten* (Frankfurt M.: Suhrkamp, 1992). The play was
premiered at the Berlin Schaubühne (1996).

> Since that's the way we're playing it ... let's play it
> that way ... and speak no more about it ... speak no
> more. (84)

To "play it that way" is a playing towards silence; to "speak
no more" invokes a latent resolution finally and irretrievably to
dispense with the convention of dramatic dialogue. This,
indeed, is an entirely consistent mode of preparing not just for
the play's ending but for the end of the theater as well.

Here, the use of "play" and "playing" points in a direction
that, as in Handke's and Müller's texts, radically reverses
relations of language and mimesis in the modern theater. In the
theater of Ibsen, Chekov, Hauptmann, Shaw, and O'Neill,
performers' minds and bodies stringently submit to and are
entirely lost in an imaginary representation implemented and
inspired by the play's use of language. In the classical modern
theater, represented action follows or is completely coordinated
with what is or is not signified in dialogic speech. But in
Beckett, Müller, and Handke (again, to name only these), the
performer is not made to act in a purely imaginary role or
situation. On the contrary, the material signifier constituted by
his/her physical presence on stage does not surrender to any
purely imaginary representation. In Müller and Handke, the
performer is foregrounded well beyond the logistics of any
dramatic role-playing; similarly, in Beckett, we have the
distinct prominence of an ambivalent vocabulary marked by
"play" and "playing," by "game" and "endgame". Even more
important, on his stage "characters continually point to the
artifice, conventions, and apparatus of the theater, and to their
own status as theatrical entities ... the actor does not so much
engage in representation, as he subverts representation by
exhibiting performance,"[20] including the delivery of a highly
effective substratum of vaudeville.

---

[20]   Michael David Fox, " 'There's Our Catastrophe': Empathy, Sacrifice,
       and the Staging of Suffering in Beckett's Theater," *New Theater*

These few and highly selective illustrations cannot of course add up to any conclusive analysis of the uses of representation in the near-contemporary theater. Still, they may well be said to draw attention to a deep disjunction between the assimilation of representational meaning and the presence of living bodies and voices and their mimesis on contemporary stages. At this late date there is a formidable difficulty, or so it seems, to revitalize the conjunction, inflecting images and fables, between the practice of mimesis and the production of meaning on stages in our theater.

Representation and Rupture in Modern Fiction

Although the theater is a special case in that mimetic practice between writing and playing is "impossibly double," the doubleness in question points to a comparable area in modern fiction where, even in the late nineteenth century, the alliance between signification and (re)semblance begins to show signs of strain. To say this is not to minimize profound differences between the two genres. In the theater, performing actors signify over and beyond what significations the text itself contains; in other words, performers serve as doubly charged agencies that bring forth their own signified, one not altogether identical with that inscribed in the words of the dramatist. As distinct from the theater, the disjuncture between representation and meaning in the world of fiction tends to be more involved from within the given patterns of ideology, consensus, and author-function. Since there are no existential agents mediating between the textually signified and its readers, the disjuncture, in Wolfgang Iser's words, is more of "a split between what is represented and what the representation stands for." If, as Iser continues, the "structure involved is that of a double meaning,"[21] how do we account for the change over the centuries in both the incisiveness and the cultural uses of the split in question?

While in fiction there is no overt space for an "impossibly double" mimesis, there is often enough and, I suggest, increasingly so a tension—ironic, sardonic, often savage— between what is mimetically rendered in the way of (re)semblance and what the representation at large is designed to convey to its readers.

The best way to come to terms with the process of dissociation between the mimetic element in representation and the work's meaning is to view it historically, against the background of earlier forms and functions in narrative. As I have suggested elsewhere, traditional narrative is marked not by any profound gap between what is represented in the course of the story and what perspective, impulse, or thought inform the process of representing. Although of course the discontinuity between the tale and the teller can never quite be obliterated, it seems possible to trace a homology of a sort between appropriation (or its absence) in the world of the text and appropriation as a force in textual production and its reception. Such homology between world-appropriating and text-appropriating practices presupposes, as I have hinted, an absence of highly differentiated social relations, interests, and ideologies. Under these conditions the "split between what is represented and what the representation stands for" was to a certain extent suspended in largely undisputed, even socially shared, perspectives on concepts and practices of nature, truth, virtue, progress, and citizenship.

To illustrate in terms of the barest of summaries, let us throw a glance at *Robinson Crusoe*. In Defoe's novel, the exigencies of an unprepared-for island experience are rendered in the spirit of a supreme challenge that can successfully be met by an ingenious series of responses marked by resolute self-

---

[21] Wolfgang Iser, *Prospecting: From Reader Response to Literary Anthropology* (Baltimore: Johns Hopkins U P, 1989) 233.

help in aid of survival through appropriation. As far as such paraphrase can hope to do justice to what is represented *in* the novel, there is not much of a "split" between the mimetic rendering of the island experience and the functional equivalent of "what the representation stands for." In fact, the representation stands for conveying a sturdy ensemble of Protestant-inspired attitudes and actions that the contemporary reader is supposed to assimilate and to make his/her own. What is represented is an agenda that, for the eighteenth-century recipient, provides a powerfully valid parable. It calls for analogical action, an undaunted resolve to take his/her fortune into one's own hands and thereby pursue, on more than merely an economic level, an appropriation of characteristic qualities, goods, and circumstances through self-mastery.

Here again, I use a concept of "appropriation" broad enough to embrace both world-appropriating and text-appropriating activities.[22] As suggested, the concept in question goes beyond Foucault's definition of discourses as, exclusively, judicial "*objects* of appropriation"[23] in that language use itself is considered as a site or agency of knowledge, pleasure, energy, and power. Hence, the links between appropriation and representation must be studied not only in relation to the exchange value of an author's works, that is, their property status but also, and at the same time, in terms of the use value of his *work*, that is, in reference to the changing functions and effects of his literary production as an appropriating agency. As far as the concept will, over and beyond its economic and juridical dimensions, encompass noneconomical and nonjuridical activities, it will be conceived in terms of

---

[22] I have explored the issue of "appropriation" at greater length in "Appropriation and Modern History in Renaissance Prose Narrative," *New Literary History*, 14 (Spring 1983): 459-97.

[23] Michel Foucault, "What is an Author?" *Textual Strategies: Perspectives in Poststructuralist Criticism*, ed. Josué V. Harari (Ithaca: Cornell U P, 1979) 148; my italics.

Aneignung, of making things (relations, books, texts, writings) one's own.

Since the nexus between representation and appropriation cannot here be pursued on a theoretical plane, let me introduce two or three modern texts in which (re)semblance and meaning in forms and functions of representational discourses have entered that state of dissociation that makes them particularly illuminating for the culture of modernity. Although unfinished at the time of the author's death, Gustave Flaubert's *Bouvard et Pécuchet* deserves our special attention because in it a radically negative version of appropriation itself emerges as a major theme. In fact, it may be said without exaggeration that this narrative comes close to being a revulsion from those classical fictions like *Robinson Crusoe* and *Faust*, where the hero's progress is through and in the image of the act of assimilating and appropriating the world and where this progress rehearses an allegory of how author and/or reader, intellectually as well as materially, are best capable of facing the challenge of their existence.

As against these classical patterns on the levels of both social function and iconic signification, the new departures in Flaubert's narrative can best be characterized by saying that the traditional links between the *representational* quality of the signified and the socially *representative* thrust behind the signifying activity become tenuous. The writer's own mode of literary production tends to be the more isolated as he turns away from the social mode of appropriation in contemporary society.

On the surface, Flaubert's narrative appears to recapitulate the whole sweep and variety of the parable of appropriation; but it does so to an altogether different effect. Bouvard and Pécuchet, two Parisian copyclerks, resolve to retire to a village in Normandy in order to dedicate the rest of their lives to successive explorations into those areas of nature, experience, and knowledge from which their previous bourgeois existence had effectively debarred them. But for them the challenge of appropriation results in a course of action marked by radical failure as well as social isolation. As the two bachelors diligently attempt to make their little world their own, as they set out to appropriate the arts of gardening, agriculture, winery, chemistry, medicine, geology, archaeology, literature, and even criticism, they neither extend the frontiers of knowledge and experience nor even confirm and reauthorize any previously appropriated body of knowledge and control over nature. Despite all their dedicated efforts Bouvard and Pécuchet permanently and increasingly "enlarge the distance between what they are studying at any given moment and their ability to cope with the problems of daily life."[24] As they read and read a vast literature of appropriation, as they proceed from authority to authority, the narrative widens the gulf between the signs of their reading and the sense of their experience, between the acquired language of their theoretical knowledge and its actual meaning in terms of subsequent actions and images.

There emerges an everwidening dichotomy between what the words and figures of their reading are representing and what, in the course of following these learned significations, is actually achieved and represented in the narrative of their reception and application. What finally signifies is the narrative of how, in the act of rehearsing its paradigm, appropriation and what authority it has enter a state of crisis. What results is some loss in the applicability of this paradigm, some decline in its validity, the defeat of its representativity.

As the two bachelors begin to dabble in the arts of writing and reading, they come up against the "assurance," the "obstinacy," even the "dishonesty" in the critical columns of their day; they are bewildered by the "idiocies of those who pass for learned, and the stupidity of others hailed as witty." Facing a deep crisis in their sense of authority, they themselves discuss the predicament of literary criticism in terms of the loss of its own representative standards:

---

[24] Gustave Flaubert, *Bouvard and Pécuchet*, trans. A. J. Krailsheimer (New York: Penguin, 1976) 10.

Perhaps one should rely on the public?
But works which met with applause sometimes displeased them, and in those that were hissed they
found something they liked. So the opinion of men
of taste is misleading and mass judgement is
inconceivable.[25]

Torn between the crumbling authority of intellectual experts
and the inconceivable legitimacy of "mass judgement,"
Bouvard and Pécuchet themselves are unable to muster any
representative response and judgement.

Their own failure and defeat is so startling because they start
out much like the traditional type of world-appropriating hero
in fiction, but rather than assimilating the world that surrounds
them so as to represent it in reference to the aims and hopes of
their own striving selves, they utterly fail in their attempt at
both world-appropriating and text-appropriating action. Finally,
at the end, when they have completely isolated themselves from
their community (and this was Flaubert's own, unfinished
design) the two inseparable friends end up as copyists at a
double-sided desk. *Aneignung* has become an impossible task:
to appropriate, to make one's own the world of nature and
society, yields nothing but defeat and, finally, despair. Having
despaired of using and enjoying the knowledge and the ways of
their world, they content themselves with copying, that is,
rewriting, not the signified of their own experience, but mere
signifiers from the books which they so miserably failed to
assimilate or translate into some meaning of their own.

Diminishing Consensus and Representation in
Henry James

The early failure in France of a poetic parable of
appropriation provides a particularly revealing foil against

---

[25]   Flaubert, *Bouvard* 1976, 140.

which the more optimistic and democratic links between the American writer and his society fall into place. At a time when Charles Baudelaire, Paul Verlaine, Stéphane Mallarmé, and Arthur Rimbaud already exemplified some determined withdrawal from any consensus-based notions of what for the poet was socially representative, the American writer from Walt Whitman and Nathaniel Hawthorne to William Dean Howells was prepared up to a point to continue to shoulder the burden of representation on the conjunctural levels of both what is mimetically pictured and what is meaningfully conveyed. In the transcendentalist tradition, the poet's version of his own representativeness receives its most sustained affirmation in the writings of Ralph Waldo Emerson, who in one of his most influential essays declares the poet to be "representative man." Coming at the end of a European Romantic tradition of homogeneity and closure in the relation of text, history, and subject, Emerson says: "the poet is representative. He stands among partial men for the complete man, and apprises us not of his wealth, but of the common wealth."[26]

For Emerson, the poet's is "the largest power to receive and to impart"; he "re-attaches things to nature and the Whole" (321, 328) and thus can "raise to a divine use the railroad, the insurance office, the joint-stock company; our law, our primary assemblies, our commerce, the galvanic battery, the electric jar,

---

[26] Ralph Waldo Emerson, "The Poet," *The Complete Essays and Other Writings of Ralph Waldo Emerson*, ed. Brooks Atkinson. (New York: Modern Library, 1950) 320; further references to this work in the text. This brief (and oversimplifying) excursion into American transcendentalism needs to be complemented by a sense of "the precariousness of this romantic performative" as adumbrated by Emerson's own awareness of "Chaos and the Dark," of "brute force ... at the bottom of society." See the fuller treatment in my essay (to which the present project is substantially indebted), "History, Appropriation and the Uses of Representation in Modern Narrative," *The Aims of Representation*, ed. Murray Krieger (Stanford: Stanford U P, 1993) 175-215.

the prism, and the chemist's retort; in which we seek now only an economical use" (210). This reads like a generous vindication of a poetic agenda for representing that world of economics, politics, nature, and science which Flaubert surrenders as a space for appropriation. But in Emerson the poetic appropriation of the world is one in which the appropriator is still believed to be close to some universal and, hence, representative human property which, in Emerson's definition, is "the common wealth." And since this "common wealth" conjoins the representations of the poet with the appropriations of "hunters, farmers, grooms and butchers" (326), not to mention the men of politics and business, the social impulse in the project of the representer and what is being signified through the represented appear to be continuous rather than discontinuous, linking spirit and matter rather than dividing them. In other words, the authority of what is representing informs, and is informed by, the authority and legitimacy of what is represented: the verbal appropriations of the poet and the material appropriations of "farmers, grooms and butchers," chemists, joint-stock companies, and politicians are made to appear related and mutually so self-supporting that they ultimately sustain a considerable space of concurrence between them.

While this American picture of hope and illusion strongly contrasts with Flaubert's treatment of the uses of appropriation, it may appear ironic that one of the greatest of Emersonian disciples, Henry James, in setting out to revise the social dimensions of his own narrative, gradually but irresistibly arrives at a position not so far removed from Flaubert's.

Since I have space only to choose one of the great Jamesian themes, the most revealing in our context appears to be the one in which the writing stands for some of the more incisive inroads into former correlations among the poetic assimilations of the writer and material appropriations of the citizen. As in the work of Thomas Mann, the erosion of consensus between them is itself represented in its most immediately perceived form: in the fiction of the artist himself, in his apartness and resistance to bourgeois respectability and the diminishing range of his own participation in the moral and political consensus of his day. The deliberate quality of his withdrawal from public affairs is turned into a theme, into a novelistic representation itself, and its most consistently mimetic form is, of course, the biographically informed portrait of characters, such as Tonio Kröger, Gustav von Aschenbach, and Adrian Leverkühn in Mann, or Neil Paraday ("The Death of the Lion"), Hugh Vereker ("The Figure in the Carpet"), Paul Overt ("The Lesson of the Master"), Ralph Limbert ("The Next Time"), and of course Nick Dormer *(The Tragic Muse)* in James.[27]

In all these representations, the artist, far from being representative of other men, either renounces the claims of middle-class life or is already an outsider, standing (in the sense of Mann) in an aloof relationship to the rest of humanity, out of harmony with at least some of the more broadly received middle-class values and attitudes.

These generally familiar moves here need to be recalled because they significantly help form the matrix of a dissociation between what is represented and what the representation stands for. The gap between the two appears at least in part to be bridged once more, yet the underlying tensions in the positioning of the artistic self vis-à-vis the world of business and politics have vastly increased. This becomes

---

[27] James himself, referring to some of these characters as "martyrs of the artistic ideal," is perfectly aware of the unprecedented and unmatched quality of their departure from "tradition ... the general complexion," from "values" hitherto taken for granted. But as against any alleged consensus on the latter, he sarcastically raises the question: "under what conceivable Anglo-Saxon star, might we take an artistic value of this order either for produced or for recognized? We are, as a 'public,' chalk-marked for nothing, more unmistakably, than by the truth that we know nothing of these values." Preface to *The Aspern Papers* (1908); cit. *The Art of Criticism. Henry James on the Theory and the Practice of Fiction,* eds. William Veeder and Susan M. Griffin (Chicago: U of Chicago P, 1986) 336.

obvious as soon as the Emersonian conception of the poet as the "sayer" and "namer" of the "common wealth," as "the only teller" of the news of the world, is critically, not to say sarcastically, redefined in relation to such public forms of activity as, for instance, a career in journalism and politics involve.

As in James' *The Tragic Muse*, the new perspective on the diminishing range of what "representation stands for" (Iser's phrase) is exemplified in the antagonism between the status of the artist and the role of the politician. This conflict leads to a defiant emphasis on the independence, the self-respect, and the uniqueness, if not the autonomy, of the function of art among other cultural practices. The Emersonian concept of art as the most intensely representative vessel of life gives way to a sense of a more self-contained, but somehow redeeming, function that precisely resides in its freedom from having to be representative. As Stephen Donadio has suggested in *Nietzsche, Henry James, and the Artistic Will*, this fiction shares "the impulse to achieve a self-definition independent of one's national or class origins, the impulse to be free of the limitations imposed by a particular time."[28]

Such hoped-for independence characterizes Nick Dormer, the central figure in *The Tragic Muse*. Although a promising politician, he begins to conceive of his future career as a liberal member of Parliament as "talking a lot of rot," which "has nothing to do with the truth or the search for it; nothing to do with intelligence, or candour, or honour."[29] Authority, in other words (and Flaubert would have agreed), is not to be found in the public sphere of power and politics; henceforth, whatever common ground there was between the representation of

---

[28] Stephen Donadio, *Nietzsche, Henry James, and the Artistic Will* (New York: Oxford U P, 1978) 90. See, in this connection, the reinterpretation of Jamesian formalism by John Carlos Rowe, *The Theoretical Dimensions of Henry James* (Madison: U of Wisconsin P, 1984) 225-37.

[29] Henry James, *The Tragic Muse* (New York: Penguin Modern Classics, 1978) 74-75; further page references in the text.

politics and the politics of representation becomes tenuous until it crumbles altogether. So Nick Dormer parts with his politically influential fiancée; he rejects "the old false measure of success" and chooses to follow his artistic ambition; he becomes a painter so as to be able to enjoy "the beauty of having been disinterested and independent; of having taken the world in the free, brave, personal way" (125).

The longing for a disinterested kind of independence, the preference for "the free, brave, personal way" must be read as symptomatic not only of the changing position of the artist in late nineteenth-century society but of the new resolve by which James himself sets out to redefine the function and the art of representation. If, up to a point in time, marked perhaps by the Joycean figure of Stephen Dedalus, the erosion of what "representation stands for" ˙ is rendered in traditionally representational forms of novelistic mimesis, the reason is not of course simply that of their undoubted resiliency. There is, at the very moment of his social alienation, the artist's attempt (as Michael Fried has shown in the work of Gustave Courbet) more resolutely than ever before to efface the distance between artist and art object, until—as in impressionism and naturalism—the representation, appearing to forget about the representer, almost comes to stand for itself, for its own fleeting light or its obstinate slice of life.

However, if it is a sense of the element of discontinuity between what represents and what is represented which, in the first place, made representation necessary, this gap, once it is turned into an abyss, begins to affect and put strains on representational form itself. Thus, the modernist link between the deepening crisis in representativeness and the nascent erosion in representational form can be seen to be anticipated in the late 1880s, in George Gissing, in Thomas Hardy's *Jude the Obscure*, and in James's *The Bostonians*. The latter in particular recoiled from what must have appeared to its author as the new vulgar forms of commercialized publishing and the bustling fervor of progressivism and its new-style canvassing.

But when this major novel, just like *The Tragic Muse,* was ill received and spitefully or, at best, indifferently reviewed, the author turned to the theater and, after that, began to experiment in and modify the narrative conventions of representational form. The results are too well known for me to specify them here, but what needs to be emphasized is that there is a connection between the represented artist's option for "the free, brave, personal way" and James's own redefinition of the representational strategy of the novel as a "direct, personal impression of life." The "direct" and "personal" quality of novelistic writing (just like the impressionism in contemporary painting) now serves as a distinguishing mark of the braveness with which the artist breaks away from that ideological authority which, in the form of a social and aesthetic consensus, had hitherto informed the standards of his representation. The "brave, personal way" helps secure a new freedom for representation from having to stand for anything; the very directness of the novel's impression guarantees a comparable freedom by which the signifying practice of the representer constitutes itself in relative independence of what (re)semblance used to dominate the novel of realism and naturalism.

Therefore, the new departure for modernist experiment in the writing of fiction may, partially at least, be understood in response to the predicament resulting from the loss in the artist's status as representative man. Now the depletion of this status is both redeemed and compensated for in terms of narrative technique and its artistry. The emerging forms of narrative immediacy, the repudiation of omniscience, the stylized modes of point of view can all, in one important respect, be understood as a formally acknowledged relief from the traditional burden of authorial representativeness. It is the "direct, personal impression," the seemingly authentic flow of individual consciousness which helps the author to leap over the crippling effects in the forms of representational closure, the ideological burden of determinacy in the public uses of language, what James in *The Tragic Muse,* coming now very close to Flaubert's *sottisier,* calls the "ignorance," the "density," "the love of hollow, idiotic words, of shutting the eyes tight and making a noise" (75).[30]

Appropriation and the New Economy of the Signifier

While the later fiction of James reveals the precariousness of the links between the traditionally mimetic forms of representation and the diminishing range of what this fiction stands for, the elements of crisis and renouvellement reach their full force only in the rise of modernist strategies of narrative. Since it is of course quite impossible here to explore the modernist turn in its richness and diversity, let me at least suggest some of the moments of rupture and transition between the Jamesian and the post-Jamesian situation by focusing on the issue of appropriation. First, let me glance at Van Wyck Brooks's *America's Coming of Age* (written in 1913-14) in which, shortly before the outbreak of World War I, the language of the dominant culture is revealingly taken to task. What Brooks, in the following passage, articulates is the complaint that the public language of politics is both unrepresentable and unrepresentative and that "ideals of this kind, in this way presented ... cannot enrich life, because they are wanting in all the elements of personal contact." Brooks notes the depth of the gulf in language between what represents personal consciousness and what is represented in public ideology:

The recognized divisions of opinion, the recognized issues, the recognized causes in American society

---

[30] There is of course a good deal of ambivalence in James's position which relates to "his posture in the marketplace, his divided ambition for both artistic integrity and popular acceptance" (Michael Anesko, *"Friction with the Market": Henry James and the Profession of Authorship* [New York: Oxford U P, 1986] 87).

are extinct. And although Patriotism, Democracy, the Future, Liberty are still the undefined, unexamined, unapplied catchwords over which the generality of our public men dilate, enlarge themselves and float (exact and careful thought being still confined to the level of engineering, finance, advertising and trade)—while this remains true, every one feels that the issues represented by them are no longer genuine or adequate.[31]

The failure, then, in the use of these concepts of politics and morality was that "the issues represented by them" had ceased to communicate any intellectual authority; the signified in the traditional language of "our public men" had exhausted its capacity for both reference and legitimation. Hence, the representational force and function of these signs were gravely impaired. What emerges from the writings of Brooks and those radical intellectuals who disowned the progressivism of the politicians is that the crisis in the representational function of language was primarily related to the erosion of a traditional type of social, cultural, and philosophical authority. Whatever stability had remained in the relation between what was representing and what was represented, in the light of this failed authority a good many public significations now appeared as "undefined, unexamined, unapplied." While in Brooks's view this crisis was diagnosed as mainly a dichotomy "between university ethics and business ethics,"[32] the latter still seemed to retain an element of representability. Language on the "level of engineering, finance, advertising and trade" continued to appear intact and was not viewed as subsumed under the crisis in appropriation which the public language of culture and politics had succumbed to.

---

[31]   Van Wyck Brooks, *America's Coming of Age* (New York: B. W. Huebsch, 1915) 166 f.

[32]   Brooks, *America's Coming* 1915, 7.

In early twentieth-century fiction, the inroads into the traditional social function of representation can most conspicuously be traced where, during or shortly after World War I, a far more radical erosion of consensus among writers, artists, and the general public led to a new political economy of signification. This was marked by hitherto unprecedented discontinuities between what used to be signified as representable and what, for the Lost Generation, was no longer so.

As an illustration let me look at a well known passage in Ernest Hemingway's *A Farewell to Arms*, which is revealing and perhaps unique because, paradoxically, it represents a crisis of signification in the hero's and, by implication, the novelist's language itself. The first person singular is Frederic Henry's:

> I was always embarrassed by the words sacred, glorious, and sacrifice and the expression in vain. We had heard them, sometimes standing in the rain almost out of earshot, so that only the shouted words came through, and had read them, on proclamations that were slapped up by billposters over other proclamations, now for a long time, and I had seen nothing sacred, and the things that were glorious had no glory and the sacrifices were like the stockyards at Chicago if nothing was done with the meat except to bury it. There were many words that you could not stand to hear and finally only the names of places had dignity. Certain numbers were the same way and certain dates and these with the names of the places were all you could say and have them mean anything. Abstract words such as glory, honor, courage, or hallow were obscene beside the concrete names of villages, the numbers

of roads, the names of rivers, the numbers of
regiments and the dates.[33]

Hemingway's character is embarrassed by the collapse of
representational function on the part of some of his signifiers.
But the embarrassment serves more than characterization; it
transcends the quandary of its speaker, the first person singular
as iconic sign and narrative point of view, so as to burden the
discursive practice of this fiction in the strategic economy of its
writing. The crisis in representation remains attached to the
characterizing icon of the first person singular and yet goes
beyond it; in other words, this crisis is both represented and
representing at the same time. Since the problem is articulated
so self-consciously, on the level of both represented character
and narrative practice, this text can be read on at least two
levels.

First, it can be read in terms of the iconic constraints in the
fictional *histoire* or figuration of character constraints that,
most immediately, are revealed in the language of the
Hemingway hero, his muteness and his modernist inability to
assert himself anywhere except in the barroom, the bedroom,
the arena, and on safari.[34] Second, and this is my immediate
concern, the text shows that the underlying crisis in
representation can be studied on the level of *discours*, in terms
of the constraints and possibilities that this novelistic writing
reveals in the ideological and aesthetic economy of its
articulation. On this level, our text reveals an extraordinarily
articulate reluctance to authorize, let alone to appropriate, not
only the dominant language of politics but also that of

---

[33] Ernest Hemingway, *A Farewell to Arms* (1929; London: Scribner, 1977)
209.

[34] See Stanley Cooperman, *World War I and the American Novel*
(Baltimore: Johns Hopkins U P, 1967) 185. This foreshadows the critical
revaluation that has long since superseded any nostalgic, even
sentimental, identification with those who flaunted their "lostness" after
the First World War.

"university ethics" (Brooks's term) and, for that matter, a certain type of journalism. There is a stark discontinuity between the given spectrum of public significations and the actually usable, much more limited, range of the novelist's signifier. When the range of what is representable is seen to be conditioned by its tenuous relation to any "abstract words"—to any positioning in generalized terms—the consequences are of course more complex than a naively referential understanding of fictional discourse can ascertain.

This complexity must be emphasized despite the fact that, as in other fictions of this period, the mimetically structured *histoire* of individual experience, especially in the love story, persists virtually unchallenged. In contrast to the as yet unbroken representational forms of this fictional figuration, the writer's performance on the level of his discursive practice is much more deeply affected. But there remains an uneasy connection between *histoire* and *discours* (a distinction made by Roland Barthes that I continue to adopt, but also adapt, to my own reading). This connection emerges when this text goes out of its way to transcribe the dilemma of representational discourse *in terms of a soldier's image* of a legitimation crisis in the uses of language. In the story, the crisis is transcribed into a spatial metaphor of the distance to, and the loss of authority in, the official language of war politics. What we have is a spatial icon of a character's physical aloofness distantiating the language of propaganda through the rain and the sheer distance from those who stood there and were told to listen. In this image, just as in that of "proclamations ... slapped up ... over other proclamations," the imperfectly achieved or reluctantly handled process of communication serves as a register of the inefficacy of the authority transported therein. When Frederic Henry heard these words, "sometimes standing in the rain almost out of earshot, so that only the shouted words came through," the transcendental signified is, as it were, acoustically neutralized, depleted in its plenitude and drowned in a gulf between the performative *Darstellung* or delivery of these words and the imaginary *Vorstellung* of their meaning.

For Hemingway's character and audience, this language has ceased to be representative precisely because, in Brooks's phrase, "ideals of this kind, in this way presented ... are wanting in all the elements of personal contact." In Hemingway's text, intellectual contact and, of course, appropriation, remained viable, if not, as Brooks maintained, "on the level of ... finance, advertising and trade," at least perhaps on that of "engineering," geography, and statistics. In *A Farewell to Arms*, "only the names of places" had "dignity," and the irony in this use of a concept like "dignity" must not detract from the observation that place names did retain some representational function and authority. If this is so, "dignity" here, presumably, is associated with a traditional sense of the conjunction between mimesis in "a local habitation and a name" and what meaning this could muster—as, for instance, in the final escape to Switzerland. Hence, it was "the concrete names of villages, the numbers of roads, the names of rivers, the numbers of regiments and the dates" which allowed for what Brooks had called "careful thought and intellectual contact," and which to Hemingway's hero did not sound "obscene" in contrast to the real obscenity in taking for granted continuity in the representational function of transcendental signifieds with so heavy an ideological liability.

In *A Farewell to Arms* place names were of course foreign, and these foreign signifiers may have been particularly suited to carrying the burden of what in our text is called "dignity." At any rate, Hemingway must have gladly used these names (much like the foreign sounds and signs of Paris, Spain, and Africa) to assist in the fictional manufacture of a world that still appeared representable precisely because its rendering was exceedingly selective, projected piece by piece, out of the most meticulously chosen and crafted materials. It was as if the choice of this material, based on meticulous scrutiny, was designed to intercept the unrepresentable and to withhold anything that did not meet the greatest rigor of authenticity. The authentic world was of course the world of things simple and basic; it was a world precluding those meanings and experiences which could *not* positively be rendered by such deceptively simple significations as "nice," "clean," and "honest."

For Hemingway, the most crucial problem, then, was one of representability. But the economy, including the simplicity of his language, is deceptive indeed when it is not at all designed to convey a comparable simplicity of meaning. This contradiction in the signification process results from the twofold demand that writer and readers place on the signifier: It is to fill in the space that remains representable. More than anything, this language is artistry in its own right, a highly fastidious medium sounding the absence of things and the muteness of emotions in the unrepresentable space between and behind the common, the trivial, and the political utterance.

What made the artful inscription of triviality so untrivial and, if I may say so, so meaningful, was that behind the fastidious language there was no blankness, no vacuity but, on the contrary, "the strongly sensed presence of things omitted."[35] The omission itself might constitute some inverted kind of pathos, the effect of understatement, the staccato accompanying the refusal to connect. Even more important, this "strongly sensed presence of things omitted" could now serve as a foil to what preciously was still representable. Hence the largeness, in Hemingway, of even the most trivial signifier: the nod, the drink, the casual greeting, the fresh shirt, the rain on the tent.

---

[35] John W. Aldridge, *"The Sun Also Rises*—Sixty Years Later," *Sewannee Review* 94 (Spring 1986): 340. Hemingway presents us with an early analogue to, say, Handke's *Kaspar*, or *Offending the Audience* (see above): The purpose of these plays is "not to present a text or to organize a performance but to be a critique in action of signification itself." (Bernard Dort, *La Représentation émancipée* [Paris: Actes Sud, 1988] 184; cit. and trans. Susan Melrose, *A Semiotics of the Dramatic Text* [London: Macmillan, 1994] 314.)

The representational efficacy of signs such as these resembled that of the names of places and rivers and the number of regiments in that their authority was not undermined by the legitimation crisis of some ideological signified. Thus, every sign that did manage to be released into signification, against the compulsion of silence and the pressure of the unspeakable, appeared so much larger for having escaped omission or obliteration.

To be sure, the price for all this economizing was high enough. Among other things, it involved a curb on the project of novelistic representation, the willingness to abstain from previously maintained appropriations of ideas and relations. But, again, the diminished range of intellectual appropriations was compensated for not just by an extraordinary precision and economy in the use of verbal signs; rather, this diminished range stood for a new and problematic dimension in the relations between the fastidious order of the signifier and the submerged presence of disorder on the level of the half-suppressed or silenced signified. In Hemingway, the signifier is held in a state of uncanny balance between its capacity for releasing and its ability to obliterate meaning. To define the quality of this balance involves an awareness of choice *and* contingency in dealing with the links and gaps of representation and in the way that the gaps are closed and the links are broken up.

Although such a definition can only be verified to the extent that it proceeds from some given text, perhaps it is possible at least to hazard a reading towards a cultural semiotics of this important direction in high modernism. The political economy in this discursive practice is to cope with the conjuncture between a highly selective range of mimesis and the precarious (dis)placement of meaning. Hemingway's artful triumph is achieved to the degree that the gap between the speakable sign and the unspeakable meaning is at least temporarily (dis)closed. Thereby the writing seeks to meet the challenge, as in the representation of war and violence, of "lostness" and silence, through the power and precision of a language that defies the burden of ideology ("sacred, glorious") under the cover of seeming triviality and tough physicality.

While this cover is scarcely lifted in *The Sun Also Rises* and a good many short stories, in *A Farewell to Arms* the response to the futility, pain, and death is doubly encoded throughout the novel. On a first level, Hemingway's representational strategies embrace the symbolic mode in reading his characters' action: Frederic Henry escapes to Switzerland and leaves the war behind. This is his way of responding to (though not controlling) the impossible alternative, and Catherine's death underlines the absolute contingency of this triumph over fear and the larger unspeakable. But at this point story and discourse, even while they continue to interact, part company. The distinction is crucial here to sound the depth of the disjunction in early twentieth-century fiction between what signified is conveyed through the traditional matter of setting and scenery, story, and character and what discursive practice is at work on the part of the author's uses of language. While the former—the *histoire*—continues to hold the mirror up to human action under given socially and politically significant circumstances, the latter—the *discours*, the specific uses of language—are much less constrained by the thematic burden of symbolic meaning. Thus, while discursive practice throughout remains in profound complicity and radical interaction with the story, the former cannot quite be reduced to or subsumed to the latter. On the contrary, modernist discourse, as in Hemingway's novel, turns against the regime of symbolic representation by repudiating the obscenities of murderous action and language and, of course, *Weltanschauung*. Hence, the political economy of silence and proscription in this discursive practice is marked by an alternative impulse, a carefully crafted tenor of deliberate toughness that is finally upheld not in the depth of any sentiment but in an artful commission to survive and so, incidentally, to resist.

Duality and Difference in Modern Representations

In conclusion, this comparative approach to representation in two major cultural media of the late nineteenth and twentieth centuries must not in the least minimize important differences between them in function and epistemology, in production and reception. These divergences should readily be granted, especially since on either side they quite specifically affect what duality we have in modern representation. In the theater, representations continue to be a matter of both performative action and iconic resemblance; as texts and bodies are conjoined in theatrical productions, the doubleness in the code of dramatic representations is born out as well as enhanced by concurrence and interaction of these two modes of cultural production and signification.

As distinct from representation in the theater, modern fiction, as we have seen, attests to different sources of performance energy in the writing. If we follow J. L. Austin's somewhat provisional distinction between performative and constative types of utterance, it is possible to trace performative forms of verbal action in novelistic language. Such performative practice can be located in a dimension of writing constituted by work. Far from bringing forth a replica, such work (in)forming writing leads to something previously nonexistent. Along these lines, Paul Ricoeur has adduced the shaping of artful form in literature as inseparable from what writing as a work is.[36]

---

[36] Paul Ricoeur, *Hermeneutics and the Human Sciences* (Cambridge: Cambridge U P, 1981). The cultural poetics inherent in the conceptual correlation between work and play, production and pleasure, must of course be seen in a context larger than this. We need to go back to Vico, Kant, Hegel, and Marx for the formation of a concept of art as production, which to this day may well be considered as the most radical antidote to a reduction of "representation" to its purely imitative or reproductive functions. For an incisive survey of this wider background, see Hans Robert Jauss, *Ästhetische Erfahrung und literarische Hermeneutik* (Frankfurt M.: Suhrkamp, 1984), esp. 77-82, 112-17.

If this is so, the mimetic component in representation is inconceivable without *techne*, no matter how much similitude (or otherwise) is achieved or intended. Clearly, *techne*, productive craftsmanship, and reference-oriented *imitatio* are not the same. In fact, the difference between them is crucial, even when this difference in the writing and reading of fiction does not exactly implicate, as in the theater, a dual epistemology comprising absent imaginary and present physical levels of action. Still, literary representation can be viewed as doubly encoded at the crucial point where resemblance and meaning part company.

In view of these highly abstract terms of a summary embracing both modern drama and fiction, it may be appropriate to conclude with an illustration that we owe to one of the contributors to this volume. In James Joyce's *Dubliners* difference and duality in modern representation achieve an exemplary form. On the one hand, these stories hold the mirror up to a circumstantial world marked by a state of stupor and inertia. Language on this level is used symbolically, in terms of fairly straightforward narrative. What along these lines is represented constitutes a plane of meanings that for the reader is available in a linear fashion. On the other hand, however, this purely symbolic mode of representation with its referential correlative (Ireland and Dublin in particular) "is sabotaged by strategically ordered signifiers, or tropes, which are marked by semantic polyvalency and disrupt the linearity of the narration, and of reading."[37] As against the overall structure of *histoire* in these representations, we have an intervention by what the same critic calls the strategies of "presentation, deformation, composition, and textual performance" (119). Disseminating and disfiguring the symbolic code of the story, these discursive uses of language constitute "meanings beyond the narration,

---

[37] Wolfgang Wicht, "'Eveline' and/as 'A Painful Case': Paralysis, Desire, Signifiers," *New Perspectives on* Dubliners, eds. Mary Power and Ulrich Schneider (Amsterdam: Rodopi, 1997) 117. Further references to this essay in the text.

they arrest the 'realistic' progress of understanding, and oblige the reader to construct an independent discourse" (141).

At this point, representation in modern fiction and representation in the (post)modern theater can be seen to converge at the point where presentation/composition (*Darstellung*) engage the symbolic code (*Vorstellung*) intent on furnishing meanings through characterization, description, and action. The point of convergence is where each genre tends to be doubly encoded. While in either case referential function and iconic form appear to persist, the reproductive process as well as its product is contested by a performative thrust of either verbal or bodily interferences. Precluding any appearance of closure or unity between what represents and what is represented, these presentational and performative energies radically disperse meaning. They explode the representational rehearsal of similitude and engage in what Wolfgang Wicht calls a larger "formation of meaning which is not any longer aligned with what is represented"(118).

James Joyce may of course be an exceptional case. But such modern representations, which on the surface appear to remove difference between what is shown and what is meant, ultimately end up undoing this removal by promoting their own rupturing force. Being subjected to contingency, the relationship between the two codes is far from being static, far from being given. In other words, modern representation—far from invariably seeking to remove difference—tends to work with it, exploiting the instability itself in the respective encodings. Both theater and fiction are capable of widening the gaps and closing the links between the symbolism in meaning and the *techne* informing the making behind the matching resemblance.

REPRESENTATION AND COMPOSITION IN JOYCE'S *ULYSSES*

Wolfgang Wicht

ABSTRACT

The narrative of *Ulysses* frequently embarks on accounts of contemporary discourses appended to religion, politics, nationalism, journalism, philosophy, and literature. The purpose of these records is to ridicule and disrupt the various registers of representation. Starting from a taxonomical distinction between what is called here *referential* (*iconic* or *indexical*) representation, *modal* representation, and *authorial* representation. I argue that Joyce's fictional text is both representative (of Dublin and the authorial stance) and antirepresentative (with regard to social and historical discourses). Joyce's specific matrix of mediation between "representation" and fictional form is brought to light through the examination of selected instances: the title of the novel, the reconstruction of the urban space of Dublin, the function of the interior monologues, the style of the "Nausicaa" episode, the intertextuality of the "Pisgah Sight" paragraph, and the materializing of utopian promises. Taken as a whole, the novel is no longer representative in the classical sense. It inaugurates a fictional construct that deconstructs the affirmative and affirmed practices of representation and authorizes itself as text, challenging the political, religious, and cultural systems of power.

The reader who draws meaning from the text of *Ulysses* is haunted by the fictional omnipresence of manifold cultural representations. He is forced to seek, as Thomas Docherty notes, "emancipation from consensus-based notions of truth, from ideology."[1] This response is rooted in the fact that the narrative of *Ulysses* frequently embarks on accounts of contemporary discourses appended to religion, colonial rule, politics, nationalism, journalism, philosophy, and literature.

---

[1] Thomas Docherty, *Alterities: Criticism, History, Representation* (Oxford: Clarendon, 1996) 35.

The purpose of these records is to disrupt and ridicule the various registers of representation that constitute the ideological spectrum of Joyce's time and simultaneously refer to the material factors in which they are generated: the practices of the Catholic Church in Ireland; the Home Rule movement; British government; anarchism; cultural institutions; and the production, distribution, and reception of news and books. Challenging a vast array of representational practices, Joyce attends to what Valente calls "his counter-representational stylistic."[2]

In what follows, a survey of Joyce's (counter-) representationalism shall be mapped out. At first, however, in face of the ubiquity of the term *representation* in critical texts, a brief consideration of its significations is in place to pave the terminological ground for what follows. A comprehensive scholarly debate of "one of the most vexed areas in contemporary theory"[3] is out of the question. It is, however, unavoidable to achieve terminological transparency to supplement and replace the routine distinction between "political," "philosophical" and "pictural/discursive" representations.[4] Moreover, somewhat out of the blue, the

---

[2] Joseph Valente, *James Joyce and the Problem of Justice* (Cambridge: Cambridge U P, 1995) 193.

[3] Jonathan Arac, "Introduction" in *Postmodernism and Politics*, ed. Jonathan Arac (Manchester: Manchester U P, 1986) xx [ix-xliii]. Arac gives an informative overview of "the tangled historicity of 'representation'" (xxi) and the current debates about it (xxi-xxviii). In contemporary philosophical thinking, the assumption has become predominant that "representation is perspectival intrinsically"; see Jerry Fodor, "Cat's Whiskers," *London Review of Books* 19.21 (30 October 1997): 17.

[4] Peter Canning, "representation," *Encyclopedia of Postmodernism*, ed. Victor E. Taylor and Charles E. Winquist (New York: Routledge, 2001) 339-41. For a political understanding of representation, see J. Roland Pennock, "Political Representation: An Overview," *Representation: Yearbook of the American Society for Political and Legal Philosophy,*

reconsideration of taxonomical distinctions forces itself upon us in spite of the term's "intrinsic perspec-tivism" and the postmodern epistemological insight that we are "caught in a double bind: ... there seems to be no possibility of 'purity' on either side, representationalist or sceptic, no avoid-ing contamination or supplementation by the other."[5] Even if the "sceptical" view prevails, the critic is in urgent need of taxonomical tools, at least to my mind, when (as in the neighboring area of narratology) the particular intricacies of representationalism in *Ulysses* are investigated.

From a traditional philosophical point of view, classical knowledge is based on the fundamental idea that what exists may be represented and what may be represented exists. The perfect ontological exchange between the idea and the object gives access to the world.[6] In fictional form, Hamlet's advice to the players poignantly represents this neo-Aristotelian, Renaissance notion of representation:

> Suit the action to the word, the word to the action, with this special observance: that you o'erstep not the modesty of nature. For anything so overdone is from the purpose of playing, whose end, both at the first and now, was and is to hold as 'twere the mirror up to nature, to show virtue her own feature, scorn her own image, and the very age and body of the time his form and pressure.[7] (*Hamlet* 3.2.17-24)

---

ed. J. R. Pennock and John W. Chapman (New York: Atherton Press, 1968) 3-27.

[5] Andrew Gibson, *Toward a Postmodern Theory of Narrative* (Edinburgh: Edinburgh U P, 1996) 75.

[6] See Pravu Mazumdar, "Écriture oder Repräsentation? Zum Standort der Archäologie Foucaults zwischen Literatur und Wissenschaft," *Internationale Zeitschrift für Philosophie* (2000) 1: 87-88 [82-101].

[7] William Shakespeare, *The Complete Works*, ed. Stanley Wells and Gary Taylor (Oxford: Oxford U P, 1988). For a magisterial discussion of Hamlet's speech and its contemporary rhetorical and normative contexts, see Robert Weimann, *Author's Pen and Actor's Voice: Playing and*

This "theory" of mimetically inspired literary representationalism essentially reappears, for instance, in Dr. Johnson's
classicist conception of representative truth, and subsequently
continues to belong to the fundamentals of the realist novel.
The concomitance between the natural and the literary inscribes
the basic principle of *affirmation* which the realist ontology of
representationalism contains, substantiated by knowledge,
empirical truth, and consensus. Toward the end of the
nineteenth century, corresponding with the decline of the
"classical" stage of capitalist economy, Enlightenmental
thinking and the natural sciences, the affirmative function of
representation surrenders to a "state of crisis,"[8] to be traced in
Flaubert, the later James and the early Joyce. In *Dubliners*, for
instance, as I tried to show elsewhere, particular formal
attributes of the narrative efface "the naïve assumption that the
meaning of the text can be generalized in monadic statements
or metaphysical essences."[9]

Despite this paradigm shift in fiction, the received
"semiotic/aesthetic and political forms of representation"[10]

Writing in Shakespeare's Theater (Cambridge: Cambridge U P, 2000)
151-79.

[8] Robert Weimann, "Text, Author-Function, and Appropriation in Modern
Narrative: Toward a Sociology of Representation," *Critical Inquiry* 14
(Spring 1988): 436 [431-47]. Drawing on Flaubert and James, Weimann
scrutinizes how "the traditional links between the representational
quality of the signified and the social representativity of the signifying
activity" become "tenuous" (436).

[9] Wolfgang Wicht, " 'Eveline' and/as 'A Painful Case': Paralysis, Desire,
Signifiers," *New Perspectives on* Dubliners, ed. Mary Power and Ulrich
Schneider (Amsterdam: Rodopi, 1997) 141 [115-42].

[10] W. J. T. Mitchell, "Representation," *Critical Terms for Literary Study*,
ed. Frank Lentricchia and Thomas McLaughlin (Chicago: U of Chicago
P, 1990) 12 [11-22]. Mitchell gives a concise introduction to the history
of the term from Aristotle and Plato, and to its most common
conceptualization as a "triangular relationship: representation is always
of something or someone, *by* something or someone, *to* someone" (*ib.*
12; 11-21). Of particular interest is also Raymond Williams's entry

continue to figure prominently in modern manuals or scholarly studies, such as Stuart Hall's Open University material on *Representation* and Susan Wells's first chapter of a book on Elizabethan drama. Hall's empirical discussion[11] significantly confuses literary *representation* with semiotic *reference*; it is trapped in mimetical categories, which do not fit in with the study of (post)modernist narratives. Wells's attempt to subsume reference "into the broader question of representation" is based on the understanding that representation is *"typical"* because "the text labors over the world and transforms it by representing it; the reader transforms the text by interpreting it.[12] For Wells, "representation" means literary representation,

---

"Representative" in *Keywords: A Vocabulary of Culture and Society* (Glasgow: Fontana, 1976) 222-25.

[11] *Representation: Cultural Representations and Signifying Practices*, ed. Stuart Hall (London: Sage Publications, 1997). Hall tells us "that languages work *through representation*," which means that they are "systems of representation" that "stand for or represent what we want to say, to express or communicate a thought, concept, idea or feeling" (4). Though Hall distinguishes this *"semiotic* approach" ("concerned with the *how* of representation") from "the *discursive* approach" ("concerned with the *effects and consequences* of representation") (6), and points to the fact that meanings may "slip and slide," his concept of "trans-coding" denotes a merely mechanical process: "taking an existing meaning and re-appropriating it for new meanings" (270).

[12] Susan Wells, *The Dialectics of Representation* (Baltimore: Johns Hopkins U P, 1985) 4, 17. Wells is aware of the fact that "the relation between the text and the world and the relation between the reader and the text are specific mediations" (17; see also Mitchell, "Representation" 1990, 12-13). Including into the "typical register" all syntactic, stylistic, and rhetorical features applied in a fictional work, Wells determinedly tells us that "the typical register of the text establishes its referential power" (19). On the other hand, Wells acknowledges that things in life are "accidental and contingent" and refuse the intersubjectivity of the typical register. She calls this quality of contingency "the indeterminate register" (64). Much earlier, Williams introduced a different and more transparent understanding of *typical.* He argues that "representative" is "typical", because it "stands *for* ('as' or 'in place of') others or other

which must be distinguished from semiotic, philosophical, and political representations. As many critics do, she ignores the fact that the presupposition of a "typical register" is a critical fallacy. As poststructuralist thinking reminds us, an infinity of registers is possible for every object. However, a sound critical judgment of *Ulysses* cannot but expose to view that the Cartesian idea of literary knowledge and form as representation (i.e., a symmetrical relation between the literary artifact and the world) is not only pertinent to the holistic paradigm of the realist novel, but noticeably to Joyce's novel as well, which, at least in some measure, is enmeshed in the reconfiguration of empirically given circumstances, based on meticulous scrutiny.[13]

To employ the notion of representation and its taxonomical distinctions is inescapable when not only the relationships between ideas (discourses) and objects are examined through a process of close interpretation, but also the reconfiguration of these very relationships within a literary composition is scrutinized. Close reading will initially make use of the typological order provided by classification. But when the question is posed—what meaning is handed down to the reader through the fictional construct—the taxonomy of representation inevitably becomes functional. Then, the difference between sociopolitical forms of representation and authorial representation triggers off extra-narrative meanings, which the reader is asked to unravel. In *Ulysses*, as I hope to show, this difference is extremely vast.

Two presuppositions may precede my taxonomical proposals. Firstly, to establish a system of coherent representations legitimizes the idea of knowing the world. But secondly, as Vicky Mahaffey reminds us, "representations—of

---

things," whereas "representation(al)" denotes "the sense of accurately *reproduced*" ("Representative," 225).

[13] Weimann has pointed to a comparable foregrounding of authenticity in Hemingway's *A Farewell to Arms*; see "Text, Author-Function, and Appropriation," 445.

what is human, what sociocultural, what divine—harden and
seem to take on the appearance of naturalness and permanence"
and "become indistinguishable from reality." Thus, representation "as a mode of substitution is a stabilizing, definite
process."[14] Only on this proviso, Hall's and Wells's
conceptions should not be dismissed in gross. They specify a
distinct mode of *literary* (not primarily semiotic or political)
representation which I call here *referential representation*. In a
broad sense, it embraces the fictional *reconfiguration* of reality
as a structured pattern of space, time, and people which might
be considered to be a section of real life (as in the realist
novel). What is represented is imagined but pretends to be
based on real facts, human beings and social relationships.
"Reference" is not restricted to the semiotic dimension in this
literary context; it includes the complex Aristotelian mimetic
triangle of object, potentially manifold form, and the means
through which particular effects on the recipient are achieved.[15]
Furthermore, referential representation accommodates two
subordinary implications. Firstly, it may focus on denoting
photographically a real or imagined phenomenon, a "thing," an
object, which is appropriated (as Mitchell suggests) in a
process of *iconic* representation. The urban space of the Irish
capital or the personal documents Bloom finds in a drawer (see
U 17.1855-67) are relevant examples, the one being an
existing, the other an imagined object of depiction. Secondly,
since "things" are not simply there but rather materially
produced and socially constituted, referential (iconic)
representation might encode social or even ideological
meanings. To mention Nelson's Pillar will most probably not
merely help to complement the urban panorama, but will also
evoke the political aspects with which the Pillar is charged. If

---

[14] Vicky Mahaffey, *States of Desire: Wilde, Yeats, Joyce, and the Irish
Experiment* (Oxford: Oxford U P, 1998) 18, 24.

[15] For a concise outline of this concept of representation in the arts, see
Mitchell, "Representation" 1990, 13-14. Wells's conception of the
"typical" is another variation of this triangle.

deep meanings are thus translated into the literary text, a
process of *indexical*[16] referential representation is established.
As I shall show below in my passage on "Dublin," to
distinguish between these two types is vital to literary
interpretation.

Acting against Hall's concocted suggestion that (de-)
constructionist approaches "put in question the very nature of
representation,"[17] more flexible, postmodern assumptions of the
concept have been proposed over the past decades.[18] Joyce
himself anticipated poststructuralist philosophy, cleverly
phrasing an aphoristic axiom in *Finnegans Wake*, which
registers that "this exists that isits after having been said we
know."[19] As Gibson suggests, "what mattered was to break with
the referential illusion, to analyse narratives as sets of
signifying practices, to explore and describe them in terms of
the codes by which they operated."[20] This insight is

---

[16] The terms *iconic* and *indexical* are borrowed from Mitchell,
"Representation" 1990, 14. Mitchell adds a third type of referential
relationship: when an object stands for something else, he speaks of
symbolic representation. For iconic representation Gibson introduces
"surface representation" (*Towards a Postmodern Theory* 1996, 81),
which amounts to "a realism of self-evidence" (82), for indexical
representation (with wider philosophical comprehensiveness) "deep
representation" (85), with the proviso that there are "no representations
that can claim incontestably to have captured deep, hidden,
metaphysically significant natures" (85).

[17] *Representation* 1997, ed. Hall, 15. On the contrary, Arac demonstrates
convincingly that Foucault and Derrida do "not attack representation"
("Introduction," xxiv; for a further discussion of this problem, see xxiv-
xxviii).

[18] A further delineation of the broad critical discussion of the "ongoing
worldwide crisis of representation" (Canning, "representation" 2001,
339) is beyond the scope of this essay.

[19] James Joyce, *Finnegans Wake* (London: Faber and Faber, 1975) 186.8-
9.

[20] Gibson, *Towards a Postmodern Theory* 1996, 69. The second chapter of
Gibson's book, "Deconstructing Representation: Narrative as
Inauguration" (69-104), deserves special mention for its incisive

theoretically essential in order to chart critically the production of meaning in *Ulysses*, which ostentatiously and uncertainly operates with continually shifting styles, shifting points of views of multiple types of narrators, the stream-of-consciousness of the main characters, internal cross-references between particular textual entities, and a vast range of intertextual correspondences.

Since the 1980s, Weimann has drawn our attention to the particular importance of the authority of the representational discourse itself, which—emerging out of the decline of late medieval allegory and romance—thrived upon the turbulent shift in the sixteenth century from the signs of forceful authority to the authority of textual signs.[21] In circumstances marked by the rise of the printing press, the success of the Protestant Reformation and concomitant erosions of feudally or clerically administered power, authors felt sufficiently unfettered in the vernacular to project the rhetoric of their own self-legitimation. Hence, "the purposes of representational practice multiplied, the matrix of representation proliferated,"[22] due to the intertwining of reflection and mirroring ("Darstellung") with functionally oriented delegation and argument ("Vorstellung"). With renewed force, this mode of *self-authorized representation* is integral to the different

---

synoptic review of (anti-)postmodern conceptions of "representation" and its pathbreaking theoretical discussion of representation and narrative. With regard to postmodernist thinking, Gibson draws the conclusion that it is "caught in an irreducible doubleness," on the one hand affirming "representability and the reality principle," and on the other hand claiming the erosion "of the very 'principle of reality'" (72). He further tells us that "in the middle ground between extremes, the ironies only proliferate" (73).

[21] See, for instance, Robert Weimann, "(Post)Modernity and Representation: Issues of Authority, Power, Performativity," *New Literary History* 23 (1992): 955-81; Robert Weimann, *Authority and Representation in Early Modern Discourse*, ed. David Hillman (Baltimore: Johns Hopkins U P, 1996).

[22] Weimann, *Author's Pen* 2000, 184.

manifestations of modernism and postmodernism in the
twentieth century, which have radically challenged and
redefined, though not utterly dismissed, the Western
representational tradition.[23] Joyce himself emphasizes the
authority of the author through which

> by its corrosive sublimation one continuous present
> tense integument slowly unfolded all marry-voicing
> moodmoulded cyclewheeling history (thereby, he
> said, reflecting from his own individual person life
> unlivable, trans-accidentated through the slow fires
> of consciousness into a dividual chaos, perilous,
> potent, common to allflesh, human only, mortal)
> (*FW* 185-186.6).

For Joyce, the single voice of the writer becomes the locus
of a hyper-representational, sublimated discourse that is able to
transcend the many voices of history and social reality. There is
no arrogance in this position, but rather the self-conscious
awareness of the necessity of authorial otherness in face of the
"historically circumscribed signifying operations."[24] The narrative enactment itself becomes a perilous, potent, common, human, mortal effort of cognition.

In theoretical terms, Weimann seeks to overcome scholarly
propositions as exemplified by Hall and Wells, revealing and
emphasizing a two-fold process: that the modalities of social
reality and ideological needs shape the form of representations,

---

[23] (Post)modernist self-authorized representation shields the work of art
against the post-industrial political, sociological, and mass cultural
"impasse of representation" or "crisis in representation," which
Weimann cogently outlines; see "Value, Representation and the
Discourse of Modernization: Toward a Political Economy of
Postindustrial Culture," *Stanford Literary Review* 10.1-2 (Spring-Fall
1993): 217; 224 [209-35]. The discussion of this problem would need
another essay.

[24] Kaja Silverman, *The Subject of Semiotics* (Oxford: Oxford U P, 1983)
129.

congruent with "the indelible role of representations in shaping modalities of social and cultural articulation," including "multiple and shifting subject positions."[25] Weimann's emphasis on the *modality* of representations may be linked to Arac's postmodern acknowledgement of "the interdependence of representation ... with history and narrative"[26] or Althusser's explanation of ideology as a "system of representations ... endowed with an historical existence and a role within a given society."[27] Natter and Jones question "the apparent unity of the object and sign," because "any materiality is attached to the representation(s) through which that materiality both embeds and conveys social meaning." If ideologies are embedded in societal materiality, "the anchors of representation are always open to disruption."[28] Modality thus implies *intentionality* or even *desire*. In other words, representation is interdependent with the practices of historically concrete social control through writing. On this premise, the practice of representation is consistently affected by "social norms and values as emblems of given relations of power."[29] I provisionally call this discursive mode of presenting power and knowledge *modal representation*. It may equally, or simultaneously, embrace the political, ideological, and literary. It constitutes the particular pattern of what Silverman calls "cultural representations," which "structure every moment of our existence" and teach the

[25]   Weimann, *Author's Pen* 2000, 257.

[26]   Arac, "Introduction" 1986, xxviii.

[27]   Louis Althusser, *For Marx*, trans. Ben Brewster (New York: Pantheon Books, 1969) 231.

[28]   Wolfgang Natter and John Paul Jones III, "Identity, Space, and Other Uncertainties," *Space and Social Theory: Interpreting Modernity and Postmodernity*, ed. Georges Benko and Ulf Strohmayer (Oxford: Blackwell, 1997) 151 [141-61].

[29]   Robert Weimann, "Representation and Performance: The Uses of Authority in Shakespeare's Theater," *PMLA* 107.3 (May 1992): 508 [497-510]. This essay offers a brilliant concise account of Weimann's seminal examination of "the difference between authority represented and author-ity representing" (509) in the Elizabethan theater.

human subject "to value only those objects which are culturally designated as full and complete."[30]

If the system of representations is open to disruption, subjective agents are also able, as Judith Butler suggests, to father (anti)representational dispositions of debate, refusal, difference, and protest. Though the subject is culturally and linguistically imprinted, he/she might realize his/her potential of acting upon the "matrices of power and discourse"[31] that constitute him or her. A position such as this obviously shapes the authorial perspective of *Ulysses*. *Authorial* representation gives form to the textual whole and to the formal ordering of the details. In a judicious essay, Lawrence calls attention to the fact that "the *labour* of language in ["Eumaeus"] has political and socioeconomic purport, which is indissolubly linked to the representation of material conditions in the chapter."[32] In other words, Joyce establishes in the text his non-conformist subject position—in "Eumaeus" and elsewhere—through the complex interaction between linguistic codification and referential representation. What the *text* unveils to the reader is that economic exploitation, colonial coercion, nationalist fundamentalism and Catholic indoctrination are the explicit subjects of authorial representation.

Modal representations figure as a dominant narrative object in *Ulysses*. From the perspective of authorial representation, they are criticized, disrupted, and negated. I propose to call this narrative anti-representational strategy, this self-authorized "putting together" at a higher hierarchical level, *auto-representative composition*. It differs markedly from the

---

[30] Silverman, *Subject of Semiotics* 1983, 177.

[31] Judith Butler, *The Psychic Life of Power: Theories in Subjection* (Stanford: Stanford U P, 1997) 5.

[32] Karen Lawrence, " 'Begarring Description': politics and style in 'eumaeus'," *A Collideorscape of Joyce*, ed. Ruth Frehner and Ursula Zeller (Dublin: Lilliput, 1998) 141 [138-55].

registers of (literary) referential and modal representation.[33] It is both representative (of the authorial stance) and anti-representative (with regard to social discourses). In a most radical and particular way, authorial composition realizes what Gibson (drawing on Heidegger, Derrida, and Vattimo) calls "the concept of 'inauguration,' " which holds that "art does not represent but inaugurates or founds a world, in that it presents itself as a new historical event or 'opening' of Being."[34] *Inauguration* puts emphasis on the fact that an auto-representative composition emanates decisively from the music and the play of words, will say, from the singular existence of the literary form. In Joyce's fiction, formal elements such as the use of Irish English, manifold poetic effects, wordplay, pastiche, taboo words, rhythm, lexical ambiguities, displacements, lists, provections, metamorphoses, shifts of style, shifts of point of view, shifts of narrative perspective, and many others are all part and parcel of authorial exhibitionism.[35] The anti-representational narrative enactment of societal modal representations is a moment and function of the literary form.

In general terms, the "founded" text of *Ulysses* is characterized by what might be called *mediation*. This word is

---

[33] A case in point is Klein's use of *representation*. Klein suggests, with regard to Joyce and Lewis, that "to be an author is to assert the power of representation, the ability to sanction through the word or image," which is produced "as a persuasive or intrinsically valuable object, one that has a real and powerful referent, whether that referent be the world outside or the processes of symbolization itself"; *The Fictions of James Joyce and Wyndham Lewis: Monsters of Nature and Design* (Cambridge: Cambridge U P, 1994) 20. I completely agree, in particular with the last part of the sentence. But the representative processes of symbolization are dramatically inconsistent with the manifold critical understandings of "representation." For this reason, terminological discrimination is apposite.

[34] Gibson, *Towards a Postmodern Theory* 1996, 88-89.

[35] McHale calls the modernist emphasis on the vocabulary "lexical exhibitionism"; Brian McHale, *Postmodernist Fiction* (New York: Methuen, 1987) 151.

meant to point at a mode of authorial composition that interrelates representationalism in its referential modes with a vast network of fictionally presented modal representations and with their (in most cases) ironic, mocking, or humorous critique through the literary form. The (re-)configuration of Dublin and *Dubliners*, of the political and ideological conditions, of the personalities of the main characters and of reliable interior monologues constructs the narrative's stabile platform, upon which the wildest (counter-)representational dances are executed.

In what follows, insights into Joyce's specific matrix of mediation shall be proffered by the examination of significant selected instances, chosen from *Ulysses*. Of necessity, this inquiry must be exemplary. It deliberately bypasses, for instance, the major, and for this reason self-evident, non-representational macrostructure of entire chapters: the textual collage of historical styles in "Oxen of the Sun" (ch. 14), the surrealist play of "Circe" (ch. 15), the catechistical game of "Ithaca" (ch. 17) and the interior monologue of "Penelope" (ch. 18). The common denominator of these different forms of presentation is the absence of the narrator (as medium). This absence at least raises the question of the structural relationship between the narrator and the other modes of representation, which must be left unanswered here.

Ulysses

In the beginning was the Title, and the Title was with Joyce. One signifier: a signifier that is a metonym of the novel's strategy of subverting representations. Conspicuously, Joyce alludes to and takes up a tradition of the realist novel, which identifies the title with the name of the protagonist. *Tom Jones*, *Silas Marner,* or *David Copperfield* are referentially representative of a main character and, indexically, of a teleologically structured biography. Correspondingly, the names are ideologically representative of the philosophy of a social class, if not of a whole age. But *Ulysses*? Even the referential subject is uncertain. Is it Bloom? Is it Stephen? Paradoxically, the heroic name "Ulysses" indicates in fact an absence, the absence of the protagonist. Strangely enough, the title does not refer to a biography, but rather to a series of events and situations on a single day. But if, premised on this shift, the eighteen episodes of the novel were loosely related to the epic's twenty-four,[36] why not the title *The Odyssey*? In point of fact, "Ulysses"/*Ulysses* produces a liminal undetermined space that does not represent what it seems to signify: neither the hero and the plot of the Greek epic nor a modern Dublin protagonist with a teleologically oriented biographical story.

Perhaps one may even guess that "Ulysses" holds out a finger towards the text-producing author himself. By common critical consent, "one of the most striking features of Joyce's book is its radical development, from one episode to another, in style, tone, and technique."[37] It is a Ulyssean task on the part of the author to visit and map the different formal realms. Understood in this way, "Ulysses" may be assumed to be representative of the metatextual level of narrative generation and of the self-authorization of the author. On the other hand, even the reader may be simultaneously identified with Ulysses, experiencing the adventures of entering all the shores and places of form and style. Speculative as these assumptions may sound, it albeit would be in line with a fundamental aspect of the fictional text, appropriately and inimitably labelled Joycean "provection" by Fritz Senn, the linguistic drive to "go beyond limits set," to carry away and be carried away.[38] "Ulysses" is a signifier in which various meanings oscillate and cohabit. In every respect, Joyce disrupts the axis of referential

---

[36] Nabokov recalls a conversation with Joyce in 1937; Joyce commented on his employment of Homer to be "a whim" (Richard Ellmann, *James Joyce* [Oxford: Oxford U P, 1983], 616, footnote).

[37] Timothy Martin, "*Ulysses* as a Whole," *A Collideorscape of Joyce*, ed. Ruth Frehner and Ursula Zeller (Dublin: Lilliput, 1998) 207 [202-14].

[38] Fritz Senn, *Inductive Scrutinies: Focus on Joyce*, ed. Christine O'Neill (Dublin: Lilliput, 1995) 39.

representation through this title, putting emphasis instead on an *undecidability* that disfigures any attempt at fixing a meaning.

Dublin

Conspicuously, the fictional world of *Ulysses* is located in a particular time and setting. The date is the 16th of June, 1904, the place the historical Dublin at this historical moment. The "Hibernian Metropolis" (*U* 7.1-2) is iconically represented through an extensive assemblage of random details. The text is dense with acute local observations. The protagonists and the minor characters are enmeshed in the local circumstances. As Martin emphasizes, "the naturalistic mode is always present— "like a shot off a shovel" (*U* 12.1918)—to undermine significance, sentiment, or solemnity."[39] Undoubtedly, Joyce's persistent reconstruction of the city throughout the text establishes a documentary image of Dublin, characterized by a convincing degree of referential accuracy. It has its focal points in particular urban sites which serve as frames to the "action" of the novel's episodes (the Martello tower at Sandycove, a terraced house in Eccles Street, Prospect Cemetery, the offices of *The Freeman's Journal*, the National Library, the pubs of Davy Byrne's and Barney Kiernan's, the Ormond Hotel, the National Maternity Hospital, the brothel district, the cabman's shelter), supplemented by a number of particular itineraries: the wanderings of Bloom about Dublin and some special routes taken across the city in "Hades" (ch. 6) and "Wandering Rocks" (ch. 10). In "Lotus Eaters" (ch. 5), for instance, Bloom perambulates within a maze of concretely named city streets, entering or passing a large number of buildings, among them a tea shop, Westland Row Post Office, Grosvenor Hotel, the cabman's shelter, a timberyard, a railway station, All Hallows Church, a chemist's shop, and a public bath. A roughly horizontal line from the west to the east is drawn in

---

[39] Timothy Martin, "Operatic Joyce," *James Joyce Quarterly* 38.1/2 (2000/2001): 35 [25-43].

"Wandering Rocks" by the journey of the Viceregal cavalcade "from the viceregal lodge" to "the lower gate of Phoenix Park," "Kingsbridge along the northern quays," "Bloody Bridge," "Queen's and Whitworth bridges," "Arran Quay," "Arran Street West," "Richmond Bridge," "Ormond Quay," "Grattan Bridge," "Dame Gate," "Fownes's Street," "Nassau Street," "Leinster Street," "Merrion Square," "Lower Mount Street," "The Royal Canal Bridge" into "Pembroke Township" and to "Haddington Road Corner," "Northumberland and Lansdowne Roads," until the final destination of the "Mirus Bazaar" is reached (*U* 10.1177-1279). In "Hades," the cortege at Paddy Dignam's funeral draws a roughly vertical line from the south(-east) to the north(-west), beginning at Sandymound and ending at "Prospect Cemetery" (*U* 6.486), moving along "Tritonville Road," and "Ringsend Road" (54), crossing "The Grand Canal" and turning into "Brunswick Street." It crosses the river at O'Connell Bridge and rattles along Sackville (O'Connell) Street, "Rutland Square," "Blessington Street," "Berkeley Street," "Phibsborough Road" and, after crossing "The Royal Canal" at "Crossguns Bridge," "Finglas Road" (*U* 6.30-458). It is noticeable that the names of Brunswick Street and Sackville Street are replaced by a catalogue of buildings and sites by the roadside, indicating perhaps the sheer length of the streets and painting a panoramic view of Dublin. One might also assume that Joyce intentionally silenced the political struggle over the renaming of Sackville Street into O'Connell Street.[40]

Street names, sites, and buildings serve as iconic local markers. They, and the "extensive use Joyce makes of newspaper cuttings, advertisements, local and topical gossip,"[41] represent the authentic, not primarily the historico-colonial, urban place of the Irish metropolis. However, as Natter and Jones note,

---

[40] See Andrew Gibson, *Joyce's Revenge* (Oxford: Oxford U P, 2002) 95.
[41] Jean-Michel Rabaté, *James Joyce and the Politics of Egoism* (Cambridge: Cambridge U P, 2001) 114.

> space is not simply a socially produced materiality
> but a socially produced—and forceful—object/sign
> system ... An appropriate theory of space as
> representation will, therefore, not only question the
> apparent unity of the object and sign, but also the
> possibility of their separation ... We are left, then,
> with space as an always already, but never
> predetermined, representation.[42]

If the city space is represented as both strictly material
(iconic) and socially encoded (indexical), the authorial
implications of referential representation multiply. Joyce's
Dublin becomes meaningful(l) on at least three distinguishable
levels. First, it renders to the reader a concrete geographical
space, which is architecturally, socially, and politically concrete
and authentic. In this way, the narrative is anchored in an
inimical Dublin/Irish setting. Through iconic representation,
Ulysses becomes an *Irish* novel. Second, the iconic
representation of Dublin functionally counterbalances, through
its documentary concreteness, all kinds of modal
representation, which Joyce otherwise tries to disrupt
methodically. Authenticity allows the text-producing author to
emancipate himself and the perspective of the fictional text
from ideology. Basically, the reader is summoned to distinguish
between the material reality, in which Irish men and women
live, and the "matrices of power and discourse" (Butler) that
constitute a second reality of values, subtly constituting the
subjects. Thirdly, since Irish history and contemporary
sociopolitical meanings are encoded in buildings, monuments,
and streets, the iconic representations potentially contain wider
indexical or even symbolic meanings. Dublin Castle *may*
signify colonial rule, the tram system the traffic and commerce
of a metropolitan (though in many ways also still provincial)
Western capital, the National Library the formation of a
national Irish culture, Nelson's Pillar the historical presence of

---

[42] Natter and Jones, "Identity, Space" 1997, 151.

British coercion or the hegemonic claim of the Protestant Ascendency. It is one of the tasks of literary criticism to examine the particular functions of the reconfigurations of Dublin sites in *Ulysses* and thus to distinguish between the material and allegorical (iconic and indexical) significations of referential representation.

In a period witnessing the efflorescence of postcolonial studies, the application of postcolonial theory to Joyce's works has resulted in a tendency of over-determined indexical allegorization. Platt, for instance, argues that Joyce's Dublin "is emphatically a colonized place," in which colonial history "is ideologically reconstructed."[43] Platt leads us to believe that "street names" are "the markers of an imperial history which has its presence stamped very firmly over the stones of a modern urban landscape. These markers carry a historical dynamic: the dynamic of colonization" (88). Similarly, Spurr suggests that for Joyce, "the architecture and planning of Dublin" forms "a concrete expression of modern colonial domination."[44] Sweeping statements of this kind, which crudely ideologize every aspect of Joyce's text, must be taken with a grain of salt. On the other hand, it would be misleading to annul all indexical meanings. Very often, the critic arrives at points at which hermeneutic problems begin. Often, textual

---

[43] Len Platt, *Joyce and the Anglo-Irish: A Study of Joyce and the Literary Revival* (Amsterdam: Rodopi, 1998) 86, 89.

[44] David Spurr, "Colonial Spaces in Joyce's Dublin," *James Joyce Quarterly* 37.1/2 (1999/2000): 24 [23-39]. A strange case of critical inventiveness is Spurr's suggestion that through the Viceroy's passage "the city [is] now seen as one great colonial space," since along the route "the cavalcade passes all the major monuments and institutions that symbolize British rule in Ireland, including the Wellington Monument in Phoenix Park, the palace of the Four Courts, the police and military headquarters of Dublin Castle, the Bank of Ireland, Trinity College, and the prosperous, mainly Protestant suburb of Pembroke Township" (33). But in this segment of "Wandering Rocks," the Wellington Memorial, the Four Courts, Dublin Castle, the Bank of Ireland, and Trinity College are not mentioned at all.

indeterminacy and critical uncertainty prevails.[45] But a careful examination of the (iconic and indexical) representationalism of textual units might increase the reliability of critical readings.

Interior Monologues

Structurally, *Ulysses* counterbalances referential representations with a vast corpus of interior monologues. As linguistic constructs, they are basically anti-representative. As Katie Wales notes, interior monologue is distinguished by "inchoate thought-processes, the flow of thoughts, abrupt topic shifts, random associations, etc. Since thought is not only verbal but non-verbal, such a style must inevitably be "symbolic" in its attempt to suggest the chains of visual images and memories, as well as other mental stimuli such as sensation, feelings etc."[46] Let me quote only two randomly selected examples:

> Ineluctable modality of the visible: at least that if no more, thought through my eyes. Signatures of all things I am here to read, seaspawn and seawrack, the nearing tide, that rusty boot. Snotgreen, bluesilver, rust: coloured signs. Limits of the diaphane. But he adds: in bodies. The he was aware of them bodies before of them coloured (*U* 3.1-5).

Stephen's famous monologic paraphrase of Aristotelian thought is preoccupied with applying aspects of the

---

[45] I want to emphasize this condition by referring to Gibson's suggestion that a "struggle over street names that began in December 1884" was one aspect of "a dynamic conflict" between the British administration and Dublin Corporation (*Joyce's Revenge* 2002, 95, 94). But I do think that this historical background does not specifically affect the iconic representation of Dublin in *Ulysses*.

[46] Katie Wales, *The Language of James Joyce* (London: Macmillan, 1992) 72-73.

philosopher's theory of color and the "translucent" to the young man's individual search ("thought through my eyes") for appropriating reality. Aristotle's philosophical thinking is by no means represented. Rather, the monologue tells us that Stephen is schooled in and probably influenced by the Greek master. The non-representational subjectivity of the utterance is emphasized through the intertwining of Aristotle with the disparate ideas of the German mystic and philosopher Jakob Boehme, who beheld the Creator in the "signatures of all things," laid open to human beings. Equally remarkable is the unsystematic and obscure reference to Aristotle, which alludes to the fact that Stephen might have a comprehensive understanding of *Of Sense and the Sensible* and *On the Soul*, but leaves it primarily to the reader to make sense of it beyond the mere reading practice of following the text. Moreover, the poetic and elliptical formation of language self-authorizes linguistic expression apart from its reference to the sea and to the beach; it is meant to generate aesthetic experience. Furthermore, "snotgreen" accomodates a cross-referential significance through its conjunction with the "new art colour for our Irish poets: snotgreen" (1.73), ironically thought up by Stephen's friend/antagonist Buck Mulligan in the first chapter. Representationalism is replaced by the presence of widening gyres of signification.

The character of Leopold Bloom, who might be considered the protagonist of *Ulysses*, is substantially created through his interior monologues. The second section of "Nausicaa" (13.772-1285) is for the most part organized as a Bloomian "speech" to himself. It anticipates the famous interior monologue of Molly Bloom in which the novel culminates (ch. 18, "Penelope"). Both monologues record the diversity of human experience, expressed through biographical bits and pieces. Disclosing the "eccentric and unpredictable mind(s)"[47] of the characters they shut out any discourse of representation.

---

[47] Derek Attridge, *Joyce Effects: On Language, Theory, and History* (Cambridge: Cambridge U P, 2000) 97.

In the fourth chapter, in which Bloom is introduced to the reader, musings about the "pleasant old times" (4.210) work in his mind, which all of a sudden are countervened by a dismal picture of Palestine:

> No, not like that. A barren land, bare waste. Vulcanic lake, the dead sea: no fish, weedless, sunk deep in the earth. No wind could lift those waves, grey metal, poisonous foggy waters. Brimstone they called it raining down: the cities of the plain: Sodom, Gomorrah, Edom. All dead names. A dead sea in a dead land, grey and cold. Old now. It bore the oldest, the first race ... (4.219-28).

This monologue is a special case of representational indeterminacy and of shifting perspectives. Firstly, with regard to the narrative process, meaning is established through structure. The text counterpoises the image of a nearly utopian place of "pleasantness" ("Pleasants street: pleasant old times"; 4.210) with the image of a dystopian place of "barrenness." In a nutshell, it is suggestive of one of the comprehensive themes of *Ulysses*: the dismantling of utopian thought. The reader might also guess that, from the authorial perspective, the "paralytic" state of Ireland is mapped out in symbolic form. But if so, the representativeness of this image is very vague. Secondly, with regard to the monologic form, Bloom's reflection upon the dead place is at this point ostentatiously non-Bloomian in its stylistic figuration. Though the mistaken inclusion of Edom in the Old Testament list of the cities destroyed by God is highly characteristic of Bloom, the poetic and rhetorical formation of the entire passage, which makes use of alliterations, assonances, anaphora, parallelism, prosody, repetition of words, semantic clusters, etc., establishes an autonomous lyrical space. This space does not really represent the geographical location of Palestine, but rather creates a poetic image of "desolation" (4.229). The form of the passage and its narrative embedding remain in a state of contradiction. After this grandiose tour de force, the narrative return from the "horror" (4.230) vision to the "natural" emotions of Bloom appears to be considerably forced. But even this change of key puts additional emphasis on the indeterminacy of representation.

Giving a narrative voice to the interior thought processes of Stephen, Bloom, and Molly, the text-producing author juxtaposes representationalism with the discontinuous expression of subjectivity. The interior monologues lack coherence; they do not unfold a consistent argument; they are not subsumed under a grand narrative. Occasionally, they change into self-subsistent thematic units. The thought processes of the three characters to some degree relate to quotidian and social reality or (in Stephen's case) the history of culture and philosophy but, what is more, the focus of attention is on individuality and the biographical peculiarities of thinking and experience, to which the activity of the reader may be added to constitute meanings from what is presented through the individual persons' minds. In this way, the narration confirms that the three characters are not representative of Catholicism, Irish nationalism, British colonialism, colonialized mentality, and Irish paralysis in general. Foregrounding the uniqueness of the individual character, the "internal direct mode of thought-presentation"[48] indicates that individual stances of nonconformity, alterity and protest might exist, which are not representative in a sociopolitical sense.

"Nausicaa"

In chapter 13, Joyce reproduces a literary paradigm of representation, faking the style of women's magazines or late Victorian popular novels. The imitation of contemporary romances adequately introduces the female main figure of the first part (*U* 13.1-770), Gerty MacDowell:

---

[48]   Wales, *Language* 1992, 75.

The summer evening had begun to fold the world in its mysterious embrace. Far away in the west the sun was setting and the last glow of all too fleeting day lingered lovingly on sea and strand, on the proud promontory of dear old Howth guarding as ever the waters of the bay, on the weedgrown rocks along Sandymount shore and, last but not least, on the quiet church whence there streamed forth at times upon the stillness the voice of prayer to her who is in her pure radiance a beacon ever to the stormtossed heart of man, Mary, star of the sea (*U* 13.1-8).

What the reader of this paragraph immediately notices is that the narrative voice is imitative; it imitates the narrators of magazine fiction, which was popular between 1880 and 1920. Scrutinizing the corpus of popular women's magazines (published in London, written by men!), Gibson highlights the fact that they "were determined by Victorian and Edwardian 'domestic ideology'" and concerned with producing "a serviceable model of English and colonial womanhood."[49] In other words, the fictional introduction to the Gerty section is a typical instance of a pseudo-realist romance,[50] which in fact epitomizes contemporary modal fictional representations, exerting "imperial, colonial, and racial"[51] as well as consumerist, behavioral, and gender control through writing. Joyce, very slyly, albeit decidedly, subverts the ostensible certainties of the "fictional" discourse through the anacoluthon

---

[49] Gibson, *Joyce's Revenge* 2002, 131-33.

[50] From a generic perspective, an omniscient narrator narrates the story. Joyce emphasizes this method through parodic imitation. For this reason, Denis Donoghue's comment on the opening paragraph that there is "not omniscient narration" is at least debatable; "The Styles of Nausicaa," *A Collideorscape of Joyce*, ed. Ruth Frehner and Ursula Zeller (Dublin: Lilliput Press, 1998) 130 [127-36].

[51] Gibson, *Joyce's Revenge* 2002, 129.

"… her who is …" The faulty order of the grammatic/syntactic construction exhibits the falsity of the shallow emotionalism of the stylistic register. The text-producing author obviously tells us that a text of this kind, which pretends to represent a social and local space, will offer a merely invented coherent view of the world. The reader is summoned not to walk into the trap laid out in alliterations, assonances, long vowels, and a chain of positively charged words, such as "mysterious embrace," "glow," "lingered lovingly," "dear old," "guarding," "quiet," "stillness," "prayer," "pure radiance," and "heart." The reader is forced to see that what he reads *is* a particular type of modal representation.

The opening description is perfectly "apposite to the agents or characters who will be featured in it."[52] Through her way of thinking and monologic expression, Gerty reveals herself as a young Dublin woman whose emotional and intellectual scope is fundamentally constituted by popular culture, class, and commercial surroundings. Adequately, the style of the narrative discourse designates a complementary phenomenon: the constitution of human subjects by enacted types of communication and the selfexpression of a human subject in terms of these subject-constituting discourses. The narrator who, on the surface and for the concrete narrative purpose, represents a concrete Dublin place at a concrete time of the day construes in fact a deceit, which aims at an affective function in the first place. As Weimann notes with reference to TV commercials, "images, texts, signifiers are set in play so as to convey desirable emotions, attitudes, states of being; but these signifiers are floating and tend to obliterate any meaningful signified."[53] Joyce introduces a type of referential pseudo-representation that coterminously is meant to deeply affect the reader. As the entire chapter brings to light, it is ideologically operational, like a TV ad, constituting "the subject within the

---

[52] Donoghue, "Styles" 1998, 130.
[53] Weimann, "Value, Representation" 1993, 231.

code."[54] All in all, the beginning of "Nausicaa" is an outstanding example of Joyce's representational games. The text is an imitation of a genre-specific referential representation of the time and place of the narrated "story." As a pastiche, it functions as the authorial composition of a discursive model, in which referential and modal representations conflate. Through this constellation, the rupture between the imitated stylistic act and the act of auto-representative composition comes to light. This difference sets free the critical evaluation of what is going on in the minds of Dubliners and also of the societal and cultural forces that subjugate the individual subject.

Within the spectrum of contemporary Joyce studies, a critical scrutiny of Joyce's appropriation of representative discourses again counterbalances the recent postcolonial trend in *Ulysses* criticism. There is, for instance, no reason to argue, as Castle does, that Gerty's "subject position of the female subaltern" is "the site of a liberatory ambivalence."[55] If every female in *Ulysses* is "subaltern," there is next to nothing left to say. If "liberatory ambivalence" shall be traced, one might find it encoded in Joyce's textual practice, but by no means in the character of Gerty. Castle mistakenly grounds his argument on the assumption that the style of "Nausicaa" is, in Bhabha's sense,[56] parodic and mimic. This, however, is exactly what it is not. The discourse of the first part of "Nausicaa," abounding in

---

[54] Mark Poster, *The Mode of Information: Poststructuralism and Social Context* (Chicago: U of Chicago P, 1990) 63; quoted also in Weimann, "Value, Representation" 1993, 231. As Suzette Henke suggests, Gerty (like Molly Bloom) "is doomed to construct a media-controlled self image"; *James Joyce and the Politics of Desire* (New York: Routledge, 1990) 138.

[55] Gregory Castle, "Colonial Discourse and the Subject of Empire in Joyce's 'Nausicaa'," *Joyce: Feminism/Post/Colonialism*, ed. Ellen Carol Jones (Amsterdam: Rodopi, 1998) 144 [115-44].

[56] "Mimicry is the fatal flaw of colonial discourse, the representation of a difference that is itself a process of disavowal" (Homi K. Bhabha, *The Location of Culture* (London: Routledge, 1994) 108; quoted by Castle, 122).

"cliché" and "*kitsch*,"[57] is perfectly, and non-parodically, imitational; it is a "*simulatio*," the installing of a kind of pre-computer-age "*virtual reality*."[58] It copies literary textual strategies in a *representational*, not a parodic, manner. The reader is summoned to critically evaluate the structure and social function of modal representation, not to make the text appropriate to pre-set theoretical assumptions.

Pisgah Sights

Frequent references to Moses and the Prophetical Books throughout the novel constitute a major thematic cluster which, as I argue in contrast to Nadel,[59] consistently deconstructs the modal representation of social and Biblical *messianic* promise and utopian thinking. In face of the ubiquity of allusions in the text, a paradigmatic investigation into the problem must again draw on a few selected examples.

Bloom's dismal vision of the barren countryside of Palestine, for instance (*U* 4.219-28, quoted above, see "Interior

---

[57] Fritz Senn, "Nausicaa," *Joyce's Dislocutions: Essays on Reading and Translation*, ed. John Paul Riquelme (Baltimore: Johns Hopkins U P, 1984) 185 [160-87]. Senn emphasizes that within the general stylistic register of "literary cliché," a large number of "stylistic metamorphoses" (184) can be registered. This may be also called a subtle undermining of representation as such.

[58] Dieter Mersch, *Ereignis und Aura: Untersuchungen zu einer Ästhetik des Performativen* (Frankfurt M.: Suhrkamp, 2002) 77-78. The imitational aspect gives substance to the recent critical readings of the Gerty section focussing on the female subject in a modern commodity culture, which Castle censures.

[59] Ira Nadel suggests that "as exile, lawgiver, prophet, nation-builder, and leader, the personal and political parallels between Moses and Joyce were explicit"; *Joyce and the Jews: Culture and Texts* (London: Macmillan, 1989) 85. In chapter 3 (84-107), Nadel gives a seminal account of the "Moses typology" (85) in Joyce's writing. For my partly diverging interpretation of the references to Moses in *Ulysses*, see Wolfgang Wicht, *Utopianism in James Joyce's* Ulysses (Heidelberg: Universitätsverlag C. Winter, 2000) 169-99.

Monologues"), disrupts the view of a blooming countryside
outlined by Agendath Netaim, the Zionist colony (191-99),[60]
which also incited Bloom's personal "pleasant" imaginings
(201-17). The passage forcefully calls to mind the Old
Testament as an intertext. In *Deuteronomy*, God's pledge to
bring the children of Israel into the land "that floweth with milk
and honey" (*Deut.* 31.20)[61] is counterbalanced by the Lord's
threat to send "many evils and troubles" upon them (31.17), if
they are "rebellious against" (31.27) him. Joyce's paragraph
dismisses the teleological course of the Biblical story, which
represents the promise made to the Chosen people that "there
will arise a Palestine, which will be nothing less than a new
Eden, Paradise regained."[62] At a later point in the novel, in
"Oxen of the Sun," the transformation of the Agendath Netaim
project into an image of "a desert land" (*Deut.* 32.10) is re-
cited. The anonymous poetic persona[63] (imitating the style of
Thomas de Quincey) reflects on "twilight phantoms...,
moulded in prophetic grace of structure," but they "fade, sad
phantoms: all is gone. Agendath is a waste land, a home of

---

[60] Even the iconic reference to the Jewish corporation, at "Bleibtreustrasse 34, Berlin, W. 15" (*U* 4.199) is a sham. In 1904, this part of Bleibtreustrasse still was a development area; eventually, a building with the street number 34/35 was erected in 1908. According to the *Berlin Directory* Agendath (or Agudath) Netaim at no time took residence there.

[61] The Bible is quoted according to *The Holy Bible* (Oxford: Oxford U P, for the British and Foreign Bible Society, 1901).

[62] Norman Cohn, *The Pursuit of the Millenium: Revolutionary Millenarians and Mystical Anarchists of the Middle Ages* (London: Temple Smith, 1970) 20.

[63] The assumption of Joyce critics to identify the voice of the passage with an interior monologue of Bloom is difficult to sustain in face of its stylistic sophistication. "Twilight" and "twilight phantoms" are signifiers which are semantically indeterminate. They might stand for the young men present in the maternity hospital (in Bloom's mood), but they might also symbolize the literary "Celtic Twilight" or utopian promises (including Agendath Netaim) in general.

screechowls and the sandblind upupa. Netaim, the golden, is no more" (*U* 14.1083-87). Gone are both the Jewish promise of Moses and the Christian promise of Jerusalem, the golden (see *Revelation* 21:18). Earlier in "Oxen," Stephen makes use of the Moses saga in order to describe (in indirect speech) his troubled relationship with Ireland, the land of milk and money: "Look forth now, my people, upon the land of the behest, even from Horeb and from Nebo and from Pisgah and from the Horns of Hatten unto a land flowing with milk and money. But thou hast suckled me with bitter milk: my moon and my sun thou hast quenched for ever. And thou hast left me alone for ever in the dark ways of my bitterness" (*U* 14.375-79). The correspondences, parallels, and echoes, established through later occurrences, augment and intensify what the text intends to say. In this case, the strategic coordination of a systematic deconstruction of the "Promised Land" myth undermines the accepted (modal) representativeness of the Moses story, annulling "the appeal of Exodus history to generations of radicals," which "lies in its linearity, in the idea of a promised end, in the purposiveness of the Israelite march."[64] What Joyce tells his Irish readers, and us, is that the Biblical and the adapted topical final views from the mountain of Nebo, or Pisgah (*Deut.* 34:1), on a wide land, which is "a land of corn and wine" (33:28), represents human, political, racial, and religious desires, whereas the unpromising end of worldly affairs rather corresponds to the image of a waste land.

Retrospectively, Stephen's inclusion of Pisgah in the list of prophetic mountains sheds some light on the parable he invents in "Aeolus," called "*A Pisgah Sight of Palestine* or *The Parable of the Plums*" (*U* 7.1057-58). Not only the "look forth upon the land of the behest" is ridiculed through its concrete political parallelism, but the promise-giving leader of his people himself is transfigured into ordinary persons of no promise at all. In Stephen's parabolic narration, two "elderly

---

[64] Michael Walzer, *Exodus and Revolution* (New York: Basic Books, 1984) 14.

and pious" (7.923) Catholic women ascend Nelson's Pillar in order "to see the views of Dublin" (7.931). They are quite unaware of the potent political symbolism of the building, erected at a central point in the city. Correspondingly, the ladies' scenic view of the roofs and churches of Dublin signifies nothing to them. Stephen's parable reveals that the two women represent a larger percentage of Dubliners in the prison-house of their social and political situation. His telling of the tale, however, contests—*as narrative*—this specimen of colonial stasis; it dislocates and questions the socially given interrelationship between the objective indexical function of the Pillar and the women's mental state of passivity, ignorance, and oblivion. The "Parable of the Plums" privileges the narrative over the ideological configurations, which it represents. The enactment of literary representation transcends what it represents.

At another level of the parable's meaning, Moses's situation becomes parabolic as well.[65] Mount Pisgah and Moses's vista of Palestine, which subsequently will be subjugated and colonialized by the Biblical Chosen People, becomes allegorically identical with Nelson's Pillar and the panorama of Dublin, symbolizing British rule over Ireland. The essential story of the Old Testament is in fact typified as the prime example of colonial subjugation.

Identifying the modal representativeness of the Moses saga with its appropriation to British colonialism, Joyce's text touches upon the problem of the contemporary representativeness of this appropriation itself, which appears in "Aeolus" as a contiguous context to Stephen's parable. It seems to be a truism in Joyce criticism that Joyce shared the "revolutionary" conception of the Moses saga, which applied the pattern of oppression and liberation to the national urge to

---

[65] "Get thee up into the top of Pisgah, and lift up thine eyes westward, and northward, and southward, and eastward, and behold [the promised land] with thine eyes" (*Deut.* 4:27).

liberate Ireland from the oppression of Britain.[66] "Parnell-as-Moses images" flourished indeed during Joyce's youth, but the "empathy between the Irish and the "Jewish case"," which "appeared in many letters and speeches during the rise of Parnell,"[67] practically ceased to have impact after Parnell's fall in 1890/91. In 1894, John Eglinton, the National Library librarian and eventual character in "Scylla and Charybdis" (ch. 9), passed an ironic judgement on "our doctrine of the Chosen People," characterizing it as, "to say the least of it, a little crude."[68] If one peruses the corpus of nationalist Irish writings at the turn of the century, it becomes obvious that references to the Moses saga were as good as nonexistent. Contrary to the accepted Mosaic accomodation, Arthur Griffith, one of the intellectual leaders of the Home Rule movement and editor of the periodical *The United Irishman*, exposed himself as the main representative of the Moses reading implied in Stephen's parable. He forwarded the idea "that the English were Jahveh's Chosen People, and Javeh had destined them to wipe out all the nations of the earth and boss this planet."[69] From this perspective, "The Parable of the Plums" might express a certain sympathy of young Stephen with Griffith's negative representation (from the Irish point of view) of the Moses myth.

A rare contemporary example of the positive citation of the Moses saga is a speech the patriotic barrister John F. Taylor extemporized in reply to a paper read by Justice Fitzgibbon

---

[66] A typical example is Theoharis's suggestion that Ireland's struggle for Home Rule "was treated in Mosaic symbols by the Irish themselves long before Joyce used it"; Theoharis Constantine Theoharis, *Joyce's Ulysses: An Anatomy of the Soul* (Chapel Hill: U of North Carolina P, 1988) 185.

[67] Neil R. Davison, *James Joyce, Ulysses, and the Construction of Jewish Identity: Culture, Biography and "The Jews" in Modernist Europe* (Cambridge: Cambridge U P, 1996) 7, 34.

[68] John Eglinton, *Two Essays on the Remnant* (Dublin: Whaley, 1894) 34.

[69] IER, "The Anglo-Israelite Destroyer of Tara," *The United Irishman*, 106 (1901): 2.

before the Trinity College Historical Society on 24 October 1901.[70] Fitzgibbon inveighed against an essay advocating the Gaelic Revival, possibly Douglas Hyde's "The Necessity of De-Anglicising Ireland" (1892), and on the whole defended a Unionist political position. It is against this, that "John F. Taylor rose to reply" (*U* 7.823), ironically imitating the voice of an Egyptian highpriest (see *U* 7.845-50, 855-59) and indirectly ironizing Griffith's procolonial reading of *Exodus* and *Deuteronomy*. Taylor's conclusion, as rendered by the figure of MacHugh in "Aeolus," is a rhetorical masterpiece of Joyce's own fictitious invention:

> *But, ladies and gentlemen, had the youthful Moses listened to and accepted that view of life, had he bowed his head and bowed his will and bowed his spirit before that arrogant admonition he would never have brought the chosen people out of their house of bondage, nor followed the pillar of the cloud by day. He would never have spoken with the Eternal amid lightnings on Sinai's mountaintop nor ever have come down with the light of inspiration shining in his countenance and bearing in his arms the tables of the law, graven in the language of the outlaw* (*U* 7.862-69).

Only the final words verbally transcribe Taylor's pamphlet. Through this tactical maneuver, the intentionality of the discourse betrays itself with a vengeance. The Bible does not indicate that the tablets were "graven in the language of the outlaw;" the biblical text does not touch upon the language question at all. The Joycean imitation of a rhetorically overdone discourse exhibits to the reader that the deliberate topical

---

[70] Taylor's argument was reported in some detail in the following day's *Freeman's Journal* and published in 1903 as a pamphlet called "The Language of the Outlaw." It is possible that Joyce was present at the meeting.

representation of a given model of modal representation is a product of specific ideological desires and political intentions. In pointblank explicitness, a commentary on the Moses story is expressed through Professor McHugh's ironic (and "uncontradicted") remark, "—That is oratory" (7.879). Stephen's subsequent interior monologue gives a final verdict, associating Moses with Daniel O'Connell and his famous rallies for the repeal of the Union in 1843:

> Gone with the wind. Hosts of Mullaghmast and Tara of the kings. Miles of ears of porches. The tribune's words, howled and scattered to the four winds. A people sheltered within his voice. Dead noise. Akasic records of all that ever anywhere wherever was. Love and laud him: me no more. (*U* 7.880-84)

The rhyme "his voice. Dead noise" stands out, annotating Mosaic, O'Connellian, Taylorian, or any other political messianic oratories. The "Mosaic passage" in "Aeolus" forms in its entirety a judgment on the modal representation of promises. It desubstantializes current readings of the original Moses saga and its diverse appropriations in contemporary political ideology. Since the oppositional interpretations are not even representative of the controversies over Irish Home Rule at the beginning of the twentieth century, the passage functionally gives point to the deliberately non-representative authorial perspective.

Materializing Representation

Finally, two examples shall be merely cited that explain to us Joyce's ironic deflation of the very processes of generating material indexical representations. Both relate to Bloom's coronation as the anarcho-socialist King Leopold I in the phantasmagoric drama of "Circe" (ch. 16). When Bloom promises his "beloved subjects" the "new era" of "the new Bloomusalem in the Nova Hibernia of the future" (*U* 15.1541-

45), this New Bloomusalem is immediately shaped up as an architectural edifice:

> (*Thirty-two workmen wearing rosettes, from all the counties of Ireland, under the guidance of Derwan the builder, construct the new Bloomusalem. It is a colossal edifice with crystal roof, built in the shape of a huge pork kidney, containing forty thousand rooms ...*). (*U* 15.1546-49)

Here as elsewhere, representations of material practices are made to comment on their submerged meanings. The New Bloomusalem is denoted as literally being a colossal edifice. Its gigantic size proves the emptiness of the vision. At the same time, the construction ostentatiously alludes to *Revelation*, substituting (among other referential details) the cubic masonry of the Biblical Jerusalem for, of all things, a huge pork kidney.[71] The meanings of both the Bloomian and the biblical constructions become ironically identical.

A little later when Bloom explains to his audience his "schemes for social regeneration," they are without delay given material symbolic shape as sculptural figures. The keeper of

> *the Kildare street museum appears, dragging a lorry on which are the shaking statues of several naked goddesses, Venus Callipyge, Venus Pandemos, Venus Metempsychosis, and plaster figures, also naked, representing the new nine muses, Commerce, Operatic Music, Amor, Publicity, Manufacture, Liberty of Speech, Plural voting, Gastronomy, Private Hygiene, Seaside Concert Entertainment, Painless Obstetrics and Astronomy for the People* (*U* 15.1702-10).

---

[71] Bloom purchases and cooks a pork kidney in "Calypso" (ch. 3).

Each of the nine muses is easily recognizable as an ideological signifier, linking pleasure and entertainment with economy, health, and astrology.[72] At the same time, the enumeration of the new nine muses tells a lie. If counted, the figures equal twelve and thus enter into an intertextual relationship with the highly symbolic number twelve in the Judaeo-Christian tradition. Banality subverts representativeness. Every level of representation becomes ridiculous: the social politics of Bloom-the-ruler, the social meanings of ceremonial representation, and the social practice of installing representative signs. Representation means falsification.

Coda

Ulysses is characterized by an extraordinary fusion of referential representations, modal representations, and anti-representative authorial composition. They are all part of a narrative composition which, presenting and not presenting representations, seeks (with Gibson's words) "to 'overcome' representation" playfully in "the ironic interdependence of the mimetic and the anti-mimetic."[73] Notably through the anti-representational style of chapters 14, 15, 17, and 18 and the distinguished quantity and quality of interior monologues, the text installs a striking dimension of non-representative narrative. The monologues are highly mimetic with regard to the subjectivity of Bloom, Stephen, and Molly, but what is going on in the minds of the protagonists is basically not

---

[72] Their plaster quality recalls Pound's *Mauberley* poem and its lament that "the 'age demanded' chiefly a mould in plaster, / Made with no loss of time"; Ezra Pound, *Selected Poems 1908-1959* (London: Faber and Faber, 1982) 99.

[73] Gibson, *Towards a Postmodern Theory* 1996, 79. Gibson suggests that this irony might help us "to grow wiser," recognizing "that any critique of representation will continually fall back into the positions from which it seeks to free itself " (*ib.*).

identical with the narrative passages representing imaginary versions of a circumstantial world.

It is through the mimetic appropriation of the "Real," vertical layers of signification and ironic distortion, that the text of *Ulysses* both endorses and disrupts representational practices. On the one hand, there is a strong element of referential representation (iconic and indexical), based on apparent verisimilitude. Differing from the realist novel, these reconfigurations do not aim at or end in representational/ epistemological closure. For this reason, they are, in a determined way, perspectival, open to indeterminacy, and the production of meaning by the reader. If, however, referential representation is a definite process, aiming at a function of affirming and stabilizing, the question—what the stabilizing moments in Joyce's representation of Dublin are—surfaces. To my mind, what Joyce tells us is (not more and not less) that Dublin is an *Irish* city which is both the focus and the promise of the *Irish* national state to come. Simultaneously, Joyce ostentatiously defines himself as an *Irish* (not a British or cosmopolitan) writer, contributing to the emergence of a new, modern *Irish* national literature. Placing, however, referential representation in juxtaposition with the peculiar non-representativeness of the interior monologues, the author also creates a structural state of balance that at the same time undermines transcendental notions of Irishness and identity.

On the other hand, as Christine van Boheemen emphasizes, the author "unsettle(s) the mirroring function of western representation. Dissemination, différance, supplementarity, invagination, *jouissance*, the Real, 'the Thing,' are embodied features and principles of Joyce's text."[74] In a particular way, the text deconstructs multiple sorts of modal representations, bringing to light the affirmative and intentional aspects they contain. Taken as a whole, the novel is no longer representative

---

[74] Christine van Boheemen-Saaf, *Joyce, Derrida, Lacan, and the Trauma of History: Reading, Narrative and Postcolonialism* (Cambridge: Cambridge U P, 1999) 194.

in the classical sense; it inaugurates a fictional construct that asserts the historical reality of Ireland and defines it as immersed in multifaceted practices of representing; it dislocates "western representation, and the canonicity of the English novel, which will henceforth be 'english'" (201), through the practicing of what van Boheemen calls "syncretic manner of representation" (1). The "unsettling" of modal representations effaces ontological fullness and disrupts the assumed identity between the signifier and the signified. Where there was a holistic representational object once, there is a gap now. In accordance with a proposition mapped out by Derrida, this mode of inauguration may be called "nonrepresentation," which "is, thus, original representation, if representation signifies also, the unfolding of a volume, a multidimensional milieu, an experience which produces its own space."[75] The author is the creator who forges in the smithy of his soul the uncreated[76] composition of a writing impelled by "the strategies that attempt a deconstruction of representation."[77]

In this position, the author is no longer a representative of hegemonic or other social forces, but rather occupies the marginal place of a noncommitted subject. He wilfully gives up the assured place of the artist within the culture. To intentionally place himself beyond the social, political, religious, and ethical constituents of society is both his triumph and aporia. Joyce's personal turning away from Catholicism, socialism, Irish nationalism and even friends and family speaks for itself. Isolation as well as artistic and "political egoism"[78]

---

[75] Jacques Derrida, "Theater of Cruelty," quoted in Arac, "Introduction" 1986, xxvi.

[76] At the end of Joyce's *A Portrait of the Artist as a Young Man*, Stephen notes in his diary, "I go to encounter for the millionth time the reality of experience and to forge in the smithy of my soul the uncreated conscience of my race" (London: Penguin Books, 1992) 273-74.

[77] Derek Attridge and Daniel Ferrer, "Introduction: Highly Continental Evenements," *Post-structuralist Joyce: Essays from the French* (Cambridge: Cambridge U P, 1984) 10 [1-13].

[78] Rabaté, *Politics of Egoism* 2001, 58.

mark the modernist vantage point that allows Joyce's uncommitted deconstructing view of the ideological realms. Unlike the functional desires of referential and modal representations, this position of critique does not go with solutions. But aporetic self-authorization is not necessarily a cul-de-sac. Rabaté has drawn our attention to the fact that the "egoistical" author objectifies himself in the authority of the work itself. The particular quality of this "transmittance" results in what Rabaté calls the principle of *auctoritas operis*, which replaces Eco's principles of *intentio auctoris* and *intentio operis*. As Rabaté emphasizes, *auctoritas operis* "can be developed for its own sake. It would thus recommend not a semiotic interpretation, but only a semantic interpretation, developed when we learn to play with the text. The reading process becomes indeed a learning process, with its own specific pedagogy."[79] As Joyce knew, inaugurational composition is a means to challenge the political, cultural and religious systems of power. He knew, as Judith Butler argues in a different context, that "the critical point of departure is *the historical present*, as Marx put it. And the task is to formulate within this constituted frame a critique of the categories of identity that contemporary [juridical, cultural, political,

---

[79] Rabaté, *Politics of Egoism* 2001, 197-203. Subtly animadverting upon recent (postcolonial, feminist, etc.) over-interpretations of Joyce, Rabaté suggests that "the ideal genetic reader" will base his readings on "two points of agreement: a radical historicization of all possible interpretive strategies, doubled with a no less historical material history of textual production" (203).

nationalist, religious] structures engender, naturalize, and immobilize."[80] In *Ulysses*, anti-representational negativity is the operative *auctoritas* of this critique.

---

[80]   Judith Butler, *Gender Trouble: Feminism and the Subversion of Identity* (New York: Routledge, 1990) 5.

OPERA AND REPRESENTATION

Karl Ludwig Pfeiffer

ABSTRACT

The essay deals with a genre/medium for which the use of the concept of representation appears to be both imperative and well-nigh impossible. It starts with the difficulties the concept has encountered, especially in a comparative perspective, in analytical theories of art and in the English court masque. The case for operatic representation is strengthened when one looks at the type of stories opera uses and at the strategies employed by librettists and composers alike to safeguard various levels of intelligibility. In such cases, opera seems to represent forms of historical and often contemporary relevance with particular force. Paradoxically, though, it is in period operas (*Zeitoper*) in which clear-cut representational/representative layers are both powerfully there and vanishing with often alarming speed. In order to explore this, the Strauss/Hofmannsthal collaboration is analyzed in some detail. Its implications—a nostalgia for representation which opera feeds but does not really satisfy—are brought out by a systematic and historical investigation into the nature, functions, and effects of the singing voice.

Representation: Shaky Concepts, Glassy Essence, and Fantastic Tricks

Representation is an elusive concept we must live with, indeed must live by. The logical difficulties of the concept are notorious. It depends, to begin with, on unstable notions of givenness. Within the tradition(s) of mimesis—one example of a representational framework—the very objects to be represented, or sometimes "imitated," have oscillated between an Aristotelian *morphe*, model works of the ancients, human nature, and moral norms, among other things. The process, or rather the *act* of representation, in its turn, is therefore not completely controlled by its supposed subject matter and takes on an ambiguous dynamics of its own. In English, but not only there, a span of almost contradictory meanings has invaded the verb *to act* itself. The act of representation may not amount to more than a simulation of its object, provided the object possesses that toughness which, for various contexts, has been described as the persistence of the real, from exchange rates to human passions and violence. But it may also develop into a fairly self-sufficient presentation or performance in which a supposedly antecedent object is demoted to a mere simulacrum, in which the reference to some prior givenness vanishes into thin air. At the very least one can say (with Paul Ricœur) that representation sparks the desire to think—and perhaps to go— beyond (what appears at some moment as) the given.[1]

It certainly is presumptuous on my part, but I do think that the difficulties involved in deciding what to consider as given—something in relation to which representation is said to take place, to be "of" or "about," to be "representation-as" (Nelson Goodman)—have had a problematic impact on phi- losophies of art, especially music. For Goodman, for instance, representation is bound up in various ways with denotation. In (instrumental) music, the representational basis consists of and in the score. Yet the score, professional music-readers ex- cepted, does not amount to much unless it is performed. While performances may differ with respect to tempo, timber, phras- ing, and expressiveness (a treacherous term in its own right), they must comply with the score. Once a single note is wrong or missing, the performance does not count as an instance of

---

[1] I take the reference to Ricœur's essay "Mimesis and Representation" from Wolfgang Iser, in whose work the instability of the given and the potential of representational acts have turned into the mainstays of a theory of literature. For present purposes see Iser's essay "Mimesis— Emergenz," *Mimesis und Simulation*, eds. Andreas Kablitz and Gerhard Neumann (Freiburg: Rombach Verlag, 1998) 696-84, 670. See also Iser's *The Fictive and the Imaginary. Charting Literary Anthropology* (Baltimore: Johns Hopkins Press, 1993) 281-96.

the work and what the work is supposed to represent, because if we admit one missing note, "we can go all the way from Beethoven's *Fifth Symphony* to *Three Blind Mice*." The "most miserable performance," on the other hand, if complete in terms of the score, does count as an instance.

Goodman says nothing about opera. But it is clear that his fearsome requirements could not apply to large traditions of composing and singing in which singers had to "complete" their parts only roughly written out by the composer. Neither could they probably apply to periods in which the composer in principle demands the singer's compliance with his score, because Goodman's separation between notes and expressive values cannot be consistently enforced in singing. Kendall Walton, in granting three remarks to opera in his large treatise on the "foundations of the representational arts," is more generous than Goodman. Unfortunately, in terms of the representational problem, these remarks are sorely beside the point (the first referring in fact to the "Peking opera" for which the problem is different anyway; the second to what Walton himself considers as one of the silly questions, here the last moments of opera characters singing away while life is ebbing away; the third asking the strange question whether it is "fictional in opera that people sing, though performers portray speech by singing").

Generally, "musical depictions"—yet another term—are relegated into a very short subchapter (Part Three, 8.6.). Here Walton admits that his examples have been limited, "rather dangerously perhaps, to the visual arts."[2] What he has to say in this subchapter about music is reasonable. It has to do with program music and less obvious, more ambiguous cases.

---

[2]   Cf. Nelson Goodman, *Languages of Art. An Approach to a Theory of Symbols* (Indianapolis: Bobbs-Merrill Company, 1968) 117, 186 f. Kendall L. Walton, *Mimesis as Make-Believe. On the Foundations of the Representational Arts* (Cambridge: Harvard U P, 1990) 165, 177, 182 (for the remarks on opera), 333-37 (for musical depictions). A later essay by Walton, "Listening with Imagination: Is Music Representational?", *The Journal of Aesthetics and Art Criticism*, 52/1 (1994): 47-61, does not change the picture substantially.

These, though, have been handled recently with greater rigor and far greater musicological expertise in a series of works by Siglind Bruhn.[3] Bruhn reminds us of Eduard Hanslick (to whom I will come back later in this essay) and Susanne K. Langer. For the latter, musical signs are presentational rather than representational. We can credit those signs with significance, but can never say what they signify. Bruhn disagrees; she asserts, correctly, that (traditional) musical language has established a highly sophisticated catalogue of intelligible signifiers. Furthermore, her definitions of and distinction between program music and musical ekphrasis (a very recent phenomenon) are precise: the first narrates and paints, suggests or represents scenes or stories (and by extension events or characters), the second narrates or paints scenes created by an artist *other* than the composer and in another artistic medium. "Program music represents, while musical ekphrasis represents."[4]

Clearly, though, terms like narrating or painting are metaphorical here. It is therefore hard to say *what* precisely a musical piece is supposed to paint, narrate, represent, or re-present. Sometimes, Bruhn speaks of "general impressions" that the composer might be likely to represent. Even if representation has come to be more widely accepted in musical

---

[3]   See especially Siglund Bruhn, *Musical Ekphrasis: Composers Responding to Poetry and Painting* (Hillsdale, NY: Pendragon, 2000), *Voicing the Ineffable: Musical Representations of Religious Experience* (Hillsdale, NY: Pendragon, 2002), *Saints in the Limelight: Representations of the Religious Quest on the Post-1045 Operatic Stage* (Hillsdale, NY: Pendragon, 2003). This is just a selection. But see also the article available on the Internet: "A Concert of Paintings: "Musical Ekphrasis" in the Twentieth Century," *http://www.eunomios.org/contrib/bruhn1/bruhn1.html* (38 pp., as of July 15, 2003).

[4]   "Concert of Paintings," 3. Cf. 4 f., 7, for Hanslick and Langer. I will take up the distinction between representation and representation (which Bruhn takes from an article by Tamar Yacobi on different representational modes in literature) later again, but with a different thrust.

theory recently, this does not mean that we know better how to get from a representational impression to the matter allegedly represented. Archetypal plots, "thematic generality," for instance, may be the abstract frameworks which one can *associate* with a piece of music. The piece does neither *imply* nor *represent* them in any compelling way (because, for instance, in Goodman's sense, any denotational connection is very hard to establish; nor could Goodman's terms of *exemplification* ["possession plus reference"] and *expression* ["figurative possession"] be applied with any ease; see Goodman's *Languages,* 46, 51, 53, 61 f.).

It may often be correct to say that opera "as a genre typically relies on integrating a verbal text into the composition in such a way that both elements, lyrics and music, when represented separately, seem to be lacking an essential complement." This thesis is almost certainly always correct as far as the words (the libretto) go. The case of musical self-insuffiency, though, does not look so simple at all. (One just has to think about many orchestra pieces or the ballet music in an opera, to say nothing about the question of a more general power, even of instrumenal music in opera.) Above all, however, to say that opera *integrates* text and music is to make a conceptual gesture or suggestion at best. To be able to *imagine* or *postulate* such integrations does not mean that one can *demonstrate* them. But then, both the cultural and personal *conditions* of such imaginations have to be looked into before one assumes that integrations take place.

I suppose that Bruhn is overstating the case for musical and operatic representation because of the religious domain that her main examples primarily explore. The case for the musical representation of religious experience can be made precisely, and not at all paradoxically, because both domains seem to be concerned with and to overlap in what is commonly called the ineffable. There appear to be "elective affinities" (in the same way that many people think there are elective affinities between feelings and music), and therefore the one can easily show up as the representation of the other. Small wonder, then, that church music constitutes such a large musical area; that it has ramified into opera; that, for example, many people are struck by the musical affinity between Verdi's operas and his *Requiem* (see also my later remarks about the oratorium and the castrati).

I think, though, that the logical difficulties of the term *representation* are not abolished, but brought under better control if one tries to stretch them out on and fasten them to historical configurations.[5] More specifically, in tackling something like opera, such configurations have to do with the media qualities of the representational apparatuses involved. Media studies—or, as I would prefer, studies of medialization, that is processes in which media, material and very often performative aspects acquire pointed relevance—have become, like gender studies and similar concerns, overly fashionable. Let me therefore prepare the ground for them by exploiting the drift of what I take to be a powerful, if perhaps unintentional example to that effect. In his essay "The Poetics of Spectacle," Stephen Orgel traces the famous quarrel between Ben Jonson and Inigo Jones back to basically identical representational concerns. While Jonson holds all "representations" to be "mirrors of man's life," Jones's aesthetics, in their turn, "derive from good Platonic doctrine and have clear moral ends." Both are working "toward similar ends" because "the antithesis between visual and verbal experience did not exist in the Renaissance, even for Jonson, in the way it does for us."[6] While language is clearly representational, every picture, in its turn and way, is a "symbol" (53). The quarrel then merely revolves around questions of representational priority and their

---

5 Unfortunately, the historical sketch in terms of musical history, linked to both aesthetic, psychologial, and indeed neurological findings and aiming at a compromise between the "formalists" and "expressionists" in the very instructive book by Anthony Storr, *Music and the Mind* (London: Harper Collins, 1992) 73-81, remains too general to be conclusive.

6 Stephen Orgel, "The Poetics of Spectacle," *The Authentic Shakespeare and other Problems of the Early Modern Stage* (New York and London: Routledge, 2002) 49-69, 50 f.

implications in terms of artistic prestige (from which financial concerns are certainly not excluded). For Jonson, the spectacle should be the *expression* of the (verbal) meaning, "the body of the work as the poetry is the soul." For Jones, also with a lot of philosophical opinion behind him, images do have meanings *and* they impress these most directly onto the soul; words can only *explain* the meaning of images (53). Thus, each awards priority to one of the two main elements. But they do not quarrel about the representational total effect.

If, however, a kind of antithesis between visual and verbal experience has sprung up, we must ask when, for whom, and through which circumstances this has happened. Orgel himself points out that critical opinion on "theatrical performance" in the Renaissance itself is divided. Some look upon spectacle as a distraction from, others as the substance of the "representation." All can borrow arguments from good authorities, including Aristotle himself (53 f.). For a while, Orgel makes both ends meet by declaring "wonder" to be the overarching goal of an inevitably "complex" spectacle (e.g., 56). Heavily charged representational modes like allegory, symbol, and myth thus appear to hold their ground as the "substance of masques" (64), because, in their interactional totality, a wonder of both spectacle and pregnancy of meaning can certainly be produced.

It is unclear, though, to what extent such elements in Shakespeare do in fact still exert such substantial representational efficacy (62 f.). Worse, much as historical (or modern) theory may assert such substantiality, it has no control on the wayward ways in which an audience may (mis)construe their import. The representational plans may be noble, but the receptional facts can be very melancholy and sometimes come close to a "perverse joke" (65). King Charles may have had his "visions of a harmonious commonwealth substantiated" in the "theatrical machine," because the "illusionist's control over the way we look at things was an important instrument of royal policy." But if this substantiation occurred "only in the realities of the theatrical machine" (68), the illusion of representational control and stability may have dawned, if not on the King himself, then at least on many others. "Milton the iconoclast" has the last word (68 f.).

Opera and Representational/Representative Overkill

I have used Orgel's *Poetics of Spectacle* not only because it is such a subtly argued piece, but also because opera is, both historically and in terms of a theory of medialization, a successor to the masque. It should therefore come as no surprise that it has been exposed to a similar abundance of representational claims. One might in fact profit by Orgel's reconciliation of Jonson and Jones and ascribe a core of representational solidity to opera which the self-relativizing complexity of—at least—Shakespearean texts had already abandoned or actively destroyed. An opera libretto may be chaotic and not amenable to verbal understanding. This, some haved claimed, is the case with some of the libretti for Verdi's operas. But normally, the language of a libretto, of what it projects in terms of plot, character, and their historical underpinnings will not meander into the representationally baffling complexity accumulated by many dramatic and prose texts. Singing certainly does not render the understanding of verbal meaning any easier. Consequently, most operas will strive to maintain a minimum level of intelligibility in other ways. This minimum, guaranteed it appears by plot, characters, and often culture—that is also intertextual or historical background—therefore normally transports a certain load of both representational and representative meaning.

I suspect, in fact, that the old and neverending quarrel about the primacy of words or music in opera, of whether the music must serve the "poetry" (Gluck), the "drama" (Alban Berg) or whether the words are merely sacrificial pawns drowned in an overwhelming operatic (that is, musical-perfomative display) is not so much about questions of primacy at all.[7] It rather derives, I suggest, from the anxiety that, without the warranty of minimal intelligibility and relatability, opera might veer into culturally, and perhaps often also psychologically inacceptable nonsense. People and cultures have a hard time welcoming or acquiescing in such a fall in "serious" or traditional art. In this (non)sense, an "anti-operatic" prejudice might amount to an extension of the anti-theatrical prejudice Jonas Barish has written on so convincingly—the fear that the performatively induced transformation of human beings on stage might create havoc in our ordinary and necessary human make-up.[8]

Indeed, opera appears to be immune from such dangers because it carries, buried or openly, social and ideological thumbprints in its construction. As in spoken drama, the implications of extra-aesthetic categories like court opera or bourgeois opera have representational repercussions in the works themselves. It is true that one cannot establish such

---

[7] For a sketch of that oft-told quarrel and its implications see, e.g., Herbert Lindenberger's *Opera. The Extravagant Art* (Ithaca and London: Cornell U P, 1984) chapter 3. Both chapters 3 and 4 in Lindenberger's book on "Opera as Representation" are important for my purposes in that they outline both representational layers ("opera has self-consciously absorbed the representational forms not only of spoken drama but of its own earlier styles and of other arts as well," 75) and their decay. See also 44 on opera's, in comparison with spoken drama's, more straightforward presentation of character. For the decay, crucial to my later argument, see for instance p. 104 about audiences "doubtless more aware of their [the so-called *Puritani* quartet of singers during the 1830s] vocal qualities and their ability to engage musically with one another than of their relationship to the particular historical context they pretended to represent."

[8] See Jonas Barish, *The Antitheatrical Prejudice* (Berkeley: U of California P, 1981), especially the chapters on Plato and the Puritans. Lindenberger has, as far as I can see, coined this term (197-210) in the wake of Barish, but does not really take up the latter's anthropological grounding of the matter, the fear of an off-limits-transformation of human beings and thereby the loss of representational control—which is much more than moral condemnation. See especially 205.

correlations consistently: Handel, composer of the Royal Academy of Music among other things, got embroiled in conflicts with an "Opera of the Nobility," and was finally subjected to the parodistic stings of a "beggar's opera." None of these terms can be really used to set up sociological-aesthetic parallels. (The terms become patently absurd when one looks at the names of the theaters, with the Opera of the Nobility for instance moving into King's Theater, Handel into Theater Royal, Covent Garden.[9]) Even so, the debate about representative (and often ideological) meanings related to and dynamically representing—both reflecting and changing cultural prejudice—can certainly be conducted quite profitably. There is no doubt that Richard Wagner, the composer who pleaded and worked most emphatically for the integration of words and music, exposed himself most conspicuously to the search for relevant meaning. One can see Wagner's efforts critically, denouncing them, in the wake of Nietzsche and Adorno, as a mixing up of music and (wrongly) interpreted literature or worse (Wagner's "anti-semitism," the dubious role of the Nibelung subject in nineteenth-century Germany). One can also appreciate the overall powerful musical effect and try to trace the subtlety of significant detail.[10]

Sometimes representational configurations are clear, but distanced and indirect. Most *verismo* operas, contrary to what one might expect and in some contrast also to literary

---

[9]   See for instance Donald Burrows, *Handel* (Oxford: Oxford U P, 1996) 179 f. and *passim*.

[10] For Germany, the many works on Wagner by Dieter Borchmeyer, Jürgen Kühnel, and others could come to mind here. But see also Kühnel's representationally, programmatically charged title concerning *Fidelio*: "'Revolutionsoper'/'Humanitätsdrama'/'Musika-lische Einweihungen in die Utopie.' '*Fidelio*-Interpretationen.'" *Fidelio/Leonore. Annäherungen an ein zentrales Werk des Musiktheaters*, eds. Peter Csobádi *et al.* (Anif/Salzburg: Verlag Müller-Speiser, 1998) 205-30. Here, the utopian "realm of freedom" of humankind united in solidarity takes sensuous shape in the music (230)—a classic case, both conceptually and materially, of representation.

naturalism, are set in some foreign "exotic" spot à la *Madame Butterfly*. Lindenberger, who points that out, quotes Adorno's generalization according to which "costume [and thus some representational drive, however naive or problematic] is an essential of opera—an opera without costume would, in contrast to a play, seem paradoxical."[11] We might not accept such a thesis without reservations. Even so, we could reinforce and enrich the representational drift allegedly produced by costume by insisting that the external props of costume exoticism are normally compounded by severe semantic, indeed ideological, and factual loads like nineteenth-century imperialism. Edward Said, among others, has argued to that effect with respect to *Aida*.

Representation Relativized: Ernst Krenek and *Jonny spielt auf* (1927)

These days, it is no longer necessary to tremble in fear of clichés if one calls the 1920s, for European and especially German-speaking areas, a period of intense (pressures and enjoyment of) modernization. The pressure was certainly felt by practitioners of the traditional arts. Music generally seemed to adopt a new matter-of-factness. Opera, for one, appeared to rise to the challenge, indeed to embrace new realities with such readiness that the years from 1925 to 1930 have been called the years of period opera (*Zeitoper*). Ernst Krenek's (1900-1991) *Jonny spielt auf* is one of the betterknown operas of that kind. It is remarkable because its composer was also a historian and theorist who had very clear ideas about what he was doing and did not hesitate, particularly in a talk for the Vienna "Kulturbund" in 1928, to make them clear to his perhaps less advanced contemporaries.[12]

---

[11] Lindenberger, *Opera* 1984, 53.
[12] I am quoting from the program produced by the Vienna State Opera for its new production of the opera in 2002/2003. The text ("*Jonny spielt auf* 1927/28," 24-47) follows the manuscript. The booklet is also useful

In spite of the clarity, Krenek's ideas about theatrical art are marked, however, by representational splits. In opera, such splits come to the forefront with special force. On the one hand, any opera, like any theatrical piece in general, must be—and, according to Krenek, normally has been—contemporary because it must reflect its times in ways the audience cannot ignore. Mozart, for one, followed the spirit of the dances of his time in his music (44). Theatrical contemporaneity has become particularly urgent after World War I. The war did not only destroy lives, but (traditional) culture and mentality as well (32). It made nonsense of the traditional role of the artist as a high priest of culture. In the opera, Max, the composer, represents that type of alienated, lonely, isolated, and unwordly artist. Krenek literally calls him, at one point "the representative of contemporary European art" ("Vertreter europäischer Kunstgegenwart," 34). His counterpart is the counterfeit violin virtuoso Daniello, owner of a precious Amati violin. In Daniello, we can identify the contemporary artist as confidence-, show-, and businessman. Between these two, the singer Anita, partly so-called feminine nature, partly career-woman, is pulled hither and thither. Jonny, the black American jazz musician, the image, as it would appear, of a principle of nature and ur-force ("Naturprinzip und Urkraft," 34), completes this sketch of contemporary artistic culture by indicating the mode in which it must be transcended. He represents and practices a kind of music whose expressive power surpasses anything Europeans have heard before. Its intensity contrasts strikingly with the chaotic falling apart of all instincts in

---

because it assembles a whole array of what one might consider as historical representationally relevant material. The only English translation of the title of Krenek's opera I have found is *Jonny Strikes Up*. For the music of a new matter-of-factness see Niels Grosch, *Die Musik der Neuen Sachlichkeit* (Stuttgart, Weimar: Metzler, 1999), especially the introduction concerning music and the "external world" and chapter 3 for *Zeitoper*. All translations of German into English in this essay are mine.

Europe, in a world abandoned by its own best people (35, 37, 44).

The conflicts that spring from this representative artistic configuration are played out in a highly contemporary setting: The scene is replete with modern gadgets—from loudspeakers, telephones, cars to railway engines, one of which in fact rolls onto the stage and nearly kills Max.

Clearly, however, Krenek does not want his opera to be misunderstood as a diagnosis of European decadence, as a piece of enthusiastic "Americanism" ("Amerikanismus") or polemical anti-Americanism, if one sees Jonny as the uncultured barbarian at the gates (27). It is not meant as a celebration, denunciation, or even mere acknowledgment of new technologies. Krenek's ire is particularly aroused by imbeciles on two fronts: those who rave about the fascination of new technologies and those who want them banned, at all cost, from the opera stage (30 f., 41). Anyone who thinks that the spirit of the times is best captured by having a man run over by a train on stage ought to be in this man's place himself—we may add: in real life (31). Furthermore, one should not lure people into the opera house by pretending they will see unprecedented technological miracles. They will soon notice that the singers sing as they do in any other opera and do not stand on their heads right from the beginning (41). It is true, as Grosch has pointed out, that the persisting presence of technical media makes us aware of the fact that music is perceptible only in forms of medialization, that Max, suddenly hearing, perhaps listening to an aria sung by Anita on the radio, is pushed out of his suicide attempt towards the end, that, in short, the communicative potentials of media are centrally "planted into" the action. But I do not see that the "characteristics" of radio reception are spread out in front of us, that, in other words, they are represented, in their technical media specificity as meaningful elements in a motivational whole. They remain, indeed, "reality fragments."[13]

---

[13] Grosch, *Die Musik* 1999, 135 f.

Krenek goes into this with pungent wit. But if opera does not represent culture and technology in any straightforward way, how (and what) does it then represent? Strictly speaking, the stage presence of cultural and technological matters is not representation at all. To make contact with the audience, any piece of theater needs levels of acquaintance and "resonance," materials, that is, without which the action in the proper sense would take place in a vacuum. Sometimes, these materials gain coherence to such an extent that they may be called subjects and topics (37). In that respect, opera, like most other arts, is an "expression of its times" ("Zeitausdruck"), a phrase, however, which in its turn is a mere tautology leading to nothing (36). Something must be there, must be going on, otherwise nothing will happen.

For a while, Krenek envisages a compromise: Plays do not give answers (to the questions possibly provoked by the materials), they just shape the question over and over again (27). But a treacherous phrase which follows that directly seems to deprive art of the cultural relevance of even the question: "Art develops on the basis of culture, but it is neither called upon nor capable of creating culture" (27). Still, however, representational impulses flare up; Krenek does not advocate escapism. We may tire of culture, may want to wallow in despair or some kind of nirvana. But once we remember that then "the Daniellos will steal our women and the Jonnies will rob us of our art," we will try to catch the train which leads us back into life (35). Is that then what we are supposed to make of the end, the fact that Max, after a narrow escape from the train which nearly kills him, and Anita leave for the U.S.?

The very strangeness of the theft-and-robbery metaphors may make us suspect that Krenek clutches at any representational straw he can still grasp, because, as a theoretical notion, representation cannot be thrown overboard. Although logically dubious, it remains conceptually necessary. As an opera *practitioner*, however, Krenek knows that opera, like drama in general (or at least the great old masters) proceeds on a basis of representational acquaintance in order, almost paradoxically, to block the formation of audience curiosity for *what* is going on, to block, in other words, consistent or even merely overall and rough representationalism. Instead, the audience must pay exclusive attention to *how* performance "strikes up" and unfolds in its own way (38). Invoking performance in the traditional terms of "the essentially, purely artistic" ("das eigentliche Künstlerische," 38) may sound like another recourse to dubious terms. But such terms can be specified descriptively, technically and operationally as a process of "scenic formation" ("Elemente, aus denen sich das Werk der Szene bildet," 40). Again, it is well-nigh impossible to do so without some faint trace of representational talk. Krenek enumerates the countless elements—music, movement, light, color, space, etc.—of scenic formation which serve to shape and sharpen the profile of the singers. The singers—or rather (and this makes for a difference indeed) "the singing human beings" (die "singenden Menschen," 40)—are also representing ("darstellend"). But now, representation appears to merge with body-based acting and thereby performance: It must contribute to the maximum "sensuous distinctness" of the singing person ("den höchsten Grad von sinnfälliger Deutlichkeit," 40).[14]

Complex as the description of that distinctness must be, it is the result of a task which in principle, though not in actual practice is staggeringly simple. The director does not have to make the opera "into," that is, a representation of something— he must simply see to it that the opera "is played" ("einfach zu spielen"). *Jonny spielt auf* is a piece without false bottom ("ohne doppelten Boden"). Nothing is going on behind things and scenes; everything is contained in and unfolds through the concrete stage process. No symbolism, no sounding for depth: "Everything which happens does not mean more than what one

---

[14] The oscillation between imitation and performance might well be the long-term fate of the German term *Darstellung*—perhaps a parallel to the range of meaning of the English verb *to act*. See Christiaan L. Hart Nibbrig, ed., *Was heißt "Darstellen"?* (Frankfurt M.: Suhrkamp, 1994).

can see." Krenek subscribes to an "unproblematic, playful operatic style for which I have found the possibly meaningless term of 'naive realism' "(42).

Literature, Representational Nostalgia, and Opera

For Krenek, the singer is therefore mainly an actor, that is, a performer. S/he must thrive on the intrinsic value of performative intensity, not on the representational pathos of the role (43). We can perhaps get closer to that intensity by looking at the seemingly more or less harmonious (in reality fairly conflict-ridden) collaboration between a writer (Hugo von Hofmannsthal) and a composer (Richard Strauss). Literature, especially in its more modern forms, might be called that privileged medium in which representation is both always built up and always torn down. Words inevitably carry meanings, they point to something they seem to represent as substitutes. Whatever can be said in one way, however, can also be said in other ways. Representational stability breaks down because the matter intimated or outlined in representational suggestions becomes itself elusive. Yet the representational impulse in words remains ineradicable.

Hofmannsthal, as a young writer, seemed to embody, or at least to promise, poetic genius. This at least is the common picture painted in literary history. For present purposes, we could define poetic genius as the ability to formally perfect representational intimations and to steer clear at the same time of representational commitments. Hofmannsthal, literay history tells us, remained faithful to his favorite topics—love, death, the role of form and ceremony—in his later work. But he did no longer couch them in the suggestive, mysterious verbal ease of his earlier work. In other words: Representation rushed in where poetic genius feared to tread before. Let me risk the guess, surely an amateurish one, that Hofmannsthal sought the cooperation with Strauss for two main reasons. In opera, he could pursue his commitment to ceremony as a kind of formalized last stronghold and a precarious fusion of the aesthetic and the sociological (aristocratic) dimensions of representation. Second, we know from his letters to friends that he felt obliged to combat a tendency in Strauss toward vulgarity, triviality, and kitsch. Consequently, even while supposedly writing the libretto as sophisticated literature, he could reinforce the representational drive of his language much more than in literature alone, because in opera the words were in constant danger of being submerged by Strauss's powerful, not to say domineering, music anyway. (Strauss is of course famous, for some notorious, for the power, the boldness of sounds and "colors" and the virtuosity of instrumentation of big orchestras.)

To make these tensions more explicit, let me refer to the Strauss/Hofmannsthal correspondence concerning *Der Rosenkavalier*. On July 12, 1910, Hofmannsthal sets forth his representational intentions for the opera:

> The point which creates a unity out of the whole thing, which keeps together both plots is precisely that Quinquin simply falls for the first young woman he meets in this intersecting double adventure. The Marschallin remains the dominating female figure, between Ochs and Quinquin. Compared to these main characters, Sophie is not so important. Please read the letter of Princess Lichnowsky which I enclose and would like to have back at some time. You will then see to what extent the ladies, this important part of our audience, feel that way. My wife, too, feels that way, and so do the wife of the publisher Fischer, the Princess Marie Taxis etc. I really want to entrust you with that now that you are getting close to and are about to compose the sentimental final scene, because the musical-spiritual unity of the whole would be damaged if we did not do justice to the Marschallin and if a strong relation between the

end of act three and the end of act one did not produce the emotional unity of the whole adventure.[15]

Hofmannsthal may not have taken his appeal to feminine
sensibility totally at face value. Still, we can detect more than a
trace of a relapse into an imitational version of representation.
This relapse occurs under the threat of musical, non-
representational autonomy. Hofmannsthal is at pains to point
this out some time later. On March 3, 1911, he declares himself
well, but not completely satisfied with the work:

> A work of art is a unity, and even the work of two
> people can turn into a unity … The music must not
> be torn from the text, the word must not be torn from
> the animated image … The dramatic character is al-
> ways between those two [the infinite human being
> and the sharply delimited puppet]. The Marshallin
> does not exist for her own sake. Neither does Ochs.
> They stand against each other and yet they belong to
> each other, with the boy Octavian in between con-
> necting them. Sophie stands against the Marschallin,
> the girl against the woman, and again Octavian
> comes in between, separating them and holding them
> together. Ochs may be as he is, still he is a kind of
> nobleman. He and Faninal are complementary, one
> needs the other, not just in this world, but in a meta-
> physical sense, so to speak.[16]

So to speak: Here, Hofmannsthal is exploring the representational potential of the opera in subtler ways. The work of art

---

[15] Richard Strauss/Hugo von Hofmannsthal, *Briefwechsel*, Gesamtausgabe,
ed. Willi Schuh, third enlarged edition (Zürich: Atlantis Verlag, 1964)
95 f.

[16] Quoted in Richard Strauss, *Der Rosenkavalier. Kompletter Text mit
Erläuterungen zum vollen Verständnis des Werkes*, comp. and ed. Kurt
Pahlen (München: Goldmann, 1980) 375 f.

seems to exist for and through itself as a relational unity. And yet that unity must have representational supplements, whether in social, metaphysical, or other terms.

Strauss, in his turn, has very different things on his mind. He complains repeatedly that there is no "really *comic* situation." More generally and importantly, he is longing for more than just one "great" moment like the restaurant entry, full of tensions even if dramatically hardly motivated, of the Marschallin (July 7, 1909, *Briefwechsel,* 74). He can imagine comic and serious *effects* without representational correlatives. In a way, he subscribes to the demand for relational unity. Because of "symphonic unity" which is imperative also for opera, he must compose one part after the other (May 4, 1909, *Briefwechsel,* 58). But with respect to opera, he is neither satisfied with Hofmannsthal's representational demands nor with his own standards of symphonic unity: "I am waiting for you and meanwhile am torturing myself with a symphony. This, honestly, is even less satisfactory than shaking May bugs from trees" (May 15, 1911, *Briefwechsel,* 115).

For the time being, the situation remains open. We can make it even more complicated, though, by dissociating both relational unity (working toward some kind of autonomy) and representational supplements (limiting autonomy) from what happens on stage even more radically. *Der Rosenkavalier* is normally included in the genre of "Literaturoper," a type of opera in which the equality of words and music is supposed to exist in particular evidence. Pahlen, in his edition and commentary, takes the final trio Marschallin/Octavian/Sophie to be a particularly beautiful specimen of such harmony (*Der Rosenkavalier,* 266). Two pages farther we must read, however, that the text loses ground not just because it is well-nigh drowned in the high musical waves, but because the simultaneity of three voices renders it unintelligible anyway for the audience. We are witnessing the fate of all similarly arranged ensembles. Pahlen generously offers compensation:

Instead, how much is there to listen to in the music,
to enjoy, to admire. The expert is offered the renew-
able experience of technical perfection, the amateur
may enjoy again and again the sensuous euphony,
the intoxicating ensemble singing and its heighten-
ing by the overwhelmingly beautiful sounds of the
orchestra (268).

In his self-exposure to perfect musical techniques and over-
powering impressionism Pahlen seems to forget his earlier con-
juring up of representational pathos: In the trio, we listen to the
"hymn of three humann voices coming from the most profound
depth of the human heart" (266).

Provisional Appraisal

Hofmannsthal's conceptual strategies, as sketched above,
are understandable. He can claim strong (perhaps more than
just) historical motivations for them. We find them also in his
ideas about marriage, the state and so forth. Opera appears to
be the medium in which the European need for a ceremonial
order, for harmonious relational structures without explicit
ideology and crude forms of conflict, can be acted out. As a
performatively dynamized tensional order opera turns into an
aesthetic icon of what an orderly, though not rigid, society
might look like. It is true that, with *Arabella,* that icon took on
aspects of the fairy tale.

Hofmannsthal demands a totality combined of what one
might paraphrase as the unity of heart, emotions, dispositions,
and atmosphere ("Gemütseinheit") and complementary
relations of character. He wants opera to display a code of
aesthetic as human(e) necessity. Once, however, that world—
the Hapsburg world of the eighteenth and nineteenth
centuries—has receded into the distant past for audiences, the
totality of *Der Rosenkavalier* falls apart into social triviality,
great and some not so great musical moments. In spite of a
network of musical motifs and subtle transitions, the music

cannot bridge the gaps between social farce and aesthetic-emotional intensity. That intensity shows up in fast-changing fragments, and in fragments only. It is, or has become, difficult for any audience to believe that the "love" between the teenagers Sophie and Octavian (both are seventeen) may overcome the program of trivial promiscuity preached by Baron Ochs.

Historical contingencies apart, this has to do with representation in opera in general. Nicholas Cook, in his book *Music, Imagination, and Culture,* has said that "for the ordinary listener if not for the connoisseur, listening to music is not, in fact, very similar to reading a work of literature."[17] Experts may keep track of form, construct formal or even metaphysical entities out of what they hear, and relate them to whichever extra-musical framework they want. But the selective, fragmentary way of amateurs picking up and remembering only the "beautiful" morsels of the music will legitimately assert itself. These selections do not so much represent, they rather re-enact the wilder and more archaic functions and effects of music.[18]

Cook is moving into cognitive science territory. Recently, this territory has been invaded by the various neurosciences. For (some of) them, art in general enhances those selective advantages that humans enjoy in reflective processes and symbolic encodings. It increases and diversifies a general creativity (exploration, experimentation, curiosity, playful behavior) necessary for survival. With the advance of culture, that creativity itself splits up into various forms. The brain faces the continuous task of binding its activities into functionally coherent ensembles. But it does not dispose of a central mechanism for that. In this as well as in other respects, Descartes was quite wrong. The partiality of functionally coherent ensembles in perception and semantic interpretation is

---

[17] Nicholas Cook, *Music, Imagination, and Culture* (Oxford: Clarendon, 1990) 171.
[18] Cf. Cook, *Music* 1990, 17, 41f., 68-70, 164, 171.

therefore liable, especially under cultural and social pressures, to misunderstand itself as representative totality. Some forms of advanced art may therefore tend to use complex aesthetic forms not to reinforce, to ennoble, or to aestheticize, but to provide relief from the burden of runaway totalities, to act out intrinsically rewarding, more or less non-representational drives in culturally attractive forms.[19]

Singing: Performative Realities, Representational After-effects

Opera takes a special position because, in using language, plot, and characters, it maintains a kind of representational façade. A comparative history of spoken drama and opera would hit upon rich mines of investigation. Moreover, the impressions produced by singing, indeed by instrumental music itself can always be related to preconceived notions, to emotional preferences of the listener which they are then thought to represent. The humdrum routine of representational gestures goes on all the time, in spite (and often because) of selective listening, in spite of Eduard Hanslick's demonstration, directed against Wagner and others, that small units of musical notes are not connected to, associated with, or representative of anything else, and that larger units therefore should be treated with representational care too.[20] Hanslick opts for a conscious, pure

[19] Let me just refer here to Wolf Singer, *Der Beobachter im Gehirn. Essays zur Hirnforschung* (Frankfurt M.: Suhrkamp, 2002) 65-67, 102, 221f., 225. For Descartes' "error" see of course Antonio R. Damasio, *Descartes' Error. Emotion, Reason, and the Human Brain* (New York: Harper Collins, 1995). In passing, I should mention that the term "representation" in the neurosciences is, of course, a strong one, since the biochemical and electrical activity of the brain and the products of this activity (consciousness in all its layers and elements) are very different indeed—the latter being, in a fairly straightforward sense, a representation of the former.
[20] See Eduard Hanslick, *Vom Musikalisch-Schönen. Ein Beitrag zur Revision der Ästhetik der Tonkunst* (1854), repr. (Darmstadt:

"contemplation" of music ("das bewußte reine Anschauen," which he then explains as "contemplative[s] Hören," 77), and thus seems to move close to what Cook relativizes: the expert's listening to the total score as a mirror of the composer's intention. Even so, the almost contradictory assembly of concepts— what could conscious *and* pure seeing-cum-contemplation consist in?—suggests at least that music, including opera is fairly immune from the "boring" dialectics of meaning, and therefore representation, for which, according to Baudrillard's *general* diagnosis in an advanced, "postmodern" twentieth century, the bell has tolled.[21] One may doubt though that the escape from representation and hermeneutic depth has been satisfactorily engineered or monopolized by the "obscene" deluge of images in modern electronic media that provide Baudrillard with one of his favorite bugbears. To a large extent, these shows are deficient, abortive forms of ritual.

Effective ritual, by contrast, is representation. But it is a representation that, while it represents, can come close to an empty form, in which the embodied aura of precise enactment takes precedence over meaning. There is ample evidence that we tend to overestimate the importance of meaning and belief of symbolic or functional depth in "traditional" ritual.[22] I am sug-

---

Wissenschaftliche Buchgesellschaft, 1981). See especially 3-12 (against the representation of emotions), 28 f; (the pointlessness of the quarrel about the priority of words or music: "Opera is primarily music, not drama," 28), 81 (the dying Henry IV in Shakespeare wants to listen to music in order to "fade away" in its non-representational element ["gegenstandsloses Element"]).

[21] See Jean Baudrillard, *Les stratégies fatales* (Paris: Grasset and Fasquelle, 1983).

[22] See various remarks by Cesáreo Bandera, R. A. Rapaport, and Jonathan Z. Smith in Robert G. Hamerton-Kelly, ed., *Violent Origins. Walter Burkert, René Girard, and Jonathan Z. Smith on Ritual Killing and Cultural Formation* (Stanford: Stanford U P, 1987) 187, 191, 195. See also, in this book, the debate on the difference between "guilt" and "excuse," running roughly parallel to deep meaning and "flat" ritualization, 245-47.

gesting now that singing in opera is one of the strongest relics of this embodied, here specifically bodily, aura of precise, virtuoso enactment. Singing intensifies auratic enactment to the detriment of representational frameworks in which ritual can ultimately be embedded, even if participants do not have to know (much about) them for a "felicitous" practice. Ritualistic precision becomes performative virtuosity, which is a form of aesthetic overstylization, because the enactment concentrates on one singer, or at most a few of them, and therefore is not socially embedded in the ordinary way. This is not a hard and fast distinction. The Catholic Church recognized the transitions, the mutual reinforcement between general ritualistic precision and specific virtuosity, early on and stuck with it for very long. It used, and soon produced, the castrati whose vocal performance has probably never been equalled, to say nothing of surpassed by any other "naturally" human or technically manipulated voice. (The last castrati sang in the Vatican, not in opera, toward the end of the nineteenth and the early twentieth century.)[23]

In terms of medialization and its impact on representation, a sharp distinction between the speaking and the singing voice must be established. By contrast, in the castrati and in virtuoso singing more generally, the distinction between the natural and the technical voice breaks down. This may sound paradoxical or perverse, since one might assume medialization to be tied up primarily with the specific, and the specifically technical-technological media in which it supposedly takes place, on which it is recorded. There is to be sure the crucial and difficult problem of "live" vs. "recorded." It is hard to get the relevant differences, concerning atmosphere, delivery, stage, and camera presence under descriptive and analytic control. It is clear, though, that the general "Benjaminian" lament about a loss of

---

[23] See my article, "Il castrato digitalizzato: Farinelli and the Medical-Aesthetic Complex." *Artefacts, Artefictions. Crossovers Between Contemporary Literatures, Media, Arts and Architectures*, ed. Angela Krewani (Heidelberg: Universitätsverlag C. Winter, 2000) 83-95.

aesthetic aura in the age of technical reproducibility is mistaken. The flexibility of camera angles for instances can compensate for the loss of live presence to a considerable extent. It is even less difficult to identify a voice and describe its essential qualities in either live or recorded versions.[24] This would suggest that the range of technical, that is performative-manipulative competence in the virtuoso singer is such that the distinction between the "technical" mastery of the voice and the "technical-technological" media in and on which it appears is of less than prime importance. With rare exceptions such as the recordings of the so-called last castrato Alessandro Moreschi at the beginning of the twentieth century, the performative-technical aspects of the singing voice assert themselves even in technologically bad recordings. Conversely, the kind of levelling perfection imposed on singing by contemporary technology has not neutralized the "dramatic" or "lyric" qualities that seem to belong naturally to one or the other voice.

---

[24] I am following Jürgen Kesting here: "For an evaluation of the [singing] human voice … there are binding natural and technical criteria." *Die großen Sänger unseres Jahrhunderts* (Düsseldorf: Econ, 1993) 76. Consequently, the metonymy "voice" for singer is admissible in this more than in other cases of a close connection between person and performance. Cf. also Jens Malte Fischer, *Große Stimmen. Von Enrico Caruso bis Jessye Norman* (Stuttgart: Metzler, 1993). For the range of natural-technical couplings see especially Fischer's glossary 599-616. At this point, a discussion (another one) of Derrida's ideas about voice, *différance*, and meaning supplements might appear imperative. I do not see, however, that Derrida ever moves into the direction taken here. Only rarely does he speak about the medialization effect of "danse, musique, volume, profondeur plastique, image visible, sonore, phonique" (*L'écriture et la différence* (Paris: Seuil, 1967) 358). He locates these elements in the tension between representation and the non-represent*able* (the unsayable like "la force" and "la vie"). The point of singing as performance is, however, that it is neutral with respect to such mythical oppositions and rather devoted to the non-representation*al*. For other hints see *La dissémination* (Paris: Seuil, 1972) 9-11, *Positions* (Paris: Minuit, 1972) 66 f. I have not checked, however, Derrida's all too abundant later work for these matters.

In any case, the singing voice may push its performative autonomy to such an extent that Kesting, with respect to the tenor Lauri-Volpi, feels obliged to attribute a sometimes "arrogant self-display" to it. Many descriptions of the ways in which a voice is "conducted" seem to fall into the worst kind of impressionism. Kesting speaks of the "intoxicating sound of Ezio Pinza's bass voice," the singer Elisabeth Schwarzkopf compares the timbre of a colleague's voice with a mixture of old port and thick cream.[25] Handled skilfully and with careful experienced expertise, however, such descriptions will set up a network of comparisons and analogies with instruments, colors, sounds and other objects capable of intersubjective perception through which something like a descriptively controlled impressionism emerges. Sometimes, indeed, the masterful self-display of the voice will aim at or is ineluctably perceived as something like representation: Kesting describes Titta Ruffo's "interpretation" of Hamlet's "To be or not to be"—soliloquy in Ambroise Thomas's opera (1868) as a "representational singing of unique intensity, vocal imagination and deep feeling" (107). But this results from a supreme play with and an exploitation of the expressive potential of the voice; it is not the interpretation of a role in the ordinary dramatic sense. Jumping to representational conclusions with respect to the expressive potentials of the voice, talk of an expression of the passions has in fact ruined a lot of writing about opera. And perhaps the voices of singers too: Kesting thinks that the identification, emotional and otherwise, with roles is one of the greatest dangers for the singer's voice. It is not an argument, but an interesting fact that Lauri-Volpi, the singer with the arrogant self-display of the voice, was probably the most intellectual singer of all times who quit singing at the age of 81.[26]

---

[25] Kesting, *Die großen Sänger* 1993, 101, 210, 503.

[26] Cf. Kesting, *Die großen Sänger* 1993, 210, 216 for Lauri-Volpi and 664, by contrast, for the burn-out case of Callas. Lauri-Volpi wrote several books in various fields far removed from his own life and singing on both of which of course he also published quite a lot.

In this crucial respect, singing carries Diderot's theory of acting in *Paradoxe sur le comédien* to an extreme. Diderot, as we know, opted for cold-blooded acting through which the actor could represent emotion precisely by not identifying with it. Rather, the actor and actress must exploit and perfect the constructional scope inherent in emotions as communicable, but not fully deterministic codes. (I am assuming, in the way of disciplines as different as neurology and systems theory, a distinction between private causally determined feelings and more or less public emotions which must be communicated, but disposed of binding codes for that only in earlier times. I do not think that Bourdieu's notion of [fine] distinctions solves the problem of communicative code.) Verbal acting proceeds in cold blood in order to perfect an expressive, to large extent also representational register; singing concentrates on cold-blooded technique to produce a mostly self-referential, representationally contingent, if expressively somehow powerful, intensity. That is why Jonathan Miller's description of the differences between a verbal play and an opera is correct. Unlike:

> a play whose dramatic virtues can be recognized on the page—and just as often disperse on the stage— the quality of an opera is not readily detectable until it *has* been performed. An unperformed opera is literally a closed book to all but a very few musicians who can visualize the action and hear the music from the score alone.[27]

Understandably, educated people like to fix meanings and represented roles to artists strutting and fretting about the stage in often outlandish costumes, singing at the top of their voice, appearing to express something at all cost and great length even while they are dying. How the interpretational habit—of which deconstruction is one the more recent offshoots—has gradually

---

[27] "Introduction," *Don Giovanni. Myths of Seduction and Betrayal*, ed. Jonathan Miller (New York: Schocken Books, 1990) vii-xiv, vii.

infiltrated all walks of life and art is an interesting, intriguing, and intricate question.[28] I am not alone in suggesting that the nineteenth century witnessed the heyday of that activity when even instrumental music—as such clearly a split from, or at best a "tacit" compliance with representational frameworks—was made to carry tremendous burdens of meaning. Beethoven's fifth symphony and many other pieces have become engulfed in associations about fate and destiny precisely because their associative potential could be used as an interpretational *ersatz* in a time for which the difficulty of speaking and arguing about such matters was clearly greater than for the Greeks or Shakespeare. That kind of interpretational greed can be indulged in even more recklessly with opera. Even so, opera singing, in spite of language and libretto, "represents" a late cultural (re)turn to a media detour toward older qualities of *phenomenality*. The most one can say in favor of representation here is that we are dealing with phenomena which, because they speak so strongly for themselves, coalesce with what they also might seem to represent.

Opera singing, then, is performative phenomenology. In my mind, this is the only phenomenology that works because an impression of phenomenality, of quasi-givenness, can only be gained and indeed fabricated by elaborate, virtuoso detours. As such, the performativity of opera must be distinguished from what some contemporary literary theory, notably in Wolfgang Iser and J. Hillis Miller, has described as the performative power of texts, the power, that is, to make something happen (in the reader).

Historical Bolsterings

---

[28] See, for instance, in my book *The Protoliterary. Steps to an Anthropology of Culture* (Stanford: Stanford U P, 2002), the Index, s.v. body, fascination, representation, ritual, theatricality. See also, more pointedly, the forthcoming book by Hans Ulrich Gumbrecht, *Productions of Presence* (Stanford: Stanford U P, 2004).

All of this does not mean that an opera chorus like "Va, pensiero, sull'ali dorate" in Verdi's *Nabucco* cannot turn into a symbol of the Italian national liberation movement; that a whole opera like *La Traviata* cannot be taken to reflect a moral-social nineteenth-century bias highly unjust to women, and so forth. But if one embarks on the search for representational horizons, they begin to pale, to be trivialized in the face of the performative power of singing as soon as one believes one has found them. Opera directors and newspaper writers in particular seem to have a hard time keeping their pronouncements on interpretational goals and results from falling into open nonsense. Singing does not exclude representational claims that the full text of an opera and sometimes even the acting of a singer seem to invite, but holds them at arm's length.

The development of opera singing argues strongly for what I am describing here as the medializing impact of vocal techniques. Opera singing can be seen as the almost accidental byproduct of textual unease, of a felt lack of power in the poetical language, including Dante's, available in Italy at the turn of the sixteenth century. At that time, the Florence Camerata tried to revitalize what they took to be the poetic power of Greek tragedy. They assumed that Greek tragedy had been sung. The idea, as such, was not wrong. But implementing it under quite different historical circumstances produced necessarily very different results. The repertoire of musical effects, the differentiation of musical instruments and techniques as well as of standards of discourse in late sixteenth-century Italian urban culture pulled the effort to re-empower poetry away from what it was supposed to resuscitate: the chanting of Greek tragedy. Demanding increased power of speech under modern conditions amounted to a stronger distinction between the ordinary and the emphatic: It pushed the effort very quickly toward a widening gap between self-sustained music (orchestral music and elaborate singing, tempered for a while by the "verbal" recitative) and other standards of speech.

This development carries severe implications. Tragedy once had the function of enacting important, indeed fateful, relations between persons and higher forms of mythological, political, or social order in various forms of heightened or "sublimated" ordinary speech. In periods of absolutism, whether real or to some extent only pro forma, the picture of a direct link between individuals and destiny meets with resistance; in "bourgeois" societies, in democracies, it is outflanked and outclassed by notions of social goals, reforms, and therapy even if it survives in both aesthetic and mental niches. While languages of fate such as the wheel of fortune survive for quite a while, the resistance to the pathos of fate is evident in layers of political and psychological calculus and in strategies of risk avoidance from Shakespeare to French classical tragedy. The risk of risk avoidance, however, lies in the decline of tragic conflict. This is why tragedy has been declared dead—as it were on the scene— continually since Euripides, in whom it took a definite literary, complex shape no longer suitable for emphatic, quasiritualistic enactments. It is also the reason why opera, in spite of obvious difficulties of its own, has fared better, on the whole, down to the present day: It replaces quasiritualistic enactment with a self-sustained, representationally neutral virtuoso performance. It eludes the competition of representational standards.

Tragedy had been the "poetic" and "dramatic" stylization of a common, often deeply anchored intuition: the relevance of persons, their emotions, intentions, and actions with respect to the "world." Opera takes the historical trivialization, perhaps even the refutation of this intuition for granted. But it pushes skeptical knowledge into the background; it re-dramatizes the intuition in a performatively virtuoso and therefore attractive form. Playing with words one could say: It re-presents, but does not represent the intuition. Individual relevance is in ruins; opera (re)creates it in a performative context where the seemingly natural (the voice and its "magic," music, rhythm) and the highly artificial (stage technology) are inextricably mixed. Once the audience has crossed this threshold, questions about cognitive, emotional, or historical—in short, about representational adequacy—can still be asked, but met with arbitrary response.

In media and cultural history, this situation is acutely experienced. In Dryden's official literary doctrines, opera overstepped the limits of acceptable or merely plausible standards of humanity. Yet his own text production frequently worked toward conditions of song. It is also significant that Enlightenment criticism is directed mainly against opera, less against oratorios and instrumental music. The representational case of the oratorio, the form to which even Handel returned after his somewhat tumultuous operatic career in London, is readily understood. With its expressive orientation toward the evocation of a higher being, it was acceptable to both religion and philosophy in their broader varieties. In that sense, the oratorio is an acceptable version of epic for periods in which secular rationalities have not expulsed the need for overarching, if vague, "religious" significance. Instrumental music represents a compromise. It dodges the potential embarrassment that may cling to the public or, in opera, quasi-public display of violent intensities, variously encoded as passions or emotions. For many, opera is difficult to accept because it invites such representational-emotional projections, which it either presents in "artificial," exaggerated, and obsolete forms or dissolves in the self-sufficiency of singing.

In the seminal essay "The Grain of the Voice," Roland Barthes tried to find a way out of the dilemma that we either predicate (interpret) too much or, intimidated by what seems ineffable, say nothing at all. There are elements in singing that can be put in the service of communication, representation, or expression (rules of the genre, coded forms of melisma, style of interpretation, etc.). There are others related to the grain of the voice, that is, the "very materiality," indeed the "voluptuousness of its sound-signifiers." A cultural tendency toward the first levels will normally produce a sentimental clarity, of which, for Barthes, the German baritone Dietrich Fischer-Dieskau is the supreme example. That type fits an "average culture" that demands expression and takes art to supply its most sophisticated forms. The so-called "Three Tenors," holding sway over large parts of the public in the mid-nineties of the twentieth century, satisfy that demand in cruder forms. The fascination of the grain of voice—that is the "friction between the music and something else," "the body in the voice as it sings ... the limb as it performs" is lost because the voices are no longer at their best.[29]

Barthes formulates the problem in a way anticipated by Hegel. This may come as a surprise, since Hegel is normally (dis)credited with a representational aesthetics. It is a mistake, however, to expect full conistency in any theory. Thus, whatever ideas Hegel may have entertained about the beautiful being the sensuous representation (the "shining" or the "illusion") of the idea, he has a very "realistic" view of opera. Hegel is very much relaxed about the "*details* of poetic execution" in the libretti of opera. These details can be "meagre and of a certain mediocrity." The "Italians" provide the paradigm here—and not just for opera. It is striking that, for a contrast, Hegel should single out Schiller, whose poems "prove very awkward and useless for musical composition." Poetry in itself, however, tends to push the use of language in problematic directions even when the comparative effect of music is not taken into consideration: It veers all too easily toward "all too ramified complications," "too difficult thoughts or profound philosophy," toward something like the grand sweep of "pathos" in Schiller's lyrics. In any case, the "bungling compilation" of Schikaneder's libretto for *The Magic Flute* "is amongst the finest opera libretti. The realm of night, the queen, the realm of the sun, the mysteries, initiations, wisdom, love, tests, and along with these a sort of commonplace morality excellent in its general principles—all this combined with the depth, the bewitching loveliness and

---

[29] Cf. Roland Barthes, *Image. Music. Text.* Essays sel. and trans. Stephen Heath (London: Fontana, 1984) 179–90, 181–82, 185, 188. Barthes of course could not have referred to the "Three Tenors."

soul, of the music, broadens and fills the imagination and warms the heart."[30]

Both Barthes's and Hegel's positions, together with similar ones in a lot of aesthetic theory, are prefigured in the situation of the Florentine Camerata. In the early modern Italian epics of Ariosto and others, the connection between literary language and aristocratic emotive norms was pushed, for a last time, into subtle complexities. In the self-ironic play of parody, however, these complexities tend to cancel each other out, to suggest the impossibility of the genre. For the Camerata, the discontent with literary language concentrates in the feeling that the sound qualities of language, which make poetic declamation fail or succeed, must be revitalized. It is in the "resounding" effect of language that the presence of both emotions and the world is immediately felt. In that respect, as I said before, even Dante's language had come to leave something to be desired.

Italian opera is perhaps the most succinctly elaborated medium of what Gramsci called the Italian "melodramatic" conception of life. Ruth Katz has told the story of "a melodramatization of 150 years of social and cultural history," tracing the ways in which Italian Renaissance literature turned literally into an "invitation to music." In various ways, the (pseudo)orality of the *novelle*, the well-nigh expiration of poetry in pastoral drama (e.g. Tasso's *Aminta*), the emphasis on the "grand production," in the *sacre rappresentazioni*, and the spectacular, but barely "literary" pathos of Senecan-Roman tragedy demanded and veered toward musical interference or far-reaching musicalization.[31] There is, furthermore, a large and

---

[30] G. W. F. Hegel, *Aesthetics. Lectures on Fine Art*, trans. T. M. Knox (Oxford: Clarendon) 1975, 2 vols. (continuous pagination), 900, 901, 945-46. Here and in what follows I am linking my analyses with passages from my *Protoliterary*, 204-22.

[31] Ruth Katz, *Divining the Powers of Music. Aesthetic Theory and the Origins of Opera* (New York: Pendragon, 1986) 177, 135. See also 87-95 on musical magic and 102-07 on monody. My account of the Florence Camerata follows mainly Robert Donington's *The Rise of Opera* (London: Faber and Faber, 1981). Ruth Katz's story is, on the whole,

ill-defined space between representational conceptions of language, like those of the Neoplatonists, and specialized, either religiously charged or relatively neutral, polyphonic music. "Sung tragedies" fashioned after the supposedly Greek model[32] were intended to occupy the space in between. The Greek way of "singing," however, changed drastically within the mixed, urbanized context of the Florentine aristocracy and the higher, professionalized bourgeoisie. Greek tragedy, in some of its early and classic representatives, may have come close to the implementation of an anthropologically "pure" or basic medium, the hypothetical unity of ritual and art. That brittle unity, or the impression of it, can be reproduced only in the form of highly "artificial" procedures of staging.

---

less concise, though sometimes more detailed than Donington's (to whom she makes no reference whatsoever). F. W. Sternfeld's *The Birth of Opera* (Oxford: Clarendon, 1993) and my own analyses overlap mainly as far as the crucial topic of metamorphoses in and through opera singing are concerend. Among the many other works consulted I would like to mention Günter Schauenberg, *Stereotype Bauformen und stoffliche Schemata der Oper* (PhD dissertation, Munich 1975), 10-32, Helmut Schmidt-Garre, *Oper. Eine Kulturgeschichte* (Cologne: Arno Volk, 1963), 18-29. The important original texts of and around the Camerata and French discussions (including opera patents by Louis XIV) are presented in Heinz Becker, ed., *Quellentexte zur Konzeption der europäischen Oper im 17. Jahrhundert* (Kassel: Bärenreiter, 1981). The state of research concerning the specific intertwining of "words" and "music," of relations between poetry, music, and dance in ancient Greece is well presented, I suppose, in Frieder Zaminer, "Musik im archaischen und klassischen Griechenland," in: A. Riethmüller and F. Zaminer, eds., *Neues Handbuch der Musikwissenschaft*, vol. 1, general editor Carl Dahlhaus (Laaber: Laaber Verlag, 1989) 113-206. Zaminer is also instructive on the beginnings of an independent "lyrico-literary" language (135). The cultural position of opera in Italy and Italian theory in more recent times has been treated meanwhile instructively in the "Habilitations" thesis by Immacolata Amodeo, *Il gusto melodrammatico. Eine medienkomparatistische Studie zum Opernhaften* (Ms. Bayreuth University 2001).

[32]   Cf. Donington, *The Rise* 1981, 82, 104-05, 112–13.

Opera, then, is a way of staging that neutralizes representation. The enchantment of performance and its very artifice is supposed to blur the boundaries between representation and enactment. This explains why opera, especially in its later Italian shamelessly "popular" form, has provoked a split of the potential audience into enthusiasts and enemies, much more so than verbal theater which continues to command attention to its intellectual and social, that is, representational implications. Conversely, opera also has spawned—apart from the literary closet plays of Wagner (Nietzsche)—much fewer interpretational controversies.

Despite the fact that opera has always exploited verbal theater for topics, themes, and plots, the difference in medium appeal is tremendous. This is most conspicuous in those forms that, for a very short time, tried to strike a balance between the two. That effort was made, for instance, in the many "intermediate" forms on London stages in the seventeenth and eighteenth centuries. Purcell's (1659-1695) "semi-operas" are the best but symptomatically short-lived examples. In the semi-operas, song and dance alternated with spoken passages. Roger North, who died in 1734 and may have coined the term, has described the dilemma of alternation quite precisely: Parts of the audience despise the music because they are interested in the represented problem. The others look upon the spoken passages as mere interruptions of the music. North, quite plausibly, opted for a separation of the "genres."[33]

---

[33] Cf. Ulrich Schreiber, "Halbe Opern: eine ganze Sache? Henry Purcell und die Anfänge der englischen Oper," *Neue Zeitschrift für Musik*, 4/148 (1987): 4-7, 5. In the present context, the most relevant introduction to Purcell is perhaps Curtis Alexander Price, *Henry Purcell and the London Stage* (Cambridge: Cambridge U P, 1984). See in particular his discussion of the problematic, sometimes downright ridiculous, "interpretations" of the "allegory" in Purcell's full (and still famous) opera *Dido and Aeneas* 1689, 229-34. A. Hutchings, *Purcell* (London: British Broadcasting Corporation, 1982) also contains valuable materials and perspectives. See also Winton Dean and John Merrill Knapp, *Handel's Operas 1704-1726* (Oxford: Clarendon, 1987), where the semi-opera is

The problem of semi-operas is abundantly obvious in Purcell's *The Fairy Queen* (1692–93), a transformation of Shakespeare's *The Tempest.* Since Shakespeare's text, even in the spoken passages, cannot be reproduced in its entirety, paraphrases become necessary. In those, the incongruity of media drifts are glaring. On the other hand, Purcell's full opera, *Dido and Aeneas* (1689), was conceived, written, and performed as a chamber opera for a very limited audience of school girls. But Dido's musicalized "message" in arias like "Ah! Belinda, I am prest" or "When I am laid in earth" seems to have engraved itself into the world's memory, as Schreiber says with self-ironic pathos: the suffering of the world is condensed in the lament of a person. It is a message, though, "from which all verbal fat has been boiled away."[34]

This "perfection" of opera, as Romain Rolland called it, arises because the language of song does not call for the disenchanting questions that spoken language might provoke. In opera, culturally critical questions concerning the authenticity—and the relevance—of emotions and motivations need not be asked. In verbal theater, such questions may easily slip into the focus of attention. In that respect, opera can never be really up to date. It will always treat the problems of yesterday and of yore. But it enacts them in a mode that makes the obsolete appear universal. In that sense, there seem to be central forms of human behavior that receive their individual and general significance only in opera. Conversely, that significance can easily degenerate into the meaningless and the absurd. Consequently, it is pointless to ask, with Adorno, how bourgeois opera can shake off its obsolete and nostalgic images

---

rightly said to have "possessed little life or propensity for growth" (141). For other sketches of the transition from various forms of "accidental" music to full opera, from the court masques to Purcell, see Reinhold Sietz, *Henry Purcell. Zeit—Leben—Werke* (Leipzig: Breitkopf & Härtel, 1955). Sietz draws attention, for instance, to the "Italianization" of court masques and to the development from there to d'Avenant and Dryden (93-98).

[34] Schreiber, *Halbe Opern* 1987, 6, 7; Price 1984, 226.

of desire and regain the status of a relevant, powerful image for the present. In the great representatives of opera, perfection is tantamount to absolute naiveté, to what Krenek called his "naive realism" mentioned above. [35]

It is the immanent dynamics of an unintended transition from various mixtures of singing and speaking, from various versions of semi-opera or less than semi-opera, to the full-blown operas of Monteverdi and their "universal" appeal that the Camerata witnessed in as little time as ten years, roughly from 1600 to 1610. In 1607 Monteverdi's *Orfeo* was produced in Mantova. In urban society, the chanting we associate with Greek tragedy would have been at least partly archaic. This is why the difference between ordinary and "poetic-dramatic" speech had to be increased. The result was singing as a highly specialized technique of its own. For a while, the Camerata group tried to replace literary-dramatic speech by what they called *recitare cantando*—clearly a compromise formula intended to reconcile the diverging pulls of realistic speech and "poetic" intensity. Soon monody—an individual switching to singing in critical and important situations—took over. This proved to be an insufficiently complex mode, and the emphasis shifted to a mixture of recitative and singing in which speech standards seemed to be preserved and yet subordinated to the lead of melody.[36] That highly unstable mixture split, in due course, into what since has been called recitative and aria. The recitative has kept close to dramatic speech. It takes care of the need to maintain at least the impression of a meaningful continuity of action. Arias soar away into expressive independence.

---

[35] Hutchings, *Purcell* 1982, 56–57; Götz Friedrich, *Musiktheater. Ansichten—Einsichten* (Frankfurt M.: Propyläen, 1986) 15, 29 or 193, 195; Adorno, "Bürgerliche Oper," *Schriften*, vol. 16 (Frankfurt M.: Suhrkamp, 1978) 24-39, 38; Romain Rolland, *Histoire de l'Opéra en Europe avant Lully et Scarlatti* (Les origines du théâtre lyrique moderne) (1895; Geneva: Slatkine Reprints, 1971) 10.

[36] Cf. Donington, *The Rise* 1981, 41, 91, 140.

In opera, the division of labor between recitative and aria has always been precarious. In the nineteenth century, in particular, the parodistic and playful handling of this division implied in *opera buffa* was subjected to more serious demands. Recitative then appeared as musically worthless. The independence of singing (*belcanto*), for Wagner on the other hand, was hard to distinguish from meaninglessness.[37] On the whole, it was of course the "boring" recitative that lost out. Once the artificial naturalness of aria is accepted, the recitative, much as it seems to represent the normalcy of speech, tends to appear artificial and unrealistic in its own way.

Opera is the early modern form in which self-sustained performance, unhampered by criteria of consistent representation, reasserts itself. For average types of rationality, this is hard to digest. Aaron Hill complained in a letter to Handel that, in opera, the "excellence of *sound*" is normally "dishonour'd by the poorness of the *sense* it is chain'd to." Hill was right, but Handel was the wrong addressee, certainly not the one on whom hopes for betterment could be built. It was Handel who, with the best of intentions, finally implemented Dryden's plans for a *Paradise Lost* opera on a smaller scale. Handel took a leading part in the 1740 operatic raid on and rape of Milton's "L'Allegro" and "Il Penseroso," supplemented by the texter Charles Jennens with "Il Moderato." From a literary point of view, there are grounds for lament. But Hill's position can easily be reversed. It then appears that Handel was able to "inspire Life into the most senseless Words." Handel himself, in a letter to Jennens, at least appeared to be highly satisfied with that mixture.

Consequently, such painstakingly precise historians as Winton Dean and John Merrill Knapp, in their book on Handel, torment themselves in vain with specious distinctions between an alleged timeless grandeur of certain Handelian figures

---

[37] Eduard Hanslick, *Vom Musikalisch Schönen* (Leipzig: Rudolph Weigel, 1854; Darmstadt: Wissenschaftliche Buchgesellschaft, 1981) 27; cf. Schmidt-Garre, *Oper* 1963, 31, 191.

(Cleopatra's "eternal seductiveness" as a "central facet of human experience") and the split between "splendid moments" and "mere" "puppet" qualities in others.[38] Or rather, they do not see that they are frequently switching between descriptive-technical analysis and value judgments both theoretically dubious and practically dated. Similarly, Dean, in his equally informative and instructive book on Georges Bizet, labors under the delusion that it is possible to balance the good and bad points of opera life. The bad points in such a picture are found in the star system, entailing the destruction of dramatic and psychological integrity. They show up glaringly in the sorry state of music criticism in Bizet's time, and in the distance that separates music and literature. The good points supposedly reside in the "dramatic" improvement of character conceptions, to which Dean devotes a whole chapter. But Dean is not at all dealing with consistency of character. He is concerned with a lack or increase in the "dramatic," that is the performative power of what may or may not be taken as a full or fragmentary character. Therefore, a dose of the playful self-irony that Nietzsche applied when he tried to make the impression of Bizet's musical-dynamic "superiority" plausible is always to be recommended. The directions taken by Prosper Mérimée's writing and Bizet's opera are entirely different, and, perhaps, seen from a present-day vantage point, neither should be burdened with notions of character: Bizet concentrates on a series of strong impressions that may or may not be attributed to "characters," while Mérimée delineates the slow and gradual falling apart of what had once appeared, as Dean has it, as a "decent human being."[39]

Descriptively, Lindenberger's distinction between the mimetic and the rhetorical orientations of opera[40] can be

---

[38] Dean and Knapp, *Handel's Operas* 1987, 18, 423.
[39] *Georges Bizet. Leben und Werk*, trans. Konrad Köster (Stuttgart: Deutsche Verlags-Anstalt, 1988); engl. *The Master Musicians Series: Bizet*, fourth ed. (London: Dent, 1978), 60-61, 62, 228-318, 283-284.
[40] Lindenberger, *Opera* 1984, 25-26.

applied to both verbal and musical theater. But the status of the mimetic, its fragments and semblances, its tendency toward indeterminacy, mostly takes very different turns. Literary-dramatic texts can be reasonably analyzed in terms of the indeterminacy into which their topics, situations, and problems, their elements of potential reference, are shifted. In opera, indeterminacy tends to approach irrelevance: The apparent referents function as triggers of unrelated, but therefore also unrelativized and somehow very real effects.

The effects are bonded not with the referents or their indeterminacy, but rather, to simplify drastically, with the nervous system. Any emotion seemingly stimulated by opera may, but need not, be attributed to anything like the destiny of characters. In that sense, Shaw's verdict that "the superior intensity of musical expression" makes Mascagni's *Cavalleria rusticana* "far more real" than Verga's play of the same title would be theoretically plausible even if Shaw's impression were shared by no one else.[41] The same would hold for Ernst Krenek's view according to which the animal(istic) effect of Weill's music in the operas by Weill and Brecht may simply push into oblivion their intellectual or socially critical "content," whether determinate or not.[42]

Efforts to identify representational horizons, that is, something the music and singing may ulteriorly point to, easily take on strained and forced qualities. Kierkegaard, to take a famous example, in his analyses in *Either/Or*, defined Mozart's Don Giovanni as the erotic-sensual genius. For Günter Schauenberg, Wagner maneuvers between the stimulation of the erotic and the repression of the sexual. For Adorno, Wagner's *Ring* presents the problematic fusion of humans dominating nature and being dominated by it.[43] While

---

[41] Quoted in Lindenberger, *Opera* 1984, 25.

[42] Cf. Schauenberg, *Stereotype Bauformen* 1975, 156-57.

[43] Schauenberg, *Stereotype Bauformen* 1975, 233; Adorno, *Versuch über Wagner*, ed. Gretel Adorno, Rolf Tiedemann (Frankfurt M.: Suhrkamp, 1978) 128-29.

controversies in literary interpretation have lost their erstwhile importance, even advanced literary theory would not dispute that the medium of literature provokes and may even need extended interpretational activities. In opera, the type of activity called interpretation is possible, sometimes even "maliciously" provoked by the intensity of what appears as expression, but also appears easily to be misplaced. The stretching of scenic immediacy toward the self-sufficiency of a magic of relations[44] in a context of unreality or even absurdity does not of course preclude interpretation. It does, however, suggest that the appropriateness of interpretational forms depends on the medium onto which they are projected.

---

[44] This is the direction which the analyses of opera are taking in Carl Dahlhaus's *Vom Musikdrama zur Literaturoper* (München: Musikverlag Katzbichler, 1983) 17. Cf. also pp. 10-12 in an essay on the method of opera analysis (pp. 9-17), in which possibilities of coming to terms with the "unreality" and "absurdity" of opera are discussed.

AFTERWORD: COMPELLING REPRESENTATION

Douglas Bruster

It seems uncannily familiar, perhaps because we have seen things start this way once before, perhaps because once seen it is surprisingly difficult to forget. A young man walks slowly through a lush and empty park holding a camera dangling from a strap. The wind jostles the limbs of trees and bushes (change is in the air). Yet even though he is clearly waiting for something to happen—to make itself present to him, as it were—he is, like us, understandably startled by the appearance of a small vehicle winding its way around a park road. The vehicle is packed with people who shout joyously as they pass him, and it is possible for an instant to think that their exhilaration is related to arriving just when they do, as though they had been invited to meet him at this time and place. They stop at a small asphalt tennis court not far from the young man. There are over a dozen of them, and they spring from the vehicle with alacrity, three of them entering the tennis court, the others lining up to watch from outside its chain-link fence. One of the three inside the court sits high in the umpire's chair; the other two commence a game of tennis, which those outside follow enthusiastically. The young man stands apart from this group, at a corner of the court but also outside it. He watches the energetic pair playing the game with bemusement; soon his reserve is put to the test when one of them chases a ball into his corner of the court. As her eyes meet his, he encourages her with a nod before she returns to the contest.

When the game resumes, our own eyes do something new. Like the spectators standing outside the court, we begin to trace the tennis ball's flight in midair, following it back and forth for a few shots. We do so for only a moment, perhaps, but it is enough to prepare us for watching the ball closely in what follows. As the game continues, one player makes a serious error, sending the ball up and over the rear fence of the tennis court near the young man. We follow the ball as it bounces and rolls at last to a stop in the grass. As the player with whom he has previously exchanged glances turns toward him imploringly, the young man graciously trots from his spot at the court's corner and, setting down his camera, retrieves the ball. Measuring its weight with a few small tosses up and down in his hand, he throws it high over the court's fence with a strong motion.

The sequence is painted with such broad and familiar strokes that, when even brief parts of it are seen again, it comes to one whole, like memories of a story learned in childhood. Certainly what this description has left out can identify it. The tennis players and spectators are, of all things, mimes; with faces painted white, and costumes that would be at home in a circus, they have mimed playing, and watching, the entire game—a match played without rackets or ball. When our eyes are made to follow the imaginary ball first through the air, then across the grass as it rolls away from the court, we, like the young man, are beguiled into their charade. This description has also left out what happens after the young man throws the ball back into the court. We watch him more closely for a while as he watches the game—also more intently this time, with chin turning ever so slightly back and forth, his eyes moving left and right in a manner that perfectly imitates those viewing a real tennis match. As he does so, we hear, at first faintly and then with increasing volume, the sound of a real tennis ball being struck before rebounding and being struck once again. The young man may hear this too, as he seems to realize something and drops his eyes as if in shame. As if to spare him embarrassment, we see him then from afar as he slowly retrieves his camera, all the while glancing back toward the tennis court as though unable to take his eyes off it. Eventually he disappears, leaving only the broad carpet of green that is the park's floor.

This is of course the celebrated close to *Blow-Up* (1966), Antonioni's first and best-known English-language film, and a motion picture that presciently captured (among other things) an emergent, widespread fascination with visual media. After all, the "young man" of the description—named Thomas in the screenplay, though the name is not heard or seen in the film—is a professional photographer who believes he has inadvertently photographed a murder in the same park in which the film ends. The broader, carnivalesque formations of the years immediately following the film's release would be writ large here as well: what the director's screenplay had called "students" became, in the film itself, the group of mimes—as if the need to present *parody* in its purest form made the latter the more desirable figures (more desirable, that is, because less individuated). They are in the film, clearly, to register something in and by the eyes of the young man. For if *Blow-Up* has momentarily advertised itself as a metaphysical inquiry into youth culture and the nature of photographic representation and its verisimilitude, the film's conclusion near the tennis court leads us to feel that its greater interest and value reside in the human dimensions of representation.

The moment of Thomas's shame follows closely upon the camera's attention to a ball that isn't there, and the aural reproduction of that same ball rebounding off rackets and court. We are not told what he feels and thinks at this moment, but his downcast eyes—as well as his turning back to watch the action on the court—suggests a realization of a certain weakness and complicity in the face of the at-hand charade and its symbolic doubles. The doubting Thomas has become credulous and painfully aware of the cost of that belief. So resonant but ambiguous is this moment of awareness (and its refusal) that a host of analytical referents offer themselves, from the "faith" in the "bad faith" of Sartre's philosophy and Debord's "society of the spectacle" to Althusser's model of interpolation, of the subject being "hailed" into subjectivity.

Yet if the era of the film leads one to any number of possible, even likely exegeses, its content offers the sequence up as a piece still provocative and vital, a story to think with and through. What it advances is, if not a *philosophy* of representation, then a *representation* of representation, a tentative answer to what Derrida called—returning here to Robert Weimann's introduction to this volume—the question of what it means that a person is "not only someone who has representations, who represents himself, but also someone who himself represents something or someone? Not only someone who sends himself or gives himself objects but who is sent by something else or by the other?" Arguably one of the most complex and profound meditations on representation in film— and, as such, adequate to Derrida's query—this final sequence offers up an artist-subject who becomes self-aware of his "sent-ness," and of his concomitant seduction into representation by a representation.

Indeed, the Sophoclean structure of this moment of realization depends upon Thomas's earlier, somewhat arrogant confidence in his ability to stand outside and capture the world of things with his camera, a kind of *skeptron* of his power. The overdetermined nature of this power—it is, for him and for those who see his pictures (even merely his camera), alternately sexual, cultural, and epistemological—parallels the topo-graphical promiscuity that the film chronicles in following Thomas's sports car on its many circular trips within London. This effortless, sometimes too effortless, traversal of boundaries appears in terms of social class as well: The film begins, we will remember, with Thomas posing as a vagrant in order to take surreptitious photographs of homeless men. The point of such insouciance seems to be our realization of representation's moral and ethical aspects.

To return to the representation of representation in this sequence of *Blow-Up* is to realize that Derrida's question cannot be answered analytically—or, if it is to be thus answered, that such an answer can be incomplete at best. For the film has continually prepared us to seek what remains absent in the look, in the recursive chain of glancing at pictures of pictures, at those who take them and scrutinize them in their turn. Whatever language we use in an attempt to explain such an absence, we return to the inescapably human center of representation. Its beguiling nature, for instance, is nowhere so convincingly portrayed as in this sequence, where Thomas's doubt (which is to say an aspect of his superiority) is tricked from him in the face of and by play. The pantomime can be said to function as pure representation: a game that doesn't bother to trouble itself with empty signifiers but yet manages to compel participation and assent.

This is of course far from saying, with Foucault, that representation has undergone a "decline." To the contrary, the tennis game sans rackets or ball stands as proleptic testimony of representation's triumph under postmodernism. As though enacting a parody of an already secular mass, these mimes—too worn out, too belated to be seen as Mephistophelean—usher empty representation front and center on the cultural stage, foregrounding the process by which it becomes itself the subject of representation. In doing so, they advertise that hollowed-out form of depiction that has in our time become an important, even dominant genre. We are no more "after" representation than we are "outside" it. As Derrida's question intimates, we are in and for representation even though—perhaps especially when—we do not recognize its agency in shaping us.

For Foucault to see the putative "decline" of representation as emanating from "the violence and endless effort of life, the hidden energy of needs" is to misrecognize its nature. Representation is not separate from need but remains its very result. *Contra* Foucault, articulation and its twin, the attention to that which is articulated, unfold from and are in direct relation to need and desire. This final sequence of *Blow-Up*, in fact, asserts its elemental value to any consideration of the subject precisely by foregrounding representation's all-too-human beginnings and ends. It is possible to sense, for instance, that Thomas's downcast eyes conceal what he realizes even as they proclaim that something is being realized, that the "energy of needs" is never hidden. That he finds himself thereafter unable not to look, unable not to acknowledge his need for the charade, speaks compellingly to the larger impossibility of remaining for very long outside representation.

GENERAL SECTION

IONA'S EARLY PRAISE POETRY AND DUNBAR'S AUREATION: CONTINUITIES AND CONTRASTS[1]

Ian S. Ross

ABSTRACT

Following a sketch of the career of Columba of Iona (d. 597 AD) as a saint, diplomat, and culture-bearer, praise poetry in Gaelic and Latin associated with him and his familia is analyzed to establish its core aesthetic principles and assess how far they are comparable with those of the Middle Scots aureate poetry of William Dunbar, a thousand years later. Comparative light on the aesthetics of the Iona poetry is sought from examination of other contemporary productions of the insular culture, including the Book of Kells. Additionally, further insights are sought by considering the structure and development of classical bagpipe music (piobaireachd), which offers the purest example of the relevant formal principles at work: the creation of tight frameworks, within which variations of increasing complexity and notable disparity are elaborated with interlace patterns, and resolution is accomplished through the return of endings to beginnings. It is suggested that behind the application of these principles by the Iona poets, and so long afterwards by Dunbar, is a quest, as Dr. Michelle Brown of the British Library staff puts it, for understanding, emulating, and transmitting the "divine rule of time, space, and substance."

Iona is a beautiful island, and it surely must foster in those fortunate enough to live there a sense of beauty. It is famous in the history of Western civilization because the pilgrim-monk

---

[1] A version of this paper was given on Sunday, 14 July 2002, at the *Tenth International Conference on Scottish Language and Literature of the Middle Ages and Renaissance*, held at Rolduc Abbey, Kerkrade, The Netherlands.

and abbot, Colum Cille, "dove of the church" in his Gaelic tongue, known to the Christian world as St. Columba, chose it for his exile from Ireland in 563. This commanding, practical, "island soldier" brought to Iona, with his Christian faith, a love of learning and a desire to share his knowledge and religion.[2] In part, he sought to do this by the example of his austere life, and in part through the creation, or inspiring the creation, of books central to Christianity, written in the beautiful majuscular script called Insular half-uncial, the earliest example of which is found in the *Cathach* ("Battler"), a psalter now in the Royal Irish Academy, Dublin, traditionally ascribed to him, once housed in a *cumhdach*, a portable shrine, and taken on to battlefields to bring victory. In addition, we believe that Colum Cille maintained a lyrical impulse, and composed or inspired the composition of beautiful praise poetry that fused native Irish literary traditions with biblical and classical ones, as well as Latin hymnology.[3]

The thesis of this essay is that the early Iona poetry exhibits aesthetic principles comparable to those found almost a thousand years later in the aureate poetry of William Dunbar, adorned with splendid eloquence as with gold, and that we find in the art productions of Columba and his *familia*, including calligraphy, metalwork, stone carving, gospel-book illumination, and poetry, one fountainhead of Scotland's creativity. Available evidence suggests that the Christian, literary, and artistic culture this holy man embodied and fostered, in time, radiated from Iona to the mainland of Northern Britain, providing a significant element of the foundation for the religious institutions of medieval Catholic Scotland and the development there of the fine arts, of which the members of the Stewart court of 1500, including its major poet Dunbar, were

---

[2]   Adomnán of Iona, *Life of St Columba*, trans. with intro. by Richard Sharpe (London: Penguin, 1995).

[3]   Thomas Owen Clancy and Gilbert Márkus, OP, *Iona: The Earliest Poetry of a Celtic Monastery* (Edinburgh: Edinburgh U P, 1997): Texts are cited by page numbers in this anthology.

the beneficiaries.

From Iona, or on his way from Ireland to that island, which he chose as the central site of his earthly pilgrimage, the white martyrdom of exile, as the Irish said, distinguishing it from the red one of death, and the green of a hermit's existence in the wilderness,[4] Colum Cille made contact with the Scots of Dál Riata (Dalriada). He ordained one of their Kings on Iona, Áedán mac Gabráin, who ruled from Dunadd in Argyll, and maintained friendly terms with Roderc son of Tuthal, King of the Christian Britons of Strathclyde, whose stronghold was Dumbarton. Roderc was the patron of Kentigern, first Bishop of Glasgow, but there is no firm evidence that the two saints met.[5] However, Columba did penetrate across the mainland's massif central into the lands of the mysterious Picts, or *Cruithne*, as the Gaelic-speakers called them, the "People of the Designs," perhaps alluding to their custom of tattooing their bodies, or perhaps to the incisions and reliefs on their standing stones, featuring abstract animal and human ornamentation. The Picts occupied northern and southern kingdoms along the Rivers Ness and Tay, and the Irish holy man perhaps contended with Pictish priests for religious supremacy in the presence of King Bridei near today's Inverness, or more likely negotiated through translators about the passage of his monks in the region. As well, Colum Cille had two English monks with him on Iona, and this suggests at least tenuous contact with the English of the mainland, possibly with Northumbria, already extending towards the Forth, which we believe to be the homeland of Dunbar's ancestors. Later to be sure, in the time of Ségéne, Columba's fourth successor as abbot of Iona, King Oswald of Northumbria, who had been baptised when in exile

---

[4]   Thomas Cahill, *How the Irish Saved Civilization: The Untold Story of Ireland's Heroic Role from the Fall of Rome to the Rise of Medieval Europe* (New York: Doubleday, 1995) 151, 183-84.

[5]   Alan Macquarrie, "The Career of Saint Kentigern of Glasgow: *Vitae, Lectiones*, and Glimpses of Fact," *Innes Review*, XXXVII.1 (1986): 3-24.

on the island, asked for a bishop to minister to the English, and
Áedán was sent in 653 to establish a daughter house of Iona at
Lindisfarne, the Holy Island near Bamborough. As well as
evangelizing northern England, this monk and his followers
brought among the English the practices of Iona, including the
founding of a famous scriptorium.

Piecing together this story of the outreach of Colum Cille
and what his successors saw as his example, we can think of an
engagement in religious and cultural missionary work by these
Irish exiles, no doubt with political or diplomatic implications
as well, among, or connecting with, the four nations whom
Bede identifies in his eighth-century *History of the English
Church and People* as making up the population of Britain:
English, British (Welsh), Scots, and Picts.[6] Moreover, Columba
was fully at home in the Latin language that united them, as
Bede tells us, "in their study of God's truth," and through this
medium, as well as in his native Gaelic, his fame endured and
had a far-reaching impact on the northern mainland.[7] Moreover,
one expressive form which Colum Cille favored, and for which
he was famous, was the chanting and singing of psalms and
hymns in praise of God, and Adomnán reports (1995: 141) the
tradition that this saint's voice was so loud that it could be
heard half a mile or even a mile away. We may think also that
Columba furthered the cultivation of the religious lyric in the
West, which has been traced back to an innovation by St.
Ambrose to comfort his persecuted congregation in Milan in
the fourth century, or so St. Augustine affirms in his
Confessions (IX.7):

> Ready to die with their bishop ... [they] decided to
> sing hymns and psalms as was the custom in the

---

[6] Bede, *A History of the English Church and People*, trans. by Leo
Sherley-Price, revsd. R.E. Latham (Harmondsworth, Middlesex: Penguin
Books, 1979) 38-39.

[7] Máire Herbert, Iona, Kells and Derry: *The History and Hagiography of
the Monastic Familia of Columba* (Dublin: Four Courts, 1996) 9-35.

East, so that the people should not lose their morale through restless anxiety; and the practice has survived to this day, and been imitated in many, indeed almost all, Christian communities throughout the world.[8]

As will be discussed below, there is some reason for speculating that Colum Cille followed the example of Ambrose and, of course, other saints, in composing hymns for people who looked to him for spiritual leadership.

Regarding Columba's enduring fame, we note that when Cináed mac Alpin (Kenneth MacAlpine), sprung from the Dál Riata and Pictish dynasties, began to unify Alba (Scotland) in the 840s, he transferred the relics of the saint to Dunkeld, and thereafter his cult survived in the royal household, with the result that in the twelfth century he was invoked as the "sword and defence of the Scots."[9] In 1123, Alexander I founded an Abbey of St Columba on the small island now known as Inchcolm, a mile and a half offshore from Aberdour in Fife,[10] and a fourteenth-century fragment of Scottish medieval plainchant survives, perhaps sung there as well as at Dunkeld, celebrating "Columba, Most Holy of Saints."[11]

To be sure, Pictish initiative in welcoming a Christian settlement in Fife, focused on veneration of relics of St. Andrew, led in time to the acceptance of this powerful apostle as the patron saint of Scotland.[12] Nevertheless, Colum Cille's

[8]   Peter Dronke, *The Medieval Lyric* (London: Hutchinson, 1968) 32-33.

[9]   Máiri Herbert, "The Legacy of Columba," in T.M. Devine and J.F. McMillan, eds., *Celebrating Columba: Irish-Scottish Connections 597-1997* (Edinburgh: John Donald, 1999).

[10]   L. Russell Muirhead, ed., *Scotland*, The Blue Guides, 5th ed. (London: Ernest Benn, 1967) 268.

[11]   Edinburgh University Library, MS 211.iv: Gaudeamus CD / Linn Record, 1992.

[12]   Richard Fawcett, *St. Andrews Cathedral*, Chris Tabraham, ed. (Edinburgh: Historic Scotland, 1999) 4.

intervention at times of national celebration and crisis was sought in Scotland, and his relics were given special prominence. The *Breccbennach Coluim Cille* ("speckled peaked one of Columba"), a tiny (9 cm high) silver shrine perhaps once containing a prayer written by the saint, is represented on a seal depicting the inauguration of Alexander III in 1249, and this shrine was carried on to the field of Bannockburn in 1314, no doubt contributing to the confidence of the Scots and the discomfiture of the English. Now known as the Monymusk Reliquary, it remains in the Museum of Scotland to remind us of the engraved, jewelled, and enamelled artwork, which devotion to St. Columba inspired.[13]

The aesthetic principles applied in this artifact are also to be found in the illuminated Gospels now associated with the foundations of the Columban monastic *familia* at Durrow, Lindisfarne, and Kells, but believed to have originated on Iona, or been inspired by work there. In this connection, the central questions of this essay are as follows. First, are these same principles present in the Gaelic and Latin poetry associated with Colum Cille? Second, are these principles discernible also in the praise poetry of Dunbar, which we style aureate? Third, can we get some further insights into these principles by considering aspects of the structure and development of the classical *pìobaireachd* unique to the culture of Gaelic-speakers? In an instructive parallel fashion, this music genre offers the purest example of the relevant formal aesthetic principles at work: the creation of tight frameworks within which variations of increasing complexity and notable disparity are elaborated with interlace features, and resolution is brought about through the return of endings to beginnings. George Henderson's investigations of the art of the Insular Gospel Books (1987) and the incisive recent research focused by Carol Farr on the Book of Kells (1997) and by Michelle P. Brown on the Lindesfarne Gospels (2003) help us understand how these

---

[13] John Bannerman, "Comarba Coluim Chille and the Relics of Columba," *Innes Review*, XLIV: 1 (1993): 14-47.

works were structured visually for display in liturgical and public worship contexts, with monks and Irish and Northumbrian aristocracy understood to be included in congregations.[14] These studies coupled with the presentation and exegesis of early Iona poetry now offered by Thomas Owen Clancy and Gilbert Márkus, together with Priscilla Bawcutt's new and impressive edition of the poetry of Dunbar,[15] allow us to pursue the question of the aesthetic principles of these art forms with the appropriate comparative materials. As well, the present flourishing of *pìobaireachd* on the coast of the Northwest Pacific, and recent studies of this art form, provide examples and information for comparative musical analysis.[16]

Irish tradition held that Colum Cille, whom we are regarding as a suitable icon for aureate poetry, was born into the royal house of Cenél Conaill of the Northern Uí Néill. These wealthy aristocrats for whom war was a way of life nevertheless had a sense of beauty and part of this heritage was their love of beautiful objects: jewelery, textiles, and sculpture. Their

---

[14] George Henderson, *From Durrow to Kells: The Insular Gospel-Books 654-800* (London: Thames & Hudson, 1987) 170-71; Carol Farr, *The Book of Kells: Its Function and Audience* (London: British Library and U of Toronto P, 1997); Michelle P. Browne, *The Lindisfarne Gospels: Society, Spirituality and the Scribe* (London: British Library, 2003).

[15] *Poems of William Dunbar*, Priscilla Bawcutt, ed., 2 vols. (Glasgow: Association for Scottish Literary Studies, 1998).

[16] R. L. C. Lorimer, "Studies in Pibroch 1," *Scottish Studies*, 6 (1962): 1-30; —"Studies in Pibroch 2," *Scottish Studies*, 8 (1964a): 45-79; —, Leaflets for *Pibroch*, vols. 1, 2: Waverley Records: Edinburgh: 1964b; A.J. Haddow, *The History and Structure of Ceòl Mór*, D.R. Hannay, ed., Glasgow: priv. ptd., 1982; Seamus MacNeill, *Pìobaireachd, Classical Music of the Great Highland Bagpipe* (Edinburgh: BBC, 1976).; —and Frank Richardson, *Pìobaireachd and its Interpretation: Classical Music of the Highland Bagpipe* (Edinburgh: John Donald, 1987); J.R. MacLeod, Surrey, British Columbia: e-mail letter, 29 October 2002, regarding the history of the Piobaireachd Club, Vancouver, BC, founded in November 1990.

scion's original name was *Crimthann* meaning "fox," but when
his vocation as a bearer of the Holy Spirit rather than a secular
warrior became clear, he was renamed the "dove" (Adomnán
1995: 242-43, 257-59). Details of his ancestry are found in an
elegy: *Amra Choluimb Chille*, composed by a learned poet, a
Fili, known as Dallán Forgaill ("dear Blind One of the
Testimony"), commissioned by a patron identified as Áed,
most likely Áed mac Ainmirech, a cousin of Columba's and
king of the Cenél Conaill, then later of Tara. Dallán seems to
have been a court poet, one of a long line of such figures who
appear in the history of Ireland and the British Isles, masters of
elaborate praise and scathing dispraise, politically useful to, or
to be bought off by, the royalty who employed them, and like
Dunbar, his Irish predecessor was well acquainted with Latin
and the learning of the Church.[17]

A preface to the *Amra* dated 1007 records a tradition that c.
590 the king of Dál Riata, Áedán mac Gabráin, and the
Northern Uí Néill high king, Áed mac Ainmerch, met at Druim
Cet, a hill near Derry, to settle pacification and dynastic
questions. Columba was in attendance, perhaps as principal
mediator. One issue was a proposal to expel the poets from
Ireland because their demands for support had become
exorbitant—the *Ollam* (chief bard), for example, had a retinue
of thirty men. Columba was successful in protecting the poets
from this measure, and thereafter he was deemed to be their
very own patron (Adomnán, Sharpe intro. 1995: 90; Herbert
1996: 265).

The *Amra* is a difficult and often obscure praise poem,
which is found first in an eleventh-century source, *Lebor na
hUidre* ("Book of the Dun Cow"). However, the royal patron
who commissioned it died in 598, and the text's language is of
an archaic cast going back to c. 600, therefore scholars believe
it provides a contemporary's view of Columba. It is indeed
likely that a prominent man, kin to Irish royalty, would be

---

[17] Clancy and Márkus, *Iona* 1997, 97-100; Declan Kiberd, *Irish Classics*
(London: Granta Books, 2001) 12.

accorded a highly wrought praise poem soon after his death. To be sure, here we have an edifying contrast to traditional heroic eulogies of the sixth century, such Ferchertne Fili's praise of Labraid Loingsech, king of Ireland in 431 B.C., who avenged his father's murder by trapping the perpetrators in a house of iron made red hot to destroy them: "Dinn Ríg [citadel of Leinster], a red wall of fire; thirty princes died in suffering. The fierce champion, Labraid, crushed them, burned them, Ireland's hero, grandson of Loegaire Lorc." Ferchertne's poem is written in an archaic verse form called *reicne déchubaid*, consisting of lines with two alliterating words or internal syllabic alliterations, linked by the last word alliterating with the first word of the next line. A concluding feature of many lines is a trisyllabic word or group of three words, marked by two or three strong stresses.

The *Amra* is also composed in this form, and the subject is likewise a *nía*, a hero or champion, but one who has gained his victories over the flesh; his strength is that of an invincible spirit and the noble qualities of this outstanding scholar and teacher, who is descended from Níall Noígiallach ("Niall of the Nine Hostages"), progenitor of the Uí Néill, are those of a warrior serving Christ (Herbert 1996: 9-12). The *Amra* has a preface invoking God's protection, and then ten sections, a sacred number, recalling the ten words or commandments given by God to Moses on Mt. Sinai, including the prohibition on the vain use of the divine name (Exodus 20:7), and the ten names of God's emanations (based on Ezekiel 1), and so on. The last word of the preface connects through alliteration with the first word of the first section, and the ending of the poem in alliterating with the opening of the first section exhibits the technique of *dunád*, which resembles the handling of the *pìobaireachd* form in music described below.

The obscurity of the *Amra* stems partly, it seems, from the archaic form of Gaelic in which it is written, and partly from the elegist's deliberate complicating of the verse, through disruption of normal word order and use of neologisms. Also,

as in later aureate verse, there are direct borrowings from Latin,
for example, *mos* (custom, habit) at III.4; *gula* (gluttony) at
V.7; and tripled in IX.3: *ius* (right), *ecce* (behold), and *certo*
(truly). Dallán shapes his verse from admiration of Columba as
a scholar, particularly for his skill in understanding law and
interpreting the Bible, and he is familiar with the saint's
sources among the Church fathers, Basil and Cassian, but
throughout he maintains a certain aesthetic distance from his
subject.

This contrasts with the perspective of Beccán mac Luigdech,
a hermit-monk devotee and distant relative of Columba, whose
two later praise-poems: *Fo Réir Choluimb* ("Bound to Colum")
and *Tiugraind Beccáin* ("The Last Verses of Beccá"), written c.
650 possibly on Iona or on nearby Rum, are also learned and
allusive, but more fluent in their alliterative patterning and use
of rhyming. They communicate more directly than the *Amra*
through their mastery of *imbas* ("poetic knowledge"), and are
more intimate in their cult-feeling of the confident appeal of a
devotee to the saint as his intercessor in heaven, but may also
be said to be part of the ancestry of "aureate" verse, in their
highly sophisticated interrelating of sense, sound, and intricate
imagery.[18]

Fire and light predominate in that imagery and, in one
direction, this links Beccán's poems to the *Amra* (II, 7-9),
which tells of the lands to the north, west, and east, shining and
blazing as a result of Colum Cille's religious endeavors. In
another direction, it connects with Dunbar's aureate poetry. For
example, there is "Ane Ballat of Our Lady," given prominence
in this paper as Dunbar's supreme example of aureate poetry.
Here Mary is hailed as a "sterne superne" and "Our licht most
richt in clud of nicht" (ed. Bawcutt 1998: 83, ll.1, 27). Also,
Dunbar's dream vision, "The Goldyn Targe," begins by
evoking the sun as a "goldyn candill," and concludes with
stanzas praising "reuerend Chaucer" for his "fresch anamalit

---

[18] Myles Dillon, *Early Irish Literature*, fifth impression (Chicago: U of
Chicago P, 1972) 76, 172; Clancy and Márkus, *Iona* 1997, 100-63.

termes celicall"; also "morall Gower" and "Ludgate laureate" for their "tongis aureate": all of these English predecessors illuminate "oure rude langage." Modestly, the Scottish poet admits his own "lytill quair" does well to be "aferit of the licht" (*ibid.* 184-92: sts. 1, 29-31).

Returning to the prototypical "aureate" elegy by Dallán Forgaill, we find there steady accretion of line linkage through alliteration of the type x + a + a; a + b + b; b + c + c, etc., varied with sequences of three words or phrases featuring parallel stress, or similarity in parts of speech, or rhetorical figures such as anaphora. Possibly there is an appropriate trinitarian implication in the *Amra*, as Columba was a servant of God the Father; imitated Christ the Son in the life he led on earth; and, like the dove in the gospel accounts of the baptism of Christ, he was the visible symbol of the Spirit of love. To be sure, triplicity is also a symbol of spiritual power found in Celtic cultures,[19] and understandably it is found in a poem portraying Colum Cille, a holy man of the highest order. The line-to-line interlacing, through alliteration and other means, is similar to Celtic knotwork and continuous line decoration of sculpture, metalwork, and book illumination, often regarded as symbolizing eternity, also to the tightly framed *pìobaireachd* musical form of much later centuries, with its inner complexities. The logic of the *Amra*'s structure, among other things, is an assertion that its subject has entered eternity, as well as a prayer that the elegist and creator of the continuous line of the poem may be taken into eternity through the efficacy of the saint. As Yeats suggested in "Sailing to Byzantium," eternity is God's artifice, which the *Amra* and other early Iona poems, also the visual art interlace designs, and *pìobaireachd* all imitate.

Continuous line aesthetics has long fascinated Gaelic-speakers and those responding to their cultural artifacts. We find this to be true at the level of sound patterning, perhaps the

---

[19]   T. G. E. Powell, *The Celts* (London: Thames and Hudson, 1963) 124.

basic form of artistic expression, in the creation, development, and dissemination of the *pìobaireachd* or *ceòl mór* form of classical pipe music, which is believed to spring from the song tradition of the *Gàidhealtachd* and was created for occasions of lamenting, gathering, salutes, and battle incitements. As appropriate, the measures are solemn and stately, or wild and stirring, and surely reach far back into the antiquity of the Irish people and their Dal Ríata offspring, the Scots, who settled in Alba, the mainland offshore from Iona, and eventually founded the kingdom of Scotland. In the twelfth century, Gerald of Wales praised the skill of Irish musicians, noting the bewitching charm of their gracenotes around the steady tone of their harps and tympana, and he declared that the Welsh imitated and the Scots excelled their Irish exemplars, but he refers to the Welsh only as playing pipes.[20] The Picts recorded some form of pipes on their standing stones, however, and the bagpipes we know today may have spread to Scotland by the fourteenth century from Europe via England.[21]

Pipers in the Highlands and Western Islands with an awareness of their heritage[22] developed *ceòl mór* ("great

---

[20] Gerald of Wales, *The History and Topography of Ireland*, trans. & intro. John J. O'Meara (Harmondsworth, Middlesex: Penguin Books, 1985) 103-04.

[21] Hugh Cheape, *The Book of the Bagpipe* (Belfast: Appletree, 1999) 25, 42, 62.

[22] The Argyll writer Neil Monroe has evoked best the deep past recalled through the piper's mastery of the art of the *pìobaireachd*: "At the end of his seven years [of apprenticeship] one born to it will stand at the start of knowledge, and leaning a fond ear to the drone, he may have parley with the old folks of old affairs. Playing the tune of the "Fairy Harp," he can hear his forefolks, plaided in skins, towsy-headed and terrible, grunting at the oars and snoring in caves; he has his whittle and club in the "Desperate Battle" ..., where the white-haired sea-rovers are on the shore, and a stain's on the edge of the tide; or, trying his art on Laments, he can stand by the cairn of kings, ken the colour of Fingal's hair, see the moon-glint on the hook of the Druids"—*The Lost Pibroch and other Sheiling Stories* (1896, London: Blackwood, 1935) 3.

music") which, before staff notation was applied to it in the late eighteenth century, was composed in a sung syllabic form known as *canntaireachd*, and so transmitted by oral tradition stemming from the composers and a chain of master teachers. Constituting generally a pentatonic melody, the vowels in *canntaireachd* sound out the principal notes, and the consonants approximate the gracenotes, embellishments in demi-semi-quavers emphasizing the theme. Tradition associates the finest flowering of the form as we know it today with the MacCrimmon family of Skye, hereditary pipers to the MacLeods of Dunvegan from the time of the seventh Chief, Alasdair Crotach (Haddow 1982: 25), who supported Dunbar's patron, James IV, in the late 1400s in asserting control of the Western Isles, and was the first of his line not to be buried on Iona.

On average, a *pìobaireachd* runs fifteen minutes, and the slowly pacing piper begins with a measured statement of the theme called the *ùrlar* ("ground" or "floor"). The piece is then built up with repetitions of three lines of music (triplicity again), embellished with the gracenotes. Alternately soft and hard in emphasis and performed with quick rattles of the fingers on the chanter, they alter the impact of the tune, since the later movements of the *pìobaireachd* build on them, and achieve their distinctive effect through the complication of these embellishments. When the ground has been played, the piper passes to "variations" of the opening three lines of music, playing repetitions of the general pattern set out by the ground, but handling the theme notes in different ways. These variations increase in complexity, giving the piper an opportunity to show the dexterity of fingering technique as he approaches the end of the piece. As this point is reached, the piper stands still to indicate a limit has been reached to the performance. To be sure, the last variation itself does not complete the *pìobaireachd*, since the piper returns to the ground once more, there being no true conclusion to this musical form, as the seeming end is the beginning.

Formally, then, classical pipe music resembles other Celtic
art work, for example, jewelry, in which serpents and other
creatures endlessly swallow tails, and abstract interlace and
knotwork designs present a unity arising from complexity,
features also to be found on the high crosses of Ireland and
Scotland—St. Martin's Cross by the abbey on Iona (which also
depicts triple-pipes), for example, and in illuminated gospels
such as the Books of Durrow and Kells, all of which manifest
the neverending line of eternity.[23] The artists in their different
media work within a tight framework: the nine notes of the
pìobaireachd; the tall upright slab, ponderous arms, and circle
of the stone cross; and the incipit or carpet-page of the
illuminated Gospel. Within these limits, patterns are
interwoven in an ever more complicated and astonishing
fashion until an acme of ingenuity is reached. The final effect
on the listener or viewer is never one of a frenzy of fantasy, but
of the repose and tranquillity of supremely well directed means
achieving a wholly satisfying end: The piper's notes fading into
silence; the carver's reliefs and incisions completing the stone
form confronting space; and script or initials and colored
designs and pictures expanding the mind and imagination
focused on the rectangular page, capturing time and
timelessness.

This combination of a tight framework, decoration through
interweaving, and more and more ingenuity in patterning, so far
described in *píobaireachd* and linked to the other Celtic art
forms, constitutes the central aesthetic and structural principles
of the *Amra*. Further insights emerge from exploring aspects of
section I, which may be considered as the *ùrlar* (ground) of
Dallán's lament for Colum Cille, dwelling on time and eternity:

> *Ní díscéoil duë Néill.*
> *Ní uchtat óenmaige,*

---

[23] MacNeill, *Pìobaireachd* 1976, 30-57; Roderick Cannon, "Highland
Bagpipe" in Derick S. Thomson, ed. *The Companion to Gaelic Scotland*
(Oxford: Blackwell, 1983) 18-21.

mór mairg, mór n-deilm.
Dífulaing riss ré as[-indet]:
Columb cen beith, cen chill.
Co india duí dó, sceo Nere:
in faith Dé de dess Sion suidiath.
Is nú nad mair, ní marthar lenn,
      ní less anma ar suí.
Ar-don—cond íath con-róeter bïu –bath,
ar-don-bath ba ar n-airchend adlicen,
ar-don-bath ba fíadat foídiam;
ar ní-n fissid fris-bered omnu húain,
ar ní-n- tathrith to-sluinned foccul fír,
ar ní-n forcetlaid for-canad túatha
Toí.
hUile bith, ba háe hé:
is crot, cen chéis,
is cell cen abbaid.
[Not newsless is Níall's land.
No slight sigh from one plain,
but great woe, great outcry.
Unbearable the tale this verse tells:
Colum, lifeless, churchless.
How will a fool tell him – even Neire [legendary
      proclaimer] –
the prophet has settled at God's right hand in Sion.
Now he is not, nothing is left to us,
No relief for a soul, our sage,
For he has died to us, the leader of the nation who
      guarded the living,
he has died to us, who was our chief of the needy,
he had died to us, who was our messenger of the
      Lord;
for we do not have the seer who used to keep fears
      from us,

for he does not return to us, he who would explain
      the true Word,

for we do not have the teacher who would teach the
    tribes of the
Tay.
The whole world, it was his:
It is a harp without a key,
it is a church without an abbot.]
    (text from Clancy and Márkus, *Iona* 1997, 104-05)

To be sure, the poet insists on the loss to his people of their
visionary pilgrim leader in the present, whose mission includes
bringing his Gospel message to their Pictish neighbors, but also
introduced is the theme of Columba's gain through settlement
in Sion "at God's right hand," that is to say in eternity, a proud
claim which is continued in the short section III:

He reached the apostles, with hosts, with archangels,
he reached he land where night is not seen,
he reached the land where we expect Moses,
he reached the plain where they know the custom of
    music,
where sages do not die.
The King has cast off His priests' troubles.   (107)

The ensuing poem elaborates in section VII on the theme of
time and eternity through tracing the path of the saint's earthly
pilgrimage and time on the Cross, this sage whose discerning
eye could see what the writers of the Four Gospels taught, and
was a poet himself, as well as founder of a hundred churches,
whose congregations were faithful to him. Colum Cille was a
descendant of *Conn Cétchathach*, the second century A.D. hero
of a hundred battles, as Dallán also tells us (VII.15), so it is
appropriate that this saint's victories in religious foundations
should equal his ancestor's in war:

Discerning the sage who reached the path of the
    four.

He went with two songs to heaven after his cross.
The guardian of a hundred churches, a wave which
    accomplishes
the sacrifice.
A mighty hero, no idolator,
he did not assemble a crooked company
who scattered under instruction.

(VII, l. 1-7, 111)

Dallán's reference to Columba going to heaven with two songs can be linked to the tradition that he was the author of two Latin abecedarian compositions in the Irish *Liber Hymnorum*. One is the learned and allusive, abecedarian *Altus prosator*, a praise-poem addressed to God the creator and celebrating His creation, which one tradition affirms was composed by the saint as he ground corn in the abbey mill for visitors. The second Columban poem is the *Adiutor laborantium*—"Helper of workers," said to have been composed as the saint was on his way to the corn mill on Iona. Such pieces have biblical and Augustinian precedents: Psalm 118 and the Bishop of Hippo's song to a popular rhythm entitled, "A.B.C. against the Donatists."[24]

The *Altus prosator* has a seven-line A introductory stanza, then 22 B to Z six-line stanzas, and a three-line Response coda. The measure is not alliterative, but each line falls into eight-syllable halves, which rhyme together:

> *Altus prosator vetustus dierum et ingenitus*
> *Erat absque origine primordii et crepidine*
> [The High Creator, the Unbegotten Ancient of Days,
> was without origin of beginning, limitless.]

In its account of cosmic history, the poem is based on assiduous study of the Bible, which correlates with the tribute

---

[24] Peter Brown, *Augustine of Hippo: A Biography* (Berkeley: U of California P, 2000) 141.

244 I. S. Ross

Adamnán paid to Columba's devotion to *lectio divina*, contemplative study of the Scriptures, as part of his monk's calling. The poet delights in employing exotic vocabulary with words drawn from Greek mythology such as *Cocytus*, *Scylla* and *Charibdis*, and he invents nouns from verbs, *praesagmen* (prophecy) from *praesagire* (to presage). These features could be related to the "Hisperic Latin" developed by Irish writers of Latin in the seventh century (cf. *Hisperica Famina* and *Lorica Gildae*), who relished complex, even bizarre, vocabulary as a form of showing off. They raided the *Altus prosator* for some of their outlandish wording, but Columba perhaps uses it to register religious awe in the face of God's mysterious power.[25] Perhaps we can find here the rudiments of the aureate style which John Norton-Smith claimed was the invention of Lydgate,[26] but which is represented in Columba's text, achieving rich poetic effects by drawing on the rich sonorities and allusiveness of the liturgy and the Old Latin and Vulgate Bibles.

If Dallán drew attention to Colum Cille's poetic gifts in the seventh section of his poem, he also captured there an essential feature of the saint's career and his era of diffusion of Christianity among the islands of Britain, recognition that the *Evangelium*, the text of the Four Gospels, was the "path" to salvation. It was therefore to be uniquely prized as a focus of devotion and inspiration for leading the truly Christian life. Hence arose the tradition of producing luxury Gospel-books in

---

[25] Jane Stevenson, "*Altus prosator*: A Seventh-Century Hiberno-Latin Poem" (unpub. U of Cambridge Ph.D. thesis, 1985); Clancy and Márkus, *Iona* 1997, 42-43.

[26] John Lydgate, *Poems*, with introduction, notes, and glossary by John Norton-Smith (Oxford: Clarendon, 1966) 192-195; A. J. Aitken, "The Language of Older Scottish Poetry" in J. D. McClure, ed., *Scotland and the Lowland Tongue* (Aberdeen: Aberdeen U P 1983) 18-49; John Corbett, "Aureation Revisited: The Latinate Vocabulary of Dunbar's High and Plain Styles" in Sally Mapstone, ed., *William Dunbar: "The Nobill Poye"': Essays in Honour of Priscilla Bawcutt* (Edinburgh: Tuckwell, 2001) 183-97.

abbeys such as Iona and its daughter-houses, where Columba's inspiration was long paramount: Durrow (County Offaly, Ireland: founded by the saint himself c. 590); Lindesfarne (Holy Island, Northumbria, 653), and Kells (County Meath, 804). Since these books were more than sources of study, and were featured in the liturgy as manifestations of Christ himself as the Word, they came to be written in the Insular half-uncial script found in Colum Cille's *Cathach*, mentioned above, and lovingly embellished in an unparalleled fashion as if with the textiles and precious jewels familiar to aristocrats, drawing on representational and abstract art, involving sacred images drawn from Early Christian usage, based on the Book of Ezekiel in the Old Testament and the Apocalypse in the New, as well as from the storehouse of Celtic, Pictish, and Saxon pre-Christian art, also art inspired by direct contact with nature.

The Durrow Gospels (c. 675) continue an earlier Anglo-Celtic MS tradition of using interlace patterns, animal, plant, and geometric, believed to have an apotropaic function through power to trap evil on the carpet pages, which follow each evangelist's symbol page and face the incipits of each Gospel. The illumination of these symbol and carpet pages, also incipit letters, makes use of traditional Celtic designs, which include cloisonné-type partitions and colors, fluted spirals, dots, and triskele patterns. The designs are dominated by interlace, as on f.192v, the sixth carpet-page immediately following the lion symbol page for St. John. Here we have zoomorphic designs for the first time, in twin panels top and bottom with red and gold serpents biting their tails to form heart patterns, and single side panels of gold and green dragons biting the rear flanks of the next one, with legs fantastically prolonged and looped (Henderson 1987: 15-17, 19-55).

The considerable artistic success of the iconographic program of Durrow is outdone by the Book of Kells, known as the Great Gospels of Colum Cille, because devotion to this saint was believed to have inspired the illuminators. It was probably completed on Iona c. 750, fairly close to the time of the completion of the Lindisfarne Gospels, c.715-20 (Brown, ~~Augustine of Hippo~~ 2000, 7-11), and fifty years or so before Viking plundering raids began, which caused this masterwork to be taken for safety to the new abbey of Kells in the early ninth century. The scale is greater than Durrow's (340 ff. 33 x 25 cm: contrasted with 248 ff. 24.5 x 14.5 cm), which was available in the original or some model form for the Kells designers, who were also conversant with the artistic advance represented by the Lindisfarne Gospels. It is a much more complex production suggesting a well-equipped scriptorium, and its central idea, so George Henderson has argued (*From Durrow to Kells* 1987, 180), seems to be that Christ is the fountainhead of the Holy Spirit and therefore is the source of everlasting life for those brought to believe in Him. As an exegete, Columba, patron and inspirer of the Book of Kells artists, emphasized this interpretation.

It is reinforced in the Gospel-Book through the full-page illuminations, either prefatory in some sense to the content of gospels, or placed in relation to key texts.[27] An outstanding example of the prefatory type is found in the assembly of the Gospel of St. Matthew, doctrinally the most influential one because of its full and clear statement of the mission of church, which Colum Cille served so devotedly. Presented with no recto or verso text, and without an allusion to a gospel narrative, is a full folio, sublime portrait of an enthroned Christ (f.32v), flanked by two peacocks (symbols of immortality), two Gospel writers, Matthew and Mark, pointing to the Book of Life that Christ holds and two winged angels. The tendrils of His hair connect with vines that represent the Eucharist sprouting from twin chalices. Perhaps this is a displaced frontispiece image meant to emphasize the analogy of Gospel-book's liturgical function to that of the heavenly liturgy presented in Revelation (Farr 1997: 145-47).

---

[27] The illuminations can be studied through perusal of *The Book of Kells*, CD ROM: produced by Trinity College, Dublin, and X Communications, 2002.

But the sublime is also found mingled with the earthy in the Book of Kells, as in examples of illuminations connected to text. Thus, St. Luke's Gospel presents a genealogy of Christ (based on 3.23-38), embellished down one margin with zoomorphic, yellow-, green-, red-, blue-colored, jewelled interlace, and at the foot of the right margin a depiction of a red-haired illuminator in green tunic and breeches, whose erect phallus is jauntily visible, a counterpoint, perhaps, to the theme of generation (Cahill 1995: endpaper right). More amazing still is the page (f.34r) devoted to the sacred anagram—Chi, Rho, Iota—which introduces the account of the nativity in Matthew, with the presentation of two words only: *autem generatio*— "now the birth." Whirlpools of energy radiate from the diamond center of the first letter, transfusing the characterizations of the four elements of earth, air, fire, and water. But there are also playful touches suggesting the witty side of Creation and Revelation: Two mice tug at a wafer (perhaps a Host) while two cats with mice on their backs look on; nearby an otter takes a fish, and far above butterflies occupy a niche of the Chi. The animal depictions are realistic, calling to mind those of the hunting scene on the St. Andrews Sarcophagus believed to be of Pictish origin (Fawcett 1999: 5). The decorative work of triskeles and knotwork abounds lavishly, alluding to the burgeoning of plants and spores. The whole seems a hymn to creation and incarnation, with the predominant red and gold of the color scheme suggesting an apogee of aureation.

A further example of an introductory type of image is the Incarnation of Christ represented by a portrait of a haloed, Byzantine-looking Mary, clasping her well-grown Child looking up at his Mother. His left hand touches her head covering and his right hand touches hers in a very human gesture (f.7v). This is found after the canon tables and opposite the synopsis of the Gospel of Matthew, beginning Navitas (f.8r). It is an innovative feature in the Columban Gospel-books, as Mother and Child are depicted Enthroned, reflecting

the elevation of Mary to the status of a Queen and venerated as
the Mother of God.

The Gospels themselves, in which Mary has a relatively
minor role, do not offer much basis for this, and Christ's form
of addressing her as "woman" is detached, to say the least
(John 2:4; 19:25). Pagans in the Middle East and Mediterranean world accustomed to "great mother" and "divine
virgin" cults, however, who became interested in Christianity,
probably pressed for something more than the austere Judaic
monotheism and patriarchalism continuing on from the Old
Testament into the New. By the middle of the second century
there began to appear Infancy Gospels, such as the Pseudo-
Matthew and Book of James, containing narratives of the birth,
infancy, youth, and high status of Mary, linked to veneration of
her as the Virgin Mother of God, in whose womb human nature
and the divine Logos were unified. In Egypt she came to be
worshipped as *Theotokos* (bearer of God), a title used by
Origen in the third century. The apocryphal narratives about her
life inspired the establishment first in the Eastern Empire, and
later in the West, of feasts in her honor, and the creation of
many mosaics and paintings of Mary in her expanded role,
associated with a Mariology assigning her imperial status as
Queen of Heaven identified with divine Wisdom. As well, she
was believed to have extensive powers as an intercessor, whose
womanly sympathy made her accessible to repentant sinners in
a way God the Father and the Son were not.[28]

The route that brought Marian devotion and image-making
to Ireland and Iona, also the Columban abbey of Kells, is not
known exactly, but they probably came via Rome. Irish visitors
to Rome, or visitors from Rome in Ireland or Iona, with eyes
for depictions of Mary might well have seen and described the
Pantheon, transferred to Pope Boniface IV by the Emperor

---

[28] Yrjö Hirn, *The Sacred Shrine: A Study of the Poetry and Art of the
Catholic Shrine* (Boston: Beacon, 1957) II. x, The Dogma of Mary; F.P.
Pickering, *Literature & Art in the Middle Ages* (London: Macmillan,
1970) 32-33.

Phocas in 609, then dedicated to the Holy Mother of God and All Martyrs (Henderson 1987: 10) or, among other Roman churches, SS. Maria Maggiore (fifth century) and Maria Antiqua (sixth century), where Byzantine-type mosaic and painting depictions evoke a regal Mother of God, especially the latter church's Maria Regina.[29] Her full, rounded face with pronounced eyebrows and attendant angel in that painting could be a memory or tradition behind the Virgin and Child portrait in the *Book of Kells*.

On Iona, Columba's kinsman and, in time, successor as abbot, Adomnán, interested himself in the plight of women in Irish society, and sought to win protection for them through as code of law: *Cáin Adomnáin* (earlier the "Law of Innocents"), which called on priests and laity to protect women, children, and churches from warfare. In part, Adamnán was inspired in this work by Columba himself, whom he records as punishing a murderer of a girl in his presence by killing him with a prayer, and forcing a druid to free a woman he had imprisoned. Carol Farr has suggested (*Book of Kells* 1997, 145) that the Virgin and Child portrait may have been included in the Book of Kells because the church for which it was produced, which we take to be the abbey of Iona, was dedicated to the Virgin, and Adamnán seems to have been responding to the veneration of the Virgin Mary established in this abbey. Subsequent commentary on the *Cáin* claimed the Holy Mother called on him to promulgate it, and that he did this for her sake. Beyond the Book of Kells, there is evidence of a Marian cult on Iona in the form of the image of the Mother and Child carved on the eighth century cross of St. Oran, which parallels the Book of Kells's depiction of flanking angels, a feature also found on the Kildalton Cross in Argyll. In Dunbar's time, when the seat of the bishop of Argyll was transferred from Lismore to the Benedictine abbey on Iona in 1507, the newly created cathedral was dedicated to St Mary.

---

[29] Richard Krautheimer, *Rome: Profile of a City, 312-1308* (Princeton U P, 1980) 97.

Above all, the theme of devotion to the Virgin Mary, still rare in the time of the Columban *familia*, is sustained in the choral hymn, *Cantemus in omni die*, by the Iona monk, Cú Chuimne ("Hound of Memory"), who died in 747 (Clancy and Markús, *Iona* 1997, 177-92). This hymn seems designed to be sung, quatrain by quatrain, by a monastic community arranged in two lines facing each other: *bis per chorum hinc et inde* ("in twofold chorus from side to side"—Stanza 2). Deliberate obscurity of the kind found in the vocabulary of the *Altus prosator* is avoided, and ordinary Church Latin provides the stock of trisyllabic rhyming words for the couplets of each stanza. A rhyming and assonantal technique, called *aicill* and found in Irish poetry from the eighth century on, is used to bind the third line's ending to the beginning or middle of the fourth one. The ideas and imagery in the poem spring from the Mariology, delighting in witty figural reversals, developed in the immediate postapostolic age, emphasizing the fact that a human mother, Mary, became the *Theotokos*, and that the miracle of the Incarnation is paramount, a lesson represented by the Mary and Son illustration of the Book of Kells:

> *Mari de tribu Iudae*
> *summi mater Domini*
> *oportunam dedit curam*
> *egrotanti homini*
> [Mary of the tribe of Judah,
> mother of the Most High lord Lord,
> gave fitting care
> to languishing mankind. — Stanza 3]
> ...

> *Per mulierem et lignum*
> *Mundus prius periit*
> *Per mulieris virtutem*
> *Ad salutem ediit.*

[By a woman and a tree
the world first perished;
by the power (virtue) of a woman
it has returned to salvation. — Stanza 7][30]

In this case, we find that the religious sensibility reflected in the Irish poet's hymn intended for performance by an assembly of monks is comparable to that prompting the aureation found in Dunbar's "Ballat of Our Lady." Each poem is praising the virtues and efficacy of the Virgin as bearer of the Word, and thus transmitter of the hope of salvation, also mediator and intercessor. To express this praise fittingly, the structural organization of interlinked assonance, alliteration, and rhyme in quatrain units chosen in each case is similar, though Dunbar triples these units for each of his seven stanzas, and his rhetoric is more highly charged. Dunbar's seven stanzas are constructed on the module a5b6, around the repeated Angelic Salutation: *Ave, Maria, gracia plena*, with key lines embellished with triple internal rhymes and supplementary alliteration. In his sevenfold structure, Dunbar dwells on the glory and grace of the maid and mother who is the "qwene of hevyne" (1.52), worthy of the highest honor as "Alphais habitakle" (1.14). While he ends with an allusion to the Crucifixion and the human ransom bought by Christ's blood, the main stress of the poem is on the mystery of the Incarnation as a victory.

Cú Chuimne's apparently simple structure also has its secrets of numerology, which indicate he exercises firmer doctrinal control over his materials than Dunbar. Of its thirteen stanzas, seven are devoted elliptically to Mary's place in divine history: who she is by descent and what was announced to her by Gabriel concerning the birth of Christ the Word; also how firm her faith was and how the Fall brought about by the weakness of a woman, Eve, coveting the fruit of the Tree of Knowledge, was negated by the power of the New Eve, who

---

[30]   Clancy and Markús, *Iona* 1997, 182-185.

returned the world to salvation by bearing the Son prepared to ascend the fatal Tree of the Cross. The second group of six stanzas is devoted first to the paradoxes of the Incarnation whereby Mary is *Theotokos*: A mother gave birth to her Father in the person of the Son, thus a creature sprang from the Creator; and she conceived a pearl for which Christians give up all they possess on earth, so gaining what is priceless, life everlasting. The final three stanzas replace narration and explanation with exhortation and prayer: Let us arm ourselves with faith to win Mary's intercession; we pray that we may escape hellfire through the redemption afforded by her merits; and let us call on the name of Christ the Word, her Son, that we may be inscribed in the Book of Life.

Thinking of the aesthetic principles present in both poems, we notice that both have tight frameworks: a chain of stanzas whose line sequences are closely tied together through alliteration, rhyme, and assonance. Within each framework, there are to be found variations on the profound theme of Incarnation of great complexity achieved though intricacy of symbolic and doctrinal allusion. These are also present features of the illuminated Gospel books to which attention has been called. Dunbar lovingly embellishes his praise of the Queen of Heaven with star and flower and songbird imagery, like the Kells illuminators of the carpet and apostle pages, also the one devoted to the Holy Mother and Child, who drew on abstract and representational designs in the arts of jewelry, weaving, and sculpture to figure the multiplicity of Creation and the centrality of the design of history in which the Fall of humanity is inevitably overcome by the Incarnation and the redemption of the Crucifixion.

The early Iona poem is specifically a hymn, a song of praise to Mary, and Dunbar's late medieval one is a "Ballat," a salute to the Virgin Mother: Each has its features of aureation calling upon the sonorities of liturgical Latin and, in the case of Cú Chuimne's poem, reflecting Gaelic learned poetry while Dunbar incorporates lexical and metrical elements from the

French *grand rhétoriqueurs*, as well as the advanced English poetry of Chaucer and Lydgate.[31]

Each poem in its own way is a song and therefore aspires to the condition of music whose archetype is the "new song before the throne" of Revelation, 14.3. Perhaps the best correlative for the musical effects of the poets is classical *ceòl mór*, for example, *Pìobaireachd Dhomhnuill Duibh* ("Black Donald's March"), composed by Iain Dubh MacCrimmon (1731-1822). This may have been the "Camerons" Gathering' which Byron tells us was heard in Brussels on the eve of Waterloo (*Child Harold*, III, xxvi; Lorimer 1964b). The poet characterizes the "war-note" as "wild and high," but the grave *ùrlar* opening the commemoration of the eponymous ancestor of the Cameron Chiefs of Locheil is strictly disciplined, and provides the framework for beautifully paced and complex variations exemplifying the aesthetic principle of interlace.[32]

The listener is thereby moved, like the reader of the early Iona

---

[31]   Alastair A. MacDonald, "Religious Poetry in Middle Scots" in R. D. S. Jack (ed.) *The History of Scottish Literature*, vol. 1, *Origins to 1660, Medieval and Renaissance* (Aberdeen U P, 1988) 97; Priscilla Bawcutt, *Dunbar the Makar* (Oxford: Clarendon, 1992) 354-57; Douglas Gray, "'Hale, Sterne Superne' and its Literary Background" in Mapstone, ed. (2001): 198-210.

[32]   The aesthetic principle of interlace in pipe music was illustrated in a CD made for me by Piper Edward McIlwaine, Vancouver, British Columbia. He plays the *pìobaireachd*, "Black Donald's March," which he learned from Andrew Wright, currently a senior piping judge in Scotland, who is considered an authority on *ceòl mór*. The extract featured the transition from Variation One Singing to Doubling, which Mr. McIlwaine identified as a "prime example of interlacing." A note he wrote on July 9, 2002 stated: "the third line of the Singling (except for the final cadence) matches the Doubling in that it replaces the Low A connectors with High A's. Also the notes preceding the High A are not stressed and therefore do not have the effect of a cadence. Similar interlacing is found in the Singling to Doubling transitions of the *Leumuath*, *Taorluath*, and *Crumluath* variations." Mr. McIlwaine also recorded on the same CD an example his *canntaireachd* version of the "March," which is based on the Nether Lorne system.

poetry, inspired by the example of Colum Cille, also the viewer of the Book of Kells and Celtic and Pictish sculpture of that long-distant era, as well as the student of Dunbar, to contemplate life and death, time and timelessness. Moreover, all these works through their combination of symmetrical and asymmetrical components, their deft articulation of similar aesthetic principles, may be seen, as Michelle Brown has written of the illuminated pages of the Lindisfarne Gospels, as representing a "quest for the understanding, emulation, and transmission of the divine rule of time, space, and substance" (*Lindisfarne Gospels* 2003, 297).

.

WILLIAM SHAKESPEARE (1564-1616):
A LIFE AND LITERARY CAREER IN
TROUBLED TIMES

Hildegard Hammerschmidt-Hummel

ABSTRACT

According to the generally accepted "Konfessionalisierungsthese," established in recent historical research, religion played the most important part in the life of each individual in early modern European history. This also applies to the famous English dramatist William Shakespeare. Based on the author's new findings, as presented in her book *William Shakespeare. His Time—His Life—His Work* (2003), this article tries to throw light on a hitherto much neglected scenario: the new legal position created by Elizabeth I's anti-Catholic legislation and its devastating consequences for her Catholic subjects. The English Catholics in Shakespeare's time were not only deprived of their rights, ostracized, criminalized, and persecuted, but also had to endure draconic punishment. On the basis of numerous new sources or ones newly made accessible, it is demonstrated that Shakespeare was born into a Catholic environment, that his parents and relatives, teachers and friends, his first employer and his literary patron were all adherents of the old faith. Just like hundreds of young English Catholics, who were educated at the new Catholic colleges abroad because Conscience prevented them from taking the compulsory Oath of Supremacy at Oxford or Cambridge, the poet, too, seems to have acquired a sound basic education in the humanities on the Continent. According to new sources, Shakespeare also played a significant role in the Catholic underground and—during the lost years—visited Rome several times. As a successful playwright in London he placed his hopes in the politically powerful Earl of Essex, as did, in fact, the whole Catholic English population. For Essex stood for a more tolerant religious policy. After the failure of the Essex rebellion, when the earl was condemned to death and executed, the dramatist wrote *The Phoenix and the Turtle* and *Hamlet*. Was Shakespeare more deeply involved in the dramatic political events at the close of the Elizabethan era than could hitherto be assumed? And is it fair to say that the devastating blow of Essex's tragic fate accounts for the fact that Shakespeare, all of a sudden, ceased writing comedies and turned to tragedy? There is circumstantial as well as hard evidence for the assumption that the poet, after he had concluded his brilliant literary career in London, made a remarkable contribution to the survival of the old religion. In the article some of the plays are briefly reviewed for explicit references to Catholic rites and concepts. Thus the poet's intimate knowledge of this culture comes to light. However, the author makes it quite clear that Shakespeare's works can in no way be "reduced" to a Catholic factional view. The poet's universal genius is fully recognized. But if viewed against the religious, political and personal background, described above, the enigmas and inconsistencies in Shakespeare's life, his evasiveness as well as the whole development of his literary activities, can be more fully understood.

In the 1580s a contemporary French observer sharply criticized the change in religion in the neighbouring country of England, decreed by law, and gave thanks to his creator that he himself—by the grace of God—had been enabled to adhere to the old forms of belief without fear and struggle of conscience. "Nothing," he stated, "is more subject unto a continuall agitation then the laws. I have, since I was borne, seene those of our neighbours, the Englishmen, changed and re-changed three or foure times, not only in politike subjects, which is that some will dispense of constancy, but in the most important subject that possibly can be, that is to say, in religion: whereof I am so much the more ashamed, because it is a nation with which my countriemen have heretofore had so inward and familar acquaintance ... "[1] These were the words of no less a person than Michel de Montaigne (1532-92). The French philosopher was afraid the adherents of the old religion might one day appear as offenders against earthly and divine majesty,[2] and asks: "What will Philosophie then say to us in this necessity? That we follow the lawes of our country, that is to

---

[1] Michel de Montaigne, "An Apologie of Raymond Sebond" in *Montaigne's Essays:* Renascence Editions, Book II. E-text [www.uoregon.edu/rbear/montaigne/2xii.htm], provided by Ben R. Schneider, Lawrence University, Wisconsin, © 1998 The University of Oregon [101].

[2] Cf. Montaigne, "An Apologie of Raymond Sebond" 1998, 102.

say, this waveing sea of a peoples or of a Princes opinions, which shall paint me forth justice with as many colours, and reforme the same into as many visages as there are changes and alterations of passions in them." His answer: "I cannot have my judgement so flexible. What goodnesse is that which but yesterday I saw in credit and esteeme, and to morrow to have lost all reputation … ?"[3] This was also the attitude maintained in England by all steadfast Catholics from Thomas More and Bishop Fisher on—including, as will be shown here—William Shakespeare.

After the renewed change in religion imposed under Elizabeth I (1533-1603), particularly after the monarch had been excommunicated in 1570 by the papal bull of Pius V (*Regnans in Excelsis*), and after the beginning of the large-scale Jesuit mission in the country (from 1580), followed by rigid anti-Catholic legislation with draconian penalties for recusants,[4] English Catholics who had remained true to their old faith or had been reconverted to it suffered not only social discrimination and loss of civil rights but often, as a consequence of the immense fines imposed on them, economic ruin and loss of freedom as well. Moreover, as their loyalty to Rome was also interpreted as loyalty to a foreign power, many recusants were accused of high treason, convicted, and executed. Many adherents of the old religion therefore sought salvation in flight, went underground or into exile, and offered active or passive resistance.

If the frightening scenario created by the politics of religion in the Elizabethan and Jacobean ages is hardly known today, then this is due largely to the fact that in the writings of mainstream English historians it was ignored, treated only marginally or played down. It is thus necessary to re-examine the textual and pictorial sources (especially those previously overlooked or not previously made accessible), to recall the

---

3   Montaigne, "An Apologie of Raymond Sebond" 1998, 102.
4   Those who rejected the Anglican divine service and especially the sacrament of Holy Communion.

most important historical dates and facts leading up to this age that so decisively shaped the subsequent course of English history and to throw light on hitherto neglected aspects of the age of Shakespeare.

In 1527 Henry VIII (1491-1547), the celebrated defender of the Catholic faith ("Defensor fidei"), commenced proceedings for divorce from Catherine of Aragon (1485-1536), to which Rome refused its consent. The great show trial of the queen took place at Blackfriars convent in London from May 31, to July 23, 1529.[5] In that year Cardinal Thomas Wolsey (?1472-1530), lord chancellor of England, was stripped of his offices. His successor, Sir Thomas More (1477 or 1478-1535) resigned in 1532 on account of the king's plans for a state church and in reaction to the submission of the English clergy. On July 11, 1531 the king separated from Catherine of Aragon without being divorced and married Anne Boleyn (?1507-1536) in secret on January 25, 1533. The new archbishop of Canterbury, Thomas Cranmer (1489-1556), formerly the king's chaplain, declared the king's first marriage null and void, on his own authority, and pronounced his second valid. In the eyes of the Roman Catholic Church, Elizabeth, the daughter born to Henry and Anne Boleyn on September 7, 1533, was illegitimate. By the Act of Supremacy (1535) the king became supreme head of the Church of England. Thomas More, who refused to take the Oath of Supremacy, was accused, condemned to death, and executed.

When Henry VIII died in 1547, his nine-year-old son Edward (1537-53) became king of England. The country was

---

[5] Eighty years later, in the same place—it was the Great Hall of Blackfriars, which now housed the famous Blackfriars Theater of his theatrical company the King's Men—Shakespeare staged the romance *The Winter's Tale*, with its trial of a wrongly accused queen, whose suffering is strongly reminiscent of that of Catherine of Aragon. Cf. Hildegard Hammerschmidt-Hummel, *William Shakespeare. Seine Zeit—sein Leben—sein Werk* (Mainz: Zabern, 2003) 258. All further references: *William Shakespeare* 2003.

ruled by a protector. In 1552 the Act of Uniformity of 1549 came into force again. Shortly before his death in 1553 Edward VI conferred on Stratford-upon-Avon the status of a royal borough, with a mayor ("Bailiff") and fourteen councillors ("aldermen"). In the same year he granted the town the privilege of (re)founding a grammar school. It was here that William Shakespeare, the son of John Shakespeare (?1530-1601), who in 1568 had become high bailiff of Stratford and a justice of the peace, must have received a well-grounded schooling.[6]

When Edward VI died in 1553, his half-sister Mary (1516-58), a Roman Catholic, succeeded to the throne. She returned the country to Catholicism and in 1554 married Philip of Spain (1527-98). In the following year (1555) the bloody persecutions of Protestants began.

On November 6, 1558 Mary acknowledged her half-sister Elizabeth as her successor—and died eleven days later. The last Catholic archbishop of Canterbury, Cardinal Reginald Pole (1500-58) died the same day. Of a total of twenty-seven dioceses ten were already vacant. Only one of seventeen Catholic bishops in office converted to the new faith, two died, two others went into exile, and the fate of one of their colleagues is not known.

Eleven bishops were arrested and died in prison. They were honoured as martyrs by English Catholics of their day.[7] There is a picture painted about ten years after Elizabeth's accession that presents a satirical view of the Roman church. It depicts Henry VIII on his deathbed, pointing to his son and successor, Edward VI, who will triumph over Rome.[8]

---

[6]   Cf. Hammerschmidt-Hummel, *William Shakespeare* 2003, 38ff.

[7]   Cf. Michael Davies, "Die Zerstörung des englischen Katholizismus durch die anglikanische Liturgiereform," *Una Voce Korrespondenz* (March/April, 2002): 89-112, 94-95.

[8]   A color reproduction of this picture, painted around 1568-71 by an unknown artist and now at the National Portrait Gallery in London—

Elizabeth I had herself crowned by a Catholic bishop in Westminster Abbey, wearing her deceased half-sister's coronation robe.[9] Both these moves were presumably intended to mislead the Catholic population. The queen did not attend the Catholic mass associated with the coronation ceremonies. She concealed her religious policy from the people. In the crisis year of 1585,[10] when war broke out with Spain, English Catholics met in Rome to work out strategies for winning England back to the bosom of the Roman Church—and Shakespeare disappeared for seven years, also visiting Rome that year—the queen was depicted with a crowned ermine near her heart.[11] This creature had the same curving form as the ermine fur in the coronation portrait. The suggestive picture was evidently commissioned by a Catholic. The Catholic population felt they had been deceived and sucked dry by their ruler. Rigorous anti-Catholic legislation that bore the hallmark of William Cecil (1520-98), Elizabeth's chief minister and closest adviser, had brought it home to them in bitter fashion that right from the start it had been the new queen's aim to eradicate Catholicism within her lifetime.[12] In 1588, a year after the execution of Mary Stuart (1542-87), on whom the hopes of English Catholics had centered, the monarch found herself exposed to attack from the Spanish Armada, initiated by

---

"Allegory of the Reformation" (reg. no. 4165)—can be found in Hammerschmidt-Hummel, *William Shakespeare*, 2003, 21, fig. 24.

[9] The coronation portrait in the National Portrait Gallery, London (reg. no. 5175) is reproduced in colour in Hammerschmidt-Hummel, *William Shakespeare* 2003, 18, fig. 21.

[10] Cf. "Motive für den Weggang von Stratford (1585)" ["Motives for leaving Stratford (1585)"], in Hildegard Hammerschmidt-Hummel, *Die verborgene Existenz des William Shakespeare. Dichter und Rebell im katholischen Untergrund* (Freiburg i. Br., 2001) 103-08. All further references: *Die verborgene Existenz* 2001.

[11] The picture of the ruler with the ermine is at Hatfield House. It is reproduced in colour in Hammerschmidt-Hummel, *William Shakespeare* 2003, 20, fig. 23.

[12] Cf. J. J. Dwyer, *The Reformation in England* (London, 1962) 21.

English Catholics in exile. After her victory, the so-called Armada portrait was painted, embodying the global claims of the monarch with positive symbols. The queen's right hand is resting on a globe.[13] A year later—presumably at the instigation of her Catholic subjects—another picture of the queen came into circulation, this time with negative symbols dominating, such as the crown that has slipped to one side.[14]

In the first year of her reign, Elizabeth re-established the break with Rome and implemented the Acts of Supremacy and Uniformity again. English Catholics resisted this imposed change in religion. Many of them attended Protestant churches regularly just as a pretense, but continued to practice their old faith in secret. Their priests were mainly disguised as servants. Their conflicts of conscience became stronger after the excommunication of the monarch (1570), and they now stayed away from the Anglican services altogether.[15]

Concerned that Catholicism might die out, William Allen (1532-94),[16] who had formerly taught at Oxford University, founded a Catholic college at Douai in Flanders (now France)

---

[13] This picture, painted by George Gower 1588, is exhibited at Woburn Abbey (inv. no. 1383). It is reproduced in colour in Hammerschmidt-Hummel, *William Shakespeare* 2003, 121, fig. 96.

[14] The copperplate engraving "Eliza, Trivmphans" (1589) by William Roger is reproduced in Hammerschmidt-Hummel, *William Shakespeare* 2003, 122, fig. 97.

[15] According to the Elizabethan parliamentary records: "... most of the *Papists* of *England* did come to our Church[?es] and heard Divine Service ordinarily, till the eleventh Year of the Queen, when the Bull of Pope *Pius Quintus* enforced not only their wilful and obstinate separation, but drew on and necessitated many of those Laws which were afterwards made against them, *an.* 13. *an.* 23. & *an.* 27 *Reg. Eliz.*" *The Journals of all the Parliaments During the Reign of Queen Elizabeth, Both of the House of Lords and House of Commons.* Collected by Sir Simonds D'Ewes. Rev. and publ. by Paul Bowes (London, 1682; Shannon: Irish U P, 1973) 30.

[16] A portrait of William Allen is in the Venerabili Collegio Inglese (Venerable English College) in Rome. It is reproduced in color in Hammerschmidt-Hummel, *William Shakespeare*, 2003, 24, fig. 29.

in 1568—with assistance from the Spanish king. The so-called Collegium Anglicum, which was based at Rheims from 1578 to 1593 on account of the turmoil of war, was not a Jesuit college, as has often been mistakenly assumed, but the training was oriented to the concepts of the Jesuits with theater and rhetoric thus occupying a prominent place. In a letter to Dr. Vendeville,[17] a friend of the Milan cardinal, Carlo Borromeo (1538-84), Allen gave a detailed account of the aims originally associated with the founding of the college:

> … our first purpose was to establish a college in which our countrymen who were scattered abroad in different places might live and study together more profitably than apart. Our next intention was to secure for the college an unbroken and enduring existence by means of a constant succession of students coming and leaving; for we feared that, if the schism should last much longer, owing to the death of the few who at its beginning had been cast out of the English universities for the faith, no seed would be left hereafter for the restoration of religion, and that heresy would thus obtain a perpetual and peaceful possession of the realm, there being no one to make reclamation, even though an opportunity should offer at the death of the Queen or otherwise. For we thought it would be an excellent thing to have men of learning always ready outside the realm to restore religion when the proper moment should arrive, although it seemed hopeless to attempt anything while the heretics were masters there.[18]

---

[17]   Vendeville was professor of canonical law at the University of Douai. After the death of his wife he became a priest and later bishop of Tournai.

[18]   "Literae D. Alani ad D. Vendevillium, 1578 or 80; MS. English College, Rome." Quoted in Thomas Francis Knox, "Historical Introduction," *The First and Second Diaries of the English College, Douay, and an*

Considerable numbers of young English Catholics from the nobility and the bourgeoisie, who were excluded from studying at Oxford or Cambridge because conscience prevented them taking the Oath of Supremacy, availed themselves of this opportunity and acquired a sound basic education in the humanities at Douai or Rheims. Those who were suitably gifted and felt called to do so could go on to study for the priesthood. As a rule their training began at the age of thirteen or fourteen.[19] In 1579, eleven years after the founding of the Collegium Anglicum, another English college was founded at Rome, with Allen's help, and still exists today. There was a lively exchange between the two institutions. The pupils at Douai/Rheims felt magically attracted to Rome and desired nothing more avidly than to be sent there.

At Allen's college—which enjoyed immense popularity and, despite the threat of severe penalties, succeeded in attracting a large and ever-increasing influx of students—teaching and learning were free of compulsion.[20] At the beginning of the seventeenth century the capacity of the old college building at Douai was already proving inadequate. Thus in 1609 a large and imposing hall was built in the Flemish baroque style, which still exists today.[21] The priests trained at Douai went into the English mission and performed their pastoral duties in the underground. They were hidden in houses belonging to the

---

Appendix of Unpublished Documents, ed. by Fathers of the Congregation of the London Oratory, with an Historical Introduction by Th. F. Knox (London, 1878) xxvi.

[19] Cf. Hammerschmidt-Hummel, *Die verborgene Existenz* 2001, 71ff.

[20] Cf. Allen to Mr. Hopkins on April 5, 1579, quoted in Dodd, *The Church History of England* II, 242. Former pupils and teachers at the college confirm that this picture is correct. Thomas Worthington, for instance, later a president of the college, who had studied under Allen, wrote: "There was no need of any written law to keep the members in discipline." Quoted in Knox, "Historical Introduction" 1878, lxxix.

[21] Cf. Hammerschmidt-Hummel, *William Shakespeare* 2003, 43, fig. 43.

English landed gentry, where secret chapels and chambers had been built.[22]

The Collegium Anglicum at Douai/Rheims and the English College at Rome were particularly disliked by the English government. In 1571, the year after Elizabeth had been excommunicated, the English parliament passed severe penal laws against English Catholics.[23] Anyone who now questioned the queen's right to the English throne was committing high treason. In 1577 Cuthbert Mayne (trained at Douai) became the first Catholic priest to be executed as a result of this legislation. That same year John Shakespeare, the highly respected and popular Stratford alderman and former mayor, refused to perform the duties of his office, without giving any reasons, and failed to attend the meetings of Stratford town council ("corporation"). He was evidently no longer prepared to act as the extended arm of the government at the local level. John Shakespeare's office was not filled again until 1586. Only once in these nine years, on September 5, 1582, did he break his resolution and attend a council meeting—however, this was obviously only to vote for his friend John Sadler, who was standing for the post of mayor. That year his son William returned to Stratford to marry and start a family.[24]

A number of prominent English Catholics, among them the rich recusant Sir Thomas de Hoghton (I) (d. 1580) of Lancashire, had already gone into exile in the first decade of Elizabeth's reign. Many were to follow them. The queen and her privy council were annoyed, but could not stop them "voting with their feet." Before fleeing to Flanders, Sir Thomas

---

[22] As at Baddesley Clinton in Warwickshire, reproduced in Hammerschmidt-Hummel, *William Shakespeare* 2003, 26, fig. 32.

[23] See "A Journal of the Proceedings of the House of Commons, in the Parliament holden at Westminster, An. 13 Reg. Eliz. A. D. 1571, which began there on Monday the 2nd day of April, and then and there continued until the Dissolution thereof on Tuesday the 29th day of May ensuing," *The Journals of all the Parliaments During the Reign of Queen Elizabeth*, 155-90.

[24] Cf. Hammerschmidt-Hummel, *William Shakespeare* 2003, 29-30.

had fortified Hoghton Tower, his family seat, and left his extensive property to his brothers, who provided him with financial aid through secret channels. He was a close friend and patron of William Allen and had helped with the founding of the Collegium Anglicum. Allen had been present at the celebrations marking the completion of Sir Thomas's rebuilding of Hoghton Tower, and had been one of the first to have the opportunity to inspect the extensive estate with its impressive gatehouse. The gatehouse and the tower of the building had been particularly strongly fortified.[25] Sir Thomas also supported Allen's college financially. In his will he set aside £100 for the purpose. It seems very likely that William Allen is identical with the teacher of the same name who had left Oxford University for exile at Louvain but had lived secretly in England from 1562 to 1565. For between 1562 and 1564 a teacher named William Allen was employed illegally and with interruptions at the grammar school at Stratford, receiving a salary from the town treasurer, John Shakespeare that was not entered in the offical accounts.[26] On the plaque in the historic classroom at Stratford Grammar School where the names of the schoolmasters are recorded, the Christian name of this teacher is omitted, although it is mentioned in the sources.[27]

As pointed out before, the large-scale Jesuit mission in England began in 1580 in the underground, under the leadership of Fathers Edmund Campion (1540-81) and Robert Parsons (1546-1610).[28] Fifty-one priests had set off from Rome in the spring. Their leaders had been strictly forbidden by the pope to make political statements or engage in political activities. In Milan, Campion and Parsons received from

[25] Cf. E. A. J. Honigmann, *Shakespeare: The "Lost Years"* (Dover: Manchester U P, 1998) 8.
[26] Cf. Hammerschmidt-Hummel, *William Shakespeare*, 2003, 31.
[27] Cf. Hammerschmidt-Hummel, *William Shakespeare*, 2003, 39, fig. 40.
[28] These details are based on Hammerschmidt-Hummel, *Die verborgene Existenz* 2001, 29-36.

Cardinal Carlo Borromeo in person the so-called "Borromeo testaments," prefabricated texts in which Catholics could profess their faith in writing. The testaments were subsequently in great demand in England.[29] John Shakespeare was among those in possession of a Borromeo testament.[30]

The group were given an enthusiastic reception at Allen's college at Rheims in May 1580, and at the beginning of June travelled incognito to London, where they were met by members of the Catholic Association, also founded at Rome early in 1580. The Catholic Association was a secret society composed of young, often aristocratic, Catholics, among them the grandson of Sir Thomas More. Its members had the task of accompanying the priests and protecting them, and preparing for them to be received in the houses of the Catholic landed gentry, but they were also to talk to young people and recommend them to attend the Catholic colleges on the continent.[31]

The mission was conducted by outstanding talents. Campion had taught at Oxford some years earlier and was regarded as the Cicero of England. The queen herself had admired him at Oxford.[32] Now the eloquent preacher was reconverting large numbers of people to Catholicism.

Campion also preached at Hoghton Tower, where Alexander de Hoghton (d. 1581), Shakespeare's first employer, was the head of the family. De Hoghton's will of 1581 is a particularly important source for a biography of Shakespeare and one in

---

[29] The head of the English seminary in France wrote to Rome in 1581: "Father Robert [Parsons] wants three or four thousand or more of the *Testaments*, for many persons desire to have them." Quoted in J. H. de Groot in *The Shakespeares and "The Old Faith"* (New York: King's Crown Press, 1946) 88.

[30] Cf. Hammerschmidt-Hummel, *William Shakespeare*, 2003, 35-36.

[31] Cf. Chap. II.3 "George Gilbert: Gründer der Catholic Association und Mäzen der englischen Missionsbewegung" ["George Gilbert: Founder of the Catholic Association and Patron of the English Mission"] in Hammerschmidt-Hummel, *Die verborgene Existenz* 2001, 44-48.

[32] Cf. Hammerschmidt-Hummel, *Die verborgene Existenz* 2001, 30.

which crucial features have hitherto been overlooked. If one accepts that in this last will and testament the frequent references to "players" do not signify actors but priests, then "play clothes" are chasubles and "instruments belonging to musics" are liturgical instruments, items required for the clandestine saying of mass ("musics")—chalices, patens etc. These are evidently code words of the Catholic underground. It was necessary for the testator, Alexander de Hoghton—a recusant, brother of the famous Catholic Sir Thomas de Hoghton, who lived in exile, and Edmund Campion's host—to be so cautious and solicitous because immediately after the beginning of the Jesuit movement to restore Catholicism priests were exposed to bloody persecution, and giving them shelter and succour was illegal and subject to severe penalties.[33]

This will contains another passage whose real significance has not previously been realized. Following on from the request that his players (i.e. priests) be taken over, Alexander de Hoghton desires his friend Sir Thomas Hesketh "most heartily … to be friendly unto Fulk Gillom & William Shakeshafte now dwelling with me & either to take them unto his service or else to help them to some good master, as my trust is he will."[34] This shows how the procurement of employment functioned in the network of Elizabethan crypto-Catholicism. The supposition that "William Shakeshafte" was a reference to no other than William Shakespeare was convincingly substantiated by the English Shakespeare scholar E. A. J. Honigmann in *Shakespeare. The "Lost Years"* (1985, repr. 1998). The name Shakeshafte had already been used by William's grandfather. Honigmann was the first to trace the tradition passed down orally in the family from generation to generation according to

---

[33] Cf. Hammerschmidt-Hummel, *William Shakespeare*, 2003, 58. See also Hammerschmidt-Hummel, *Die verborgene Existenz*, 2001, 91-99.
[34] Cf. Honigmann, *Shakespeare. The "Lost Years"* 1998, 136.

which Shakespeare had lived with the de Hoghtons for two years as a young man.[35]

According to the antiquary and biographer John Aubrey (1626-97), Shakespeare "had been in his younger yeares a schoolmaster in the countrey."[36] As a rule, Aubrey's knowledge was obtained from reliable sources. In the case of Shakespeare he was able to draw on information from the actor William Beeston (?1606-1682), whose father, Christopher Beeston (d. 1638), had been a member of Shakespeare's theater company.

Gillom and Shakeshafte alias Shakespeare were not servants but superior staff, evidently Catholic tutors or private teachers in the testator's household. This is also Honigmann's view. It was customary, in the circles of the Catholic English gentry of that time, to employ private and unlicensed Catholic teachers. This is also in line with Aubrey's "schoolmaster" thesis.

The two young men were also high-ranking officials in a secret society and were paid for their services for life.[37] The organization in question was evidently the Catholic Association, which had—as has already been mentioned—been founded in the summer of 1580. At Hoghton Tower its members must have protected, among others, the Jesuit priest Edmund Campion and his companions. As was first proved in

---

[35] Honigmann, *Shakespeare: The "Lost Years"* 1998, 28-30. Sir Bernard de Hoghton, the head of the family, confirmed this tradition to the author in November 2002.

[36] Cf. "William Shakespeare," *Aubrey's Brief Lives*. Ed. with the Original Manuscripts and with an Introduction by Oliver Lawson Dick [1949]. (Harmondsworth: Penguin, repr. 1978) 437-38, 438.

[37] These research findings were published in chap. C.II of my book *Die verborgene Existenz*, 2001: "Kopf [Leader]: Thomas Sharp - £ 3 / 6 s / 8 d / Erster Rang [First rank]: Fulke Gyllom, William Shakeshafte [= Shakespeare], Thomas Gyllom, Roger Dugdale - je [each] £ 2 / Zweiter Rang [Second rank]: Thomas Coston, Thomas Barker, Robert Bolton, Thomas Ward—je [each] £ 1 / Dritter Rang [Third rank]: Roger Dickinson, William Ormesheye (alias Ascroft)—je [each] 13 s / 4 d" (97). The members, eleven in all, were also to be paid a full year's salary after Hoghton's death.

2001, the young Shakespeare commemorated the martyrdom of Edmund Campion in an extremely accomplished elegy.[38] In *Twelfth Night* Shakespeare alludes to an interrogation of Campion in the Tower—and to the years of his hermit-like seclusion at the Jesuit college in Prague.[39]

In 1581 Campion and his companions were betrayed by a Crown spy. Elizabeth was secretly present at Campion's first interrogation, but then revealed herself and asked the prisoner whether he acknowledged her as queen of England. When Campion affirmed this, the monarch offered him life, freedom, wealth, and honors. But Campion would also have had to recognize Elizabeth as the spiritual authority—a condition he could not meet. He was accused of high treason, severely tortured, condemned by false testimony, and cruelly executed.[40] The Catholic Church beatified him in 1886 and canonized him in 1970.

Two other priests died with Campion because William Cecil was determined to set a warning example: Sherwin was

---

[38] "The scowling skies did storm and puff apace, / They could not bear the wrongs that malice wrought; / The sun drew in his shining purple face; / The moistened clouds shed brinish tears for thought; / The river Thames awhile astonished stood / To count the drops of Campion's sacred blood. / Nature with teares bewailed her heavy loss; / Honesty feared herself should shortly die; / Religion saw her champion on the cross; / Angels and saints desired leave to cry; / E'en heresy, the eldest child of hell, / Began to blush, and thought she did not well." The text is to be found under "Thomas Pounde of Belmont" in Henry Foley, *Records of the English Province of the Society of Jesus.* 7 vols. (London, 1877-1882; New York, 1966) III, 623. The poem was originally attributed to Pound, but this was shown to be incorrect, primarily through stylistic comparisons. If the young Shakespeare was indeed the author—and all the indications suggest this—and if he was using an idea that came from Parsons, this is renewed confirmation that when the Elizabethan cartographer John Speed spoke of "This papist and his poet" (1611), he was indeed alluding to Robert Parsons and William Shakespeare. Cf. Hammerschmidt-Hummel, *Die verborgene Existenz* 2001, 32-34.
[39] Cf. Hammerschmidt-Hummel, *Die verborgene Existenz* 2001, 34-36.
[40] Cf. Hammerschmidt-Hummel, *Die verborgene Existenz* 2001, 31.

executed vicariously for the English seminar at Rheims and Bryant for the English College at Rome. As the architect of the anti-Catholic penal laws, Cecil was particularly hated by English Catholics. Shakespeare later caricatures him as Polonius in *Hamlet* and has him die like a rat.

Parsons, the second leader of the mission, was Campion's equal and was similarly successful in his mission work. He was a shrewd tactician and strategist, and succeeded in escaping his pursuers and leaving England under the protection of the Spanish ambassador.

Parsons subsequently became the leader of the Catholic mission.[41] He established further English colleges and secret printing presses in France and Spain. His most important college—it functioned as a continental bridgehead with direct links with the Catholic underground in London (Blackfriars)—was situated at St. Omer, south of Calais. This college, founded in 1593—the massive complex of buildings can still be admired today[42]—attracted large numbers of pupils and had two theaters, a store of theatrical equipment, and a separate school of rhetoric. Supported by the pope, the king of Spain and the French aristocracy, Parsons had developed political and military strategies to restore Catholicism in England, by force if necessary. The attack on England by the Spanish Armada in 1588 was the result of his initiative—as was the appointment of William Allen as a cardinal by Pope Sixtus V in 1587. In the event of a Spanish victory Allen would have become archbishop of Canterbury.[43]

According to the Rheims Report of 1579/80, the Jesuit missionaries were particularly successful in the north of England, obviously in Lancashire, and also in a relatively small "province," by which—it appears—Warwickshire was meant,

---

[41] Cf. the account given in Hammerschmidt-Hummel, *Die verborgene Existenz* 2001, 37ff.

[42] Illustrated in Hammerschmidt-Hummel, *William Shakespeare* 2003, 45, fig. 44b-c.

[43] Cf. Hammerschmidt-Hummel, *William Shakespeare* 2003, 56.

where within a very short time around 5,000 people were reconverted to the Catholic faith.[44] In this "province," where the mission was so successful, was Stratford. It was there that fierce Catholic resistance developed. It was part of the diocese of the bishop of Worcester, who complained in a letter to Cecil about the dangerous recusancy there.[45] At Allen's college it was known that the government had lists of the names of those who were reconciled with Catholicism and reprisals were feared. The English ambassador in Paris, who was particularly annoyed by the run of young English Catholics on Rheims, was already thinking of such action. He advised his government to impose severe penalties on the parents of students should they fail to recall their sons.[46]

The English government was evidently quick to follow the advice of its ambassador to France, reprisals being taken in 1580: 140 citizens of the realm—presumably parents of students at Rheims—were summoned before the Queen's Bench in London, one of the highest courts in the land. This seems to have been an immediate reaction to the Jesuit mission.[47] But the real answer was the draconian anti-Catholic legislation of 1581, passed in the spring, which made not only

---

[44] Cf. Hammerschmidt-Hummel, *Die verborgene Existenz* 2001, 54-55.

[45] Cf. Hammerschmidt-Hummel, *Die verborgene Existenz* 2001, 52; see also Hammerschmidt-Hummel, *William Shakespeare* 2003, 28.

[46] According to the so-called Rheims Report (1579-80): "... the English Ambassador resident at Paris, seeing and hearing that very many noble youths were travelling hither, and that some were becoming priests, others religious, but all going to the seminaries, is reported to have said that he would advise his mistress and her counsellors to take early steps with regard to this matter by the imprisonment of the parents, unless they not only kept their sons at home, but also recalled them thither." *The Douay College Diaries, Third, Fourth, and Fifth, 1598-1654*, eds. Burton and Williams, II, 560. The chronicler comments: "Yet they arrive daily, and they are of such standing that now there are among us the heirs and eldest sons of good families, whom their parents desire to be made priests" (II 560-61).

[47] Cf. Hammerschmidt-Hummel, *Die verborgene Existenz* 2001, 55ff.

those engaged in the mission but also their converts guilty of high treason.[48] Further, even more severe penal laws against adherents of the old faith were to follow.[49]

Catholic priests and believers were now threatened with heavy fines and stiff prison sentences. Anyone over sixteen who failed to attend protestant worship was fined £20 a month. Anyone who employed a schoolmaster who refused to follow the new religion was fined £10 and sent to prison for a year. Anyone who knew of such infringements of the law and failed to report them within twenty days was deprived of his income and property and sentenced to life imprisonment.

One-third of the confiscated property went to the queen, one-third to the poor of the parish, and the remaining third to the denouncer.

England was now covered by a network of informers and spies. The ones most feared were lapsed Catholic priests who were often in possession of confidential information from the English colleges at Rheims/Douai and Rome. For a time William Allen had to fear for the lives of his pupils, a spy named Baines having suggested poisoning the college well.[50]

The same spy whose false testimony brought about Campion's downfall in 1581 had already betrayed the young priest Thomas Cottom (1549-82) in 1580. His brother, the

---

[48] Cf. Hammerschmidt-Hummel, *Die verborgene Existenz* 2001, 17, and Hammerschmidt-Hummel, *William Shakespeare* 2003, 25f.

[49] The following account is based on the chapters "Die antikatholische Religionsgesetzgebung unter Elisabeth I. und Jakob I." ["The anti-Catholic religious legislation under Elizabeth I and James I"] in Hammerschmidt-Hummel, *Die verborgene Existenz* 2001, 16-21, and "Die antikatholischen Strafgesetze unter Elisabeth I. und ihre Folgen" ["The anti-Catholic Penal Laws under Elizabeth I and their Consequences"] and "Zur Lage der Katholiken unter Jakob I.: Enttäuschung und Widerstand" ["On the state of Catholics under James I: Disillusionment and Resistance"] in Hammerschmidt-Hummel, *William Shakespeare* 2003, 16-28 and 237-42.

[50] Cf. Hammerschmidt-Hummel, *William Shakespeare* 2003, 48-49.

Stratford schoolmaster John Cottom (?1547-1616), thereupon lost his job.[51]

In 1585, the year when war broke out between England and Spain and English Catholics met in Rome to discuss (even military) strategies for re-catholicizing their country, a further anti-Catholic penal law was passed. All Jesuits and priests were banned from England under penalty of death. Anyone who helped them was also condemned to death and their property confiscated.

Students at the English colleges on the continent who did not return and take the Oath of Supremacy were guilty of high treason and, if arrested, were accused and condemned to death. Anyone who helped Jesuits, priests, or their colleges and students was sent to prison. Parents who had their children educated on the continent without the approval of the government were fined £100.

The penal law of 1593 required convicted Catholic recusants over sixteen to be registered, and they could only move freely within a radius of five miles. If they failed to obey, their property could be forfeit. Those whose annual income was under £40 had to submit to the new religion or swear to leave the country. Anyone who swore the oath and broke it faced the death penalty.

The situation created by this legislation had disastrous effects on Catholics in England. For them and their priests and monks England became one great prison. In Act II, Scene 2, Hamlet alludes to this when he says, "Denmark's a prison" ["Denmark" meaning England].

The wretched plight of his contemporaries was depicted in detail by William Allen, with an indirect appeal to his brothers in faith throughout the world:

> If they [our fellows in the catholic faith through Christendom] might see all the prisons, dungeons, fetters, stocks, racks, that are through the realm

---

[51] Cf. Hammerschmidt-Hummel, *Die verborgene Existenz* 2001, 48-50.

occupied and filled with catholics; if they might behold the manner of their arraignment even among the vilest sort of malefactors; how many have been by famine, ordure and pestiferous airs pined away; how many by most cruel death openly despatched; how many have suffered proscription and condemnation to perpetual prison; how many have been spoiled and otherwise grievously punished by forfeiting to the Queen 100 marks for every time they hear mass; how many gentlemen and others, persons of wealth, are wholly undone by losing thirteen score pounds by the year for not coming unto the heretical service; how many have lost all their lands and goods during life for flying out of the country for their conscience sake; ... how many wander in places where they are not known, driven into woods, yea surely into waters ... to save themselves from the heretics cruelty; how many godly and honest married couples most dear one to another by the imprisonment, banishment, flight of either party are pitifully sundered; how many families thereby dissolved; into what poverty, misery and mishap their children are driven; what numbers thereby run over sea into most desperate wars and fortunes, or by better luck and fortune go to the seminaries or other service to pass their time during their parents calamity.[52]

Precarious as the situation of English Catholics and their priests was during Elizabeth's reign, it deteriorated still further under James I, who succeeded Elizabeth in 1603. The scenario is one of increasing gloom that is reflected in Shakespeare's great tragedies, written during this period. Catholics in England and Ireland had hoped their situation would improve under

---

[52] Allen, quoted in Knox, "Historical Introduction," *The First and Second Diaries of the English College* 1878, lxviii-lxix.

James, who, after all, had conspired with the pro-Catholic opposition circle around the earl of Essex. Robert Devereux, second earl of Essex (1566-1601), and his friend Henry Wriothesley, third earl of Southampton (1573-1624) had been working secretly to establish James as Elizabeth's successor in the event of her death, as the queen had inexcusably neglected the question of the succession virtually to the end. The Scottish king had promised the English Catholics tolerance.[53] So despite being oppressed, persecuted, and deprived of rights, the suffering Catholic population in the 1590s had cause to hope for improvement. This was also the case with Shakespeare, who in this decade wrote the comedies in which he drew on his impressions of Italy and the Mediterranean world and the histories in which, pillorying the evils and the suffering of earlier ages, he held up a mirror to his own time.

Contrary to all expectations, however, the new king did not repeal any of the anti-Catholic penal laws. In fact, under him the situation actually worsened. At the beginning of 1605 James announced that it had never been his intention to accord the "papists" tolerance. He said he would give them a further year to reconsider their position, then he would make the laws stricter and have them executed.[54]

Once more English Catholics had been deceived. The French ambassador repeatedly interceded for them. When he presented James with a petition on April 1, 1604, the monarch threw it on the floor in violent anger and stamped his feet on it.[55]

Violent armed resistance began to form among sons of the Catholic landed gentry in the Midlands, not far from Stratford, who were related to Shakespeare's mother and whose fathers were in prison as recusants or had been financially ruined or

---

[53] Cf. Hammerschmidt-Hummel, *William Shakespeare* 2003, 190 and 237f.

[54] Cf. G. B. Harrison, *A Jacobean Journal. Being a Record of those Things most Talked of During the Years 1603-1606* (London, 1941, repr. 1946) 194.

[55] Cf. Harrison, *Jacobean Journal* 1946, 127.

executed. The plan to blow up the fully assembled Parliament at Westminster on November 5, 1605 was an act of Catholic revenge intended to strike at the center of state power and topple the protestant regime. The plot was foiled at the last minute. Those involved were detected, seized, and taken to the Tower.

Guido (Guy) Fawkes (1570-1605), who was to have set off the explosion but was caught before he could do so, was brought, passing under the name of Johnson, before the king on November 6, 1605. "When Johnson was brought to the King's presence, the King asked him how he could conspire so hideous a treason against his children and so many innocent souls which never offended him. He answered that it was true; but a dangerous disease required a desperate remedy."[56] This argument echoes almost word for word Hamlet's statement in IV, iii, which appears to be an allusion to the Essex rebellion: "Diseases desperate grown, / By desperate appliances are reliev'd, / Or not at all." Fawkes told the Scots present, including the king, that "his intent was to have blown them back to Scotland."[57]

The conspirators were condemned to death and executed with extreme cruelty. The fifth of November is celebrated in England to this day as an occasion of rejoicing, with innumerable fireworks set off throughout the country.

After the Gunpowder Plot the hunt was on for the Jesuits Henry Garnett (1566-1606) and John Gerard (1564-1637). While Gerard, disguised with a false beard and a wig, succeeded in escaping via the secret meeting place for fugitive priests at Blackfriars,[58] Garnett the Superior was caught, after a long siege, in the chimney of a Catholic country house. After a trial for high treason which, particularly on account of the defamatory and wounding speech of Sir Edward Coke, the Crown prosecutor, is reminiscent of the show trials in

---

[56] Cf. Harrison, *Jacobean Journal* 1946, 244.
[57] Cf. Harrison, *Jacobean Journal* 1946, 244.
[58] Cf. Hammerschmidt-Hummel, *William Shakespeare* 2003, 263.

totalitarian states in the twentieth century,[59] Garnett was condemned to death and executed.[60]

The situation of English Catholics was desperate. In 1613 they were prohibited by law from carrying weapons.[61] One bill of that year—which was not passed—would have required them to wear red caps and colored stockings.[62] Not until the Catholic Emancipation Act was passed in 1829 were English Catholics granted equality of status with their protestant fellow citizens—in legal theory at least. English historians have played down the Catholic persecutions of those days. Catholics are still barred from succeeding to the throne. The "Merrie England" image of the Shakespearean era still conveyed—often ingenuously—is a myth.

****

It is essential to adduce this historical, religious, and political background to understand William Shakespeare's development and literary activity. The initial impulse to look into the enigmas and inconsistencies in Shakespeare's life came

---

[59] As recounted in Hammerschmidt-Hummel, *William Shakespeare* 2003, 241, Coke used the remainder of the trial, which lasted only one day, to defame the Jesuit Superior with polished phraseology, to humiliate him and finally to put him on a level with a common criminal. Garnett, Coke said, was a man with many names. He was an Englishman and a gentleman by birth. Educated at Westminster and then Oxford, he had first worked as a corrector for the printer Tottel and was now himself being "corrected" by the law. By profession he was a Jesuit and a superior. The latter designation was indeed fitting, for in his diabolical treason he was superior to all his predecessors. He held the degree of a doctor of the Jesuits, and this was, to put it bluntly, a doctor of the five d's: "of dissimulation, of deposing of Princes, of disposing of Kingdoms, of daunting and deterring of subjects, and of destruction."

[60] Cf. Hammerschmidt-Hummel, *William Shakespeare* 2003, 241.

[61] Cf. Hammerschmidt-Hummel, *William Shakespeare* 2003, 242.

[62] Cf. Peter Vansittart, "Frighted with false fire," *The Spectator* (August 31, 1996): 30.

to the author from a picture of the dramatist, the Flower portrait,[63] which she was able to prove to be genuine in 1995 with the aid of experts at the Bundeskriminalamt (German Federal Office of Criminal Investigation) and medical specialists.[64] The portrait is dated 1609. When it was subjected to X-ray examination in 1966, a valuable fifteenth-century Italian Madonna was discovered underneath the picture of Shakespeare.[65] Shakespeare probably inherited this picture from his Catholic mother, who died in 1608. Pictures of the Virgin Mary, like the Borromeo testaments mentioned above, rosaries, and other "Catholic" objects constituted a threat to the lives of their owners in the England of those days. Thus painting over the picture of the Madonna was probably one of the safest and most elegant solutions. For the reasons stated it

---

[63] Color reproductions of the—restored—Flower portrait, which is part of the Royal Shakespeare Collection at Stratford-upon-Avon, appear in my books *Das Geheimnis um Shakespeares "Dark Lady." Dokumentation einer Enthüllung.* (Darmstadt: Primus Verlag, 1999) 94, fig. 15, *Die verborgene Existenz* 2001, front cover, and *William Shakespeare* 2003, 199, fig. 133.

[64] See my essays: "Ist die Darmstädter Shakespeare-Totenmaske echt?," *Shakespeare-Jahrbuch* 132 (1996): 58-74. "Neuer Beweis für die Echtheit des Flower-Porträts und der Darmstädter Shakespeare-Totenmaske. Ein übereinstimmendes Krankheitssymptom im linken Stirnbereich von Gemälde und Gipsabguß," *Anglistik* (September 1996): 115-36; "Shakespeares Totenmaske und die Shakespeare-Bildnisse 'Chandos' und 'Flower'. Zusätzliche Echtheitsnachweise auf der Grundlage eines neuen Fundes," *Anglistik* (März 1998): 101-115; "What did Shakespeare Look Like? Authentic Portraits and the Death Mask. Methods and Results of the Tests of Authenticity" in *Symbolism* first ed. Rüdiger Ahrens (New York: AMS, 2000) 41-79.

[65] The X-ray photographs were taken at the Courtauld Institute in London in 1966, but today they are neither there nor in the Royal Shakespeare Collection at Stratford-upon-Avon. They were published in the *Illustrated London News* (June 18, 1966). Details are reproduced in Hammerschmidt-Hummel, *Die verborgene Existenz* 2001, 12, fig. 1a, and Hammerschmidt-Hummel, *William Shakespeare* 2003, 200, fig. 134.

seemed advisable to submit the hitherto unproven Catholicism thesis to a thorough re-examination.

Investigations conducted on the basis of a number of new sources or ones newly made accessible have yielded astonishing positive results[66] so that today we no longer have to rely on conjectures regarding Shakespeare's religious affiliations. He was born into a Catholic environment; his parents and relatives, teachers and friends were adherents of the old faith. As a son of Alderman John Shakespeare, who had married Mary Arden, daughter of the gentleman Robert Arden of Wilmcote,[67] the young Shakespeare must have attended Stratford Grammar School—evidently, as was customary, from the age of seven to fourteen, i.e., from 1571 to 1578.

The name of his teacher, Simon Hunt (d. 1585), who was employed at Stratford at the handsome salary of £20 a year, can be found, together with the names of the other (known) schoolmasters at King Edward VI School, on the plaque in the classroom in the old building, which has been preserved.[68] In 1575 Hunt professed his Catholicism, hitherto practiced in secret, went to Douai, studied for the priesthood at the English seminary there, became a Jesuit in Rome, and in 1580 was appointed English confessor (penitentiary) at the Holy See. His predecessor in the office was Robert Parsons, who—as has been mentioned—embarked that year on the secret Jesuit mission to England with Edmund Campion.[69]

---

[66] These are presented in Hammerschmidt-Hummel, *Die verborgene Existenz* 2001, and in Hammerschmidt-Hummel, *William Shakespeare* 2003, which draws on the former.

[67] For this reason, and because he had amassed substantial property, he was later able to apply—successfully—for a coat of arms. Cf. Hammerschmidt-Hummel, *William Shakespeare* 2003, 15, fig. 18, and 16.

[68] The classroom and the plaque with the names of the schoolmasters are illustrated in Hammerschmidt-Hummel, *William Shakespeare* 2003, 38, fig. 37 b, und 39, fig. 40.

[69] Cf. "Simon Hunt: Lateinschullehrer in Stratford-upon-Avon und jesuitischer Beichtvater am Stuhl von St. Peter in Rom" ["Simon Hunt:

Like many English Catholics who sent their sons to the
continent to study at Douai (and other colleges founded later),
the Shakespeares must also have provided their son William
with such an education, and there are numerous indications that
this was at William Allen's Collegium Anglicum from 1578 to
1580.[70] At that time, Allen's college—transferred to Rheims
for reasons of safety from 1578 to 1593—was still the only
educational institution for young English Catholics. In *The
Taming of the Shrew* Shakespeare alludes to Rheims as a seat
of learning and uses knowledge he could only have acquired
there.[71]After that, the young Shakespeare—as has already been
mentioned—entered the aristocratic Catholic household of
Hoghton Tower.

Shakespeare's education, at school and afterwards, under
Catholic auspices and his first, illegal appointment in an aristocratic Catholic household corresponded, as has been shown, to
the typical career of young English Catholics in the Elizabethan
era. The further—mysterious—course of his life, his sudden

Schoolmaster in Stratford-upon-Avon and Jesuit Penitentiary at the Holy
See at Rome"] in Hammerschmidt-Hummel, *Die verborgene Existenz*
2001, 48, and Hammerschmidt-Hummel, *William Shakespeare* 2003, 30.

[70] Cf. "John Shakespeare: Karriere und Konfession" ["John Shakespeare:
Career and Religion"] in Hammerschmidt-Hummel, *Die verborgene
Existenz* 2001, 50-62.

[71] It is extremely significant that the dramatist himself, in this context,
expressly mentions Rheims. In *The Taming of the Shrew* Lucentio is
introduced under the false name of Cambio (which characterizes him) as
a young scholar who "has been long studying at Rheims; as cunning in
Greek, Latin, and other languages" (II, i, 80-82): Shakespeare must have
been alluding to the Collegium Anglicum since he was familiar with the
names of its classes. In *Notes & Queries* (March 5, 1938) Richard H.
Perkinson pointed out that Rheims in the age of Shakespeare (because of
the English College that had been transferred to the French city from
1578 to 1593) would have been "recognized as the most important
source of Catholic activity in England rather than as a seat of general
culture." Cf. also The Arden Edition of *The Taming of the Shrew*, ed.
Brian Morris (London: Arden Book Company, 1981) 201. Cf.
Hammerschmidt-Hummel, *Die verborgene Existenz* 2001, 80ff. .

disappearances at times of crisis (1585, 1601, and 1613), the many enigmas and inconsistencies in his literary work, and his consummate depiction of profound human suffering bear the stamp of his allegiance to a forbidden religious faith and his involvement in the Catholic underground.

Shortly after his arrival in London in 1592, presumably coming secretly from Gravesend in a boat—as returning Catholics usually did—[72]Shakespeare was already a well known and envied author. That he had spent the preceding seven "lost years" (1585-92), about which Shakespeare scholars had hitherto known nothing, on the continent and at Rome was demonstrated on the basis of new findings in *Die verborgene Existenz* (2001).[73] What activity Shakespeare

---

[72] Anthony Skinner and Richard Acliffe, for instance, were seized at Gravesend when—coming from Calais—they were about to row up to London in a small boat. When they were interrogated on December 18, 1591, it turned out that they were Catholic recusants who had been abroad for eight years, spending the greater part of this time at Rome. Skinner had been a servant of William Allen, who, as has been mentioned, was appointed a cardinal by Pope Sixtus V in 1587 and, had the Spanish Armada been victorious, would have become archbishop of Canterbury. Acliffe had been in the service of Bishop Cassano. Cf. William Harrison, *An Elizabethan Journal. Being a Record of those Things most Talked of during the Years 1591-1594* (London, 1928) 86.

[73] In the authentic pilgrims' book no. 282, with entries from the period 1580 to 1656, of the time-honored English pilgrims' hospice in Rome that was mentioned as early as 726 and was affiliated to the newly founded Venerable English College in 1579, the author discovered, in October 2000, pseudonyms which contain part, or the whole, of the name of the small English town of Stratford, and which evidently denote none other than William Shakespeare. The many indications she amassed all suggested that Shakespeare, then twenty-one, had precipitately left—perhaps had to leave—Stratford at the end of February 1585, after the christening of his twins, Judith and Hamnet, and travelled to Rome, where a number of English Catholics had assembled that year to discuss strategies for returning England to the Catholic faith. In addition, Shakespeare's Stratford Grammar School teacher Simon Hunt—as has been mentioned—held the office of penitentiary at the Holy See. The first entry in the pilgrims' book no. 282 that points to

engaged in in the "lost years" has now become apparent from a newly interpreted passage in a contemporary source that confirms the findings published in 2001 in a totally unexpected fashion. The text in question is the strongly autobiographical *Groats-worth of Wit* (1592) by the dramatist Robert Greene (1558-92), who had studied at Cambridge and Oxford.

Greene's work had already provided Shakespeare's biographers in the past with evidence that William Shakespeare was active in London in 1592 as a playwright and a newcomer to the stage and was causing something of a stir. The author of *Groats-worth of Wit*, whose own life had been ruined by excesses and was nearing its close, made spiteful and envious allusions to his successful young rival, attacking him with unusual vehemence. He abused the new star of the stage as an "vpstart Crow, beautified with our feathers, that ... supposes he is as well able to bombast out a blanke verse as the best of you: and beeing an absolut *Iohannes fac totum*, is in his owne conceit the only Shake-scene in a countrey."[74] If Greene's

---

Shakespeare is "Arthurus Stratfordus Wigorniensis" (April 16, 1585), i.e., "Arthur (from) Stratford (in the) diocese of Worcester," the second is: "D. Shfordus Cestrensis" (April 8, 1587), apparently an amalgamation of "Sh[akespeare]" and "[Strat]fordus" together with a reference to the diocese that included Lancashire, where the dramatist held his first appointment. Finally, the third entry, "Gulielmus Clerkue Strat-fordiensis" (September 22, 1589), in effect "William, secretary from Stratford," seems a particularly clear reference to William Shakespeare, with "Clerkue" denoting his work in the service of English Catholicism. Shakespeare may have been in Rome again in 1591—after 1585, 1587 and 1589. This is suggested by the recognizable biennial rhythm and the suspicious fact that among the entries for 1591 one name has been completely scratched out—presumably with a sharp quill. Cf. the epilogue in Hammerschmidt-Hummel, *Die verborgene Existenz* 2001.

[74] The complete sentence runs: "There is an upstart Crow, beautified with our feathers, that with his *Tygers hart wrapt in a Players hyde*, supposes he is as well able to bombast out a blanke verse as the best of you: and beeing an absolute *Iohannes fac totum*, is in his owne conceit the onely Shake-scene in a countrey." From *"Greenes Groats-worth of Wit"* (S.R.

allusion to Shakespeare's name ("Shake-scene") showed who his invective was directed against, his reference to a passage in Shakespeare's early history Henry VI (part 3) makes it unmistakably clear who is being attacked and abused here: "that with his *Tygers hart wrapt in a Players hyde* supposes he is as well able to bombast out a blanke verse as the best of you."[75] Shakespeare's original line is: "O tiger's heart wrapt in a woman's hide" (I, iv, 137).

In *Groats-worth of Wit*, however, there is another particularly telling passage which Greene launches into an attack on Shakespeare. This one depicts the encounter between Roberto, a scholar, writer, and playwright in whom we recognize the author himself and a young actor from the country, elegantly dressed, self-assured, but anonymous, whom the English historian A. L. Rowse thought some years ago he could identify as William Shakespeare.[76] On the basis of the new discoveries now made about Shakespeare's forbidden Catholicism, his training at a Catholic college on the continent and his employment in the Catholic underground, it is now possible to substantiate this thesis.

In the dialogue between Roberto and the anonymous actor, the stranger affirms that he has been an author in the country, can produce a fine speech, and once wrote "morals" (=morality plays). This information is very revealing and corresponds with traditional knowledge of Shakespeare's life up to this point. However, the most revealing statement from the actor, who remains nameless, refers to his activities in the preceding seven

---

Sept. 20, 1592) in E. K. Chambers, *William Shakespeare. A Study of Facts and Problems*. 2 Vols. (Oxford: Oxford U P, 1930, repr. 1951) II 188. Cf. also Ingeborg Boltz, "B. Shakespeares Leben" in *Shakespeare-Handbuch*, ed. Ina Schabert, 4th ed. (Stuttgart: Kröner, 2000), "6. 'Johannes Factotum,'" 147, and Hammerschmidt-Hummel, *William Shakespeare* 2003, 90.

[75] "From Robert Greene's *Greene's Groats-worth of Wit* (S.R. Sept. 20, 1592)" in Chambers, *William Shakespeare* 1930, II, 188.

[76] Cf. A. L. Rowse, *Shakespeare the Man* (London: Macmillan, 1973) 59-60.

years (1585-92), when, he self-confidently declares, he was "an absolute Interpreter to the puppets." This statement is coded, but its meaning becomes apparent if one considers it, like Alexander de Hoghton's will of 1581, against the background of the illegality of English Catholicism. "Puppet" then evidently signifies "player." And the code word "players" had already been used by Alexander for the priests he had concealed at Hoghton Tower. This would make the "Interpreter to the puppets" a person who is in the service of Catholic priests, playing the role of a kind of mediator.[77] This passage can thus be regarded as additional written confirmation that in the seven "lost years" (1585-92) Shakespeare performed offices for priests—evidently as a member of the Catholic Association within the framework of the forbidden Jesuit mission in England. His purchase, in 1613, together with three trustees, of the eastern gatehouse at Blackfriars, which, as has already been mentioned, gave shelter to persecuted Catholic priests and adherents of the old religion,[78] conforms perfectly with this scenario and substantiates the interpretation put forward here.

A further source that has now yielded new material for Shakespeare scholars provides evidence for the first time of where Shakespeare stayed on his continental travels, where he, so to speak, "pitched his tents." In *L'Envoy to Narcissus* (1595)[79] the Elizabethan author Thomas Edwardes mentions a

---

[77] Cf. Hammerschmidt-Hummel, *William Shakespeare* 2003, 70.

[78] Cf. "Shakespeares Beitrag zum Überleben des englischen Katholizismus: Hauskauf in Blackfriars (1613)" ["Shakespeare's Contribution to the Survival of English Catholicism: Purchase of a Building in Blackfriars (1613)"] in Hammerschmidt-Hummel, *Die verborgene Existenz* 2001, 116-20, and "Das Vermächtnis an den katholischen Untergrund und Rückzug nach Stratford"—"Hauskauf in Blackfriars" ["The Legacy to the Catholic Underground and Retreat to Stratford"—"Purchase of a Building in Blackfriars"] in Hammerschmidt-Hummel, *William Shakespeare* 2003, 259-66 and fig. 167.

[79] The only extant copy is in Peterborough Cathedral Library. It was reprinted by Rev. W. E. Buckley in 1878 for the Roxburghe Club (61 and 62). Reproduced in C. M. Ingleby, L. Toulmin Smith and F. J.

number of prominent writer colleagues, enabling us to identify them by using not their own names but those of characters in their most important or most popular works.[80] By far the most eminent of these authors is Shakespeare, whom Edwardes calls "Adon"—after Shakespeare's famous epic poem *Venus und Adonis*, which had already been reprinted several times in the 1590s. This sensuous and erotic poem, dedicated to the young earl of Southampton, was immensely popular with Shakespeare's contemporaries, especially among educated young people.

Edwardes says that Shakespeare, the author of *Venus und Adonis*, who the subsequent part of the text is about, constitutes the center of the poets and exerts a great influence. In so doing, Edwardes reflects the general opinion of the bard of Avon, but goes one step further by conveying to us a few characteristics of Shakespeare the star poet. Edwardes describes Shakespeare's pen as "bewitching," but says that this author "differs much from men" and that his "golden art" moves us "To have honored him with baies." He also explains what exactly distinguishes the great poet from his fellow-men. It is his contacts with monastic communities, with whom he finds shelter.[81] This is the only way the phrase "Tilting under Frieries" can be interpreted. The significance of this statement has not previously been recognized. "Frieries" is a reference to monasteries or monastic communities. The expression "Tilting

---

Furnivall, comps., *The Shakspere Allusion-Book: A Collection of Allusions to Shakspere from 1591 to 1700*, re-edited, revised and re-arranged, with an introd. by John Munro (1909), re-issued with a pref. by Edmund Chambers. 2 Vols. (London: Oxford, 1932) I, 25-26.

[80] Thus "Collyn" is a reference to Edmund Spenser, who wrote of "Colin Clout," glorified "Albion" (England) in *The Faerie Queen* and is the author of an elegy on Sir Philip Sidney. "Rosamond" is an allusion to Samuel Daniel, "Amintas" to Thomas Watson and "Leander" to Christopher Marlowe.

[81] Cf. Hammerschmidt-Hummel, *William Shakespeare* 2003, 165.

under Frieries" thus means "pitching one's tents under monastery roofs or in the shelter of monasteries."[82]

Shakespeare's esteem for the various forms of monastic life that were no longer to be found in the England of his day, as they had been abolished under Henry VIII, becomes apparent at various points in his literary works.[83] Edwardes's poem *L'Envoy to Narcissus* of 1595 now provides written evidence that Shakespeare stayed at monasteries on the continent. This corresponds perfectly with the newly interpreted written source presented above, according to which in the so-called "lost years" (1585-92) Shakespeare acted as "absolute Interpreter to the puppets [= priests]," thus functioning as a mediator in the service of priests.

It is only in relation to this historical context that the dramatist's clandestine life becomes accessible to us, enigmatic passages in his works acquire meaning, many of his texts

---

[82] Hammerschmidt-Hummel, *William Shakespeare* 2003, 165.

[83] Officially, at least, there were no longer any monks in England in Shakespeare's day. Thus they were no longer a significant feature of English towns and rural areas, as they had been before the schism under Henry VIII. Before the Reformation their presence was to be felt particularly in the cityscape of the capital, with its numerous monasteries and churches. In the Elizabethan and Jacobean ages they only survived in the Catholic underground and the prisons. But precisely for this reason monks play all the more prominent a part in quite a number of Shakespeare's plays. Banished from real life, they are put on stage by the dramatist, recalled to people's awareness and at the same time honoured with a memorial. In sonnet no. 73 the poetical "I" laments the "Bare ruined choirs where late the sweet birds [monks] sang". In the plays, monks act as counsellors to people hard pressed and in need. They are clever, knowledgeable, benevolent, sympathetic, forgiving and magnanimous. They are able to help and, particularly, show paths that can be followed even when the situation appears hopeless for those involved and their conflicts seem insoluble. Derogatory remarks about monks, such as were almost proverbial in England around 1650—for instance in the rhyme "a friar a liar"—are absent from Shakespeare's works. Cf. Hammerschmidt-Hummel, *William Shakespeare* 2003, 234-35.

appear in an entirely new light, that we understand why Shakespeare kept back around half his plays,[84] and answers verified by scholarship can be given to questions previously unanswered. Shakespeare's hidden existence in the illegal scene of English Catholicism is the key to the great unsolved problems in his life and literary work.

With his history play *Henry VI*, probably written at the beginning of 1592 (or even earlier), Shakespeare, then twenty-eight, eclipsed the established dramatist Robert Greene and challenged the great dramatic talent Christopher Marlowe (1564-93). As a crypto-Catholic, Shakespeare may have met Marlowe, the government spy, in Rheims in 1587.[85] Immediately after Greene's malicious and insulting attack on

---

[84] These appeared for the first time in the First Folio Edition of 1623, the first collected edition of the dramas, compiled by John Heminge and Henry Condell, close friends and actor colleagues of Shakespeare, and containing the engraved portrait of him. They are marked with an asterisk(*) in the list of abbreviations of Shakespeare's dramas given in Hammerschmidt-Hummel, *William Shakespeare* 2003, cf. 335.

[85] In that year Philip II, at the urging of exiled English Catholics led by the Jesuit priest Robert Parsons, was preparing to assemble his Armada to attack England, and Marlowe was in Rheims to spy on the English College there. In his play *The Massacre of Paris* Marlowe mentions the Collegium Anglicum in a way that would please the English government, attributing to the French king (Henry III) beside the corpse of Cardinal Guise, whom he has had murdered, the words: "Ah this sweet sight is physic to my soul, /... / Did he not draw a sort of English priests / From Douai to the Seminary at Rheims, / To hatch forth treason 'gainst their natural queen?" Christopher Marlowe, *The Complete Plays*, ed. by J. B. Steane (Harmondsworth: Penguin Books, repr. 1972) (V, 2, 99) 109-11. In his report, however, Marlowe is said to have spoken positively of the English "papists" there and to have called the English protestants "hypocritical asses." The late Oxford historian A. L. Rowse remarked: "... Marlowe was said to think that 'if there be any God or any good religion, then it is in the Papists,' because the service of God is performed with more ceremonies, 'as Elevation of the Mass, organs, singing men, shaven crowns, etc. And that all Protestants are hypocritical asses'", A. L. Rowse, *William Shakespeare. A Biography* (New York: Harper & Row, 1963) 115.

Shakespeare, the printer and dramatist Henry Chettle (?1560-
?1607) did not only defend the new star of the stage but praised
his character and the quality of his writing and hinted that he
had long been known in higher circles.[86] In 1598 another
contemporary, Francis Meres (1565-1647), placed Shakespeare's works on a par with those of the great classical
authors.[87] But Shakespeare was also a cult author for educated

---

[86] "The other [Shakespeare], whome at that time I did not so much spare,
as since I wish I had, ... (especially in such a case) the Author [Greene]
beeing dead, that I did not, I am as sory, as if the originall fault had
beene my fault, because my selfe have seene his demeanor no lesse civill
than he exelent in the qualitie he professes: Besides, divers of worship
have reported his uprightnes of dealing, which argues his honesty, and
his facetious grace in writting, that aprooves his Art," Ingleby et.al., *The
Shakspere Allusion-Book* 1932, I 4.

[87] "As the Greeke tongue is made famous and eloquent by *Homer, Hesiod,
Euripedes, Aeschilus, Sophocles, Pindarus, Phocylides* and *Aristo-
phanes*; and the Latine tongue by *Virgill, Ovid, Horace, Silius Italicus,
Lucanus, Lucretius, Ausonius* and *Claudianus*: so the English tongue is
mightily enriched, and gorgeouslie invested in rare ornaments and
resplendent abiliments by *Sir Philip Sidney, Spencer, Daniel, Drayton,
Warner, Shakespeare, Marlow* and *Chapman.* *** As the soule of
Euphorbus was thought to lived in *Pythagoras*: so the sweete wittie
soule of *Ovid* liveds in mellifluous & hony-tongued *Shakespeare*, witnes
his *Venus* and *Adonis*, his *Lucrece*, his sugred Sonnets among his private
friends, &c.
As *Plautus* and *Seneca* are accounted the best for Comedy and Tragedy
among the Latines ? so *Shakespeare* among y[e] English is the most
excellent in both kinds for the stage; for Comedy, witnes his
Ge[n]tleme[n] of Verona, his *Errors*, his *Love labors lost*, his *Love
labours wonne*, his *Midsummers night dreame*, & his *Merchant of
Venice*: for Tragedy his *Richard the 2. Richard the 3. Henry the 4. King
Iohn, Titus Andronicus* and his *Romeo and Iuliet*. As *Epius Stolo* said,
that the Muses would speake with *Plautus* tongue, if they would speak
Latin: so I say that the Muses would speake with *Shakespeares* fine filed
phrase, if they would speake English." "Palladis Tamia. Wits Treasury,
Being the Second part of Wits Common wealth. 1598" in Ingleby et. al.,
The Shakspere Allusion-Book 1932, I, 46-48, 46. Elsewhere Francis
Meres mentions, as one of "the best for Comedy amongst us" "Edward

young people in England. In 1600 the students of Cambridge performed a play in which homage is paid to the incomparable author William Shakespeare. The anonymous author of the two-part play *The Return from Parnassus*[88] ridicules this and has an enthusiastic undergraduate named Gullio say, in effect, that even though the foolish world may esteem Spenser and Chaucer, he will honour "sweet master Shakespeare," place his epic poem *Venus and Adonis* under his pillow and have his portrait hanging in his study.[89] In 1623 the first complete edition of Shakespeare's dramas had to be attached to a chain in the library of Oxford University. The most read scene was the parting scene in *Romeo and Juliet*, as can be seen from how worn the pages are.[90]

Though it has not previously been recognized, Shakespeare's literary work is astonishingly closely linked with specific events and developments of the age, which was particularly dominated by one subject—the change in religion imposed by the government. This is apparent in his early history *King John*, in which there are clear references to Elizabeth and the consequences of her religious policy.[91] John

---

Earle of Oxforde" (47). In the 1580s Edward de Vere, earl of Oxford (1550-1604) had his own company of actors, who performed once at court, but otherwise played in the provinces. They were no rivals for Shakespeare's company (The Chamberlain's Men, from 1603 The King's Men), which was formed in the early 1590s and soon rose to the top.

[88] Altogether there are three "Parnassus" plays by an unknown author: *The Pilgrimage to Parnassus*, *The First Part of the Returne from Parnassus* and *The Second Part of the Returne from Parnassus*. They were written between 1598 and 1602 and were performed at St John's College, Cambridge. They are among the so-called "university plays" written by students.

[89] Cf. "Return from Pernassus, Part I. 1600" in Ingleby et. al., *The Shakspere Allusion-Book* 1932, I 67-69, 68. Cf. also Hammerschmidt-Hummel, *William Shakespeare* 2003, 99-100.

[90] Cf. Hammerschmidt-Hummel, *William Shakespeare* 2003, 145.

[91] The connections are discussed in part III of Hammerschmidt-Hummel, *William Shakespeare* 2003: "Das dramatische Schaffen I: Historien,

does not recognize the supremacy of the pope and is excommunicated. His subjects are released from their loyalty to him, as he is now a heretic. Anyone who kills the excommunicated king is to be honored like a saint. The bull excommunicating Elizabeth issued by Pope Pius V in 1570 was similarly worded.

In *King John*, more directly than in other plays, Shakespeare focused on a burning problem of his time: Could and should Elizabethan Catholics remain loyal to a queen Rome had declared a heretic? Were they obliged to obey a heretic? The conflict their consciences faced seemed insoluble. In *King John* Shakespeare offers what from a Catholic point of view would seem a practicable solution. At the end John is reconciled with Rome and so receives back the crown from the hands of the papal legate. Elizabeth, of course, did not follow this example.

Annoyed at the use of English history on the stage for political purposes, the monarch, in 1599, had her senior censor, John Whitgift, archbishop of Canterbury (?1530-1604),[92]

Lustspiele und eine frühe Tragödie—König Johann" ["The Dramatic Works I: Histories, Comedies and an early Tragedy," see "King John"]. Cf. 117ff.

[92] Whitgift had previously been bishop of Worcester, the diocese to which Stratford-upon-Avon belonged.   It was from him that William Shakespeare and his bride, Anne Hathaway, acquired their marriage licence after just one reading of the banns at the end of November 1582 (before the beginning of Advent, when marriages could not take place). They seem to have tricked Whitgift by giving the bride's residence wrongly, claiming that she was from Temple Grafton although Anne Hathaway was really from Shottery, near Stratford, a village that belonged to the parish of Holy Trinity Church in Stratford, where the incumbent was a protestant. At Temple Grafton, however, John Frith officiated, an elderly man who had remained a Catholic priest and who, according to the sources, took care of "diseased hawks"—evidently a reference to the suffering adherents of the old religion. In a contemporary puritan report on the situation ("A survei of the state of the ministerie in Warwickshier") he is stated to be "an old priest & Unsound in religion; he can neither prech nor read well, his chiefest trade is to cure hawkes that are hurt or diseased, for which purpose manie doe

prohibit the printing of plays with English history as their subject.[93] Her neglect of the succession had led to her being compared to Shakespeare's Richard II, who neglected his royal duties and was deposed.[94] Shakespeare reacted promptly to the new ban: In 1599 he wrote *Julius Caesar*, a Roman-history play at the center of which is an on-stage tyrannicide. Thomas Platter the Younger, a Swiss doctor, saw the play at the Globe Theater on September 21, 1599.[95] In the spring of 1599

---

usuallie repaire to him ..." Vol. X, 5, of the *Dugdale Society*, quoted in Schoenbaum, *William Shakespeare* (London: Oxford U P, 1975) 71. Ian Wilson comments: "In other words, he was a Catholic, but too old and in too small and unimportant a parish for it to be worth turning him out of his living." *Shakespeare: The Evidence*. (London: St. Martin's Press 1993) 57. Cf. also Hammerschmidt-Hummel, *Die verborgene Existenz* 2001, 99-102.

[93] Cf. G. B. Harrison, *A Last Elizabethan Journal. Being a Record of those Things most Talked of During the Years 1599-1603* (London: Routledge, 1933) 21, and Hammerschmidt-Hummel, *William Shakespeare* 2003, 88 and 126.

[94] Not without reason did the queen almost constantly suspect sedition in the last years of her life. That she also considered Shakespeare's *Richard II* dangerous and saw in it an allusion to herself is apparent from statements she made in connection with the official report of the historian William Lambarde (1536-1601) on 4 August 1601. Since January 1601 Lambarde had been in charge of the records and documents of the Tower. On the occasion of his report he had a conversation with the queen, who referred to Essex's attempt to depose her. In this connection, he wrote, Elizabeth had spoken of the reign of Richard II and had said, "I am Richard II. know ye not that?" In the further course of the conversation she had declared that "this tragedy was played 40^{tie} times in open streets and houses." Scholars are convinced that Elizabeth was referring to Shakespeare's *Richard II*. Cf. Hammerschmidt-Hummel, *William Shakespeare* 2003, 189.

[95] "Den 21. septembris nach dem imbißeßen, ettwan umb zwey uhren, bin ich mitt meiner geselschaft über daß waßer gefahren, haben in dem streüwinen dachhaus die tragedy vom ersten keyser Julio Caesare mitt ohngefahr 15 personen sehen gar artlich agieren; zu endt der comedien dantzten sie ihrem gebrauch nach gar überauß zierlich, ye zwen in mannes undt 2 in weiber kleideren angethan, wunderbahrlich mitt

Shakespeare[96] came out publicly as an enthusiastic adherent of the earl of Essex. Essex, the good-looking favorite of Elizabeth[97]—but he was also, as recent historical research has shown, an extremely capable politician and statesman[98]—fell into disgrace after abandoning his Ireland campaign, but primarily because, without witnesses and without a mandate to do so, he had negotiated with the Irish Catholic rebel leader, Hugh O'Neil, Earl of Tyrone. Essex was the political rival of Robert Cecil (1563-1612), who was physically deformed, but intellectually brilliant.[99] The queen had given the son of William Cecil, for so many years her chief minister and adviser, the opportunity to make a distinguished career. Robert

---

einanderen." ["On 21 September, after dining, at about two o'clock, I crossed the water with my companions and in the thatched playhouse saw the tragedy of the first emperor Julius Caesar skilfully performed by about fifteen persons; at the end of the comedy they danced, as is their wont, most gracefully and wondrously together, in pairs, dressed alternately in men's clothes and in women's."] *Thomas Platter d. J. Beschreibung der Reisen durch Frankreich, Spanien, England und die Niederlande 1595-1600.* Im Auftrag der Historischen und Antiquarischen Gesellschaft zu Basel. Hrsg. v. Rut Keiser. 2 Bde. (Basel/Stuttgart: Schwabe & Co. AG, 1968) II, p. 791.

[96] The most famous—and oldest—likeness of Shakespeare, which came into the possession of the National Portrait Gallery in the nineteenth century, is the so-called Chandos portrait. A colour reproduction of it appears in Hammerschmidt-Hummel, *William Shakespeare* 2003, facing the title page and on page 94, fig. 79.

[97] The portrait of the earl of Essex at Woburn Abbey shows him as the victor of Cádiz. It is reproduced in colour in *William Shakespeare* 2003, 172, fig. 114.

[98] In *The Polarisation of Elizabethan Politics. The Political Career of Robert Devereux, 2nd Earl of Essex, 1585-1597* (Cambridge: Cambridge U P, 1999) the Australian historian Paul E. J. Hammer comes to the conclusion that the traditional image of Essex as a political lightweight, a gambler, an incompetent military leader, even a "playboy of the western world," is a caricature and urgently in need of revision.

[99] The portrait of Robert Cecil is exhibited at Hatfield House and reproduced in colour in Hammerschmidt-Hummel, *William Shakespeare,* 2003, 173, fig. 115b.

Cecil succeeded his father and continued the latter's policies. William Cecil[100] had been the architect of the strict anti-Catholic legislation. English Catholics regarded him and, later, his son, as their worst enemies. Essex, on the other hand, was their great idol. He was at the center of the oppositional Essex circle—largely pro-Catholic—together with his closest friend, the Catholic earl of Southampton,[101] Shakespeare's patron, friend, and rival. With the tragic failure of the rebellion and the execution of Essex, the oppressed and deprived English Catholics, including Shakespeare, lost the man on whom they had placed their hopes. Was Shakespeare more deeply involved in the dramatic political events at the close of the Elizabethan era than could hitherto be assumed? By interpreting new textual and pictorial evidence and decoding, for the first time, the allegorically enigmatic Shakespeare poem "The Phoenix and the Turtle," the author has succeeded in offering a plausible answer to this question.[102] We can be certain that Essex's tragic fate did have drastic consequences for the dramatist's life and literary work. It is fair to say that it is this devastating blow that accounts for the fact that Shakespeare, all of a sudden, ceased writing comedies and turned to tragedy, something for which no convincing explanation has hitherto been offered.[103] Thus *Hamlet*, the

---

[100] The portrait of William Cecil, also at Hatfield House, is also reproduced in color in Hammerschmidt-Hummel, *William Shakespeare* 2003, 173, fig. 115a.

[101] The portrait of the earl of Southampton, which is in the National Portrait Gallery (Montacute), is reproduced in colour in Hammerschmidt-Hummel, *William Shakespeare* 2003, 96, fig. 82.

[102] Cf. my lecture "William Shakespeares 'The Phoenix and the Turtle': Notate zur Entstehung des Werk und zur Entschlüsselung seiner Figuren als historische Persönlichkeiten," given at the annual conference of the Deutsche Shakespeare-Gesellschaft at Weimar on April 26, 2002, published in: *Anglistik. Mitteilungen des Deutschen Anglisten-verbandes* (Sept. 2003): 71-84.

[103] These remarks are based on the new research findings presented in part IV of Hammerschmidt-Hummel, *William Shakespeare* 2003, 171-200.

tragedy of the sensitive prince in a "rotten" state, has to be seen as the dramatist's reaction to the tragic outcome of the bitter power struggle at the end of the Elizabethan era. With this play, as with the encoded political allegory "The Phoenix and the Turtle," written immediately after the death sentences passed on Essex and Southampton,[104] Shakespeare created an incomparable memorial to the dead Essex.[105] The Catholic prayer Horatio says for the dead Hamlet in V, ii—"And flights of angels sing thee to thy rest"—corresponds to the one Essex repeated twice on the scaffold, praying that God might send down his angels to lead his soul to heavenly joys.[106] There is also a visual allusion to this in the emblem on the title page of the text published in 1603.[107] Around seventy years ago, the eminent English Shakespeare scholar John Dover Wilson remarked that his religious feelings had been slightly injured by this scene.[108]

Six months after Essex had been executed, a French delegation under Marshal Biron came to London on a state visit. Biron was Henry IV's closest friend and had also been a friend of Essex. Demonstratively clad in black mourning, with no insignias of honor or bravery, he rode with his companions

---

[104] Cf. "Shakespeares Klagegedicht 'Phönix und Taube'" ["Shakespeare's Elegy 'The Phoenix and the Turtle'"] in Hammerschmidt-Hummel, *William Shakespeare* 2003, 191ff.

[105] See "Das dramatische Schaffen II: Tragödien und Problemstücke - Hamlet" ['The Dramatic Works II: Tragedies and Problem Plays, see *Hamlet*'] in Hammerschmidt-Hummel, *William Shakespeare* 2003, 207-22.

[106] John Dover Wilson, *Shakespeare. Der Mensch. Betrachtungen über Leben und Werk nach einem Porträt.* (Hamburg: Schröder, 1953) 120.

[107] See fig. 146 in Hammerschmidt-Hummel, *William Shakespeare* 2003, 210, where it is pointed out in the caption that the victim (Hamlet/Essex) is depicted in the form of a chained fish, with the arrow that has pierced the body of the fish merging into plant- or flower-like forms that reach upward, rising to a dove and the angels of heaven.

[108] Dover Wilson, *Shakespeare* 1953, 120.

to his audience at the palace of the queen,[109] whose humiliation could not have been greater. They spoke about Essex. Elizabeth is said to have shown her guests his head.[110] Against this background it appears understandable that, shortly after, the old queen should have refused to take food, suffered severe behavioral disorders[111] and felt faint at the opening of Parliament on October 27, 1601.[112] But it also explains why the famous and highly esteemed author William Shakespeare— despite being called on twice to do so—refused to extol the deeds of the dead monarch.[113] A year later, Biron was accused of treason, condemned to death and not pardoned by his king. He was executed in the same manner as Essex.[114]

∗∗∗

---

[109] Harrison, *A Last Elizabethan Journal* 1933, 201: "At the Court it is much noted that the French wear all black and no kind of bravery at all, wherefore Sir Walter Ralegh rode by night to London to provide himself with a plain black taffeta suit and a black saddle." See also Hammerschmidt-Hummel, *William Shakespeare* 2003, 209. Raleigh had previously been showing the distinguished French guests the sights of London and Westminster.

[110] Harrison, *A Last Elizabethan Journal* 1933, 202: "In her discourses with the Duke the Queen spake of the Earl of Essex, sharply accusing him of ingratitude, rash counsel and obstinately refusing to ask pardon, ... Some also report that she showed the skull of the Earl to the Duke and the Frenchmen in her closet, or fastened upon a pole ...."

[111] "The Queen in these days is quite disfavoured and unattired, and these troubles waste her much. She disregardeth every costly dish that cometh to the table, and taketh little but manchet and succory pottage .... She walks much in her privy chamber, and stamps with her feet at ill news, and thrusts her rusty sword at times into the arras in great rage." Harrison, *A Last Elizabethan Journal* 1933, 202.

[112] "It is said by some who were present that the Queen in all her robes would have fallen if some gentlemen had not suddenly cast themselves under that side that tottered and supported her." Harrison, *A Last Elizabethan Journal* 1933, 207.

[113] Cf. Hammerschmidt-Hummel, *William Shakespeare* 2003, 196-97.

[114] Cf. Hammerschmidt-Hummel, *William Shakespeare* 2003, 209.

After this tragic political event that deeply affected the minds of his contemporaries, Shakespeare wrote no more history plays and comedies—with the exception of *Henry VIII*—but only tragedies and dark problem plays, and, at the end, romances.

This close interplay between his life, his work, and the events of his time is a consistent phenomenon with Shakespeare and characteristic of his existence as an author. It can also be demonstrated in the conclusion of his brilliant literary career. In 1613 the celebrated dramatist arranged his retreat from London,[115] before retiring to Stratford.

If one takes a closer look at *Henry VIII*, staged at the Globe Theater in 1613 and revealingly entitled *All is True* by Shakespeare (and/or his co-author John Fletcher), clear expressions of the author's own opinion become apparent, for instance the allusions to the outrageous events of English history under Henry VIII. In the prologue the dramatist warns his audience that much of the content of this history play will offer no occasion for joy. They must not expect laughter but grief, pity and tears.[116] Here Shakespeare is speaking directly to his public, which—as is well known—occurs very rarely in his work. One example is the prologue to the fifth act of *Henry V* (1599). Still full of optimism, the playwright alludes to Essex,

---

[115] See "VI. Das Vermächtnis an den katholischen Untergrund und Rückzug nach Stratford" ["VI. The Legacy to the Catholic Underground and Retreat to Stratford"] in Hammerschmidt-Hummel, *William Shakespeare* 2003, esp. 259-66.

[116] "I come no more to make you laugh; things now / That bear a weighty and a serious brow, / Sad, high, and working, full of state and woe; / Such noble scenes as draw the eye to flow / We now present. Those that can pity, here / May, if they think it well, let fall a tear, / The subject will deserve it. Such as give / Their money out of hope they may believe, / May here find truth too. Those that come to see / Only a show or two, and so agree / The play may pass, if they be still and willing, / I'll undertake may see away their shilling. / Richly in two short hours. Only they / That come to hear a merry bawdy play, / ... Will be deceiv'd ..." (1-17).

viceroy and supreme commander, who had set off for Ireland with an army in the spring of 1599. Shakespeare, too, is infected by the general elation and elsewhere in the same play writes the rousing and inspiring line "Now all the youth of England are on fire."

The politically explosive message in *Henry VIII* must have met with a mixed reception. But Shakespeare evidently paid no heed to this or to his own danger. Shortly after this he must have embarked for the continent (probably on a vessel belonging to the shipping magnate John Jackson) to travel to Rome. This must have happened secretly and without an exit permit, as was usual among English crypto-Catholics at the time. When Shakespeare acquired one of the most important institutions of the Catholic underground, the eastern gatehouse at Blackfriars, in March 1613, Jackson was one of his three trustees. By buying this property, the dramatist made a considerable contribution to enabling Catholicism to survive in England. By appointing trustees he ensured that it would continue after his death.[117]

Seven years after Shakespeare's death, a serious accident occurred in the northern gatehouse of Blackfriars. In 1623, during a clandestine service in a secret Catholic church on the third story of the building, the floor caved in, plunging a hundred people to their deaths, among them the guest preacher, Father Robert Drury, a well-known Jesuit priest who had previously been rector of the English College at St. Omer.[118] It was never established whether the disaster was due to sabotage.

When Shakespeare (together with Fletcher) wrote *All is True/Henry VIII* he had already completed his life's oeuvre with the romance *The Tempest* and had taken his own leave of his public with Prospero's profound epilogue. For *All is True*

---

[117] Cf. Hammerschmidt-Hummel, *Die verborgene Existenz* 2001, chap. V, 116-20, and *William Shakespeare* 2003, 259-66.

[118] See "Die Katastrophe von Blackfriars (1623)" ["The catastrophe of Blackfriars (1623)"] in Hammerschmidt-Hummel, *Die verborgene Existenz* 2001, 127-47.

there was an external occasion. In 1533, as was outlined at the beginning, Henry VIII had already broken with Rome by secretly wedding Anne Boleyn while still married to Catherine of Aragon. With this step he had pointed English history in a new direction, and one which was painful for Catholics. In 1613 exactly eighty years had passed since all this happened.

When this play in which Shakespeare had dared to make Catherine of Aragon—the queen Henry had repudiated—the secret heroine was performed at the Globe Theater on June 29, 1613 (St. Peter's Day), the thatched roof of the theater was set alight when cannons were fired. It was the very scene in which Henry and Anne Boleyn meet for the first time. Whether this happened by chance or was done deliberately is a question which, as far as the author knows, is first raised and discussed in *William Shakespeare. Seine Zeit—sein Leben—sein Werk* (2003)—against the background of the numerous arson attacks on English churches evidently carried out by militant puritans[119] and the malicious mockery which Shakespeare's close friends and actor colleagues, who only just managed to escape the flames, were exposed to from puritan quarters.[120]

---

[119] The question is considered in detail in Hammerschmidt-Hummel, *William Shakespeare* 2003, 269, where the author concludes that the circumstances as a whole point primarily to radical puritans, but that other protestants would also have had reason to try to prevent the performance of *All is True*. Both groups would have been likely to take offence at a history play about Henry VIII in which Catherine of Aragon, a Catholic, was made the secret protagonist. Neither group would have been prepared to accept a comprehensive Catholic revision of England's recent protestant history on the stage of the Globe Theater. Such considerations add substance to the suspicion that the Globe Theater fire on St Peter's Day 1613 was started deliberately. Since the Gunpowder Plot of 1605 there had been an increasing readiness to resort to terrorist violence as a means of achieving political and religious aims. This, too, supports the contention that the incident may have been an arson attack.

[120] The anonymous contemporary ballad *Sonnett upon the pittiful burneinge of the Globe playhowse in London*, which expresses a covert gloating satisfaction at the misfortune, was presumably composed shortly after the fire. It was evidently the work of a puritan. The six stanzas all end

Shakespeare, evidently, had already left London before the Globe Theater fire; he presumably spent much of the summer at Stratford and then travelled to Rome once again. In October 1613 he arrived there and lodged at the pilgrims' hospice of the English College. As in the "lost years" he used the name of his home town, Stratford, as a pseudonym.[121] But this time he chose the Christian name "Ricardus" together with the surname "Stratfordus." "Richard" was the name of his last surviving brother, who had died in February 1613.[122]

After his return Shakespeare retired for good to his Stratford refuge. In 1597 he had acquired an elegant residence there with a large garden and later, by buying additional land and tithe rights, had created for himself an existence independent of the favour of princes, far away—as Montaigne had phrased it— from the "waveing sea of a peoples or of a Princes opinions" with all their "changes and alterations of passions."[123]

---

with the refrain "Oh sorrow, pittiful sorrow, and yett al this is true," which ironically echoes the title of the play—*All is True*. Cf. Hammer-schmidt-Hummel, *William Shakespeare* 2003, 266-68.

[121] In the course of research carried out in October 2000 the author discovered, among entries for 1613 in the pilgrims' book no. 282 of the English College at Rome, the name "Ricardus Stratfordus."

[122] Cf. Hammerschmidt-Hummel, *Die verborgene Existenz* 2001, 163.

[123] Montaigne, "An Apologie of Raymond Sebond," 102.

Illustrations

1. "William Shakespeare—authentic portraits and montages." Picture quotation from: *William Shakespeare. Seine Zeit—sein Leben—sein Werk* (Mainz: Philipp von Zabern, 2003), cover illustration. From left to right: the Chandos portrait (c. 1594-99), the restored Flower portrait (1609), the Droeshout engraving in the First Folio edition (1623), the death mask (1616), the Flower portrait before restoration (1609), a BKA montage of Chandos/Flower (1995), the funerary bust, a BKA montage of death mask/funerary bust (1995).

2. Historic Grammar School, Stratford-upon-Avon: Classroom. Picture quotation from *William Shakespeare. Seine Zeit—sein Leben—sein Werk*, illustration 37b.

3. Salle Jardine de France (1609/10). New building of the Collegium Anglicum, Douai, founded in 1568. Picture quotation from *William Shakespeare. Seine Zeit—sein Leben—sein Werk*, illustration 43.

4. Rome in the year 1588. Fresco in the Vatican Library. Picture quotation from *William Shakespeare. Seine Zeit—sein Leben—sein Werk*, illustration 62.

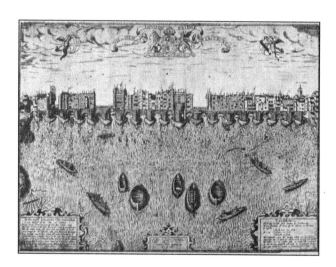

5. View of London Bridge from the East with small boats. Engraving, 1597. Picture quotation from: *William Shakespeare. Seine Zeit—sein Leben—sein Werk*, illustration 66a.

6. "Elizabeth I in Parliament. Title picture of the published parliamentary records from the reign of Elizabeth I. On the queen's right her chief minister and closest adviser, William Cecil, Lord Burghley." Picture quotation from *William Shakespeare. Seine Zeit—sein Leben—sein Werk,* illustration 25.

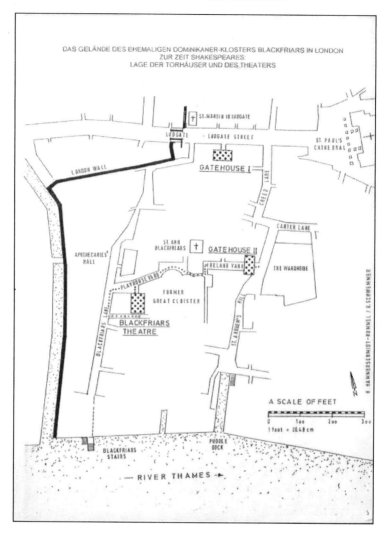

7. H. Hammerschmidt-Hummel / Udo Schwemmer, Site plan of Blackfriars in London at the time of Shakespeare with Gatehouse I, Gatehouse II and the Blackfriars Theater according to textual and pictorial sources, newly made accessible. Picture quotation from *William Shakespeare. Seine Zeit— sein Leben—sein Werk,* illustration 162.

8. Corner of the site of New Place (Chapel Street/Chapel Lane), Shakespeare's residence at Stratford-upon-Avon. Picture quotation from *William Shakespeare. Seine Zeit—sein Leben—sein Werk,* illustration 150a.

ORIENTALISM RECONSIDERED YET AGAIN: ALEXANDER KINGLAKE'S *EOTHEN* (1844) AND THE DISCOURSE OF EASTERN TRAVEL

Ralph Pordzik

ABSTRACT

The following essay engages with Alexander Kinglake's *Eothen, or Traces of Travel brought home from the East* (1844), one of the most controversial travel books of the nineteenth century. The aim is to locate the text within the larger dynamic of Victorian travel discourse—a dynamic in which texts addressing the Oriental "other" are endowed with new creative potential but are also inherently delimited by their ideology of getting into a direct and unmediated relationship with the other. As I shall argue, *Eothen* not only brings to the fore the crisis of perception gradually making itself visible in Victorian culture but it also helps to augment it. For Kinglake, travel writing is a form of cultural intervention; travelogues simulate social situations that closely follow western views and arrangements, i.e., they create some form of intermediary space that constantly stimulates the imagination and inspires travellers to make judgements not so much on the cultural other than on their own culture. In Eothen, this intervention takes the form of a highly ambiguous narrative which seeks at once to overcome irreconcilable contradictions and to veil the material and political conditions which demand a powerful discourse of otherness—in this case the conditions of Orientalism and the institutional power over the East it claims.

Travel writing: Signification and Legitimation

In his pathbreaking study *Orientalism* (1978), Edward Said writes that during the entire nineteenth century the Orient was a "favorite place for Europeans to travel in and write about. [There] developed a fairly large body of Oriental-style European literature very frequently based on personal experiences in the Orient"—works, according to Said, which "rely on the sheer egoistic powers of the European consciousness at their center."[1] In this paper, I would like to offer a different account, putting into a cultural frame certain of the opposing moves and ambiguities of Kinglake's travelogue *Eothen, or Traces of Travel brought home from the East* (1844), referred to by Said as an "undeservedly famous and popular book" and a "pathetic catalogue of pompous ethnocentrism and tiringly nondescript account of the Englishman's East ... Like many other travellers he [Kinglake] is more interested in remaking himself and the Orient ... than he is in seeing what there is to be seen."[2] My aim is to correct the impression of careless and prejudiced writing in *Eothen* and to arrive at a more sympathetic understanding of this important and innovative work. In the paper, I shall try to locate Kinglake's travel record within the larger deconstructive dynamic of Victorian travel discourse, a dynamic in which texts addressing the cultural other are strategically enabled but also inherently delimited by their underlying assumptions and demarcations, by their trying to get into a putatively direct and unique relationship with the other.

Said is perfectly right when he argues that, owing to the epistemological crisis of late Victorianism, the more self-assuredly provocative, intense and "imperial" travel accounts were written and published in the second half of the century.[3] It is the travellers' tireless "capacity for wonder" which can be regarded as one of the most striking aspects of this type of literature. Wonder, as Raymond Williams puts it, "overrides the determinism of the system ... it is the kind of miracle that happens."[4] However, wonder may also emerge as a miracle delib-

---

[1] Edward Said, *Orientalism. Western Conceptions of the Orient* [1978]. Reprinted with a New Afterword (London: Penguin, 1995) 157-58.

[2] Said, *Orientalism* 1995, 193.

[3] Said, *Orientalism* 1995, 166–69. See also Manfred Pfister, "Robert Byron and the Modernisation of Travel Writing," *Poetica* 31 (1999): 464-75, 468-69.

[4] Raymond Williams, *The English Novel: From Dickens to Lawrence* (London: Chatto & Windus, 1971) 52.

erately manufactured in order to gloss over the writers' difficulties in coming to terms with the foreign cultures they seek to
portray. As Said argues: "Travel books or guidebooks are about
as 'natural' a kind of text, as logical in their composition and in
their use, as any book one can think of, precisely because of
this human tendency to fall back on a text when the uncertainties of travel in strange parts seem to threaten one's equanimity."[5] Fantastic or marvelous renderings of the other can thus
emerge as a kind of ersatz or strategy in travel discourse, taking
the place of the "articulating code"[6] displaced in the process of
remodelling the framework that produces it. Alexander Kinglake's travel classic *Eothen* is a telling case in point.[7] Here, the
shock of the individual encountering a foreign and 'marvellous'
culture is reflected in the book's highly erratic style and vacillation between different forms of reportage, diary, and portrayal
that fail to combine into a conclusive whole. Several times the
narrator sets out to explore in greater detail scenes or incidents
that attract his attention for a time but then fails to control or
incorporate them meaningfully at all. For Kinglake, it seems, it
has become next to impossible to mould the different "traces of
travel brought home" into an orderly narrative of cause and
effect. His account of the East provides the most fantastic kinds
of growth, lore and cliché in an almost purely supplementary
fashion; what runs through it is a paradoxical energy, a loss of
customary settlement, which in its constant repetition appears
implausible because misplaced.

What is the reason for this aesthetic "failure"? As I shall argue here, nineteenth-century travel writing not only brought to
the fore the crisis of perception gradually making itself visible

[5]   Said, *Orientalism* 1995, 93.
[6]   Karl Ludwig Pfeiffer, "Gilbert and Sullivan, or the Cultural Poverty of
      Systems Theory," *Anglistentag 1997. Giessen: Proceedings*, ed.
      Raimund Borgmeier et al. (Trier: wvt, 1998) 337–46: 340.
[7]   Alexander Kinglake, *Eothen, or Traces of Travel Brought Home from
      the East* [1844], with an introduction by J. M. Scott. (Geneva: Edito-
      Service S.A., 1969).

in Victorian culture; in fact, it also helped to augment it. Travel discourse should be regarded as a form of cultural intervention; travelogues simulate social situations that closely follow western arrangements and assumptions, they create some type of artificial, intermediary space that constantly motivates and instigates the traveller's consciousness, moving him or her to make judgements not so much on the other than on his or her own culture. In *Eothen*, this intervention takes the form of a pleasurable narrative which seeks at once to overcome irreconcilable contradictions *and* to mystify the material and political conditions that demand a powerful discourse of otherness—in this case the conditions of Orientalism and the cultural and institutional power over the East it claims. Yet, as narrative *Eothen* ultimately fails to deliver that containment and instead may be seen to foreground precisely those problems which it works to efface or overcome. The result is a radically ambivalent text which exemplifies a moment of historical crisis in Victorian culture. This crisis is the struggle to produce a coherent discourse adequate to the complex requirements of travel writing during one of its most important transformative stages: With the old certainties and convictions threatening to dissolve, new forms of knowledge must be acquired in a complex process of mediation relating views and patterns of meaning drawn from widely different and often conflicting fields of experience. Divorced from his primary cultural affiliations and ways of life, Kinglake has to find a place for the unfamiliar and the new in his received repertory of modes of description and evaluation. The more he struggles to integrate these new elements, however, the more he distances himself from his present ideal of literary representation and mediation, the established Victorian model of dialogue and cultural containment, the then—according to Raymond Williams—only "common mode of interpreting all our existence."[8] Consequently, the very conflicts

---

[8] Raymond Williams, *Culture and Society*. (London: Chatto & Windus 1958) xviii. For a detailed account of Williams's idea of culture in a wider educational frame see Rüdiger Ahrens, "Education in Raymond

which the weakened order generates from within are construed
as attempts to subvert it from without (by an assumed "alien"
other), and that order strengthens itself by simultaneously re-
pressing dissenting elements and eliciting consent for this action via cultural production.[9]

Another way of seeing this has been proposed by Dean
MacCannell in his attempt to define European travel writing in
the context of the emergence of modern tourist industry.[10] According to his view, the European middle classes observed with
irritation the growing fragmentation of the modern age[11] and
tried to respond to it by reintegrating its diversified components—science, history, art, and morality,—thus constructing
new orders of the absolute. In this they were assisted by the
expanding possibilities of the tourist industry which produced

---

Williams's *Theory of Culture*," *Modernisierung und Literatur.
Festschrift für Hans Ulrich Seeber zum 60. Geburtstag*, ed. Walter
Göbel, Stephan Kohl and Hubert Zapf. (Tübingen: Gunter Narr, 2000)
259–67.

[9] For this concept of subversion in literature and culture see Paul Brown,
"'This thing of darkness I acknowledge mine': *The Tempest* and the
Discourse of Colonialism," *Political Shakespeare. Essays in Cultural
Materialism*, ed. Jonathan Dollimore and Alan Sinfield (Manchester:
Manchester U P, 1994) 48–71.

[10] MacCannell, *The Tourist. A New Theory of the Leisure Class.* [1976].
(Berkeley: U of California P, 1999).

[11] The phrase is MacCannell's; see *The Tourist* (quoted above). One cannot
escape the feeling that he wrote his study under the influence of George
Lukacs's *History and Class Consciousness: Studies in Marxist
Dialectics* (1923) which had appeared in English translation in 1971.
Lukacs had tried to prove that the effects of capitalism were
fragmentation and reification; under such circumstances, he claimed,
every human being becomes an object or commodity and wholeness and
community finally disappear. This specifically modern discontinuity,
MacCannell seems to suggest in accordance with Lukacs, can only be
overcome by an act of mental will, an act through which individuals can
join one another by imagining the 'common bond' of travel between
them and thus break the rigidity imposed upon them by tyrannical
outside forces.

modern alternatives to the disparate experience of everyday life. Subsuming perceived moments of social and cultural difference to their own perspectival domain, middle class travellers took every effort to make them appear as an orderly series of formal representations and forge them into a unified design. Constructing these new totalities, however, they simultaneously effected the "differentiation"[12] of culture into ever more distinct and marketable experiences; they artificially preserved and remodelled the non-modern and the "primitive" (e.g., in the Romantic age), thus affording it a major position in western commodity culture.[13] As MacCannell writes: "The dialectics of authenticity lead to a progressive development of spurious structure, ever further removed from domestic life, as modern man is driven ever further in his quest for authentic values and his true self." And he concludes: "The end is an immense accumulation of reflexive experiences which synthesize fiction and reality into a vast symbolism, a modern world."[14]

MacCannell's critique has the merit of dispensing with the time-honored myth that there can ever be some kind of "equal footing" between the traveller and his "object," a fully reliable mode of recognizing cultures absolutely different from our own. From the very outset, the middle classes as the bearers of modern practices of travelling, sight-seeing and exploration pressed others to adapt themselves to their own understanding of the world, their established modes of production and consumption. In return, they preserved and musealised the indigenous and the exotic as valuable signs[15]—a dubious gift, as it

---

[12] MacCannell, *The Tourist* 1999, 13.

[13] MacCannell, *The Tourist* 1999, 13. For the marketability of travel experiences see also John Urry, *The Tourist Gaze. Leisure and Travel in Contemporary Societies* (London: Sage, 1990) 5 f.

[14] MacCannell, *The Tourist* 1999, 23 and 152.

[15] Cf. Groys, "Unsere Welt auf Reisen," 35; MacCannell, *The Tourist* 1999, 198. For the view of the other as sign see Jonathan Culler: "the tourist is interested in everything as a sign of itself.... All over the world the ... tourists are fanning out in search of the signs of Frenchness,

served mainly to repress and control their own consuming desire for the local or marginalized other and the allegedly "primitive." Their writing thus gained materiality through the desires and fantasies played out in its interpretations of otherness—interpretations that, by making the unconscious conscious, replaced ideologies of western identity with less accessible assumptions.

In historical terms, it can indeed be said that in the nineteenth century, English travellers held a certain form of cultural authority over the Orient. Said's critique of western travel practice is therefore not, as Christoph Bode once remarked, "beside the point."[16] Already in the eighteenth century, there existed a growing body of literature based on personal experiences in the Orient. William Beckford (1759–1844) springs to mind immediately as one prominent writer; Eliot Warburton (*The Crescent and the Cross*, 1845) and Richard Burton (*Personal Narrative of a Pilgrimage to Al-Madinah and Meccah*, 1855–56) are obvious examples for the Victorian century. As travellers in the Orient, these writers felt the urge to protect themselves from the "unsettling influences"[17] of the East, the "eccentricities of Oriental life, with its odd calendars, its exotic spatial configurations, its hopelessly strange languages, its seemingly perverse morality."[18] They also tended to simplify these complexities and to reduce them to a series of "detailed items presented in a normative European prose style."[19] Not only defining but also carefully "editing" their version of the Orient, they turned their

---

typical Italian behaviour, exemplary Oriental stances, typical American thruways, traditional English pubs." "Semiotics of Tourism," *American Journal of Semiotics* 1 (1981): 127–40, 127.

[16] Christoph Bode, "Alexander Kinglake, *Eothen or Traces of Travel Brought Home from the East* (1844) oder Wie man sich nicht ansteckt". *West Meets East: Klassiker der britischen Orient-Reiseliteratur.* (Heidelberg: Universitätsverlag C. Winter, 1997) 49–67: 64.

[17] Said, *Orientalism* 1995, 166.

[18] Said, *Orientalism* 1995, 166.

[19] Said, *Orientalism* 1995, 167.

encounter with the East into a specific kind of cultural situation or *méthode experimental* (Emile Zola) affording them the right to systematize, exclude, displace, and bring into focus.

More than other travel writers of his time, Kinglake was aware of the subjective viewpoint inherent in his account; he didn't believe in the possibility of seeing the Orient "firsthand," from the angle of a "person immersed in it."[20] What he seems to have had in mind was a sensibly restored as well as *exotic* and pleasurable picture of Oriental life and manners. Fragments of experience, such as those supplied by travel, served as material, but the narrative shape and the figures were constructed by his writer-traveller, for whom 'experience' consisted mainly of circumventing the unruly life forms of the East with definition, portrait, chronicle, and characterization. What distinguishes Kinglake from those who preceded him is that he did *not* care to excise from his rendering of the Orient anything that might have ruffled Victorian sensibilities, that contradicted the demand for unified experience. On the contrary, *Eothen* is a wildly comic and often defiant provocation of middle class readers' expectations and values. It is linked to a particular form of literary activity intervening in a Victorian mental and institutional framework and directing itself against the forces of constriction and alienation and the practical spirit of the "uncultured" middle classes. Addressing himself to his close friend Eliot Warburton (1810-25), Kinglake writes in the preface:

> The very feeling, however, which enabled me to write thus freely, prevented me from robing my thoughts in that grave and decorous style which I should have maintained if I had professed to lecture the public. Whilst I feigned to myself that you, and you only, were listening, I could not by possibility speak very solemnly. Heaven forbid that I should talk to my own genial friend, as though he were a

---

[20] Said, *Orientalism* 1995, 196.

great and enlightened Community, or any other respectable Aggregate![21]

The marked disrespect for common values and a common
manner of address signals Kinglake's critique of the pretentiously informative and often plainly mediocre travel report of
his time. Presenting his own work as a travel diary in disguise
everybody can buy and read who actually *wants to* ("the familiarity of language … may be laid to the account of our delightful
intimacy"[22]), he manages to reach the casual Victorian reader
unaccustomed to such frankness in literary writing. What the
implied reader will find in the book is not, however, congruent
with what he may experience in the East as a historically "real"
and, most of all, material place: "It is right to forewarn people
… that the book is quite superficial in its character."[23] From the
beginning, *Eothen* exhibits a keen awareness of the impossibility to get into contact with the world of the cultural other "as it
really is"; the particularities of time and space are deliberately
downplayed as ornamental and profane:

> One's mind regains in absence that dominion over
> earthly things which has been shaken by their rude
> contact; you force yourself hardily into the material
> presence of a mountain or a river, whose name be-
> longs to poetry and ancient religion, rather than to
> the external world; your feelings, wound up and kept
> ready for some sort of half-expected rapture, are
> chilled and borne down for the time under all this
> load of real earth and water, but, let these once pass
> out of sight, and then again the old fanciful notions
> are restored, and the mere realities which you have
> just been looking at are thrown back so far into dis-
> tance, that the very event of your intrusion upon such

---

[21] Kinglake, *Eothen* 1969, 2.
[22] Kinglake, *Eothen* 1969, 3.
[23] Kinglake, *Eothen* 1969, 3.

scenes begins to look dim and uncertain as though it belonged to mythology.[24]

How can the excuse for a travel account so self-professedly free from all genuine representation be "its truth" and "righteous[ness] in matters of fact"?[25] How can such a book ever hope to convey plausible impressions "which were really and truly received at the time" of the writer's "rambles"?[26] It seems only fair to assume that encountering the East has worn away Kinglake's emotional balance and inbred rationality of time and space. In the Orient, he is confronted with antique splendour and fierceness, with boundless distance, deserts, and the "sublime melancholy" of Eastern mentality. But these can only be thought and written about when they are not experienced directly, as the above statement seeks to point out. Thus, whenever Kinglake's traveller happens to come upon something he does not expect or is not prepared to cope with, he must resort to prefabricated images of the other to represent what is otherwise unsayable. Overwhelmed by the scope and the awful dimensions of the world surrounding him, he runs risk of losing the referential power he claims for his travelogue. The following passage, recounting a trip to Beirut, amply demonstrates this threat: "nearly all my knowledge of the people, except in regard of their mere costume and outward appearance, is drawn from books and despatches. To these last I have the honour to refer you."[27] Or another passage, describing the death of a group of monks whom the plague had summoned to "taste of real death": "… and though I have no authority for the story except an Italian newspaper, I harbour no doubt of its truth, for the facts were detailed with minuteness and strictly corresponded with all that I knew of the poor fellows to whom they

---

24 Kinglake, *Eothen* 1969, 52.
25 Kinglake, *Eothen* 1969, 4.
26 Kinglake, *Eothen* 1969, 4.
27 Kinglake, *Eothen* 1969, 89.

related."[28] The act of immediate experience is even more dramatically revealed as an act of recognition in the following scene depicting the similarities between the geographic location of Samothrace in Turkey and Homer's aesthetic conception of it (who probably never saw the original site):

> I think that this testing of the poet's words by map and compass may have shaken a little of my faith in the completeness of his knowledge. Well, now I had come; there to the south was Tenedos, and here at my side was Imbros, all right, and according to the map, but aloft over Imbros,—aloft in a far away heaven was Samothrace, the watchtower of Neptune!
> So Homer had appointed it, and so it was: the map was correct enough, but could not, like Homer, convey *the whole truth*. Thus vain and false are mere human surmises and doubts which clash with Homeric writ![29]

"Fact imitates fiction," one feels like exclaiming here.[30] But are we really supposed to regard Kinglake's casual references to cultural pre-texts as some kind of artistic pose, an illustration of his peculiar notion of "sentimental truth," his "liberty to tell as little as one chooses" about countries already "thoroughly and ably described"?[31] Or is this another exhibition of epistemological insecurity, a sign of the European writer's inability to give an orderly shape to his divergent experiences in the

---

[28] Kinglake, *Eothen* 1969, 126.
[29] Kinglake, *Eothen* 1969, 55.
[30] It is tempting to see the map as a guiding metaphor in *Eothen*. According to Jurij Lotman, maps are examples of plotless texts, and once we draw a line from A to B, they acquire a plot: Action is introduced. The narrator's rambles signify, so to say, the only textual event in the book, namely that of the endless introduction of new events, landscapes, objects, and characters.
[31] Kinglake, *Eothen* 1969, 4.

East? As I shall argue here, the seemingly disconnected moments of expression in *Eothen* are neither romantic nor self-congratulatory; in fact, they result from Kinglake's difficulty to overcome the fragmentation of his modern perspective and to turn his first-hand experiences into a unified or absolute design. They signify the problematic situation of a self caught between conflicting symbolic orders, a situation encoding the drama of definition of self and other in varying and often uneven relations. Said, in *Orientalism*, fails to see this problem, arguing instead that Kinglake's

> ostensible purpose ... is to prove that travel in the Orient is important to "moulding of your character— that is, your very identity", but in fact this turns out to be little more than solidifying "your" anti-Semitism, xenophobia, and general all-purpose race prejudice ... Although Kinglake blithely confesses to no knowledge of any Oriental language, he is not constrained by ignorance from making sweeping generalizations about the Orient, its culture, mentality, and society. Many of the attitudes he repeats are canonical, of course, but it is interesting how little the experience of actually seeing the Orient affected his opinions. Like many other travellers he is more interested in remaking himself and the Orient ... than he is in seeing what there is to be seen.[32]

My question here would be: How can an author write about what he sees when the discourses at hand are not really suited to meet this demand for unprejudiced accuracy and truthfulness? How is he to make reliable observations if the official repertory of verbs and adjectives fails to accommodate the material vision of the East opening in front of him? Said himself argues that European writers and scholars were forced to con-

---

[32] Said, *Orientalism* 1995, 193.

front a set of "imposing resistances"[33] to their common modes
of representation but he misinterprets the urgency of this conflict in the case of Kinglake's travelogue. The Victorian travel-
ler-writer seems to have been aware of the fact that the various
data of experience gained from travelling can always be organized to generate specific feelings and beliefs. All habits and
social attitudes, he seems to tell us, are residues of cultural experiences of this or a related order, separated from their original
contexts and transformed in the individual mind. To insist on
the natural value of the local and the authentic, as Said does, on
the unique and specific status of cultural ensembles as prolon-
gations of the world of concrete fact and actuality, is of no real
purchase here: We cannot, in any intuitive sense, "see" or
"feel" the Orient. No single person who shares in the real life of
a specific culture owns the privilege to convey the authentic
value of this experience. We stand apart observing the pulse of
everyday life in a particular side street or market in Beirut, for
instance, or, attending a performance in Cairo, turn into dilettante ethnographers, if we do so at all. The given discourses or
linguistic and cultural arrangements rule out the possibility of
authenticity in the very act of producing it. This is not to say
that there is no such thing as an autonomously felt identity, no
real or grounded fear of being cut off from personal relationships and positive communal experience. If committed to the
page or voiced within the orbit of the officially accredited media, however, this feeling automatically turns into a *representation* of otherness, not the (other) thing itself.

Containment and Subversion

Looked at from this angle, it becomes obvious that Kinglake
can never really manage to overcome the loss of original experience. As he himself concedes: "there will often be found in
my narrative a jarring discord between the associations prop-

---

[33] Said, *Orientalism* 1995, 193.

erly belonging to interesting sites, and the tone in which I speak of them."[34] Or: "the traveller ... tells you of objects, not as he knows them to be, but as they seemed to him." "His very self-ishness ... compels him, as it were, in his writings, to observe the law of perspective."[35] This brings us back to our initial point of analysis, namely the problem of transcending cultural contradictions and of harmonizing the conflictual perceptions governing the text. Kinglake's ambivalence in this respect—his unconscious foregrounding of cultural experiences he actually seeks to efface or contain—is dramatically borne out in several passages describing his encounter with a particularly "weird" kind of otherness. A case in point is the scene in which is de-picted a female white slave held captive in a citadel near Cairo. Kinglake describes her as "very young," though "extremely fat. She gave me the idea of having been got up for sale,—of hav-ing been fattened, and whitened by medicines or by some pecu-liar diet. I was firmly determined not to see any more of her than the face."[36] Although described as "Circassian," the slave should be regarded as a projection of the writer's own Euro-pean (imperial) self here, reflecting the cultural fears and anxie-ties associated with being a western traveller in the Orient. Ar-tificially "whitened" and "fattened," and subjected to the same treatment the imperial explorers meted out to many Eastern nations in the past, she marks the "return of the repressed," perversely thriving, as it were, on the cultural power and pre-dominance of "whiteness" in the East. In all her fatness and vulgarity, the slave connotes degeneracy, disorder, and a "de-monic repetition"[37] threatening the western writer's stable and integral self. She represents everything that Kinglake is afraid of in the Orient, all that might dissuade him from his premedi-tated course. At the same time, she is not entirely without power. For at the heart of the colonial stereotype, there always

---

[34] Kinglake, *Eothen* 1969, 4.
[35] Kinglake, *Eothen* 1969, 6.
[36] Kinglake, *Eothen* 1969, 226.
[37] Homi Bhaba, "The Other Question," *Screen* 24 (1983): 18–36, 18.

lies the fact of a disruptive threat that needs to be admitted. If Kinglake's cliché declares the slave to be rapacious and overwhelming in all her obesity, then even as it marks her as inferior to himself, it announces her power to violate and thus requires the imposition of restraint if such power is to be curtailed ("I was firmly determined not to see any more of her than the face"). Thus, the colonial stereotype continues to disturb: it is always, as Paul Brown puts it, "impelled to further action,"[38] propelling the narrative to move on. All this is due to the fact, however, that there prevails in Kinglake's Oriental world a dense atmosphere of uncertain dreams, fables and "fresh wonders"[39] infinitely multiplying themselves past resolution and definiteness, so that the traveller's patterns of classification and description ultimately fail to structure it.

As a rule, *Eothen* registers the dissonant voices of the other only in an effort to contain and control; this effort fails for reasons easily discernible in the text. What the traveller tries to repress or stow away returns within the space of his own narrative, because as a writer and dilettante interpreter of other cultures he clearly depends on what he thinks he can relegate to an outer sphere or foreign existential domain. As a consequence, the text as a whole produces an increasingly self-reflective and self-contradictory discourse on cultural difference. This discourse comes to the fore especially in the narrative's treatment of religious issues. On the one hand, Kinglake's narrator confronts all forms of religious zeal in what has become known as an expression of "public and national will over the Orient."[40] Referring to the fasts of the Greek Church in Smyrna, e.g., he writes that they

> produce an ill effect upon the character of the people, for they are not a mere farce, but are carried to such an extent, as to bring about a real mortification

---

[38] Brown, "'This thing of darkness I acknowledge mine,'" 1994, 58.
[39] Kinglake, *Eothen* 1969, 91.
[40] Said, *Orientalism* 1995, 194.

of the flesh. The febrile irritation of the frame, operating in conjunction with the depression of the spirits
occasioned by abstinence, will so far answer the objects of the rite, as to engender some religious excitement, but this is of a morbid and gloomy character; and it seems to be certain, that along with the
increase of sanctity, there comes a fiercer desire for
the perpetration of dark crimes. The number of mur-
ders committed during Lent, is greater, I am told,
than at any other time of the year.[41]

What comes along as a satirical account of an especially
weird form of spiritual devotion may also be seen as a reasonable critique of religious seduction, written in the spirit of a
specifically western tradition of secular enlightenment and agnosticism. Looked at from this angle, Kinglake's record is one
segment in a vast body of Victorian writing based on the common faith in a universally accessible reality that can be experienced and interpreted by all and agreed upon in a kind of continued, sensible dialogue. Being another western traveller in
search for the "real" Orient, why should Kinglake not be entitled to brandish acts of intolerance which threaten to destroy
the integrity of others or to ridicule habits that imperil the idea
of democracy? However, Kinglake's position in this respect is
not as unequivocal as it may seem at first. Later on in his book,
he gives a compelling account of the plague in Cairo, claiming
it is unavoidable for the traveller

that after a little while the social atmosphere of Asia
will begin to infect him, and, if he has been unaccustomed to the cunning offence by which Reason prepares the means of guarding herself against fallacy,
he will yield himself at last to the faith of those
around him; and this he will do by sympathy, it
would seem, rather than from conviction. I have

---

[41] Kinglake, *Eothen* 1969, 66.

been much interested in observing that the mere
"practical man," however skilful and shrewd in his
own way, has not the kind of power that will enable
him to resist the gradual impression made upon his
mind by the common opinion of those whom he sees
and hears from day to day. Even amongst the English (though their good sense and sound religious
knowledge would be likely to guard them from error) I have known the calculating merchant, the in-
quisitive traveller, and the post-captain, with his
bright, wakeful eye of command—I have known all
these surrender themselves to the really magic-like
influence of other people's minds.[42]

Again, what is foregrounded here is the threat of a disruptive
other unbalancing the western self, something strange and disconcerting that needs to be dealt with; but this time it is also
tentatively affirmed as a valuable force helping the individual
adapt himself to an alien environment. Like other travellers
before him, Kinglake seems to feel his detached powerlessness,
and perhaps also a kind of willingness to enter and become part
of what he sees. Yet the issue is more complex; in a mysterious
kind of way, the Orient seems to remain barred to the westerner's full participation—rational or mystical—in it. At surface level, all the perceived habits pertaining to the Arab world
can be interpreted rationally; thus, the pilgrims journeying to
Palestine are "a well-disposed, orderly body of people, not
strongly enthusiastic, but desirous to comply with the ordi-
nances of their religion,"[43] and the worshippers of Terra Santa
can be derided as religious hypocrites who steadily embrace the
"sticks and the stones" from a "calm sense of duty," not "working out," but *transacting* the great business of salvation."[44]

---

[42] Kinglake, *Eothen* 1969, 116–17.
[43] Kinglake, *Eothen* 1969, 173.
[44] Kinglake, *Eothen* 1969, 165.

Kinglake seems to impose on all these people his own brand of scepticism ("patient reason [fighting] her slow battle against Asiatic prejudice"[45]), seeking to privilege the rational element by turning it into an undeniable absolute. What finally shows *him* to be relying on what he appears to exclude is his frank statement that he has had the heart to talk about the "pernicious effects" of the weird and ex-centric *bizzareries* of the Orient— "yet to these I owe most gracious and beautiful visions!"[46] Drawn ever deeper into the contradictions of his own discourse, Kinglake can no longer reduce the incongruities before him, and it won't help anymore to proclaim the hand that put down such words as "seized by some false angel"[47]; denigrating the superstitions of the Arab peoples, Kinglake inadvertently fore-grounds their positive and possibly enriching qualities. He points out, e.g., that it was the natives' adhering to their inher-ited rules and beliefs that secured their survival during the time of the plague: "The Orientals … have more quiet fortitude than Europeans under afflictions of this sort, and they never allow the Plague to interfere with their religious usages."[48] He even goes so far as professing to have benefited from their approved strategies of survival while staying at Constantinople:[49] having come into contact with a "plague-stricken corpse" and believ-ing himself doomed to death, he repudiates the "contagion the-ory," and from that time "went wherever I chose, without tak-ing any serious pains to avoid a touch …, and so … was able to

---

[45] Kinglake, *Eothen* 1969, 34.
[46] Kinglake, *Eothen* 1969, 67.
[47] Kinglake, *Eothen* 1969, 68.
[48] Kinglake, *Eothen* 1969, 216.
[49] It must be seen as an indirect confirmation of this belief when the reader is told, by and by, that *all* died of the plague, "my banker, my doctor, my landlord, and my magician…. A lad who acted as a helper in the house I occupied lost a brother and a sister within a few hours. Out of my two established donkey-boys one died. I did not hear of any instance in which a plague-stricken patient had recovered" (*Eothen*, 234). The only survivor of the plague is, of course, Kinglake himself!

live amongst the dying without that alarm and anxiety which would inevitably have pressed upon my mind, if I had allowed myself to believe that every passing touch was really a probable death-stroke."[50] When finally he overcomes a strong and delirious fever he had mistaken for the plague,[51] this must be interpreted as a symbolic victory over the western mindset and its irreducible tendency to create threatening images of otherness—a process repeating itself, as it were, in colonial history: First the dominant order has to produce a potentially dangerous other before it can confirm its own strength of will and power of anticipation in overcoming its resistance to it.

The reader may believe this episode to be true or not, but what it shows is that there are features in Kinglake's representation of the Orient which disrupt the recognition of his account as merely solidifying "anti-Semitism, xenophobia, and general all-purpose race prejudice."[52] At surface level, Kinglake utilizes religious attitudes for his own worldly interest, revealing their alleged spuriousness and reworking them into a kind of cultural façade behind which the Oriental hides his true inner, rational being; yet at closer inspection it becomes apparent that it is the very religion he defames that accounts for the exceptional cultural encounters and stunning moments of rich experience that make the book worth reading! Here, the plague together with the folklore and the motives of religious superstition that accompany it is seen to operate not for the colonizer but for the colonized, for those who suffer from humiliation and who find in their inherited belief a powerful and resistant force against imperial domination. Almost obsessively, the narrator returns again and again to the topic, recounting numerous instances of native suspense of reason and logic in the midst of the ravages of the disease: "when an Osmanlee dies [of the plague], one of his dresses is cut up, and a small piece of it is sent to each of

---

[50] Kinglake, *Eothen* 1969, 40–41.
[51] See Kinglake, *Eothen* 1969, 235–37.
[52] Said, *Orientalism* 1995, 193.

his friends as a memorial of the departed—a fatal present ... for it too often forces the living not merely to remember the dead man, but to follow and bear him company."[53] There seems to be in this a secret quality beyond the narrator's rational grasp of things, something he almost compulsively returns to, reports and comments on, and tries to fathom, even though it evades his rational faculties and puts into doubt his agnosticism. It is this quality existing by and for itself, something impossible to subsume or accommodate to the requirements of the westerner's discourse and rationally biased attitudes.

Conclusion

What all this demonstrates is that an alternative space beyond colonial appropriation—in this case, the plague as a "mysterious and exciting"[54] force in a "degenerate," late-imperial setting and site of resistance against western rationalism—can only be presented through Orientalist discourse, since the officially recognized discourse of Eastern otherness is the only one at hand. Obviously, Kinglake's narrator can only mediate the "truly oriental"[55] excess of the plague through that very discourse, and so the discourse itself may be said to produce the unusual and contradictory form of resistance against western prejudice emerging in the text. *Eothen* registers, if only momentarily and with alternating success, a radical ambivalence at the heart of western discourse of travel in the Orient, demonstrating that it is a site of permanent struggle over signs and meanings rather than a homogeneous style or schema of perception. In its ambiguity it radiates a sense of *intervention* and *interpellation* which reminds us of the fact that the "handling" of Oriental culture can always be adapted to suit the purposes of specific narratives. As I have attempted to show

---

[53] Kinglake, *Eothen* 1969, 39.
[54] Kinglake, *Eothen* 1969, 38.
[55] Kinglake, *Eothen* 1969, 38.

above with specific examples, opposing moves and strategies of writing and definition—such as those governing Kinglake's text—encode struggle and contradiction even as, or rather because, they strive to insist on the legitimacy of established patterns of Victorian narrative discourse.

On the whole, then, *Eothen* is a perfect model of ideological intervention in western travel writing; it requires the conflict with the other in order to demonstrate its own power as narrative: Struggle and conflict therefore precondition the announcement of the writer's victory over otherness, over the potentially disruptive forces that once again have been subsumed to the preordained idea of Victorian culture as unified experience, as a "common faith" and "common way of life" in the sense of Raymond Williams's theory of culture. Without really acknowledging it, *Eothen* requires and produces the other—another continually undermining and dispersing the narrative's power of conviction. No matter how much Kinglake refers his readers back to Oriental clichés and stereotypes, no matter how strongly he strives to emphasize the absolute difference between the westerner and the Arab, his account serves as a kind of "limit text"[56] in which the characteristic operations of western Orientalist and travel discourses may be revealed—as instruments of domination and "register[s] of beleaguerment"[57] (the best example being Kinglake's lengthy description of plague-ridden Cairo and his ironic identification with the Oriental other as *both* become interstitial) or as a site of radical cultural ambivalence. These operations produce techniques and patterns that seek to infuse and efface western institutional power; they are also, however, driven into contradiction and disruption. It comes as no surprise, therefore, that Kinglake finally registers, albeit rather subliminally, his difference from the other itinerant "European[s] ignorant of the East,"[58] claim-

---

[56] Brown, "'This thing of darkness I acknowledge mine'" 1994, 68.
[57] Brown, "'This thing of darkness I acknowledge mine'" 1994, 68.
[58] Kinglake, *Eothen* 1969, 224–25.

ing the privilege of genuine access to Oriental culture after having shared *their* predicament and having adopted *their* rules
and methods. Receiving all signs and attributes of his rescued
identity as a traveller—his surviving the plague, his procurement of dromedaries formerly belonging to victims of the
plague, etc.—from the Orientals, he can now wind his way out
of the "pest-stricken" city of Cairo to embrace new adventures.
He may return to his former self-assurance as a British traveller
and agent of a powerful colonizing nation (and indeed does so
towards the end of the narrative[59]), but this change will not
again pass unacknowledged, for it will draw attention to the
way it presents a passage from self to other that is apt to subvert the order it sets out to reconfirm.

---

[59] See page 295, *Eothen*, where the narrator loses some words on the
Christians of Damascus who, "with all the claims of superior intellect,
learning and industry, were kept down under the heel of the Mussulmans
by reason of their having *our* faith. I heard, as I fancied, the faint echo of
an old Crusader's conscience, that whispered, and said, 'Common
Cause!'"

MEDITATION UPON LIFE AND DEATH: THE NOTION OF DEATH IN THE POETRY OF EMILY DICKINSON AND TAO YUANMING

Liu Dan

ABSTRACT

Emily Dickinson and Tao Yuanming are two great reclusive poets. The first part of this comparative study is to explore the two poets' different and similar viewpoints on life and death. The second part of this paper is to analyze their ideas from their religious influences, their social and cultural backgrounds and their inner worlds as well. In the long run, this comparative study might serve to reveal the fundamental philosophies that help to form the Chinese and American writers' notion of death on the whole.

Biographical Discrepancies

Sometime between 1630 and 1638, Emily Dickinson's earliest American ancestors left for a raw British outpost in Connecticut. Some two hundred years later, Emily Dickinson, possibly one of the greatest women poets in world literary history, began her seclusion and continued her creation of poems that granted her fame more than one hundred years after her death. Sometime between 380 AD and 420 AD, Chinese literary history recorded some great poems composed by a great poet—Tao Yuanming. Apparently, these two poets, one being a man, the other a woman, with one thousand and two hundred years between them, have nothing to do with each other. However, Tao's idea of retreating to the country life and life of simplicity found echoes years later from Emily Dickinson who lived on the other side of the Pacific Ocean. More importantly, a close reading of the death poems composed by the two poets would turn out to be thought-provoking for those who are concerned with cross-cultural communication. It is amazing to find these two poets' notion of death could be so similar while each maintains its unique originality. This comparative study tries to analyze the two poets' ideas of life and death from their religious influences, cultural angles, and their inner worlds.

Thematic Similarities

Of the nearly 1,800 poems by Emily Dickinson that readers today have the possibility to read, one third deal with the subject of death and examine death from the viewpoint of the living, the dying, or the dead. Toward the end of his life, Tao Yuanming composed three elegies for himself. All these three poems examine death from the point of view of the dead. The first describes the scene when the speaker is put into the coffin; the second focuses on the relatives' mourning for the dead; the third depicts the way to the tomb. More importantly, the two poets' attitude towards life and death turn out to be quite similar. For one thing, they agree that death is something quite natural. Thus there is no need to be afraid of it. Tao Yuanming writes in his "Requiem" No.1: As death displaces every life for sure,/ An early death can't be called premature." [1] Similarly, Emily Dickinson writes in her poem No.712: "Because I could not stop for death,— / He kindly stopped for me— / The carriage held but just ourselves— / And immortality." [2] The tone of the two poems is calm and even casual. The narrator in Dickinson's poem, reckoned to be the author herself, is too

---

[1] Rongpei Wang, *A Comparative Study of English Translations of Tao Yuanming's Poems* (Beijing: Foreign Language Teaching and Research Press, 1999) 373.

[2] Richard Wilbur, ed., *Emily Dickinson: Selected with an Introduction and Notes* (New York: Dell Publishing Co. Inc, 1960) 77.

busy and too contented to stop her life. Death, who is pictured here as a kind and considerate gentleman, stops to call her to go with him in the carriage. Hence, death is a natural process that surely will occur in a person's life journey.

Secondly, their death poems demonstrate the two poets' viewpoint towards fame and material goods by depicting the dead person's behavior upon death. In Dickinson's poems, the dead gives away all her keepsakes. "I willed my keepsakes— signed away / What portion of me be / Assignable—."[3] In another poem, "Death is a Dialogue Between," we can trace the poet's relationship to New England Transcendentalism. For transcendentalists, human body and outward nature are merely "clothes" or "an overcoat of clay" as Dickinson puts it in her poem. What they care about is the "Over Soul." Under the influence of Transcendentalism, Dickinson attacks the over-emphasized idea of materialism and commercialism. In Tao's poem, the dead cares no more about gain or loss, right or wrong. He writes, "Ten millennium after I am gone, / My fame or shame will cease to linger on."[4] For him, there is only one thing regrettable— "That I did not drink enough wine when alive." From these lines, we can sense his optimistic attitude toward death. When death is coming near, readers can find no worry, no anxiety, and no fear from the two poets' writing.

Thirdly, the two poets record the reaction of their beloved upon their death, which reflects the heart-felt grief and love between the living and the dead. In Tao's poem, he writes, "My tender children cry for me in vain / While my friends are shedding tears." Also, in "Requiem" No.2, he writes, "The Kith and Kin weep in a mournful mood." In "Requiem" No.3, "My relatives may have some lingering grief."[5] In his later life, Tao lived together with his young son's family. His daughter-in-law treated him very well, and Tao loved the family very much. In Dickinson's poem, we find "The eyes around—had wrung

---

[3] Wilbur, *Emily Dickinson* 1960, 58.

[4] Wilbur, *Emily Dickinson* 1960, 373.

[5] Wang, *Translations of Tao Yuanming's Poems* 1999, 379, 383.

them dry— / And Breaths were gathering firm …"[6] For
Dickinson, death and love are closely related to each other. In
"I Have Never Lost As Much But Twice," Dickinson explicitly
expresses the idea that life without love is death. Readers can
sense the deep love between the two parts. The living are
crying and mourning for the dead. More than that, the living are
begging before the door of God, hoping God will return their
beloved.

Differences in Symbolic Expression

As two poets from two different cultures in different times,
Tao and Dickinson demonstrate their different notions of life
and death as well. First of all, Emily Dickinson's death poems
are distinctive for their direct, simple, and diverse images.
Actually, she depicts death from different perspectives. As for
Tao, death is a simple thing. Death is death. In his poems, he
uses such images as "wild grass," "frost," "vast expanse" and
"poplars" to describe death scenes. In Dickinson's poems, a
mantel clock, a fly, the setting sun, the porcelain, and even a
gentleman can serve as symbols of death. In "A Clock
Stopped—Not the Mantel's," Dickinson compares a stopped
clock to the end of life, the sudden cessation of life and time. In
another often quoted poem, "fly," which is open to several
interpretations, becomes the symbol of death. For one, as an
insect, it is related to the rotten and putrid flesh, which easily
reminds people of rotten corpses and death. It can also be
regarded as the verb "to fly" which means to move or float in
the air. The second interpretation suggests the Christian belief
of salvation. People can be chosen and saved by God after their
death. They can float in the air to go to heaven. Dickinson's use
of different symbols of death greatly demonstrates her use of
Romantic imagination.

---

[6]   Wilbur, *Emily Dickinson* 1960, 58.

Secondly, readers may witness Dickinson's ambiguous ideas of immortality, whereas in Tao's poems, he tends to believe there is no life after death. In the fourth stanza of Dickinson's poem No.712, the narrator tells the reader explicitly that they are driving towards a country cemetery where the house of death, a fresh grave, can be seen. By then, both the narrator and the reader realize the destination of this trip. Then the last stanza indicates that the trip is eternal and endless because the "house's heads were toward eternity." This poem suggests the existence of immortality and eternity. Though the body of a person may be put into a grave, the journey of the soul cannot be stopped. However, in "I Heard a Fly Buzz – When I Died," Dickinson ends her poem quite ironically without the expected vision of immortality. The fly interposes between the dying person and the light. "Light" here is actually a pun. It can mean the light from the dying person's window; more importantly, it suggests the radiant light in the Heaven. Ferlazzo suggests that in this poem Dickinson gives up the hope of immortality, and Barton Levi St. Armand thinks that this poem "is similar to hundreds of mortuary effusions that dwell on the details of deathbed scenes."[7] In Tao's "Requiem" No.1, he writes, "My spirit is dissolved into thin air, / With my frame in the coffin lying there;"[8] in No.3, "What else is there for the clay." Therefore, as far as Tao is concerned, death is the end of people's lives, and there is no life after death. When a person dies, he is unaware of any losses or gains.

As a poet living in the later half of the nineteenth century America, Emily Dickinson's death poems clearly indicate the poet's characteristic as a Romantic writer. While Tao's ideas of death are more philosophical, Dickinson's death poems create a kind of combination of sad thoughtfulness, repressed terror, slight shiver, mild humor, and sometimes even bitter satire. For example, in the poem "It was just this time, Last year, I died,"

---

[7]   Barton Levi St. Armand, *Emily Dickinson and Her Culture* (Cambridge: Cambridge U P, 1984) 56.

[8]   Wang, *Translations of Tao Yuanming's Poems* 1999, 373.

which has been regarded as her "most obviously hostile autobiographical poem,"[9] she describes herself as a corpse. In another poem, "I Never Lost As Much But Twice," we can sense her deep grief and sorrow due to the parting of her beloved. Emily Dickinson makes full use of her unique imagination to reflect her various perspectives on death. As for the Chinese poet, Tao's requiems for himself were written at the close of his life. He uses a matter-of-fact attitude to depict death. "What else is there for the dead man to say? / Underneath the hill his body turns to clay"[10] clearly demonstrates his idea of death. It makes no difference how long a person is to live. Death means going back to the earth. People once again become part of Nature. Death is a natural course.

Cultural Backgrounds Compared

From the analysis above, we may note the similarities and differences of the two reclusive poets' ideas of life and death, which might be analyzed through their respective religious influences, social and cultural backgrounds, and their inner worlds as well. Dickinson's notion of death is closely related with her religious uncertainty. At the time of Dickinson's birth, the churches of her hometown Amherst were Orthodox Congressional with services attended twice on Sundays and with daily Bible reading encouraged at home. Sermons stressed man's depravity, the necessity of conversion, the immense impact of death, and the idea of eternity and immortality. Although Dickinson rejected the dogmas of Calvinism, the fact that her community was occupied with Calvinist eschatology indicates that she could not be freed from its influence. Thomas H. Johnson points out in his *Emily Dickinson* that the poet clung to the traditional (Calvinist) orthodoxy even in her moments of severest doubt. Puritanism, one of the major

---

[9]   Elizabeth Phillips, *Emily Dickinson: Personae and Performance* (University Park: Pennsylvania State U P, 1988) 87.

[10]   Wang, *Translations of Tao Yuanming's Poems* 1999, 383.

religious influences in Dickinson's life, emphasizes the faith to God. During the 1820s and 1830s, the Second Great Awakening was in full force trying to rejuvenate Puritan zeal through a series of religious revivals. Because of the parting and death of her beloved relatives and friends, she opposed the idea of a higher power (namely God), as influencing her every move and thus governing her thoughts and beliefs towards life. Readers may find different images of God in her poems— burglar, banker, and father. In her death poems, Dickinson tries to explore final answers to these important religious questions, and hopes to get closer to the secret of death.

Some critics claim the three major thought-systems of Confucianism, Taoism, and Buddhism have all exerted profound influence on Tao Yuanming's creation in his lifetime. However, written two years before his death, Tao's requiems are greatly influenced by the Neo-Taoism, which emerged as the prevailing religion to replace, or at least to supplement, the previously popular Confucianism. In Tao's other poems, we can also trace the influence of Taoism. Actually, it has been calculated that Tao has quoted about 133 times from *Zhuangzi*, a book recording ideas of Zhuangzi, one of the founders of Taoism. The requiems reflect Taoist's belief that there is no life after death, or in other words, nothing remains after death. Once people die, that is the end of everything. Upon this point, he disagrees with the idea that people may still exist in some form after death. For him, the frame or the body, the flesh of human beings will be integrated with nature after his death.

Another important factor that may inspire the two poets' ideas lies in the social and cultural backgrounds and their personal life journeys as well. Born to a prominent family, Dickinson was educated at Amherst Academy. She also spent a year at the Mt. Holyoke Female Seminary, but left because of her dislike of the religious atmosphere there. In her twenties, she still led a busy social life, but gradually she became more and more reclusive with each passing year. By her thirties, she stayed home and withdrew when visitors arrived. But mentally she did not withdraw from the outside world. She was a passionate letterwriter and kept reading newspapers. More than 1,000 letters survived after her death, which actually become important documents for critics to understand and analyze her writing. During her lifetime, women were disqualified by their sex from entering public life. Unlike her father who was busy with his work in the public world, Emily was relegated to the private sphere. However, as a resolute, independent, unusual woman, Emily challenged men's fitness to rule in either professional or in domestic spheres. She refused to publish her poems when she was alive. For one thing, it was not common for women to publish their works. More importantly, she was reluctant to adapt her poems to fit the trends at that time. America in the 1800s also witnessed choices between the pursuit of material goods or the spirit, the soul. Dickinson chose to withdraw from the outside world willingly for the reason that she wanted to turn to her inner world to retain the individuality and freedom of her spirit. Her bold use of death imagery serves to explain the originality of her poetry. As a strong-minded person, she refused to change to appeal to others. It is quite natural for her to make full use of her unique imagination to depict death.

Tao lived in the Chinese period of Disunity, the transition of Chinese history between the powerful Han and the intellectual Tang Dynasties. During his lifetime, Tao experienced the transition of three dynasties, then emperors, endless wars, pestilence, and famine. Much of China was confused and disillusioned by the competing claims of power. During the years 394 and 406, Tao worked for some officials five times and each time went back to his hometown. Finally, in the year 406 when he was 41 years old, after serving for a time in the bureaucracy of the Jin Dynasty, Tao withdrew completely from the imperial life and began his simple country life and made his living by working hard in the fields. He was sorry for the flaws of the society and held different political views. For him, living in this kind of corruptive society became a process of suffering.

It is no wonder then to find Tao's philosophical and sometimes even satiric attitude toward death. Though the topic of death has been regarded as taboo in Chinese culture, Tao reveals a poet's willingness to accept death calmly. There were so many pains for the living that death actually became a way for people to be saved from all the troubles and miseries of the present life.

Similar Inner Worlds

Last but not least, we can explain the inner worlds of the two poets to trace the sources of their creation. One thing the two recluse poets had in common lies in the fact that they never withdrew from people mentally. Through letters and their friends, they exchanged ideas of life and death, and yet kept their spiritual independence in their inner hearts. Emily Dickinson began to consider life and death quite early in her life. She had known of the death of Amherst people since her childhood. Death of her beloved is probably the emotional matrix of her death poems. For instance, upon hearing the news of her aunt's death, she wrote in one of her letters, "Blessed Aunt Lavinia now, all the world goes out, and I see nothing but her room, and angels bearing her into those great countries in the blue sky of which we don't know anything …"[11] Dickinson expressed the grief she felt. She spoke of sobbing, crying, and weeping bitterly. In her inner world, she was pondering on life and death and love, the central themes in her poems. As Fatima Ahmed Albedrani indicates, "Death assumes the form of love, which is, paradoxically, a form of creativity. Emily Dickinson's life without love is death, and her death in love is life. Love becomes life, life love, and death dies into life."[12]

---

[11] Thomas H. Johnson and Theodora Ward, eds., *The Letters of Emily Dickinson*, 3 vols. (Cambridge: Harvard U P, 1958) 2: 354.

[12] Gudrun Grabher, Roland Hagenbüchle and Cristanne Miller, eds., *The Emily Dickinson Handbook* (Amherst: U of Massachusetts P, 1998) 187.

As for Tao Yuanming, as early as in 413, Tao wrote three poems on "Flesh, shadow, and spirit," expressing his ideas on death. "Plunge yourself in Nature's Course with sheers. / And then you won't have any joys or fears. / When your life has reached its destined date, / It is no use complaining of your fate."[13] Similar ideas can also be found in his requiems. After he returned to dwell in the country, he kept in touch with a group of scholars living near him. Among them we find Liu Yimin, Zhou Xuzhi, who together with Tao, are regarded as "Three-Recluse in Xunyang." Liu, Zhou and a famous monk named Huiyuan were members of the famous "White Lotus Society" on Lushan Mountain. They gathered together to learn Buddhist doctrines. For them, the human spirit would leave human flesh to live independently when a person dies. In the long run, it would regain its life through samsara (trans-migration), thus becoming immortal. Their ideas are closely related with the teachings of Buddhism—flesh and spirit are independent. It is impossible to decide which one is superior. During one of their gatherings, they urged Tao to join in their society, but Tao declined. In later part of his life, after witnessing so many troubles in the present life, Tao's view on death became even more materialistic.

"Love and death are the most significant themes. Both are the expression of the spirit, each of which annuls the past 'tract' of life but opens another and better life as immortality."[14] It is no wonder that so many poets worldwide touch upon death in their poetry. Confucius said years ago, "Till you know about the living, how are you to know about the dead?"[15] In Confucius's viewpoint, only when people get to know the meaning of life, can they truly understand death. Shakespeare has Hamlet say in his famous soliloquy, "To be or not to be, that is the question." After hesitation and pondering, Hamlet

---

[13] Wang, *Translations of Tao Yuanming's Poems* 1999, 167.

[14] Grabher, et al., *Emily Dickinson Handbook* 1998, 187.

[15] John B. Khu, et al., *The Confucian Bible Book 1 Analects: English and Modern Chinese Versions* (Beijing: World Affairs Press, 1997) 167.

chooses to live to revenge and fight against seas of troubles. Different people from different cultural backgrounds show their interest in this theme. After exploring the fundamental meanings of death in Emily Dickinson's poetry and Tao Yuanming's requiems, we detect the two poets' similar and different interpretations of death. Actually, by creating these poems on death, by showing their dissatisfaction with their present lives, the two poets demonstrate pursuit of a happy and ideal life. This might be the fundamental source of their artistic creation.

EMPIRES OF KNOWLEDGE: THE IMPERIAL ARCHIVE AS FORMATION STRATEGY OF CENTER/PERIPHERY RELATIONS

Sandra Gottfreund

ABSTRACT

In the discursive terrain mapped out by the terms archive (M. Foucault, Th. Richards), imperialism, and race, this article sets out to explore representations of Africa under and for Western eyes in late Victorian respectively early modernist texts (H. Rider Haggard, J. Conrad). The archive as discursive junction of knowledgeable facts in the service of the "nation in overreach" is a strategy of power/knowledge. As such, it is vital to the contemporary struggle to fight modernization's by-products of alienation and the eroding plausibility of western subject conceptions. Yet accumulating knowledge about the Other in order to stabilize the (white male) self, works to overtax the code of "the West and the rest." In Haggard's "writing Africa" to restore masculinity, that input overload to the archive is still overwritten by recourse to pseudo-scientificity and action. *Heart of Darkness*, though, foregrounds the designing maneuver of imperialist myth-making. It stages the archive's very constituents as being "hollow at the core." Although there are still blind spots owing to the specific codes of imperialist worlding, the differences producing and maintaining the system of imperialism are subjected to second-order inspection so that the text bears out a significant semantic innovation in its move from "essences" to observer-dependent "differences."

System Building

Economic, military, and political power is not enough: empires need "knowledgeable" Others. Fictions of Empire such

as *King Solomon's Mines*[1] and *Heart of Darkness* therefore can
be read as literary transformations of Africanist knowledge:
They draw from and feed into an "archive Africa"[2] as
hegemonic discursive junction of "facts" in the service of the
nation in overreach.

Although written at a time when the Empire was still fairly
alive and kicking, the archive as encoded in the narratives is
already a symptom of crisis: An ongoing process of
modernization and disenchantment triggers the alienation of the
(white male) subject and calls for a new attempt at cultural self-
definition via an Other abroad. Accumulating knowledge about
this Other, however, disrupts the efficacy of the binary
construction of "the West and the rest" by its sheer amount and
diversity. The texts emerge as indices as to how and how far
the overtaxing of the archive can still be handled, whether the
representational crisis threatening whiteness with loss of self
can be warded off, be written over by action or whether
narrating Africanist experience is inconclusive at best,
increasingly barring the devices of imperialist myth-making.

Contextualizing the fictions of Empire in the setting of
modernization is to locate them in a complex and unfinalized
process that still is background of contemporary critical
discourses, among which postcolonialism more than any other
of those "post"-terms undermines the "pastness" of colonialism
optimistically implied by the prefix. "Post" is thus not to be
taken as synonymous with "de-" or "ex-". Rather, it indicates a

---

[1] *King Solomon's Mines* represents the plethora of the altogether fairly
similar Haggard-texts, which are under consideration here.

[2] This usage of "archive" is indebted to Thomas Richards, *The Imperial
Archive. Knowledge and the Fantasy of Empire* (London: Verso, 1993).
Richards takes the term from M. Foucault's *Archaeology of Knowledge*
but zeros in more closely than the *Archaeology,* which defines archive as
the sum total of discursive rules characterizing an epoch. On the other
hand, the focus seems to broaden in comparison to Foucault's
concentration on the practices of the national state. Yet, considering that
the archive is property of a national state, albeit one "in overreach" (cf.
Richards, *Imperial* 1993, 1), this delineation seems problematic.

second order observation[3] able to mark the blind spots of any given binary construction, e.g. that of white self and black other: It signifies "a procedure an 'ana-': analysis, anamnesis, anagogy, and orphosis that embodies an initial forgetting."[4] Consequently, modernization always includes an awareness of gaps in knowledge, of the still unknown, the not-to-be-known, or of the fragmentary and relative nature of knowledge in general. It engenders the subject's alienation from itself, when "subject" as a consequence can no longer signify a self-aware entity.

Such existential insecurity calls for defence by definition, production, and appropriation of the world as orderable and controllable text: An imperial archive as imagined/desired sum total of knowledgeable facts becomes strategy of power/knowledge.[5] Difference here seems to be controllable by bureaucratic overview and organization. The perpetuation of stereotypes serves to ensure navigating in the increasingly rough waters of the formerly unequivocal hegemony of center over periphery.

Even though Africa was still a fairly uncharted territory around 1850, it could no longer be called "unknown": the profitable slave-trade and expeditions for the sake of territorializing had prepared the thoroughgoing inscription of the dark Other in the Scramble for Africa in the last quarter of the nineteenth century. What was encountered was read on the matrix of contemporary hegemonic discourses as prejudiced constructions rooted in the given religious and mythological

---

[3] Niklas Luhmann, *Die Gesellschaft der Gesellschaft* (Frankfurt: Suhrkamp, 1998) 144.

[4] Jean-Francois Lyotard, *The Postmodern Explained: Correspondence 1982-1985*, eds. Julian Pefanis and Morgan Thomas (Minneapolis: U of Minnesota P, 1993) 80.

[5] The term is used in the Foucauldian sense as power and knowledge producing and conditioning each other.

epistémé.[6] New situations hence were not at all completely incomprehensible but grounded in a legitimate and limited admission of difference as exotism, primitivity, and adventurous potential.

Expeditions and conquests underlay a continent's "discovery" for the text and carried a substantial part of the Africanization of Africa whose perception was formed and transported by the mechanisms of text production: travelogues focusing on exotic detail, the adventure genre, scientific and philosophical treatises merged in intention. Eventually, the texts presented what was discourse already: like all knowledge, theirs was language referring to language, not seeing but interpreting.[7] True to the *epistémé* of the late-nineteenth and early-twentieth centuries, *énoncés* about the Other were discourses of the excluded in opposition to the normativity of a center with signifying power. The western subject's ex-centric move hence invariably resulted in centric discursification: an "epistemological determinism"[8] foregrounded the already "known" features and reduced to palimpsestic status what did not fit.

As archive of popular and axiomatic "truths" Africanist speech, similar in function to Said's *Orientalism*, furnishes a systematic *langue* by means of which Africa can be made transparent as a store of knowledge to be ordered: "State power thus turned upon inscription, upon the absorption of events into

---

[6]   Cf.: "… colonial discourse is highly self-referential in that what it considers to be a fact does not reflect historical reality, but the preconceptions of the colonialist who produces the discourse in the first place" (Vera Nünning and Ansgar Nünning, "Fictions of Empire and the Making of Imperialist Mentalities: Colonial Criticism as a Paradigm for Intercultural Studies," *anglistik & englischunterricht* 58 (1996): 7-32, 17).

[7]   Cf. Michel Foucault, *The Order of Things: An Archeology of the Human Sciences 1966* (London: Routledge, 2002).

[8]   V. Y. Mudimbe, *The Invention of Africa: Gnosis, Philosophy and the Order of Knowledge* (Bloomington: Indiana U P, 1988) 75.

the prodigiously dispersed writing machine."[9] True to the motto "There is no sin as great as ignorance,"[10] the center strives to overcome the fear of the unmapped colonial uncanny by classifying, listing, canonizing, excluding and deforming raw knowledge into a structure.[11] Resting on the belief in the possibility of an archive as "imagined sum of all that was known or knowable,"[12] Empire goes text, an elaborate bureaucracy becoming the imperial construction's backbone.

Attempts to make the Other visible in order to rule and consume it appropriate its multiple stories and reduce them to the always already known. By means of textualizing alterity, semantic stability[13] can emerge as "knowledge" and "truth":

---

[9]   Richards, *Imperial* 1993, 111.
[10] Rudyard Kipling, *Kim* (1901; London: Penguin, 1994) 160. *Kim* renders a vivid instance of the constitution of archives. Emerging in the centric "crowded rooms of easy London" (234) as by-product of the knowledge production of the Fellows of the Royal Society, "bald-headed gentleman who know nothing of the army" (234), application and extension to the colonies in the form of an "Ethnological Survey" (217) is undertaken by emissaries of the center and members of colonial space (Hurree Chunder Mookerjee). The participation of the Indian Other is index to the centre's hegemony: Mookerjee is "MA of Calcutta University" (217), with "the ambition to write FRS after his name" (233). Ready to praise the delights of European literature, he is all too willing to forget he is just "R 17" (217). In the sense of Th. Macauley's "Minute on Indian Education," hegemony emerges out of a consensus generated by education (see also A. Gramsci's comments on the role of the intellectual in colonized societies).
[11] The Other in its space seems to withdraw from definitory fixation in a kind of *différance* because the transplantation of discourses undermines the links to their constitutive lifeworlds. Therefore, the center is likely to develop a certain paranoia leading to excessive signification. This is markedly obvious in the discourse on masculinity where the overdrawn signification suggests fragility that is probably one reason for isolating masculinity off into male clublands.
[12] Richards, *Imperial* 1993, 11.
[13] Cf. Luhmann, *Gesellschaft* 1998, 673.

Africa turns into myth.[14] Being nothing more than a sign
system, it is read as depoliticized, dehistoricized fact, as natural
denotative entity. This gesture establishes a world without
ambiguities by (mis)understanding the contingent as natural;
the constructedness (and motivatedness) is hidden by structures
signified as intranscendable. Pretending apoliticality by
suppressing its origins in signifying practices (and the
signifying practice as such) the myth has manifest political
implications: the will to knowledge becomes territorializing
will to power. In order to neutralize the dangers of the Other,
an Empire of Knowledge emerges, establishing a construction
of Africa as reality of the West.

The Ideology of the Other as Ideology of the I

In Haggard's case, this "writing Africa" is a conservative
and patriarchal attempt at restoration. The necessity to question
the binary patterns fixated in and by the archive still is only
latent. Endeavoring to save Western civilization, the texts try to
counter the disenchanted world by remythifying the Africanist
archive, i.e., by reproducing and reaffirming the always already
known. A pseudoscientific confirmation of English superiority
serves to overwrite the input overload to the archive and
maintains the illusion of the knowledgeability of the Other as
ideology.[15] This strategy can be read as one variety of early
modernist writing: The discourses are transported on into
modernism where they reveal an inner logic between

---

[14] The conception of myth is indebted to Roland Barthes, *Mythologies*
(1957; London: Vintage, 2000).

[15] The term "ideology" is used in T. Eagleton's sense as an attempt to
fixate meanings and world views in support of the powerful, as maps of
meaning purporting to be universal truths while being historically
specific understandings only. Ideology serves as unexamined ground of
experience; it governs perceptions, judgements, and the sense of what is
normal or deviant. See *Literary Theory: An Introduction* (London:
Blackwood, 1996) 13/14, 117.

imperialist and fascist mentality by subduing relative and plural perspectives in an ideology of blood and race.[16]

Consequently, throughout the body of Haggard's writing (social) Darwinistic discourses serve to stress their affiliation to empirical "truth" and hegemonically endow other discourses with plausibility and authority. Western aggression is transformed into pseudoscientific anthropological terminology; the seemingly neutral scientific tone underlines the superiority toward the object of knowledge. Thus the Africanist Other hardly ranks above the ape ("'I believe the baboons are almost as human as the Bushmen'") or is even equated with it via hyphenization ("ape-man").[17]

Only at the very start is this Other a source of insecurity, an "unreadable," a "fearful fascination":[18] the lack of differentiatedness is complained about;[19] the incongruity of white subject and Africa confuses the European sense of direction. Jungles, streams, morasses, darkness, and prairies undermine Western concepts of measure and progress. Likewise, the Other's zero language confronts the center's will to know and evokes its desire to control.[20] Briefly, ever-withdrawing knowability suggests an "Africa-syndrome," both physically and mentally.[21] Fascination hence is mainly due to the challenge of Western knowledge patterns yet the surmounting

---

[16] The term "race" is used in spite of its political incorrectness since it is still valid as social construct and category of differentiation. For reasons of readability it is not marked with inverted commas to signify its constructedness. The same goes for "black" and "white" which are used in the structuralist sense as semiotic terms marking one or the other side of the distinction.

[17] Haggard, "Allan's Wife," *Allan's Wife and Other Tales* (Leipzig: Tauchnitz, 1890) 87; *She* (New York: Signet, 1994) 2.

[18] Haggard, *Child of Storm* (London: Cassell, 1925) 37; *Ayesha: The Return of "She"* (New York: Dover, 1978) 8; *The People of the Mist II* (Leipzig: Tauchnitz, 1894) 25.

[19] Cf. Haggard, *The People of the Mist I* (Leipzig: Tauchnitz, 1894) 99.

[20] Haggard, *King Solomon's Mines* (London: Penguin, 1994) 239.

[21] Haggard, *King* 1994, 72; *She* 1994, 234.

of these challenges is always already implicit.[22] Confusion, moreover, never implies a sanctioning of deconstructionist thinking suggested by She: " '... to other eyes than ours the evil may be the good and the darkness more beautiful than the day, or all alike be fair.'"[23] Boundary-maintaining male power of signification always overwrites the insecurity embodied by Africa in highly "imaginative geographies."[24]

White maleness encompasses anthropological, ethnographic, botanical, zoological, and linguistic discursive power. Hence Haggard's narrators appear as amateur ethnographers, adventurers, hunters, researchers, and translators. Almost chameleon-like intellectual and adaptive faculties allow transgression and invasion into colonial space without ever really destabilizing the self-description as individualized subjects.[25] Africa, in principle, is understandable because it is already discourse. Its mythemes are familiar, just "'our old friends, the Darkness and the Dawn in an African shape.'"[26] A further feature of the acquisition/production/maintenance of power/knowledge are monarch-of-all-I-survey scenes[27] from the position of "keen observer"[28] which work towards the Other's quasifascist permeation. Resulting from a fetishization of the gaze, a mappable and controllable panopticon emerges.[29]

[22] Cf. Haggard, *She* 1994, 98.

[23] Haggard, *She* 1994, 203.

[24] Cf. Edward W. Said, *Orientalism. Western Conceptions of the Orient* (1978; London: Penguin, 1995) 84.

[25] White also acts *under cover* by nominal indigenising: "... we had elected to pass by our Zulu names in Zu-Vendis." cf. Haggard, *Allan Quatermain* (London: Penguin, 1995) 181.

[26] Haggard, *People I* 1894, 83.

[27] Mary Louise Pratt, *Imperial Eyes. Travel Writing and Transculturation* (London: Routledge, 1992) 201.

[28] Haggard, *Wife* 1890, 20; *Child* 1925, 320.

[29] See Haggard, *People I* 1894, 117; *King* 1994, 95. Mapping signifies appropriation, both of a concrete geographical (Haggard, *Allan* 1995, 271) and a mental kind (Haggard, *She* 1994, 131, 301).

Appropriately, landscape is surveyed, measured, described and read as nature related to man, as an effect obtaining between object and observer,[30] as aesthetic, hostile or as means of subsistence. Knowledge primarily is an ocular effect enforced by the observer's elevated position, technological aids, and the masculine "rhetoric of presence":[31] the Western subject is seeing-man,[32] its utterances founded in an empiricity overwriting their discursive contingency.

Thus, Africa under Western eyes is a panorama of geography, flora, fauna, and human Otherness. Resources are sketched, indigenous flowers and animals described. Botanical knowledge is increased by the discovery of new species; yet integrating them into the classificatory patterns characteristic of western knowledge is possible. Regarding zoology, even the seemingly alien can be integrated since species are retraceable to generic types.[33] Likewise, treasures of the soil are listed, justifying the signification as "a veritable Eldorado."[34] The classification mania rampant in all the texts signifies the white subject anchored in a bureaucratic state,[35] and it is this very classifying and inscribing which makes the Western subject, seemingly delimited by leaving the center, harden into a clearly sketched entity in colonial space again.

Language is power as an instrument of command, appropriation and illustrating status; hence polyphony is part of the subject's strategy. Not only is it equipped with academically acquired language competence; learning the

---

[30] "… a landscape, no less than a text, is "read" by mutable "interpretive communities," each with its distinct "horizons of interpretation'" (Chris Fitter, *Poetry, Space, Landscape: Toward a New Theory* (Cambridge: Cambridge U P, 1995) 8.

[31] Pratt, *Eyes* 1992, 205. e.g., Haggard, *King* 1994, 95; *Ayesha* 1978, 216; *Wife* 1890, 123; *Child* 1925, 265; *Allan* 1995, 200.

[32] Pratt, *Eyes* 1992, 7.

[33] Cf. Haggard, *King* 1994, x, xi; *She* 1994, 61, 71, 127.

[34] Haggard, *Allan* 1995, 146.

[35] E.g., Haggard, *King* 1994, 33/34.

Other's language is easy as well, "being simple in its construction"—even dialectal differences are manageable and object to scholarly analysis.[36] The texts render African expressions with English translations,[37] the center being aware of (and quick to put to use) the fact that translating is interpreting: "I translated, expressing my opinion at the same time ..."[38] The act of translation turns into one of conquest for

> translation means precisely not to understand others who are the original (inhabitants) but to understand those others all too easily—as if there were no questions of translation—solely in terms of one's own language, where those others become a useable fiction: the fiction of the Other.[39]

Tribute to the texts' popularity and unequivocal insertion into the monologic reading of Africa are repetitive plot-elements, clichés, truth formulae, all-too-transparent authenticity gestures and mechanical renderings of ritualistic crises of representation haunting the white subject. Basically a gesture intended to enhance diegetic plausibility, those moments of failing speech,[40] however, are of a purely rhetorical kind. As part of the fascination they exert, they are just temporary barriers to be transcended by a finally "authentic" description of Africa. Hence, the texts present themselves as "true story,"[41] structured as diary entries with footnotes added subsequently by the narrator/writer or as eye witness accounts framed by

---

[36] See Haggard, *King* 1994, ix, 240; *Allan* 1995, 155; *Ayesha* 1978, 13.
[37] Cf. Haggard, *Allan* 1995, 97.
[38] Haggard, *King* 1994, 58.
[39] Eric Cheyfitz, *The Poetics of Imperialism: Translation and Colonization from* The Tempest *to* Tarzan (Oxford: Oxford UP, 1991) 105.
[40] E.g. Haggard, *King* 1994 , 77; *Allan* 1995, 138.
[41] Haggard, *King* 1994, xi.

editor fictions. Moreover, editorial asides[42] furnish additional information or corrections, drawing from the benefits of hindsight. This allows to appropriate and reproduce the Other's history as "true"; likewise, replicas of manuscripts, maps, illustrations, facsimiles, and transcriptions of diverse languages suggest authenticity. Paratextual part of literary convention are dedications to supposed Africa-experts preceding almost every text. Boosting the narrative's credibility, they simultaneously serve to affirm the competence of the patriarchal network by allowing "to show them [the others] as they are, in all their superstitious madness and blood-stained grandeur."[43] Frequent recourse to comparison is an attempt to tie the unknown, be it climate, architecture, size relations, danger situations or landscapes, back to de-alienating discourses. A kind of intellectual anticipation takes place: It is held that there is nothing that cannot be known or grasped, for "[t]he unknown is generally taken to be terrible."[44] This mounting of comparisons in the name of sense-making clearly indicates the constructedness of Africa: Comparing is an expression of lack and as such an attempt to overwrite the gaps Africa still presents to the European archive. This project, however, is bound to get stuck with the "like": Africa is never original but always only a European product, though one, that in Haggard's texts is still taken as "natural" hegemonic construction to be defended at all costs.

The Other then is the result only of its very representational dispossession;[45] its relevance is reduced to the function of research object and source of information:[46] in the context of

---

[42] E.g., Haggard, *She* 1994, 157, 178, 181; *Allan* 1995, 108, 141, 156; *King* 1994, 5, 16, 69; *Child* 1925, 3, 26, 30.

[43] Haggard, *Child* 1925, v.

[44] Haggard, *She* 1994, 29.

[45] Cf. Gail Low, *White Skins / Black Masks: Representation and Colonialism* (London: Routledge, 1996) 268.

[46] On the other hand, aware of knowledge as power, absolute secrecy is essential to secure the white position: "The objects of our journey have

the "fact-finding mission"[47] useful pragmatic know-how as regards locale, language, and inhabitants is found in the "common" *alter*.[48] Knowledge signified as near-intellectual is attributed to medicine men of an indefinite, frequently mythical age[49]; a kind of time warp additionally refers it back to white origins.[50]

If the texts cast alterity as object of research, etho/ethnological observations reveal a markedly phenotypical orientation which is why, true to the contemporary body/black-white/soul-distinction, the gaze mostly captures female figures. Western features are recognized benevolently; an absence of English dress is mentioned with slightly voyeuristic undertones and habitually associated with shamelessness.[51] A cognate discursive mechanism rules the representations of African warriors: Physical details are depicted with hardly repressed homoerotic undertones. Making the Other an object of aesthetics and consumption, the Africanist gaze is full of *lustangst*. Careful stagings of supposed authenticity list height, size, and accessories; the fur added as fig-leaf only reinforces nudity by its association with animal life. It is, however, this very connection to fauna or aesthetic items which sanctions

been kept a dead secret" (Haggard, *King* 1994, 40). Such paranoia, the fear of having one's fundamental stabilizing codes deciphered, is an inevitable by-product of the archive (cf. Richards, *Imperial* 1993, 150).

[47] Said, *Orientalism* 1995, 84.

[48] E.g., Haggard, *People I* 1894, 86; *People II* 1894, 279; *Allan* 1995, 101; *She* 1994, 28.

[49] The written word counts as signifier of civilization as it implies historicity. Hence it is rarely attributed to the Other: Only Ayesha (as white queen) owns academic institutions, libraries (Haggard, *Ayesha* 1978, 186), and a remote Tibetan monastery offers "opportunities of antiquarian research" (Haggard, *She* 1994, 170). Otherwise, merely Zu-Vendis, appreciated by the whites for its aristocratic structures, provides "written records" (Haggard, *Allan* 1995, 148).

[50] See Haggard, *King* 1994, 16; *She* 1994, 62.

[51] Cf. Haggard, *King* 1994, 117, 125, 162; *People I* 1894, 283.

potentially (homo)erotic pictures by transporting them back onto discursively safe terrain.[52]

The information thus assembled in the texts is ordered into archives.[53] An authoritarian discourse monopoly makes the West sole historiographer. History emerges as normative discourse of power/knowledge[54]; any discontinuity is seen within the continuity-framework of Western history, working to blot out the arbitrariness of the sign. The center invents the Other in its pastness[55] and organizes the transport of its myth back to the center: the narrator of KSM dedicates his story to his son studying to be a doctor, Holly in *She* writes for the dons of his university enclave, and selected specimen of alterity are sent to exhibition.[56] The re-import into the metropolis leaves the constructs of knowledge to archive processings encoding political instrumentalization.

Even though discourses refer to scholarly curiosity, philosophical or academic interest[57] as strategies of anti-conquest,[58] power/knowledge as signified by the archive is of immediate political, military and first of all material significance.[59] It is a tool of Empire building and the resultant

[52] See Haggard, *King* 1994, 101.
[53] Haggard, *Allan* 1995, 146.
[54] See also Robert Young, *White Mythologies: Writing History and the West* (London: Routledge, 1990) 4.
[55] Cf. Haggard, *King* 1994, 15, 101; *Allan* 1995, 24.
[56] See Haggard, *People II* 1894, 47. Exoticism was imported massively for exhibition in zoos and fairs (cf. Colonial Exhibition Amsterdam 1883, Paris World Fair 1889; Antwerp World Fair 1894, Paris Exhibition, 1900): "The world's fairs accomplished a tremendous amount of socialization. Under the guise of entertainment, they carried an ideology of whiteness ... to a global audience. Through art, ethological displays, eugenic contests, and souvenirs expositions privileged whiteness." cf. Valerie Babb, *Whiteness Visible: The Meaning of Whiteness in American Literature and Culture* (New York: New York UP, 1998) 137.
[57] Haggard, *She* 1994, 78; *Child* 1925, 145; *Ayesha* 1978, 149.
[58] Cf. Pratt, *Eyes* 1992, 7.
[59] Haggard, *Allan* 1995, 68; *Child* 1925, 217.

hegemony then in a circular move furthers "the introduction of our wider ways of thought and foreign learning and influence"[60] into colonized space.

Such white power is the Other's alienation. Hegemonic speech practices transport a significant delegitimation[61] (such as naming the Hottentot Cheat in *The People of the Mist*). The exclusively Western possession of signification destroys the agreement of *Alter* and its environment by overwriting black sense-making, condemning the subaltern to mere mimicry or baring them of any articulation whatsoever. A "blank darkness"[62] "calling" for white inscription emerges.

The project archive thus cuts both ways: Silencing Africa, it re-enforces the voices of the subject positions believed to be under siege in the center. Consequently, the discourse of masculinity is reaffirmed in the ideal of the gentleman. It includes a strength of will mentioned ad nauseam, a cult of modesty harking back to knightly tradition, a concomitant stressing of the strictly immaterial motivation of the mission as well as a notion of duty understood as martyrdom in the name of the *white man's burden*. Gentlemanly reputation is also founded on physical appearance, and emblems of progress, be they weaponry, monocles or false teeth, and on strictly binary

---

[60] Haggard, *Allan* 1995, 200.

[61] Such liberties are strictly denied to the Other: "'… it is not decent that they should call a white man by their heathenish appellations to his face'" (Haggard, *King* 1994, 58). Hierarchies are clearly demarcated. Representational dispossession (cf. Low, *White* 1996, 268), parallel to material and territorial privation, is the white agency's privilege: "'There was a certain assumption of dignity in the man's [Umbopa's] mode of speech, and especially in his use of the words 'O white men,' instead of 'O Inkosis,' which struck me. 'You forget yourself a little,' I said. 'Your words run out unawares. That is not the way to speak'" (Haggard, *King* 1994, 40).

[62] Cf. Christopher Miller, *Blank Darkness: Africanist Discourse in French* (Chicago: U of Chicago P, 1985). for a graphic illustration see Haggard, *Nada the Lily* (London: George G. Harrap, 1925) 216.

discourses of class and nationality[63] where "upper class" and "English" are to "lower class" and "non-English" as colonizer is to colonized. A sometimes outspokenly homoerotic subtext in the (quasi-)celibate male universe of the texts is readable as outflow of a regeneration fantasy of beleaguered masculinity[64] to be had only in male bonding.

In the same vein, patriarchy works as legal discourse. Its constitutive freedom of action is rewritten as license to kill in colonial (free) space, constructed via *Genesis* 1.28 and the concept of the civilizing mission. Hunting as classical *topos* of imperialist discourse is index to the symbolical-ritualistic appropriation of alien space. Weapons, major signifier of masculinity, emerge as grotesque arsenal of fetishes in front of an atavistic Africanist setting.[65] A scientific, in contemporary discourse: Darwinistic dimension justifies the "trigger-happy approach"[66] and makes white hunters become active part in the project of selecting the fittest only.

---

[63] For a detailed analysis of the gentleman-code in Haggard see Bernhard Reitz, "Der *Christian gentleman* als imperiales Konstrukt in den Afrika-Romanen Henry Rider Haggards," *anglistik & englischunterricht* 58 (1996): 73-90.

[64] An *in-nuce* embodiment of both poles in the Victorian debates about education and suffrage for women as well as alternative scripts of femininity is to be found in J. Ruskin's *Of Queen's Gardens* (1864) and J. Stuart Mill and H. Taylor's *The Subjection of Women* (1869).

[65] Cf. "'Three heavy breech-loading double-eight elephant guns, weighing about fifteen pound each, to carry a charge of eleven drachms of black powder ... Three double-500 Expresses, constructed to stand a charge of six drachms, sweet weapons, and admirable for medium-sized game ... or for men, especially in an open country and with the semi-hollow bullet ... One double No. 12 central-fire Keeper's shot-gun, full choke both barrels ... Three Winchester repeating rifles (not carbines), spare guns ... Three single-action Colt's revolvers, with the heavier, or America pattern of cartridge'" (Haggard, *King* 1994, 37/38). See also *King* 1994, 63; *She* 1994, 127; *Child* 1925, 241; *Allan* 1995, 66.

[66] John Mackenzie, *The Empire of Nature: Hunting, Conservation and British Imperialism* (Manchester: Manchester U P, 1988) 95.

Clearly congenial with this discursive network are code, structure, and emplotment of the classical adventure narrative[67] with shares in the various discursive arenas evoked by Haggard's texts. Adventure mainly is escape from eroding masculinity in a center marked by closed borders[68] and boredom.[69] The context of affluent society, cultivated land and "cultivated" people effects "idleness and over-feeding,"[70] as typical markers of domestication within the subject. Neither challenge nor provider of action, the center condemns to a passivity which is admitted as signifier of alterity only. If the discourse of masculinity just holds limited sway over the center owing to modernizing tendencies and the decline of the Old Society marked by property and patronage, loss of male status is imminent. Answer to this is the definition of Africanist space as arena to revitalize manhood by inscribing it with adventurous potential.[71] Desire for the Otherness encoded here makes the temptation of *going native*, a kind of cross-dressing investing into a temporary suspension of ethics, vie with the imperative of a strict line of demarcation. The discourse of contagion sketches Africa as dirty, slimy, stinky, malarious[72] and—by metonymy, so are its inhabitants: "It is trying to sit in the company of a score of black people and many thousand flies."[73] Hence, whites take preventive measures and erect *cordons sanitaires* like walls, ditches, and fences to keep their distance from the common Other. A regeneration/re-appropriation of outdoor-masculinity is achievable only via a

---

[67] Cf. Nünning and Nünning, *Fictions* 1996, 12.

[68] Cf. Haggard, *Allan* 1995, 3.

[69] Cf. Haggard, *King* 1994, 6.

[70] Haggard, *Allan* 1995, 10.

[71] Soon, however, the decline of this potential is also registered in Africa and attributed to Baedeker-/Cook-tourism in the wake of the Scramble for Africa. cf. Haggard, "'Elephant Smashing' and 'Lion Shooting,'" 1894; and F. Harrison, *Regrets of a Veteran Traveller*, 1897.

[72] Cf. Haggard, *Allan* 1995, 136; *She* 1994, 63, 73, 122.

[73] Haggard, *People I* 1894, 256; cf. *Allan* 1995, 26, 31.

token black exhibiting numerous white signifiers and "little or nothing of the negroid type"[74] as temporary quasi-gentleman. Yet transracial connections like these are always bound to end: It is either the spectacularly heroic death of the black partner or his deliberate retreat into apartheid which affirms the myth of the eternal color line and "saves" white. Likewise, the atavistic potential of the pseudo-transracial performance of *going native* is reflected and overcome as transitory experience only so that the boundary between barbarism and civilization is kept from blurring.[75]

Another strategy of liberating and revalorizing manhood is war. The texts parade dead or mutilated bodies. Their excessive and highly redundant wallowing in blood exhibits a crypto-fascist anonymization which is carried by a "poetics of war,"[76] clothing carnage in metaphors of cultivation and class.[77] The technologization of genocide is the index to both cultural superiority and the coincidence of the advent of the machine gun and the Scramble for Africa. Just as in the case of *going native*, whites recognize the potential regression inherent in war but always have safeguarding pseudoscientific or psychoanalytical discourses to fall back on: either the Other is "bred to be butchered"[78] or mass murder is the result of the indomitable *id* manifesting itself.

Brief spells of border crossings hence never lead to more than a patriarchally encoded superficial questioning of the

---

[74] Haggard, *Child* 1925, 8.

[75] "In each case, the hero shares some of the qualities of the savage sidekick, but the doubling or mirroring process is lopsided: white always overshadows black." Cf. Patrick Brantlinger, *The Rule of Darkness. British Literature and Imperialism, 1830-1914* (Ithaca: Cornell U P, 1988) 59.

[76] Robert H. MacDonald, *The Language of Empire: Myths and Metaphors of Popular Imperialism, 1880-1918* (Manchester: Manchester U P, 1994) 18.

[77] Cf. Haggard, *Allan* 1995, 238, 77.

[78] Haggard, *Nada* 1925, 76.

binary code nature/civilization: Nature is only a means of
regenerating the latter; any idea of the binaries being woven
into each other is valid exclusively with reference to the
feminine part of civilization. In a move again consistent with
the permanent effort to hold the fortress of masculinity, what is
foreclosed in order to hold masculinity "pure," namely the very
otherness of the same, is attributed to woman:

> I dare say that the highly civilized lady reading this
> will smile at an old fool of a hunter's simplicity
> when she thinks of her black bead-bedecked sister:
> ... And yet, my dear young lady, what are those
> pretty things round your own neck? – they have a
> strong family resemblance, especially when you
> wear that *very* low dress, to the savage woman's
> beads. Your habit of turning round and round to the
> sound of horns and tom-toms, your fondness for
> pigments and powders, the way in which you love to
> subjugate yourself to the rich warrior, who has
> captured you in marriage, and the quickness with
> which your taste in feathered head-dresses varies—
> all these things suggest touches of kinship; and
> remember that in the fundamental principles of your
> nature you are quite identical.[79]

Phallo- and ethnocentrism converge in zeroing on woman as
singular site of the dangerous implicatedness of *ego* and *alter*.
"Woman" thus safely frozen into Otherness, any internal
differentiation merely reiterates the constitutive binary
paradigms of Victorian gender discourse: Embodiments of
conformist infantilized stereotypes face marginalized (read:
atavistic) women figures as part of the colonial uncanny, sure
to be centerd though by the hegemonic binding power of
patriarchal narrating.

---

[79] Haggard, *Allan* 1995, 4.

The consequential irrelevance of the category of woman as regarding plot, however, is compensated for on the level of civilizational discourse: here white beleaguered womanhood goes sign and justification of imperial mission. Feminine conformity being vital to the English imperial efforts, the ideal woman is coded as reproductive and conservative. The conception of gender hence resonates with the male self-description via a racialized Other in the application of analogous signifying practices: just as in the discourse of race, physical attributes laden with second-order meanings here turn bottom line of the construction of social sex.

"Atavistic" black or mixed-race female figures on the other hand call for stabilizing reactions on the matrix of the horror of miscegenation, the chief problem accompanying the always already sexually connoted conquest of foreign "virgin" territory: Sexuality becomes a major intersection zone of imperial power relations since the possibility of degeneration and crumbling hierarchies is starkly foregrounded. Thus, the black woman is reduced to a frightening and seductive sign, sexualized and tabooed for endangering the color line. To escape that threat to male integrity, she is removed, preferably not without prior declarations of the impossibility of interracial relationships.

The dominant presence of the Victorian discourse of sexuality features strongly in the sexualized landscapes. They represent a specific kind of imperialist worlding as well as a further instance of containment strategy necessitated by the need to keep gender boundaries intact.[80] Consequently, while

---

[80] Landscape, in this case a rock formation, is also made to bear the burden of explicitly racist discourse, underlined by recourse to the "scientificity" of craniology: "… I perceived that the top of the peak … was shaped like a negro's head and face, whereon was stamped a most fiendish and terrifying expression. There was no doubt about it; there were the thick lips, the fat cheeks, and the squat nose … There, too, was the round skull … and, to complete the resemblance, there was a scrubby growth of

the texts advertise themselves as depicting more or less celibate clublands with "not a petticoat in the whole history,"[81] they compensate for that gap by means of a sexualised topography allowing manhood eventually to overcome the ontological insecurity marking two Freudian dark continents: the female body and Africa. This mapping is romanticizing first—"the east began to blush like the cheeks of a girl"[82]—only to move on to an explicitly erotic semiology which, being attributed to a landscape makes possible the subliminal articulation of fantasies by means of sanctioned signifying systems.

The adventurers in *King Solomon's Mines* start out at the top of the landscape mapped out as woman lying on her back. "[P]an bad water"[83] marks the female head as site of degeneracy. In the course of the search across "Sheba's Breasts" only explicitly genital body parts are foregrounded:

> These mountains ... are shaped after the fashion of a woman's breasts, and at times the mists and shadows beneath them take the form of a recumbent woman, veiled mysteriously in sleep. Their bases swell gently from the plain, looking at that distance perfectly round and smooth; and on the top of each is a vast hillock covered with snow, exactly corresponding to the nipple on the female breast.[84]

Legs and arms are rendered as mere rudiments; the mouth of the treasure cave, though, corresponds with the potentially castrating vagina,[85] entry signifies "... to enter the very womb

---

weeds or lichen upon it, which against the sun looked for all the world like the wool on a colossal negro's head" (Haggard, *She* 1994, 58).

[81] Haggard, *King* 1994, 3.

[82] Haggard, *King* 1994, 68.

[83] Haggard, *King* 1994, 21.

[84] Haggard, *King* 1994, 77.

[85] Cf. Haggard, *Nada* 1925, 196.

of the earth."[86] The veil motif seems to tone down sexualisation,[87] yet implies the hymen as hiding a potentially dangerous female sexuality. The uneasiness encoded in the veil, however, eventually is a permeable boundary to be transgressed. The adventurers habitually tear it and find their way across the "extinct volcanoes" which Sheba's Breasts, in a geologically demythifying move, turn out to be.[88] Reaching the womb—source of life—signifies both an annihilation of the threat of female sexuality as well as the arrival at the site of wealth—a discursive fusion prepared for by the compass as icon of male rationality rendered beside the body-as-map right from the start.[89]

Furthermore, ethnocentrically constructed difference keeps the white male subject from losing ground. The discourse of race, unremittingly evoked by the texts, functions along the lines of a hauntingly simple discursive grammar: Black is what is defined as black. This fixation by naming presupposes an indexical function of language with such a manifest link of signifier and signified that a tautological effect of signature can emerge: "the precoded signature of being—race, gender, ethnicity, et al.—is self-confirming ground of its own raison d'etre, enfolding origin and end in a quest that has always already arrived at its destination."[90]

Hence, if the Other is taken out of amassing and animalization at all, its characteristics turn out to be negative ones. In a circular move of logic, they are racial features again, especially lack of self-discipline, intemperance, and "native

---

[86] Haggard, *She* 1994, 268.
[87] Cf. Haggard, *King* 1994, 78.
[88] Haggard, *King* 1994, 77.
[89] Cf. Anne McClintock, "Maidens, Maps and Mines: *King Solomon's Mines* and the Reinvention of Patriarchy," *Women and Gender in Southern Africa to 1945*, ed. Cheryl Walker (London: James Currey, 1990) 97-124, 115.
[90] Kimberley W. Benston, *Performing Blackness: Enactments of African-American Modernism* (London: Routledge, 2000) 285.

idleness" which furnishes the chief argument for declaring *alter*'s space as uncultivated and appropriating it. Superstition is opposed to white scientific knowledge. A convenient textual strategy illustrating the workings of hegemony is making the Other articulate its inferiority and praise the whites for taking up their burden. Similar to this staging of the Other's consent with its negative evaluation by the center, the *topos* of cannibalism is tribute to the logic of the victors: the Other has to be conquered in order to neutralize its threat to the center. Moreover, the accusation of regression implicit in anthropophagy also legitimates one way of mythifying exploitation: Wealth then is just reward of a legitimate intervention into at once barbarian and barbaric societies. In its being cast as mere by-product of benevolent white *mission civilatrice*, any base economic motivation is suppressed so that the gentleman-ideal can be maintained and the patriarchal signifying chain be restored. A second strategy consists in presenting the contact zone as ahistorical: Framed like this, the economic genesis of wealth likewise remains a blind spot, allowing to keep up the non-mercenary façade of the quest.[91]

This multilayered (re-)construction of WASP-mentality and patriarchal networks embodies a substantial revitalization: In a quasi-vicarious regeneration of both masculinity and *Englishness* in do-or-die situations, the hero's function in Haggard's texts consists of a representative enactment of power fantasies; the exotism imported into the center is index to the fullness of the victors' luxury.[92]

Decoding Impossible?

---

[91] "'Wealth is good and if it comes into our way we will take it, but a gentleman does not sell himself for wealth'" (Haggard, *King* 1994, 141).

[92] Cf. Jan Nederveen Pieterse, *White on Black: Images of Africa and Blacks in Western Popular Culture* (New Haven: Yale UP, 1992) 95.

Heart of Darkness, by contrast, already testifies to a substantial loss of archival authority. Any attempt to grasp alterity is doomed to failure even if the edifice's pillars are still nominally present. Like civilization, though, they turn out to be "hollow at the core."[93] Moreover, those fault lines are no longer counterbalanced by the narrative act, although homodiegetic narration framing a further embedded first person narrative (G. Genette's metadiegesis), is usually a means of establishing "authenticity," or at least credibility as verisimilitude. In *Heart of Darkness*, though, the layered narrative merely foregrounds the complexity of experience and the difficulties of coming to terms with narrating. To be sure, the frame-narrator attempts to establish a situation of commonality ensuring communicability so that Marlow, as autodiegetic narrator, may relate his subjective experience to an audience sharing his specific cultural code. Thus, to a certain degree, framing contains Marlow's fragmentation of reality.[94] Yet, tentatively, this compensatory quality is subverted when even the first narrative moves towards an autotelism[95] that indicates in how far heteroreferentiality to the metanarrative of imperialism is bereft of its stabilizing function.

In addition, Marlow's absorption of other people's narratives into his own (as pseudo-metadiegeses) signifies how his self-assuredness is eroded: A decentring takes place which, via metalepsis, even enters into the frametale.[96] The possibilities of retrospection are exploited to the degree of a remark like "'The mind of man is capable of anything—

---

[93] Joseph Conrad, *Heart of Darkness* (London: Penguin, 1995) 95.

[94] Cf. Christoph Reinfandt, *Der Sinn der fiktionalen Wirklichkeiten: Ein systemtheoretischer Entwurf zur Ausdifferenzierung des englischen Romans vom 18. Jahrhundert bis zur Gegenwart* (Heidelberg: Winter, 1997) 211.

[95] "Between us, there was, *as I have already said somewhere*, the bond of the sea" (Conrad, *Heart* 1995, 15; italics mine).

[96] Cf. the thematization of the title in both narratives (Conrad, *Heart* 1995, 62, 124).

because everything is in it, all the past as well as all the future.'"[97] Yet the epistemological potential attributed to the narrating subject with its benefits of hindsight is undermined:[98] reassuring moments of seeming suture of signifier and signified are pathetically few and far between, just an English book and the bond of language linking Marlow and Kurtz.[99] Otherwise, morphology is no longer morpho-logical:[100] any certainty of designation flounders. Flags do not indicate their nation; signatures are illegible and perishable.[101] Signs make no sense at all[102] or only signify in processes of dangerously delayed decoding,[103] testifying to meaning no longer being just "out there." They are unreliable and the resulting uncertainty cuts deeper than a mere pun on Kurtz being so tall and bares any knowledge as falling pitiably short.[104]

Hence, telling is struggling, work comparable to repairing a boat[105] and just as provisional. Links are strenuously

---

[97] Conrad, *Heart* 1995, 63.

[98] Cf. Diana Knights, "Structuralism: Joseph Conrad, *Heart of Darkness*," *Literary Theory at Work: Three Texts*, ed. Douglas Tallack (London: Batsford, 1987) 9-28, 18.

[99] Cf. Conrad, *Heart* 1995, 65f., 82.

[100] Cf. Richards, *Imperial* 1993, 54.

[101] Cf. Conrad, *Heart* 1995, 64.

[102] E.g., "'It was the stillness of an implacable force brooding over an inscrutable intention. I had to keep guessing ... to discern, mostly by inspiration, the signs;'" "'Whether it meant war, peace, or prayer, we could not tell. We were cut of from the comprehension of our surroundings'" (Conrad, *Heart* 1995, 60, 62).

[103] Ian Watt, *Conrad in the Nineteenth Century* (London: Chatto & Windus, 1980) 214. cf. Conrad, *Heart* 1995, 75, 94.

[104] Tzvetan Todorov, *Genres in Discourse* (Cambridge: Cambridge U P, 1990) 109. See Conrad, *Heart* 1995, 97.

[105] "'I like what is in the work,—the chance to find yourself. Your own reality—for yourself, not for others—what no other man can ever know. They can only see the mere show, and never can tell what it really means'" (Conrad, *Heart* 1995, 52).

overtaxed[106] in this endeavor to achieve narrativity as logical coherence, for incommunicability is a curse in a world constructed as language, a signifier of utter isolation:

> He was just a word for me— ... Do you see him? Do you see the story? Do you see anything? ... No, it is impossible; it is impossible to convey the life-sensation of any given epoch of one's existence,— that which makes its truth, its meaning—its subtle and penetrating essence. It is impossible. We live as we dream—alone ...[107]

With metanarratives as ultimate horizon of intelligibility and guarantee of transparency losing ground because of increasing social fragmentation and differentiation, any heart, any essence, any kernel is inaccessible and incommunicable. The subject is reduced to its constructions of the Other and to its own complementary emergence out of this very reflexivity. Sense becomes an observer-dependent construct. What remains is the imperative of going on narrating to regain a modicum of subjectivity which, in order to express itself, must needs avail itself of language.

The resultant blurring of the boundary between subject and object, however, in *Heart of Darkness* is mainly an expansion of Marlow into the Other. Subjectivity is on his side clearly because Africa remains a rather abstract site of the enactment of white sense-making attempts. As such it is removed into the prisms of readings while simultaneously proving inaccessible to white modes of cognition. The "fascination of the abomination"[108] is a challenge which cannot be rendered in, let

---

[106] Cf. those between the Intended's voice and the sounds of Africa or the gesture linking both women figures (Conrad, *Heart* 1995, 100, 121/122). See also Knights, "Structuralism" 1987, 20.

[107] Conrad, *Heart* 1995, 50.

[108] Conrad, *Heart* 1995, 20.

alone be mastered by words.[109] Its darkness indissolubly is
object of desire indicative of lack and source of fear. The urge
to narrate again and again does not even halt at describing a
void: neither does the map passage identify Africa nor is
verisimilitude sought for by accumulating details, be they
botanical, zoological or ethological, for reality effects.[110]
Replacing the monarch-of-all-I-survey scenes of classical
adventure narration with an atmosphere of alienation and near-
claustrophobia, not even the trite representations of Africa as
(female) body, as prehistoric, or terra incognita establish
knowledgeability.[111]

As a consequence, technology, conventional sign of victory
over nature, is futile to the point of parody.[112] A "stream of
manufactured goods," mostly of little value, pouring into
Africa evokes a mere "trickle of ivory."[113] Pseudoscience is still
part of the imperialist project as knowledge production,
basically, however, it is a two-fold dead-end road: neither do
clients return to testify to change nor would changes be
measurable.[114] Science turns absurdity, becomes an empty
confirmation of a sheer private theory. Never are its
constructions grounded in fact, never are they subjected to the

---

[109] "'Could we handle that dumb thing or would it handle us?'" (Conrad,
Heart 1995, 49).

[110] Conrad, *Heart* 1995, 21. Cf. Roland Barthes "L'effet de réel, "
Littérature et Réalité (Paris: Seuil, 1982) 81-90.

[111] Cf. Conrad, *Heart* 1995, 54, 99, 59, 62, 69/70.

[112] "It appears the French had one of their wars going on thereabouts. In the
empty immensity of earth, sky, and water, there she was [a French man-
of-war], incomprehensible, firing into a continent. Pop, would go one of
the eight-inch guns; a small flame would dart and vanish ... and nothing
happened. Nothing could happen. There was a touch of insanity in the
proceeding, a sense of lugubrious drollery in the sight ... " (Conrad,
Heart 1995, 30/31).

[113] Conrad, *Heart* 1995, 37.

[114] "'This is my share in the advantages my country shall reap from the
possession of such a magnificent dependency'" and "'... moreover, the
changes take place inside, you know'" (Conrad, *Heart* 1995, 27).

test. Science sees only what it projects. It becomes patent metonym of the increasingly tautological behemoth characterizing the imperialist project at large.

A paper-shuffling functionary, signifier of the economy and administration, belies his sterile and abstract efficiency in his attempt to keep track of keeping track.[115] His single-minded devotion to his red tape of files and columns is deadly for "'... as long as there was a piece of paper written over in accordance with some farcical law or other made down the river, it didn't enter anybody's head to trouble how they would live.'"[116] Empire as text is starkly demythified, when the accountant's transactions are juxtaposed with the "groves of death:"[117] Money has a genesis here, one paid for by the chain gang's sufferings. The business of empire has clearly turned monocausal and monoglot empire of business.[118]

Hence, the hero's function as imperial "emissary of light"[119] remains an empty space. The travesty of this figure embodied by Kurtz enacting what Africa is to white—utter licence, no religion, no resistance to temptation, but colonial, alien horror—reveals an unstoppable gap. Draining transparency and eroding unequivocal signification leave but a voice behind.[120] When closure is out of sight and incomprehensibility reigns supreme, fractures of the façade of imperialism are strongly foregrounded. Nonetheless, there are still blind spots left over from the specific codes of imperialist, binary worlding. Thus, *Heart of Darkness* fails to envoice an Other. In that the text leaves black a more or less silent blank, a gap emerges which

---

[115] Cf. Richards, *Imperial* 1993, 3.

[116] Conrad, *Heart* 1995, 70.

[117] Conrad, *Heart* 1995, 38.

[118] Cf. Edward W. Said, "Two Visions in *Heart of Darkness*," *Culture & Imperialism* (London: Vintage, 1994) 20-35, 25.

[119] Conrad, *Heart* 1995, 28.

[120] Cf. Conrad, *Heart* 1995, 79, 93.

signifies a certain confirmation of imperialist thought.[121] Furthermore, instances of explicit racism, be it Fresleven's lynch justice or the Aunt's infantilization of Africans as in need of being weaned from barbaric habits,[122] abound and also contaminate Marlow as narrator in his pseudo-metadiegeses: Conventionally, technological know-how is denied to the Other; "nigger" is a term unquestioned.[123] Marlow's Africanist experience is strongly marked by the negativity of things inappropriate: The fireman is depicted to the point of ridicule;[124] a positive description bows to convention and is sanctioned by its conformity to racialist presuppositions:

> They shouted, they sang; their bodies streamed with perspiration ... faces like grotesque masks ... bone, muscle, a wild vitality, an intense energy of movement that was as natural and true as the turf along *their coast* (italics mine)... They were a great comfort to look at. For a time I would feel I belonged still to a world of straightforward facts; but the feeling would not last long.[125]

---

[121] Chinua Achebe's accusation of Conrad as a "bloody racist" started the postcolonial wave in Conrad criticism. In spite of the significant re-reading stimulated by his essay, his analysis is hardly useable here owing to the almost unproblematic assumption of identity of narrator and author. See "An Image of Africa: Racism in Joseph Conrad's *Heart of Darkness*," *Joseph Conrad: Third World Perspectives*, ed. Robert D. Hamner (Washington: Three Continents, 1990) 119-30. The quote mentioned above is found on p. 124.

[122] Cf. Conrad, *Heart* 1995, 23, 28. The relevance of woman as stronghold of imperialist thinking in the center is emphasized by the fact that it is the aunt's mediation which makes Marlow part of the "Workers" in the first place.

[123] Conrad, *Heart* 1995, 76, 81.

[124] Cf.: "'... to look at him was as edifying as seeing a dog in a parody of breeches and a feather hat, walking on his hind legs'" (Conrad, *Heart* 1995, 64).

[125] Conrad, *Heart* 1995, 30.

Just like the mis/displaced fireman, however, can be reconstructed as a Western product,[126] there is in the description of the dancers also an acknowledgement of belonging accompanied by the implicit insight that the white observer is the one unbelonging. This displacement leaves room for deeply destabilizing perceptions: "'No, they were not inhuman that was the worst of it—your suspicion of their not being inhuman.'"[127] To be sure, this argument *ex negativo* is hardly able to deconstruct imperialist thinking, but it suggests a nascent cultural relativism, a hint of the binaries as hierarchies being implicated in each other: Hence, ideas and idols are separated by a dash only; drums could be bells, London is dark; Kurtz's voracity foregrounds the cannibals' discipline. He is no "bearer of the torch" but an invader.[128] The propagated multicausality of imperialism rooted in missionary, altruistic and economic benefits is reduced to the catch-all term "ivory." Encountering the detribalized African guard, Marlow is cast into the perspective of being looked at as Other: Amassing and de-individualization as *topoi* of imperialist world-making are conferred onto the agents of the discourse in a turn of the tables.

Yet denying language to the Other is a sign that boundaries are not really conceived of as transgressible. The Other's incomprehensibility always runs the risk of working to mute it completely.[129] Dialogue and an en-voicing of the subaltern thus cancelled out, there is only the indelible trace of delegitimation carried by hegemonic speech practices. This very represen-tational dispossession, however, becomes thinkable as "striking back" onto its perpetrators: Right from the start, the discourse of colonialism is undermined by the counter-memory of subjugated knowledges. Even if the term "exploitation" as

---

[126] Cf. Conrad, *Heart* 1995, 64.
[127] Conrad, *Heart* 1995, 62.
[128] Cf. Conrad, *Heart* 1995, 20, 39, 15, 70/71, 95.
[129] Cf. Conrad, *Heart* 1995, 108.

semantic "odd man out" is not mentioned, it serves as subtext: "germs of Empire"[130] are ambiguously source of contamination or continuation. Language, even one as hallowed by tradition as "the ensemble of linguistically based practices unified by their common deployment in the management of colonial relationships,"[131] is no more monolithic and unequivocal than English history: the narrator foregrounds Britain's own colonized past, his choice of present perfect[132] suggesting a relativity, a near-synchronicity when progress is the only imperialist temporality.

Moreover, *Heart of Darkness* empties the imperial conquest as generic plot of its structural function. Despite the overt quest-pattern, the percivalesque conventions of an immaterial object of search as well as change and improvement effected by reaching it[133] are parodied. The attitude of expectation built up by the prologue as a quasi-sea-tale and the club-like male atmosphere are undermined by plot-reduction to a minimum: Nothing really happens.[134] Already the metaphor used for Marlow's telling by the first narrator[135] signifies the transcending of the adventure plot: There is no kernel, no heart of darkness. It is rivets missing. In this absence, there is no manhood to be restored: Kurtz is as light as a child and compared to an enchanted princess.[136] Masculinity is intimated only in the form of black woman as site of body plus

---

[130] Conrad, *Heart* 1995, 17.

[131] Peter Hulme, *Colonial Encounters: Europe and the Native Caribbean 1492-1797* (London: Routledge, 1986) 2. See also the definition of colonialist discourse "as the set of codes, stereotypes, and vocabulary employed whenever the relationship between a colonial power and its colonies is written or spoken about" (Nünning, *Fictions* 1996, 10).

[132] Conrad, *Heart* 1995, 18.

[133] Cf. Reitz, *Christian* 1996, 83.

[134] Cf. "The 'mythological' narrative (of action) is present only to allow the deployment of a 'gnoseological' narrative (of knowledge)" (Todorov, *Genres* 1990, 104).

[135] Cf. Conrad, *Heart* 1995, 18.

[136] Cf. Conrad, *Heart* 1995, 72.

mistress:[137] By reliance on a locus classicus of adventure-writing, the text plays on the ever-present abominable fascination of miscegenation yet the single white man's burden is one of the gang, Marlow having to carry Kurtz.

With civilization gone simply for lack of butchers, policemen, pavements, and censoring public opinion,[138] ivory becomes the new substitute for transcendence. Switching registers as easily as this implies a crisis of legitimacy so severe as no longer to be overcome by hegemonic narratives: Tearing off a telling postscript is just a desperate measure to restore plausibility.[139] Likewise, "voice" is no more presence and transparency despite Marlow's attempts to decode "'The horror'" with a vengeance in order to achieve coherence. Yet his metadiegesis is never fully reduced to complete dissolution into the logic of Kurtz, as the Russian's and the Intended's tales are.[140] However, even if things fall apart in the periphery, the center still needs to hold, united in the unassailable belief in the closed system of imperialism. With Marlow grasping the chance to counter his sense of (male) displacement and the insight into the incommunicability of experience, the conventional parameters of the representational domain of imperialism are maintained: Marlow allows Kurtz's fiancée to turn "talking Kurtz" into pure monologue, for only by insisting on the discursive features of the *mission civilatrice* can she remain metonym of European womanhood and Western civilization as modelled on the universe of separate spheres.[141] Already his decision to visit the Intended is owing to the mere impression of her on a photograph and, as a consequence,

---

[137] Cf. Conrad, *Heart* 1995, 99.

[138] Cf. Conrad, *Heart* 1995, 81.

[139] Conrad, *Heart* 1995, 115.

[140] Cf. Conrad, *Heart* 1995, 87-96, 118-123.

[141] Cf. Conrad, *Heart* 1995, 116. see also: "'They—the women—I mean—are out of it—should be out of it. We must help them to stay in that beautiful world of their own, lest ours gets worse'" (Conrad, *Heart* 1995, 80).

Marlow's readings further serve to freeze her into posturing.[142]
Trapped in her function as wife-to-be even though "'the
horror'" is substituted for by a proper name, her name remains
encoded as "'your name'"—sufficient and still workable as
image of order as patriarchy.[143] It is, nevertheless, increasingly
foregrounded as an empty signifier after all, a violence done to
arrive at suture just as in a circular move Kurtz remains
unequivocal site of sense proper to her with any arbitrariness
cancelled out.

With the center unable/unwilling to perceive that the
stabilizing *langue* has long begun to disintegrate into *paroles*,
meanwhile the former bearer of the logos has already been
caught in the brevity of "'Mistah Kurtz—he dead.'"[144] "The
voice" has ceased to speak, for there is an other *sujet
d'enonciation* now emerging out of the very gap of white
senselessness.

The Category of Option

"If the subject is to extend its colonizing sway over things
and stamp them with its indelible presence, then systematic
knowledge of the word is essential."[145] In Haggard's texts, the
male subject creates, or rather, re-creates himself as occupant
of a stable subject position in this very colonizing sway. By
affirming hegemony in colonial space in the midst of a crisis
threatening *Englishness*, this position of power basically rests
on an assumption of the Other's full knowledgeability. Yet the
drive to know is "to some extent in contradiction with the
power it exists to promote … it must at once master its object
and confront it as other, acknowledge in it an autonomy it

---

[142] Cf. Knights, *Structuralism* 1987, 23/24.

[143] Conrad, *Heart* 1995, 123. Cf. Anthony Fothergill, *Heart of Darkness*
(Milton Keynes: Open U P, 1989) 106.

[144] Conrad, *Heart* 1995, 112.

[145] Terry Eagleton, *The Ideology of the Aesthetic* (Oxford: Blackwell, 1990)
73.

simultaneously subverts."[146] Hence, the uncanny "lability and fugacity of the referent,"[147] the fear of the nomadic is overwritten with totalizing constructions since "in a world depleted of significance ... myth can furnish just those ordering, reductive schemas necessary to elicit unity from chaos."[148]

As result of the complexity of the imperialist endeavor as politics, aesthetics and epistemology all in one,[149] signifying systems go nature; they acquire plausibility within the (here still) closed system of imperialism. The claims to truth, authenticity and reality they seem to satisfy remain unquestioned so that the world emerges as Western text, readable and controllable. In a paradoxical move, darkness is simultaneously maintained and illuminated. Whiteness thus can present itself as invisible self-generating norm despite its dependence on an Other constructed as dark. An "identitarian authority"[150] develops establishing an unequivocal communi-cability of reality, which still manages to overwrite the input overload to the archive.

In *Heart of Darkness* on the other hand, language is paradigm and obsession but no longer a transparent medium of worlding.[151] Staging the draining plausibility of imperialist

---

[146] Eagleton, *Ideology* 1990, 73/74.

[147] Simon Gikandi, *Maps of Englishness: Writing Identity in the Culture of Colonialism* (New York: Columbia U P, 1996) 190.

[148] Eagleton, *Ideology* 1990, 318.

[149] Cf. Said, *Visions* 1994, 26.

[150] Edward W. Said, *Culture and Imperialism* (London: Vintage, 1994) 378.

[151] This is most emphatically regretted by F. R. Leavis. In *The Great Tradition* (London: Chatto & Windus, 1950) he censures *Heart of Darkness* for Marlow's abstractness of language which "muffles" (177) any "awareness of the possibilities of life" (2) with its "adjectival insistence upon an inexpressible and incomprehensible mystery" (247). Accusing Conrad of "making a virtue out of not knowing what he means" (180), Leavis reads this inconclusiveness as failure in that he sees literature as crystallization of fundamental values which are on the defense elsewhere. If the decline of the West is not to be averted by

reality conceptions, it radically undermines its supposed "naturalness" by revealing its affirmative contribution to the maintenance of given power relations. In a kind of re-entry, the very differences mapping out the system of imperialism are submitted to second-order inspection: what is called attack is actually defence; slaves are almost exclusively referred to as "criminals," exiled and alienated guards belong to the "reclaimed;" Europeans are "Workers," just like Kurtz's victims are "rebels."[152] Language sanctions imperialism's life lies. There is, however, no alternative register available to confront it.[153] Ambivalence is ineluctable. Uneasily, the narrative vacillates between language perceived as increasingly disintegrating and the desire to see language as guarantee of stable and unwavering signification. Loath as Marlow is to admit it, the awareness of the archive's claim to unequivocal language being merely a "doomed and ineffective defence against a world which cannot be hunted, trapped, known"[154] is nevertheless inescapable.

The resultant displacement of the subject is being desperately out of reach of any sense-making prop. Hence, a definite communicability is increasingly replaced by the sheer persistence in narrating owing to the recognition of having to resort to language to be subject at all: "'… I have a voice, too, and for good or evil mine is the speech that cannot be silenced.'"[155] Since reality is dissolving into heterogeneous voices and going on narrating is paramount, there are no finalized integral entities, no last words, no sutures, no closure

---

close reading (cf. Eagleton, *Literary* 1996, 30), the possibility of existential insecurity also haunting the sacred precincts of art must be blotted out or else the text is "marred" (Leavis, *Tradition* 1950, 174) and "minor" (173).

[152] Conrad, *Heart* 1995, 37, 33, 28, 96.

[153] Cf. Conrad, *Heart* 1995, 54-56.

[154] Peter Conrad, *The Everyman History of English Literature* (London: Dent & Sons, 1985) 561.

[155] Conrad, *Heart* 1995, 63.

anymore: crying, dying, lying, and story telling[156] are only tentatively probed as provisional endings.

Gradually, the notion of "reality" is replaced by one of possibility, of contending constructions whose designing maneuvers move to the limelight.[157] Thus, the process of sense-making is transferred from mimetic reproduction of conventional communication about reality to the self-referentiality of the text. *Heart of Darkness* bears out a significant semantic innovation in this move from "essences" to observer-dependent "differences" as result of the structural conditions of modernity. The blind spots of binaries and their implicatedness in each other are foregrounded; distinctions cry for an explanation of who made them. In that the text replaces the presence of a single stable voice with a cacophony of conflicting *énonciations*, the respective knowledges, perceptions, and perceptional gaps go constructs of an observer, and this insight into the constructedness of the metanarrative of imperialism takes over its previous constructiveness.

A deconstructionist proviso for every single sign[158] must be perpended, if only in fictional space. Yet if one takes the constructedness of every reality into account, this lets a wider option of reflection shine through.

---

[156] Cf. Fothergill, *Heart* 1989, 86.

[157] Cf. Peter Zima, *Theorie des Subjekts: Subjektivität und Identität zwischen Moderne und Postmoderne* (Tübingen: Francke, 2000) 307/308.

[158] Cf. Luhmann, *Gesellschaft* 1998, 1146.

THE PROBLEMS OF ADAPTATION: THE CASE OF JOSEPH CONRAD'S *THE SECRET AGENT*

Nic Panagopoulos

ABSTRACT

Although today Conrad is widely acknowledged as one of the foremost prose stylists in the English language and a bold innovator of the novel form, it is easily forgotten that during most of his lifetime his work met with scant critical acclaim and a noticeable lack of commercial success. This not only frustrated his literary aspirations, but also left him in terrible debt and poor health too. He often tried in vain to make his writing more appealing to the general reader by regularly changing the subject matter and setting of his novels, or by experimenting with different literary forms.

The Secret Agent was intended from its inception as a "book to produce some sensation."[1] This aim was not to be achieved through "sensationalism," however, but by basing the tale on a widely discussed subject at the time: the Greenwich Park bombing. While writing the serial version for *Ridgeway's Militant Weekly*, Conrad confided to Methuen that "my mind runs much on popularity now,"[2] while in a letter to John Galsworthy he revealed his eagerness to make "Mr & Mrs Verloc effective for the amusement of a public."[3] Nevertheless,

---

[1] Frederick R. Karl and Lawrence Davies, *The Collected Letters of Joseph Conrad*, Letter to J. B. Pinker (Cambridge: Cambridge U P, 1988) 3: 459-460.

[2] Karl and Davies, *Collected Letters* 1988, 3: 370-371.

[3] Karl and Davies, *Collected Letters* 1988, 3: 339-340.

the book version of *The Secret Agent* which he regarded a "perfectly genuine piece of work" that afforded him "one of the minor satisfactions"[4] of his writing life, sold less than 3,000 copies in Britain in its first five years of circulation, and was branded by one critic "too sordid to be tragic and too repulsive to be pathetic."[5]

It is understandable, therefore, that Conrad would wish to try his hand at a more popular and potentially lucrative artistic medium such as the stage. There were other incentives too. John Batchelor claims that involvement with the theater offered Conrad "welcome distraction from the isolated business of writing fiction,"[6] especially during the war which exacerbated his perennial anxiety and ill-health. Altogether Conrad wrote three plays which were all adapted from his own fiction: a fact which, according to Amy Houston, suggests that "he did not find the dramatic medium itself directly inspiring."[7] It may also have been an attempt to bring his existing work before a wider audience in the hope that the universal recognition which had eluded him as a novelist may have been won, in some measure, in the theater. In 1916 Conrad helped Macdonald Hastings with his dramatization of *Victory,* which was eventually produced by Henry Irving in 1919 and ran at The Globe from the 26th of March to the 14th of June the same year. John Batchelor argues that it was the relative success of this project which prompted Conrad to consider writing his own plays.[8] In a letter to Eric

---

[4] 1920 Author's Note to Joseph Conrad, *The Secret Agent*, edited with an introduction and notes by Martin Seymour-Smith (London: Penguin, 1963).

[5] Norman Sherry, *Conrad: The Critical Heritage* (London: Routledge & Kegan Paul, 1973) 21.

[6] John Batchelor, *The Life of Joseph Conrad* (Oxford: Blackwell, 1993) 244.

[7] Amy Houston, "Joseph Conrad Takes the Stage: Dramatic Irony in *The Secret Agent*" *The Conradian*, Autumn (1998): 55-69, 55.

[8] Batchelor, *Life of Conrad* 1993, 244.

Pinker from the time of his collaboration with Hastings and Irving, Conrad wrote:

> You will admit I have some faculty of dialogue ... the bulk [of my work] *is* dramatic. And if I can only learn to adapt my faculty for dialogue and drama to the conditions of the stage, then ... I am not ossified yet. I am still impressionable and can adapt my mind to various forms of thought—and perhaps art.[9]

Yet, even before this production, Conrad seems to have harbored an unfulfilled dramatic urge. John Galsworthy, speaking from personal experience, informs us that Conrad "had fitful longings to write for the stage,"[10] and the fact that he wrote novels instead was essentially due to the limitations which the dramatic medium "imposes on word painting and the subtler efforts of a psychologist."[11] Max Beerbohm, responding to Conrad's promising adaptation of "To-morrow" entitled *One Day More*, opines that Conrad was "just the sort of person who ought to be coaxed into writing plays,"[12] but this opinion is not shared by most critics—especially those who saw the production of *The Secret Agent*. Galsworthy himself claims that, had Conrad began by writing for the stage, "he would no doubt have become one of the greatest dramatists of our time,"[13] but diplomatically adds that, it was just as well that he hadn't, because the world would then have lost an even greater novelist.

---

[9]   Quoted in Batchelor, *Life of Conrad* 1993, 244.
[10] John Galsworthy, introduction to *Laughing Anne & One Day More*, by Joseph Conrad (London: Castle, 1924) 5.
[11] Galsworthy, *Laughing Anne* 1924, 5.
[12] Max Beerbohm, "Mr. Conrad's Play" in *Around Theaters* (London: Rupert Hart-Davis, 1953) 384.
[13] Galsworthy, *Laughing Anne* 1924, 6.

The general consensus is that the conventions and requirements of the two artistic forms are too distinct to allow an easy transfer of technique from one to the other. To add to this inherent difficulty, Conrad had expressed mixed feelings about the "requirements of the stage" which, at times, appeared to him "as a great and august mystery," and, at others, vanished "before [his] meditations, into thin air."[14] He also seems to have nursed a certain dislike for actors, calling them, rather unkindly, "a lot of *wrongheaded* lunatics pretending to be sane."[15] As Amy Houston observes: "In this context of meagre theatrical experience and even less theatrical interest, it seems unlikely that Conrad could produce a full-length play of any merit."[16] Nevertheless, Conrad confessed that writing and staging a play was his "dark and secret ambition," for the chance to do which he would "sign an agreement with the Devil himself ... and think the experiment worth trying."[17] In hindsight, this reference to Faust's legendary pact with the Devil, itself the subject of theatrical adaptation, seems to have been less than propitious.

Conrad began thinking of adapting *The Secret Agent* in 1919, and completed the first draft early in 1920. While engaged in this project we see him contemplating the dramatization of other novels, including *The Arrow of Gold* and *Under Western Eyes*, and he confided to Pinker that there was "a fascination in doing a thing like that over in another medium," provided "one were certain of intelligent interpretation."[18] He did not seem to feel this certainty, however, and the adaptation of *The Secret Agent*, like most of

---

[14] Joseph Conrad, *Joseph Conrad: Life and Letters*, ed. G. Jean-Aubry, 2 vols. (London: Heinemann, 1927) 2: 268.

[15] Joseph Conrad, *The Collected Letters of Joseph Conrad*, eds. Frederick R. Karl, Laurence Davis, 4 vols. (Cambridge: Cambridge U P, 1991) 1: 419.

[16] Conrad, eds. Karl and Davis, *Collected Letters* 1991, 1: 57.

[17] Conrad, ed. Jean-Aubry, *Life and Letters* 1927, 2: 276.

[18] Conrad, ed. Jean-Aubry, *Life and Letters* 1927, 2: 276.

Conrad's fiction writing, was attended by grave misgivings. In the 1920 Author's Note to the novel he admits:

> Lately, circumstances ... have compelled me to strip this tale of the literary robe of indignant scorn it has cost me so much to fit on it decently years ago. I have been forced, so to speak, to look upon its bare bones. I confess that it makes a grisly skeleton.[19]

Indeed, Conrad wondered whether this story "of utter desolation, madness and despair,"[20] might not be totally unpalatable for a theater audience out for an evening's entertainment, yet, in a letter to Galsworthy, he expressed his ardent wish to make them "swallow their supper and think it fine too."[21] Although confessing that he couldn't have "any pretensions to dramatic gifts,"[22] he nevertheless hoped that his career was "exceptional enough to have that evolution in it ... recognized as a manifestation of creative art."[23] Having completed the adaptation, however, he confided to R. L. Megroz that he had not enjoyed writing the play, for it had meant "cutting all the flesh off the book."[24]

Conrad's primary concern was to put across his own distinctive "ideas as to the artistic reproduction of life," and he was anxious that the adaptation should be as Conradian as possible. Thus, while taking care not to strain "stage conditions unduly for the sake of originality," he allowed himself the liberty of "stretching them out" in order to fit his conception of

---

[19] 1920 Author's Note in Joseph Conrad, *The Secret Agent* (1907; London: J. M. Dent and Sons Ltd., 1947).

[20] Author's Note in Conrad, *Secret Agent* 1947.

[21] Conrad, ed. Jean-Aubry, *Life and Letters* 1927, 2: 225.

[22] Conrad, ed. Jean-Aubry, *Life and Letters* 1927, 2: 257.

[23] Conrad, ed. Jean-Aubry, *Life and Letters* 1927, 2: 277.

[24] R. L. Megroz, *A Talk with Joseph Conrad and a Criticism of His Mind and Method* (London: Elkin Mathews, 1926) 31.

art.[25] At the same time he wanted to produce a genuine dramatic work and not allow it to become "a mere exercise in intellect, ... style," or "over-refined sentiment,"[26] as he felt Henry James had done with his own plays. To compensate for his relative lack of authorial control and to give the audience some psychological insights into the characters, Conrad furnished the actors with an abundance of stage directions dealing with every aspect of line-delivery, intonation, and posture. At times these are almost patronizing and reveal the insecurity of an old, established novelist having to play the role of a new, untried playwright. The extended stage directions also express Conrad's mistrust of the actors in their ability to interpret and communicate his meaning to the audience, for most of them, he claimed, "have no imagination."[27] While revising the play, however, he cut many of the more intrusive ones out, sensing that he was overstepping his jurisdiction as a playwright, and had to allow the actors more scope in interpreting their parts.

In the autumn of 1922 the task of producing the play was assigned to Harry Benrimo who appeared to Conrad to be a trustworthy collaborator and one who understood his "conception of stagecraft."[28] The play was scheduled to open on November 2nd at the Ambassadors Theater in the West End of London. Conrad had earlier rejected a proposal by Calthrop to stage the play at the Aldwych during July and August of the same year because he felt that many Conradians would be out of town for the summer, and the principal drama critics would be replaced by their understudies in the press. *One Day More* had ran for only three days in 1905, and Conrad wanted to give *The Secret Agent* every possible chance of success, particularly since he sensed that this was to be his last opportunity of displaying his dramatist's skills. Taking into consideration the

[25] Conrad, ed. Jean-Aubry, *Life and Letters* 1927, 2: 227.
[26] Conrad, ed. Jean-Aubry, *Life and Letters* 1927, 2: 273.
[27] Conrad, eds. Karl and Davis, *Collected Letters* 1991, 4: 218.
[28] Conrad, ed. Jean-Aubry, *Life and Letters* 1927, 2: 276.

difficulties he had encountered in the novel's adaptation, Conrad contented himself with the hope that the play would be a *"succèss de curiosité"* based on the theater-going public being curious enough to want to see what a novelist of his standing and reputation had produced in a different medium. He trusted it would run for about six to eight weeks, unless the protagonists gave some exceptional performances to "fascinate people"[29] which, in any case, could not be guaranteed. The financial returns would, therefore, be limited, unless the same people came to see it more than once: an unrealistic expectation, Conrad admitted, for a play like *The Secret Agent.*

The run-up to the production proved every bit as nerve-racking as the tense period before the completion of a novel. Conrad's vexations during this time are revealed in his letters and also faithfully recorded by Mégroz who interviewed him and set down their discussion in *A Talk with Joseph Conrad.* In June 1922 Conrad had revealed to Eric Pinker his fear that the play may "sink unsung" which would constitute a "great disaster"[30] for him and, as the production began to take shape, he became ever more personally involved in it. In October he attended a number of the rehearsals and wrote to his publisher: "I discover in myself rather to my surprise an extreme interest in the production." He was dismayed, however, at finding two of the principals miscast: The actor playing Chief Inspector Heat was not authoritative enough (he was too young and tall), while Clifton Boyne who played the Professor seemed intent on interpreting his part without the slightest regard for Conrad's wishes. Conrad wrote to Benrimo complaining that not a single one of his stage directions had been "even so much as indicated" by the latter during rehearsals. On the plus side, Miriam Lewes seemed to have got into the character of Winnie quite well, while Freddie Paisley's rendition of Stevie was found to be "excellent."[31] Some last minute changes were made

[29] Conrad, ed. Jean-Aubry, *Life and Letters* 1927, 2: 273.
[30] Conrad, ed. Jean-Aubry, *Life and Letters* 1927, 2: 272.
[31] Conrad, ed. Jean-Aubry, *Life and Letters* 1927, 2: 277.

to the script to compensate for the weaknesses of the cast, while Act III, the salon scene, was reduced in importance by being turned into the second scene of Act II.

As the production entered its final phase Conrad complained to Aubry about feeling an extraordinary irritation regarding "that damned piece," as he called it.[32] Such was his nervous tension, in fact, that he was unable to attend the first night in person and sent Jessie who reported afterwards that she had had "*the* evening of her life."[33] Instead, Conrad agreed to be interviewed by Mégroz in a nearby hotel, but kept dashing to the reception to inquire if there were any messages from the theater. It is sad that having invested so much hope in the dramatization of *The Secret Agent*, its author never actually saw it in performance.

The play closed on November 11th, 1922, ten nights after it had opened, amidst what Frank Swinnerton described as "the worst 'press' of any play of any pretensions that we have seen in recent years."[34] Not even Conrad, in his worst bouts of depressive gloom, could have imagined the critics' "awe-inspiring" unanimity in damning his play which he likened to a "chorus of parrots."[35] He protested that "even a play written by an angel could not have stood up against the weight of a unanimous press"[36] and claimed that his had effectively been "put to death" by it. Indeed, as Hermon Ould points out, "only the richest management can keep a play on long enough to weather the storm of a bad Press,"[37] and the management of the Ambassadors Theater did not seem to fall into this category.

---

[32] Joseph Conrad, *Joseph Conrad: Lettres français*, ed. G. Jean-Aubry (Paris: Gallimard, 1929) 178.

[33] Conrad, ed. Jean-Aubry, *Life and Letters* 1927, 2: 282.

[34] *Bookman*, 56, New York, February 1923, 739-40, in *Joseph Conrad: Critical Assessments*, ed. Keith Carabine, 3 vols. (London: Routledge, 1992) 3: 701.

[35] Walpole 1929, 169, in Houston 1998, 60.

[36] Conrad, ed. Jean-Aubry, *Life and Letters* 1927, 2: 279.

[37] Carabine 1992, 3: 698-99.

The acting was, on the whole, deemed satisfactory but not so the play. Most critics agreed that Conrad had not demonstrated an adequate understanding of the requirements of the stage and should have invested more time in improving his playwrighting technique. *The Times* critic put it in a nutshell when he wrote: "Mr Conrad is a great novelist, but not yet a great dramatist."[38] Alfred Capus granted that *The Secret Agent* "contains all the elements of a moving play," but argued that Conrad had lost his way by "trying to blend his narrative with political side-issues." It is indicative of Conrad's failure to balance the political and domestic themes of the play that this critic got the impression that "a few random pages of essays [had] been wedged into the story."[39] The play's structure was particularly criticized. One critic reported hearing that "the construction of the play was infantile"[40] and even Galsworthy had to admit that Conrad did not seem to know how to "keep his line of action clear."[41] What is undoubtedly true, and what most reviewers agreed on, is that Conrad would have done better to have written an original play, because he was too restricted by the content of the novel to give a true account of himself as a dramatist.

John Galsworthy, who among Conrad's contemporaries has given us perhaps the most balanced critique of the play, claimed that we have in this case "a salient illustration, not only of the difficulty of adaptation, but of the fundamental difference between novel and drama as a medium for presenting life."[42] Indeed, the usual difficulties of adaptation are augmented in the case of *The Secret Agent* by the fact that it is not a realist text, dealing with a conventional subject and containing stock characters. Thus, in adapting it for the stage,

---

[38] *The Times*, 3 November 1922, in Jocelyn Baines, *Joseph Conrad: A Critical Biography*. (London: Weidenfeld and Nicolson, 1960) 428.

[39] *The New World of the Theater*, ed. J. T. Grein (London: Martin Hopkinson, 1924) 2-3.

[40] Frank Swinnerton in Carabine, *Critical Assessments* 1992, 3: 701.

[41] Galsworthy, *Laughing Anne* 1924, 10.

[42] Galsworthy, *Laughing Anne* 1924, 8.

Conrad was confronted with virtually insurmountable stylistic
and formalistic problems. These forced him to completely
reassess his work, and he claimed that he "had no idea what the
story was about till [he] came to grips with it in the process of
dramatization."[43] The fact that it does not work on stage should
not grieve us, though, for, in comparing novel and play, we are
not only afforded a better understanding of Conrad's narrative
technique, but also gain valuable insights into the problems of
adaptation in general.

The particular work was probably chosen for adaptation
because of its dramatically potent plot which contains multiple
reversals of fortune, culminating in the tragic fall of its
protagonists. For Aristotle, the family ("oikos") was the ideal
micro-environment in which to develop a tragedy, but the more
the tragic plot ("mythos") progresses, the more the core of the
family is destroyed.[44] *The Secret Agent* is essentially "a
domestic drama" in which all the members of a household are
destroyed after wittingly or unwittingly becoming embroiled in
irresolvable conflicts, emanating from the structure of the
society in which they live. These conflicts have an archetypal
quality, for they represent the clash of universal opposites in
life: private/public, masculine/feminine, reason/feeling,
justice/retribution. Besides its general tragic framework, the
plot of *The Secret Agent* is particularly reminiscent of
Aeschylus' *The Agamemnon*, for both show a man returning
home to his wife after many trials and tribulations abroad, only
to be murdered by her for having sacrificed their "child" in the
course of his "campaigns."

Of course, there are many differences between the two
works, besides the basic generic one. In Conrad's novel Stevie
is not, strictly speaking, the couple's child, but, being mentally
retarded and physically abused by his real father, he has
become the object of his sister's maternal affections and,

[43] Conrad, ed. Jean-Aubry, *Life and Letters* 1927, 2: 234.
[44] Stephen Halliwell, *The Poetics of Aristotle*, translation and commentary
(Chapel Hill: U of North Carolina P, 1987) ch. 13, 14.

consequently, Verloc's dependent. His function, however, is essentially the same as Iphigeneia's in Aeschylus' trilogy: He represents the innocent victim whose pathetic death sets the tragedy in motion. Verloc is a very ignoble Agamemnon, in keeping with the squalid urban landscape of Victorian London in which this modern tragedy is set. His social prestige is limited to the respect of his wife and mother-in-law, whom he provides for, and the trust of the small anarchist community that congregates regularly in his shop. He was once held in some esteem by his employers for services rendered, but this has waned considerably in recent times and, when we first see him, he is at a low ebb in his fortunes. It is worth noting, however, that like Agamemnon who survives the battlefields of the Troy, only to be killed in the traditional warrior-haven of the home, Verloc does not meet his doom in the course of his subversive activities abroad, but in the comfort of his living room.

In contrast to her mock-heroic husband, Winnie does attain near tragic status by virtue of her maternal passion, which gives her the moral force to stab the "murderer" of her "child" in a moment of consummate grief and instinctive savagery. Conrad explicitly associates her with mythical heroines of the past when he describes her "biblical attitude of mourning" over Stevie's death ("the covered face, the rent garments; the sound of wailing and lamentation") as well as her pose of "perfect immobility," which is said to express "all the potential violence of tragic passions". However, neither the dramatic potential of its central situation, nor its pseudo-tragic protagonists could of themselves guarantee the successful dramatization of *The Secret Agent*.

The problems that Conrad had to address in adapting the novel fall broadly into three categories: time, space, and narrative. It is well known that the time-organization of *The Secret Agent* is far from conventional. The central event, the Greenwich bombing, is not narrated directly, but needs to be gradually uncovered by the reader in a kind of extended "delayed decoding" stretching over many chapters. One of the novel's greatest technical achievements is the way it enacts a series of time shifts which circumnavigate the central event by transporting us forwards and backwards in time, as well as presenting it from a variety of different perspectives. The reader is also obliged to reconstruct the simultaneity of many events which take place on the night Verloc is stabbed, even though their narration is dislocated and prolonged so that they appear to have taken place over a far longer period of time. This virtually unlimited freedom to organize and restructure time—which the novel form offers and which *The Secret Agent* relies upon for much of its dramatic tension—does not apply to the stage which, due to its mimetic character, is governed by far stricter rules of chronological representation. Not only does dramatic time have to remain as close as possible to real time regarding the sequence of events, but the duration of events represented on stage cannot vary significantly from the duration of the actual events being portrayed.

Conrad was thus obliged to iron out the novel's temporal dislocations in keeping with the demands of the target medium and to show a far closer correlation between cause and effect. The explosion is located at the end of act I, while acts II and III depict the reactions of the police and anarchists on the one hand, and Lady Mabel's party guests, on the other. Again, Conrad reveals the details of the Greenwich bombing gradually, but the suppression of information concerning the central incident, which worked so well in the novel, loses much of its force in the adaptation. Not only would much of the audience seeing the production be already in possession of the crucial facts, but the "hole-in-the-center" modernist device is largely out of place in a realist play that needs to be far better grounded in concrete incident and cannot wallow in ontological uncertainty to the same extent. Regarding the concentration of time, Acts II to IV of the play depict events taking place over a single afternoon, but the fact that the explosion has already been precisely located between acts I and II creates a subtle imbalance in the play which is not visible in the novel due to the latter's temporal ambiguities. The events which are seen to follow, and therefore emanate, from the central incident in the play far outweigh those that are seen to contribute towards it, whereas in the novel both appear to be equally important, and there is also an effective blurring of cause and effect. Some attempts are made to prolong dramatic time in the adaptation, but there is far less scope for this kind of chronological manipulation here than in the novel. The stage directions, for example, are often employed to suggest a slowing down of the action by focusing attention on certain details, but this is more obvious in reading than in performance and, as has already been noted, Conrad cut most of these out before the play was staged. Where dramatic time does seem to slow down sufficiently for the audience to penetrate the situations depicted is during some of the characters' longer speeches, particularly Vladimir's exposition of his bomb-throwing philosophy to the dumbfounded Verloc in act I, and Verloc's long-winded explanations of Stevie's death, before he is stabbed in act IV. It is not by chance that these scenes are among the most effective in the play.

The formal restrictions of the target medium posed even greater technical problems for the adaptation than the modernist time organization of the novel. Besides being telescoped to fit dramatic form, the story was restructured into four acts entitled, (I) The Private Life, (II) The Under World, (III) The Upper World, and, (IV) The Issue. This division, according to Paola Pugliatti, was "meant not only as a temporal re-ordering of the fabula but also as a sort of rationalization of the general meaning of the play."[45] What this critic fails to point out, however, is that by logically "deconstructing" his novel in order for it to fit neatly into a conventional dramatic format, Conrad was fatally oversimplifying it. Moreover, the need to keep the setting as simple as possible means that most

---

[45] Carabine 1992, 3: 714.

of the scenes take place in Verloc's shop, including the crucial interview between Verloc and Vladimir in which the idea of the Greenwich bombing is introduced.

This solution, however, creates more problems than it solves. Firstly, it is difficult to believe that the first secretary of a major foreign embassy would personally visit a seedy little shop in Soho to instruct one of his employees on how to carry out their subversive activities. Besides the fact that such an arrangement shows a careless disregard for the methods which an agent provocateur would actually employ (something which Conrad is very careful to avoid in the novel), Vladimir is presented outside his natural habitat, and his character loses much of the authority it possesses in the novel. Another effect of showing Vladimir visit Verloc at home, besides implying that the diplomat is incompetent and doesn't know his business, is to suggest that the world of international espionage invades the Verlocs' private domain from without, rather than destroying it from within, as is the case in the novel.

The fact that Conrad had far less space in the adaptation meant that he had to concentrate much more on the domestic theme of *The Secret Agent*, even at the cost of weakening the story artistically by detracting from its generic ambiguity. The different requirements of the realist stage explain why, in the process of adapting the novel, he discovered that it was not so much about Verloc, as about Winnie. As he claimed in the author's note that was written around the same time as the play, this was "Winnie Verloc's story" and all the other characters are "grouped about her and related directly or indirectly to her tragic suspicion that life doesn't stand much looking into."[46] However, the greater significance given to the domestic tragedy in the adaptation, albeit constituting a thematic focusing of the original story, creates a serious structural imbalance in the play. This is particularly evident in the end of the final scene when Winnie, instead of committing suicide, is shown going mad

---

[46] Conrad, Author's Note, *Secret Agent* 1920.

after Ossipon has tried to flee from her in horror. At this point Heat arrives at the shop to wrap things up, followed by the Professor, and the play ends with the policeman and the terrorist exchanging words over a deranged Winnie who is raving incoherently on the floor. The curtain goes down with the representatives of legality and political extremism standing on either side of the tragic figure symbolizing innocent humanity, whom they have destroyed between them. But this dramatic tableau fails because the character of the Professor is not as well established in the play as it is in the novel, and his symbolic significance is not evident to the audience which has probably forgotten him by the final scene. In response to Arnold Bennet's criticism of the ending, Conrad confessed, "I simply lost for the moment whatever I may have had of the stage sense in me."[47] Yet, the weakness of the play's final scene is indicative of more than just a temporary lapse on the part of the dramatist; the Professor casually strolling into Verloc's shop in the final act just to take his portion of the blame for the tragic outcome of events highlights the way in which the political theme of *The Secret Agent* appears superfluous and contrived in the adaptation.

It is not surprising that Conrad went wrong with the structure of the play, particularly when it came to balancing the tale's two themes. His insistence on keeping as close to the novel as possible, coupled with the spatial restrictions applying in the target medium, meant that many of the characters are too sketchily drawn to warrant their inclusion in the play. Jocelyn Baines points out that the play contains "a bewildering number of minor characters who confuse the action and do not leave enough room for the development of the major characters or of the central situation."[48] Conrad defended the inclusion of certain characters or scenes which may appear superfluous from the point of view of action on the grounds that the central

---

[47] Conrad, ed. Jean-Aubry, *Life and Letters* 1927, 2: 282.
[48] Baines 1960, 248.

situation depicted in the play is "purely illustrative." As he confessed to John Galsworthy, the real subject of the tale is "*not* the murder of Mr Verloc by his wife and what subsequently happens to her. It is all a matter of feeling." Thus, characters such as Winnie's mother and Vladimir, which could hypothetically have been cut to save space, are all "closely to the point"[49] for Conrad, because they play a vital role in establishing the "feeling" of *The Secret Agent*.

Yet, this "feeling" which is so masterfully conveyed in the novel, and which many of the characters rely on for their raison d'être and veracity, could not so easily have been reproduced on stage where a far stricter economy applies, and, as Galsworthy points out, "cruel obstacles" are "put in the way of the sustained mood."[50] As a result, some characters do appear strikingly out of place: The anarchists, in particular, with their revolutionary posturing, seem irrelevant to the domestic tragedy which the play focuses on, and are not developed enough individually to appear anything other than caricatures. Galsworthy claimed that "the feeling and illustrative value" of the situations and characters "could have been preserved, and even increased"[51] if Conrad's dramatic technique had been up to the task, but the problem is more complicated than Galsworthy suggests. Conrad could not have been "attending only to the plain sense and clear connexion of the story,"[52] as he claimed he was doing in the play, while including characters and scenes whose main function is suggestive. There is a fundamental incongruity between the realist method employed in the adaptation and the impressionistic quality of the tale itself. The problem is not merely one of space, but of style.

As has already been noted, the play is essentially realistic which means that the development of the plot and logical consistency of the action takes precedence over the creation of

---

[49] Conrad, ed. Jean-Aubry, *Life and Letters* 1927, 2: 257.
[50] Galsworthy, *Laughing Anne* 1924, 9.
[51] Galsworthy, *Laughing Anne* 1924, 13.
[52] Conrad, ed. Jean-Aubry, *Life and Letters* 1927, 2: 227.

atmosphere or mood. Such a strategy may be Aristotelian, but it does not suit such an evocative work as *The Secret Agent* and highlights how important for its overall effect is the narrative method employed in it. As Galsworthy was the first to point out, "*The Secret Agent* was a novel of atmosphere [that] depended for its triumph on innumerable subtleties, and the fidelity of a sustained mood." These qualities, Galsworthy argues, could not have been transferred to the stage which "falls far short of the novel" as "a faithful vehicle of mood" and where "selection is dictated by physical conditions beyond [the dramatist's] control."[53] Indeed, some of the most memorable descriptive scenes in the novel, such as the famous cab ride scene, or the Assistant Commissioner's "walk on the wild side" of London, are cut in favor of weak, expositional scenes that serve to elucidate the plot. An example of the latter is the salon scene in which Michaelis talks with his Lady Patroness (called Lady Mabel in the play) and which Galsworthy called "dead wood"[54] in its dramatic version. The opening scene too does little more than establish Winnie's personal history and motives for marrying Verloc, as well as Stevie's blind trust in his brother-in-law in preparation for the boy's fatal employment in the Greenwich bombing. Moreover, it is undramatic and clumsily written: Verloc is called a "good man" for Stevie's consumption far too often, while Winnie repeats ad nauseam that "things don't bear much looking into." This scene sets the tone of the adaptation in which there is an overreliance on repetition in order to unequivocally establish the characters' motives. The result, as Frederick Karl observes, is that "the dramatic implications" of the tale "are lost in the retelling of important action."[55] Thus, in contrast to the novel which is both gripping as a narrative and powerfully evocative at the same time, the play is neither effective drama in its own right, nor

---

[53] Galsworthy, *Laughing Anne* 1924, 9.

[54] Galsworthy, *Laughing Anne* 1924, 10.

[55] Frederick R. Karl, *A Reader's Guide to Joseph Conrad* (New York: Noonday, 1960) 292.

does it succeed in conveying the tale's characteristic atmosphere of urban squalor and moral decay.

Not only does the straightforward realism of the adaptation not suit the particular work being adapted, but it conflicts with Conrad's poetics in general. This is testified by both the adaptation of the novel for the stage and the revisions Conrad made to the serial version to produce the book. In fact, the method employed in each case seems to have been exactly the reverse. While in the adaptation Conrad had to "strip the tale to the bone"[56] due to the limited space at his disposal, in revising the serial version for the book, he expanded his material considerably. As Harold E. Davis points out in his excellent essay on Conrad's impressionism, "at least one whole chapter (X) is inserted, the closing scenes are more than twice the length, and page after page of descriptive details are added."[57] The effect of this is to "fill in the bare action by an enlargement and clarification of the mood"[58] which, for Conrad, was the essence of the experience. Furthermore, the rich descriptive details added to the serial but cut from the adaptation are vital for *The Secret Agent's* effectiveness, for they serve to suggest rather than state the real subject of the tale. This relates to one of the basic principles of literary impressionism, which is the avoidance of direct reporting. As Ford Maddox Ford wrote regarding "the method," "you must render: never report. You must never, that is, write: 'He saw a man aim a gat at him;' you must put it: 'He saw a steel ring directed at him.'"[59] Yet, this is exactly the opposite of what Conrad does in the adaptation where he repeatedly resorts to simple exposition and the reporting of events that have previously occurred to reinforce the plot's inevitability. Thus, it is clear that what is missing

[56] Conrad, Author's Note, *Secret Agent* 1920.
[57] Harold E. Davis, "Conrad's Revisions of *The Secret Agent*: A Study in Literary Impressionism," *Modern Language Quarterly* 19:3 (1958): 244-54, 244.
[58] Davis, Conrad's Revisions 1958, 245.
[59] Davis, Conrad's Revisions 1958, 245.

from the stage adaptation is precisely that impressionistic method that gives the novel its force and is so characteristic of Conrad's style in general.

Another factor that weighed against the success of the adaptation was the difficulty of transforming the narrator's voice. The novel employs a third-person narrator who could be removed without ostensibly affecting the plot. However, although this narrator does not participate in events and can assume a certain degree of detachment, his highly subjective narrative and limited perspective mirror the isolation and mutual incomprehension of the characters he describes, as though he too were one of them. Furthermore, although he enjoys a privileged point of view and can often shed light on motives and causes, his partial omniscience does not give him the authority to judge or interpret events. He is generally content to describe what he sees, allowing the facts to speak for themselves, in a way that reflects the disavowal of authorial omniscience that Conrad made one of his trademarks. Indeed, Paula Pugliatti suggests that the narrator's avoidance of explicit judgement "seems to be a transposition in terms of narrative technique of Winnie's recurring statement that life doesn't stand much looking into."[60] In other words, the narrator appears to be both clinically detached and personally involved in the events he is describing. In this respect he resembles the author himself who claimed to be detached from the squalid setting of his tale, but not at all unconcerned with the plight of his characters. As Conrad wrote in the 1920 author's note:

> the whole treatment of the tale, its inspiring indignation and underlying pity and contempt, prove my detachment from the squalor and sordidness which lie simply on the outward circumstances of the tale.[61]

---

[60]   Carabine 1992, 3:706.

[61]   Conrad, Author's Note, *Secret Agent* 1920.

It is clear, therefore, that the narrator serves a very important function in *The Secret Agent* and his absence from the play could not easily have been compensated for by the dramatic devices at Conrad's disposal.

One of the ways in which Conrad attempts to translate the narrator's voice into theatrical terms is by presenting a commentary on the action from a variety of different perspectives. Thus, each character in the play is mirrored by an opposite who offers an alternative interpretation of events in keeping with his or her different philosophy and station in life. That it was Conrad's intention to make perspective a central concern of the play is confirmed by his comment to Galsworthy that the implications of the story arise not so much from "a conflict of motives or passions but simply from various points of view."[62] However, the play's preoccupation with perspective is only apparent after close textual analysis, and seems to have been lost to the audience watching the production who were probably confused by the plurality of voices it contains. The critics too picked up on the wordiness of the play: Galsworthy remarked that Conrad did not appear to know how to "economize his words,"[63] and Alfred Capus observed that "his figures are lost in random scenes and excess of talk."[64] To a certain degree, this misunderstanding was to be expected, for the reader of a novel can pause, reflect upon and compare different episodes and characters in order to understand their narrative function, but the spectator of a play cannot. Moreover, perspectivism was a relatively new artistic concept at the time Conrad was writing and his lack of experience as a playwright meant that he was unable to successfully adapt this central concern of his prose fiction to the stage. The result is a play which contains too much dialogue that is not particularly dramatic or directly relevant to the central situation, and not

---

[62] Conrad, ed. Jean-Aubry, *Life and Letters* 1927, 2: 257.
[63] Galsworthy, *Laughing Anne* 1924, 10.
[64] Grein, 2.

enough action. Indeed, it is debatable whether such a subjective narrative as that of *The Secret Agent* can be represented dramatically in any way. As Colin Tucker, the producer of the 1992 BBC television version, points out: "The forms of novel and the drama are crucially dissimilar: the subjective experience of the reader who becomes involved in a narrative at his or her own pace is entirely opposed to the passive role of the audience, which is forced to respond to events imposed on it." Thus, Tucker concludes, "there is no such thing as adaptation" and the best one can do is create a "parallel event which connects with the original work in obvious superficial ways ... but which depends for its artistic life on something new and different."[65]

In adapting *The Secret Agent*, Conrad was not prepared to change the original story in any way and tamper with what he saw as "the truth of [his] conception." In order for the adaptation to be as "Conradian" as possible, all "extraneous sentiment,"[66] as he put it, had to be avoided. However, this rather inflexible attitude meant that the play contained the seeds of an obvious failure, even before it was unveiled to the public and torn to shreds by the press. For, rather than transferring the essence of the novel to the stage, it was an attempt to reproduce it as a play without sufficient regard for the inherent differences between the two artistic mediums. As Galsworthy pointed out, one "cannot approach the stage successfully without a profound respect and a deep recognition that its conditions are the essentials of an appeal totally distinct from that of a novel."[67] Conrad may have understood this general truth in theory, but his stage version of *The Secret Agent* shows that he was unaware of its implications for the practical business of adaptation. The "parallel events" that Colin Tucker and Alfred Hitchcock were later to produce from

[65] Joseph Conrad, ed. Gene M. Moore, *Conrad on Film* (Cambridge: Cambridge U P, 1997) 193.
[66] Conrad, ed. Jean-Aubry, *Life and Letters* 1927, 2: 234.
[67] Galsworthy, *Laughing Anne* 1924, 10.

Conrad's novel, for television and the cinema respectively, prove that *The Secret Agent* is adaptable, provided one takes into consideration the interdependence of content and form and the fact that no work of art can possibly remain the same when translated into a different medium.

WHEN THE SYMBOL SWERVES:
SPATIAL DESIGNS AND MEANING-SLIDES IN
CHARLES PALLISER'S
THE QUINCUNX [1]

María Jesús Martínez Alfaro

ABSTRACT

Charles Palliser's first novel—*The Quincunx: The Inheritance of John Huffam* (1989)—recaptures the atmosphere of nineteenth-century England while weaving an intertextual net that both absorbs and transforms the defining features of Victorian realism. Taking as a starting point the fact that Palliser sets out to write not a pastiche but a parodic/defamiliarized version of the novel's numerous intertexts, my paper focuses on the question of whether the symbol of the quincunx, on which the novel's complex structure is based, partakes of this same dynamics in which contemporary meanings are conveyed through already existing forms. To do so, my analysis delves into the various meanings ascribed to the quincunxial design in other contexts, not directly related to literary fiction, and contrasts them with the ones that derive from the novel's play with its own compositional space.

> Quizá la historia universal es la historia de la diversa
> entonación de algunas metáforas. [2]
> – *Jorge Luis Borges*

---

[1]   The research carried out for the writing of this article has been financed by the Spanish Ministry of Science and Technology (Department of Humanities and Social Sciences), BFF2001-1775.
[2]   "Perhaps universal history is the history of the diverse modulations given to a few metaphors." (My translation). Jorge Luis Borges, "Otras inquisiones" in *Obras completas*, VII, ed. Carlos V. Frías (Buenos Aires: Emecé Ed.) 14-16.

It was in 1989 and after more than a decade of careful research that Charles Palliser (Massachusetts, 1947) published his first novel, *The Quincunx: The Inheritance of John Huffam*. This novel powerfully recaptures the atmosphere of Edwardian England and recreates the rich textures of nineteenth-century fiction by combining Dickens's masterful narrative technique with the suspenseful plots of Wilkie Collins's works. The protagonist of the story is young John Huffam, who lives with his widowed mother, Mary, in a fairly idyllic rural estate in the North of England. Yet the widow, and ultimately John, have mysterious enemies who manage to gradually trick them out of their money. As a consequence, they are forced to leave behind their life of relative comfort in the country and end up fighting for survival in the deprived areas of nineteenth-century London. Constantly threatened and pursued, John comes to understand that he may be entitled to one of the largest fortunes in England. He then starts digging into his family's past to find out the truth about his origins as well as the whereabouts of a hidden will that can surely turn him into a rich heir.

As Umberto Eco had done after publishing *Il nome della rosa* (1980), Charles Palliser wrote a fairly long "Author's Afterword"—added to the 1993 edition of the novel—where he reflects on his role as a fiction writer and on the actual writing of *The Quincunx*. The first issue he focuses on is that of the unavoidable gap existing between the author's intention and the readers' reception and interpretation of a literary text. In this respect, Palliser seems to have found three main kinds of response to his novel.

Some, reading the novel as if it had been written in about 1850, had seen no reason to look for ambiguities. Others had had their suspicions aroused to a greater or lesser degree and had observed elements that were not consistent with the novel's appearance of being written almost a century ago. Many, however, had become deeply suspicious as they read, and one said—very gratifyingly—that the last sentence had forced him to start the book again from the beginning.[3]

Even if all agreed on the fact that the novel is highly indebted to Dickens, critics and early reviewers of the novel, who are but a special kind of reader after all, similarly responded in (significantly) divergent ways. Thus, some among them saw *The Quincunx* as a mere imitation of Victorian fiction, "clever, but merely a trick,"[4] entertaining though completely pointless in the sense that Palliser's recreation showed "nothing except the fact that it can be done."[5] A second group of critics, though, detected the work's "modern sensibility"[6] behind its strikingly Victorian façade: the lack of closure, the crucial questions that are never answered, the novel's self-conscious character, its postmodernist quality, etc. Finally, there is a third group of critics—corresponding to Palliser's "deeply suspicious readers"—who analyzed the novel in depth[7] concluding that *The Quincunx* is not an imitation but

---

[3] Charles Palliser, "Author's Afterword" in *The Quincunx: The Inheritance of John Huffam* (1989; London: Viking, 1993) 1203.

[4] Robert Taylor, "*Quincunx*: Clever but Merely a Trick," *Boston Globe* (7 Feb. 1990): 38.

[5] Linnea Lannon, "Greed Expectations Mystery Unlocks in a Dickensian Tale of Five Families," *Detroit Free Press* (28 Jan. 1990): 1L.

[6] Charles Matthews, "Dickensian Echoes Keep Me Pages Turning High Five Times for Quincunx," *San José Mercury News* (11 Feb. 1990): 19. See also Benjamin Griffith, "Twists of *Quincunx* Tease Mind, Touch Emotions," *Boston Globe* (7 Feb. 1990): 38; Steven Marcus, "A Post-Modern Romp in Dickens's London," *Newsday* (28 Jan. 1990): 24; David Walton, "Of Heroes, Villains & Intrigues. A Labyrinthine and Compelling First Novel, Researched for 12 Years, Recalls Vivid Victorian Tones, and Rings with Real Life," *Philadelphia Inquirer* (28 Jan. 1990): H01.

[7] See Susana Onega, "Charles Palliser," *Post-war Literatures in English* 19 (1993): 1-12; "The Symbol Made Text: Charles Palliser's Re-writing of Dickens in *The Quincunx*," *Revista Alicantina de Estudios Ingleses* 6 (1993): 131-41; "Mirror Games and Hidden Narratives in Charles Palliser's *The Quincunx*," in *Theme Parks, Rainforests and Sprouting Wastelands: European Essays on Theory and Performance in*

a clever parody of nineteenth-century fiction which turns out to be written by three of its characters: the protagonist, John Huffam, and two Punch-and-Joan puppeteers called Pentecost and Silverlight. John and the puppeteers also narrate most of the 125 chapters, and the complementarity of their accounts together with the mixture of historical and literary episodes throughout the novel suggest the blurring of boundaries between history and literature and their levelling to the same— fictional—status. This fact aligns *The Quincunx* with other postmodernist historiographic metafictions by authors like John Fowles, Peter Carey, Umberto Eco, Peter Ackroyd, Graham Swift, and Jeanette Winterson, to name a few. Thus, even if Palliser's work is, unquestionably, an immense monument to Victorian fiction, one should not overlook the fact that the nineteenth-century novel is being treated in *The Quincunx* as a literary resource to write fiction in and for the present. The reader gets lost in a maze of Victorian intertexts only to discover the way in which the latter have been absorbed, but also transformed and put at the service of a completely different project.

Apart from the novel's Victorian intertexts, the other recurring element in Palliser's work is, of course, the quincunx. According to Ian MacNiven, the quincunx was originally "a planting pattern not uncommon in medieval and Renaissance arboretums: five trees arranged like the dots on the five of dominoes."[8] It is this arrangement of five trees and five marble statues (from which the central tree and statue have been removed) that John finds at the front of the building intended by his great-great-grandfather, Jeoffrey Huffam, to be a mausoleum. John soon learns that the planting pattern near the Old Hall of the Hougham estate is also a reproduction of the

Contemporary British Fiction, eds. Richard Todd and Luisa Flora (Amsterdam: Rodopi, 2000) 151-63.

8   Ian MacNiven, "The Quincunx Quiddified: Structure in Lawrence Durrell" in *The Modernist: Studies in Literary Phenomenon* (Rutherford: Fairleigh Dickinson U P, 1987) 235.

original Huffam shield: an arrangement of five quatrefoil roses, like the five on a die, from which the shields of the other branches of the Huffam family derive.

Significantly, the quincunx is much more than the novel's title and a recurrent element in the diegesis, where it variously appears as a planting pattern, a heraldic device, a design engraved on the family's crockery and cutlery, a booby-trap to protect a safe, etc. It is also the key to the novel's formal structure: there are five parts (each entitled after the five family branches: the Huffams, the Mompessons, the Clothiers, the Palphramonds and the Maliphants), five books in each part, and five chapters in each book. Just as the reader walks farther into this quincunxial labyrinth of a text, so does the main character try to find his bearings—his place in the complex genealogical tree of the Huffam family—by reconstructing the pattern that will open the safe where Jeoffrey Huffam's second will is kept. This pattern is also reproduced on an old wedding card that contains the coats of arms of the five families arranged to form another quincunx or, more precisely, a quincunx of quincunxes (each corresponding to one of the five families). To all these quincunxial designs, one should add the quatrefoil roses that appear at the beginning of every Book: The novel's paratext[9] is thus made to underline the fact that the twenty-five books occupy in the work as a whole, a place parallel to that of the twenty-five quatrefoil roses in the heraldic device of the quincunx of quincunxes.

The pervading presence of the quincunx in Palliser's novel is then no less overwhelming than that of Victorian fiction. Yet

---

[9] Gérard Genette uses this term to refer to the text's title, subtitle, epigraphs, illustrations, notes, and other kinds of accessory signals which surround the text and sometimes comment on it. The relations between the paratext and the body of the text are the basis of paratextuality, one of the five categories of transtextuality. Gérard Genette, *Palimpsestes. La littérature au second degré* (Paris: Seuil, 1982) 8-14.

if we admit, as I have shown elsewhere,[10] that Palliser set out to write not an imitation but a parody of the novel's numerous Victorian intertexts—not a pastiche of Dickens but a defamiliarized version of the latter's works[11]—in order to express through it a postmodernist worldview, we may as well ask ourselves whether the symbol of the quincunx partakes of this dynamics in which contemporary meanings are conveyed through already existing forms. An affirmative answer to this question would lead us to face the gap between author's intentions and reader's interpretations that Palliser refers to in the already mentioned "Author's Afterword." Though he openly admits there that he is playing with Victorian fiction—a self-conscious play in which he "wanted to obey the conventions and yet break the rules"[12]—he seems to have chosen the figure of the quincunx almost by chance. He wanted the reader to feel that there was a design emerging from the apparent randomness of events, which led him to the idea of a pattern based on numbers. Since three, four, and six failed to work, he arrived at five "by nothing more than the process of elimination"[13] and he did so fairly late, when most of the novel was already written. In other words, he did not choose five because of the archetypal and number symbolism of the quincunx. Moreover, he decided that he "wouldn't get involved in that because I couldn't take on an extra complication at that late stage. It also seemed to me that it wasn't going to be relevant … It's not something that I'm interested in, either."[14] And yet, after the New Criticism's "intentional fallacy" and

[10] María Jesús Martínez, *Text and Intertexts in Charles Palliser's* The Quincunx (Ann Arbor: U of Michigan P, 1996).
[11] For a view of *The Quincunx* as a pastiche of Victorian fiction, see Christian Gutleben, *Nostalgic Postmodernism. The Victorian Tradition and the Contemporary British Novel* (Amsterdam: Rodopi, 2001) 42-45.
[12] Palliser, "Author's Afterword" 1993, 1212.
[13] Palliser, "Author's Afterword" 1993, 1217.
[14] In Susana Onega, "An Obsessive Writer's Formula: Subtly Vivid, Enigmatically Engaging, Disturbingly Funny and Cruel. An Interview with Charles Palliser," *Atlantis* XV (1993): 269-83, 271.

poststructuralism's "death of the author" what Palliser intended or, rather, did not intend in as far as the symbol of the quincunx is concerned, should by no means be seen as an obstacle, but as a challenge to produce our own interpretations of the spatial design that governs the novel.[15] This is also part of the prerogatives that intertextuality confers on the reader, who is free to establish his/her own intertextual connections, regardless of the author's intentions or conscious design when writing the novel.

In "La littérature et l'espace," Gérard Genette reflects on the paradox of talking about space in literature. For the literary work to be perceived as such it should be read, and reading is, in all appearance, an essentially temporal experience. Yet space is a dimension as relevant to literature as it is to other, traditionally considered spatial arts, such as painting and architecture. Even architecture, the spatial art par excellence, does not talk about space, but rather, Genette says, it is space that talks through it, in it, and about it. Similarly, there is a literary spatiality that goes beyond the spaces (settings) depicted in the text, a spatial dimension that is "active et non passive, significante et non signifiée, propre à la littérature, spécifique à la littérature, une spatialité représentative et non représentée."[16] This being so, Genette goes on to analyze what he refers to as "aspects de la spatialité littéraire" or, what is the same, the diverse ways in which the spatiality he rightfully claims for literature can be approached. I would like to call

---

[15] Palliser encourages this attitude when he sets himself apart from the John Fowles of *The French Lieutenant's Woman*, a novel, he says, spoilt by "too much Fowles coming and explaining." By contrast, he sees his fiction as "not expository" but "experiential": the reader should feel things, should be left to his/her lot and find his/her own interpretations instead of being told them. In Onega, "Interview" 1993, 282.

[16] A spatial dimension that is "active, rather than passive, signifying, rather than signified, proper to literature, specific to literature, a spatiality that represents, rather than being represented." (My translation). Gérard Genette, "La littérature et l'espace" in *Figures II* (Paris: Seuil, 1969): 44.

attention to two of these aspects as particularly relevant to my analysis of *The Quincunx*. Firstly, there is the undeniable spatial dimension of the written text,[17] the appearance of the words on the page, the disposition of paragraphs and, beyond that, the arrangement of the whole discourse in the book considered as "une sorte d'object total," that is, the book as "total object." Moreover, there are certain effects (of repetition, parallelism, symmetry, etc.) which demand a perception of all the moments that make up the reading experience as simultaneous, as united in the space of the book.[18] Secondly, though to Genette this is the last mode of literary spatiality, there is the view of literature as a vast atemporal domain, an infinite (Borgesian) library where the past is simultaneous with the present, and where, in Proust's words, "la temps y a pris la forme de l'espace."[19] In what follows, then, I will concentrate on (the relationship between) these two aspects of literary spatiality in Charles Palliser's novel. The latter has a wide scope: If *The Quincunx* is a node in the infinite web, the infinite library of literature and culture, one has to focus on a limited set of intertextual relations in the hope that they will illustrate the complex ways in which this text relates to others. This is, of course, a heuristic device, a useful strategy one has recourse to for merely practical reasons. Yet critics and reviewers tend to foreground the novel's Victorian intertexts

---

[17] Among the authors who later developed Genette's insights, Carl Darryl Malmgren refers to this particular aspect of literary spatiality as "iconic space": the space generated by the fact that the speech act on which a narrative rests must be recorded on some sort of physical medium. He also comments on the way in which the text's physicality is often used metatextually in contemporary fiction by systematically foregrounding any of the four levels of iconic space he distinguishes: alphabetic, lexical, paginal, and compositional. Carl Darryl Malmgren, *Fictional Space in the Modernist and Postmodernist American Novel* (Lewisburg: Bucknell UP, 1985) 39, 45.

[18] Genette, "Littérature" 1969, 45-46.

[19] "Time has taken the form of space." (My translation). In Genette, "Littérature" 1969, 48.

while they comment on the quincunxial design of the novel as merely a clever trick on the author's part. It is my contention, though, that this quincunxial design lends itself to the same kind of intertextual analysis as the novel's plot, characters, settings, and narrative style(s). Consequently, the potentially infinite intertextual relations that one can establish between this novel and other texts can be reduced to a manageable size by focusing on Victorian literature in general and Dickens in particular, but it can equally be dealt with from the perspective provided by the quincunx as both icon and symbol.

In an iconic mode of representation the physical qualities of the sign correspond to those of its referent. As an iconic embodiment of the quincunx, then, Palliser's novel duplicates it in the structural design of the text. The potential of this iconic space is exploited at a compositional level by self-consciously playing with the arrangement of the different sections that make up the novel and which the reader must consider simultaneously as a spatial whole (Genette's view of the book as "total object"). In a symbolic mode, by contrast, the correlation of sign and referent is arbitrary, it belongs to the realm of ideas rather than the domain of sensory forms. The symbolic meanings of the quincunx and the number five come from old and they cannot be kept at bay when reading Palliser's novel. According to Georges Matoré, an "image often retains, in its profoundest depths, the traces of its original values, and we could apply to it what we have said elsewhere of the word: the image remembers. It is at once potential and nostalgia."[20] Thus, the image of the quincunx takes us back to the past, as much as the novel's Victorian intertexts do, and becomes a powerful intertext itself, an intertext that combines a visual design, a pattern, and the archetypal and symbolic connotations that were long ago ascribed to it in contexts not directly related to the realm of literary fiction. This combination is best

---

[20] In Wendy B. Faris, *Labyrinths of Language. Symbolic Landscape and Narrative Design in Modern Fiction* (Baltimore: Johns Hopkins UP, 1988) 2.

represented by Sir Thomas Browne's detailed study of quincunxial patterns in *The Garden of Cyrus*, which will be the starting point for the development of my analysis. Eventually, the way in which the past is made present in the text by means of the quincunx as a spatial design will lead us to consider how the traditional symbolic meanings of the quincunxial pattern are altered in this postmodernist work of fiction. In this light, the relationship between *The Quincunx* and the conventions of nineteenth-century realism is not unlike that between the novel and the quincunxial figure: The text follows the rules, and yet, it breaks them.

I

The quincunxial design is much older than the techniques and devices of Victorian realism. As early as 1658, Sir Thomas Browne published two essays entitled *Urn Burial* and *The Garden of Cyrus*. They appeared in one single volume and, though some of the themes in *Urn Burial* are relevant to Palliser's enterprise—particularly Browne's comments on the difficulty of translating the meaning of an artifact from the past to the present—it is the second essay that interests us here. Significantly, the epigraph to *The Garden of Cyrus* is a sentence from Quintilian, which is the very same sentence that constitutes the epigraph to Palliser's novel: "*Quid Quincunce speciousius, qui, in quamcumque partem spectaveris, rectus est?*"[21]

The initial subject of *The Garden of Cyrus* is Cyrus the Younger's method of planting trees by fives in the shape of a

---

[21] "What can be more beautiful than a quincunx, which is straight from whatever point you view it?" (My translation). This straightness that Quintilian highlights refers both to the ever-regular structure of the symbolic design and to the moral rectitude it is meant to stand for. Yet both kinds of straightness—that of the formal pattern and that of the principles that govern the main character's behavior—will become suspicious in the course of Palliser's work.

quincunx, that is, in the shape of an X (a tree at each corner of a rectangle/square and one at the center) so as to produce a continuous plantation in the form of a network. Browne's essay relates this quincunxial network to a Hermetic microcosm, figuring the whole world (the works of nature and those of man) and, what is more, the intelligible continuity of the universe. It is not hard to see how a net is an appropriate figure of continuity; what is perhaps less easy to grasp is its appropriateness as a figure of intelligibility. If this can be explained somehow, Palliser's enterprise will appear all the more striking since what *The Quincunx* eventually suggests is the impossibility of reaching a definite interpretation of the events narrated along so many pages. As John Huffam admits, he "could continue for ever to hear new and more complicated versions of the past without ever attaining to a final truth,"[22] and the same goes for the reader.

According to John Irwin, the key to *The Garden of Cyrus* is the connection that Browne establishes among numbers (the number five), letters (V, the Roman symbol of five), and geometrical shapes (the decussation, or X shape).[23] It is on this relationship that we must focus in order to understand how the figure of the quincunx relates to the notion of intelligibility. Thus, the quincunxial network is to Browne not only an orderly disposition of the physical world. It is, first and foremost, an "Originall figure," the pattern of the Garden of Eden, for "since even in Paradise itself, the tree of knowledge was placed in the middle of the Garden, whatever was the ambient figure, there wanted not a center and rule of decussation."[24] Accordingly, if the quincunx is a God-given design, then it must express the basic relationship between man and the universe, between

---

[22]   Charles Palliser, *The Quincunx: The Inheritance of John Huffam* (1989; London: Penguin, 1990) 1029.

[23]   John T. Irwin, *The Mystery to a Solution. Poe, Borges and the Analytic Detective Story* (Baltimore: Johns Hopkins U P, 1994) 141.

[24]   Thomas Browne, "The Garden of Cyrus," in *Sir Thomas Browne. The Major Works*, ed. C. A. Patrides (London: Penguin, 1977) 333.

knower and known. As John Irwin points out, the various modes of intelligible representation of the world (i.e., mathematics, language, and geometry) are contained within a quincunx, joined together as physical inscription in the above-mentioned relationship among numbers, letters, and geometrical shapes. That is why this formal pattern imposed on nature can be said to schematize the interface between the mind and the world.[25]

The notion that there is a necessary (because original) correspondence among numbers, letters, and geometrical shapes is, of course, a belief shared by a variety of mystical philosophies, alchemy and the cabala among them. This belief grounds a series of practices based on the sense of a complete noncontingency, and thus necessary meaningfulness, of every detail created by an absolute intelligence. This is the case, for instance, of the numerical interpretation of the letters in a name, such as the Tetragrammaton.

If God is responsible for the origins of the quincunxial pattern in the world, John's ancestor, Jeoffrey Huffam, is the designer of the quincunxial device in the diegesis. Significantly, the reader is informed that Jeoffrey Huffam identified the quincunx with his name to the point that he intended to celebrate the latter when he planned the big new house in the Hougham estate in the form of an H.[26] In Hebrew, the number five is represented by the letter H, which appears twice in God's name, thus becoming the letter added by God himself to Abra(h)am's name after His blessing (Genesis 17, 5). Susana Onega interprets this as a hint of the divine nature of John's ancestor, which is in turn supported by the fact that Jeoffrey Huffam's archenemy changed his name from Abraham to Nicholas (a familiar equivalence with Satan) and that this Nicholas fathered John Huffam's own devilish enemy, Silas

---

[25] Irwin, *Mystery* 1994, 143.
[26] Palliser, *Quincunx* 1990, 860.

Clothier.[27] Eventually, all this brings to the fore the metaphysical quality of John's quest, thus taking us back to the quincunxial planting pattern and MacNiven's remark that "the quincunx of trees ... is said to be the key to the lost Templar treasure [which can be either] a treasure of gold and precious stones [or] *a gem of spiritual knowledge, a gnosis.*"[28] In more than one sense, then, John's confrontation with his enemy stands for the eternal combat between good and evil, a combat in which man strives for spiritual knowledge.

The complex relationship that exists between the quincunx—the figure—and *The Quincunx*—the novel—can also be traced back to the doctrine of archetypes. As Borges points out in "El Golem":

Si (como el griego afirma en el *Cratilo*)
el nombre es el arquetipo de la cosa,
en las letras de *rosa* está la rosa
y todo el Nilo en la palabra *Nilo.*[29]

Similarly, the quincunx is present in *The Quincunx* both as formal device and as generator of symbolic meanings. Yet,

---

[27] Onega, "Symbol" 1993, 134. For his part, Browne sees the "h" added to Abra(h)am's name as "the character of Generation" (i.e., fertility). Thus, if Abraam had not had this letter added to his name, he would have remained childless. For this same reason, his wife Sarai became Sarah. Browne supports this approach with the fact that in the cabala the "mother of Life and Fountain of souls" is Binah, whose seal and character is H. Browne, "Garden" 1977, 381-82. In the light of Browne's view, it is just appropriate that the name that appears in the first place in all the genealogical trees scattered throughout the novel should be H̲enry H̲uffam, H. H. The double H presents him as a kind of patriarch, the "source" from which all the branches of the family spring.

[28] Ian MacNiven, "Quincunx" 1987, 235 (emphasis added).

[29] "If (as the Greek asserts in the *Cratylus*) / the name is the archetype to the thing, / the rose is in the letters of *rose* / and the whole Nile in the word *Nile.*" (My translation). Jorge Luis Borges, *Antología poética 1923-1977* (Madrid: Alianza, 1981) 59.

according to Browne, the quincunxial pattern owes its name "not only unto the Quintuple number of Trees, but the figure declaring that number," that is, the Roman letter V, "which being doubled at the angle, makes up the letter X, that is the Emphaticall decussation, or fundamental figure."[30] In other words, by doubling the Roman V—at once letter, numeral, and geometrical shape—we get an X figure—also a Roman letter, which represents the number ten as well as the decussation of the quincunx.

The structure of the novel is based on a similar doubling, which is carried out at different levels. Each part has five books. The first three books in each part constitute a V shape that gives way to an X figure once books IV and V are added— a quincunx of books, with book III at the center and the other four at the corners. Similarly, the V shape formed by parts one, two, and three is projected downwards from its angle to form another X when parts four and five are added. The stability (regularity) of this pattern—made by repeatedly doubling two fives (V) joined at their apexes (X)—is reinforced by the sphericity of its nature: $5 \times 5 = 25$ (five chapters x five books = twenty-five chapters in each part), $25 \times 5 = 125$ (twenty-five chapters x five parts = one hundred and twenty-five chapters in the novel). Five is a spherical number because, when it is multiplied by itself, it always circles back to end in itself no matter how many times the process is repeated ($125 \times 5 = 62\underline{5}$, $625 \times 5 = 312\underline{5}$, etc.). Browne suggests the ultimate significance of this sphericity in noting that five is one of the numbers that make up the mystical name of God. Since the letters that compose the Tetragrammaton (Y, H, V) are respectively the tenth, fifth, and sixth letters of the Hebrew alphabet, and since ten, five, and six are all spherical numbers, these letters encode God's essence.[31] Accordingly, if the number five ultimately stands for an intelligence which is absolute and infinite, a novel based on this number at the levels of both content and form

---

[30]   Browne, "Garden" 1977, 328.
[31]   Browne, "Garden" 1977, 382.

suggests, initially, at least, the same notions of perfection, stability, and all-inclusive intelligibility: a flawless formal pattern imposed on a complex but well-devised plot that leaves no loose threads in the end.

It is interesting to note that, in Browne, the quincunx is not only an appropriate image of divine wisdom or man's intellectual approach to the universe, but also of the way in which man *sees* the world: "It is no wonder that this Quincunciall order was first and still affected as grateful unto the eye: For all things are seen Quincuncially."[32] Browne thus associates the decussation with human vision: As the rays of light come to the eye, the cornea and the lens refract them to produce the corresponding image on the retina. It is actually a kind of V shape that governs the path of the rays of light to the lens and from the lens to the retina.

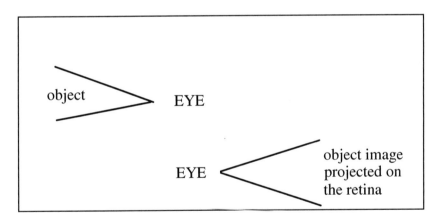

When the eye "captures" an object, the cornea and the lens (re)produce an inverted image of it. Significantly, the image of the object constitutes not a mirrored reflection of the same object as is found in the outward world but, rather, a diagonally mirrored reflection, an inversion in which up becomes down, and left becomes right.

---

[32] Browne, "Garden" 1977, 376.

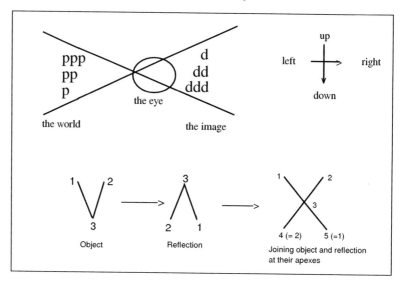

It is worth noting that the V shape can be doubled at its angle (decussation), but it can also be doubled at its open end (the rhombus or lozenge). It is little wonder, then, that if the decussation represents in Browne the path of vision that runs from outer to inner—from object to brain—the rhombus should stand for the path that runs from inner to outer—from brain to object. According to John Irwin, this is what happens, for instance, when a painter projects an internal image onto the (external) canvas of a picture: The artist treats the picture plane as "the base of two pyramids pointing in opposite directions, the apex of one being the eye-point of the artist and the apex of the other being the central vanishing point toward which all the orthogonals perpendicular to the picture plane recede," that is, a point at the center of the plane that recedes ad infinitum.[33]

Formulated in this way, the relationship between the decussation and the lozenge/rhombus strikingly recalls the two principles on which the structure of Palliser's novel is based: the diagonally mirrored reflection and the *mise en abyme*. These are the same principles that govern the arrangement of

---

[33] Irwin, *Mystery* 1994, 144-45.

the five quincunxes on the wedding card Miss Lydia Mompesson—an old cousin of John's grandfather—shows John during one of their conversations. Though Miss Lydia's explanations and John's deductions refer literally to the quincunx of quincunxes on the wedding card, formed by the coats of arms of each of the five families, they ultimately throw light upon the novel's structure. Each part consists of a quincunx of books; each book, in turn, is made up of five chapters, and so, it contains another quincunx *en abyme*. Moreover, the patterns in each part are reflected by those in the part diagonally opposed to it, and the same applies to the books within each part. In as far as the wedding card is concerned, this reflection is based on the way in which colors (black, white, and red) are combined in each quincunx of roses. When it comes to the text, the pattern emerges from the arrangement of narrative voices, that is to say, from the ways in which the narrative instance remains the same or varies in the chapters of the books that make up the novel's five parts, as I will explain later on.[34]

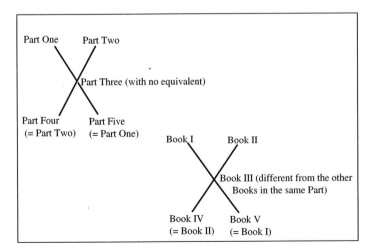

---

[34]   See also Onega, "Symbol" 1993, 136-38.

Miss Lydia's card contains twenty-five quatrefoil roses—that is, roses made up of five elements, four petals and a bud—arranged in fives to form five quincunxes. Each quincunx, like each part, corresponds to a family. Each quatrefoil, with its five elements, is the equivalent to a book, with its five chapters. And the different tinctures in the quatrefoils' buds and petals relate to the different narrative instances in each of the chapters. As Miss Lydia is not sure whether she will find the card or not, she and John try to work out the pattern—which the latter desperately needs to open a safe and retrieve a will—by using whatever details Miss Lydia can remember. She explains that the quincunx of quincunxes represents the union of the two founding families: the Huffams and the Mompessons. The quincunx comes originally from the Huffam crest, but all the families descended from Henry Huffam's adopted variants of it. It is for this reason that, though at first sight the design of the quincunxes in each of the family's devices seems to be identical, various tinctures are used to mark the difference.[35] In the Huffam version, the four quatrefoils at the corners have white petals and a black bud, while the arrangement of tinctures in the central quatrefoil is precisely reversed: black petals and a white bud. The Mompesson design, Miss Lydia adds, is the same, except that the central quatrefoil has red petals.[36] In order to work out the other versions of the device from the ones they know, Miss Lydia suggests relying on an important heraldic principle: the diagonally mirrored reflection, according to which the first and fifth quincunxes should be identical, just as the second and the fourth, while the central one must be different from them if the logic of the pattern is to be maintained.

---

[35] At this stage, it might be a good idea for the reader of this article to set pen (one black and one red) to paper and try to reproduce the coats of arms of the five families as John does, that is, beginning with the Huffam and the Mompesson designs, in this order, and working out the others from these two.

[36] Palliser, *Quincunx* 1990, 1013.

As this pattern is reproduced at the textual level, the issue of narrative voice becomes most relevant: Just as in every quatrefoil of the heraldic device the petals and buds are painted in two different tinctures, the five chapters in every book are narrated by two different narrative instances—except from one book, the *central* one, devoted entirely to the diary written by John's mother, Mary (part three, book III). In the quincunx of quincunxes the only quatrefoils that change are the ones at the *center* of each quincunx. Accordingly, books I, II, IV, and V remain *the same* throughout the *five* parts: The first chapter is narrated by John and the other four by the puppeteers. Then, the central books of parts one and five (diagonally opposed to one another) change in the same way: The puppeteers narrate the first chapter and John the remaining four. Finally, the same parallelism exists between the central books of parts two and four: The first chapter, narrated by John, is followed by four chapters narrated not by the puppeteers but by a third narrative instance: Miss Quilliam in part two and Mr Escreet in part four.

Book III in part three also changes and, in addition, it is not equal to any of the books in the other four parts. In fact, this central book must be approached with John's doubts about the color of the central bud in mind, doubts that arise when Miss Lydia at last manages to find the wedding card containing the arrangement of the (tinctured) quincunx of quincunxes:

> As we had anticipated, the arrangement was symmetrical with the first and the fifth, like the second and the fourth, elements exactly reflecting each other, and the Huffam motif was indeed the first as I had suggested it should be. The crucial central quincunx was identical to the second and the fourth, except that the bud in the middle quatre-foil appeared—as predicted— not to be white. But what was it? ... it was very difficult to make out whether the central bud was filled with dots or was entirely

black—or was even white with slight discolorations of the paper.[37]

The textual equivalent of "the crucial central quincunx," in John's words, is, then, Mary's diary, which occupies the central book of the part at the center of the novel (from chapter 61 to chapter 65). Mary started writing this diary when John was still a child. It was originally intended to inform her son of basic events that had taken place before his birth, but that he was still too young to understand. The first two sections of the diary (chapters 61 and 62) are written in their country estate at Melthorpe and go over some of the events already told by John in the initial chapters of the novel, though now these events are presented from Mary's point of view, instead of John's. The remaining three sections of the diary (chapters 63, 64, and 65) are written in London and provide information about Mary's life while John was kept away from her by their enemies. These sections also show the way in which Mary's narration evolves into a diary aimed at herself rather than her son. Thus, chapter 65 takes the form of a rather incoherent account, as could be expected from a woman who is tired, weak, and drugged. Chapters 62, 63, and 64 are arranged like the equivalent chapters in the other four books, but chapters 61 and 65 are different from any other. The chapter that is placed at the center of the whole novel (chapter 63) presents no peculiarity; it is similar to chapters 62 and 64 and, in this sense, the novel can be said to have a stable center. Yet the quincunx formed by the five chapters of Mary's diary is not the last one in this recursive structure of quincunxes-within-quincunxes, as chapter 61 contains, in turn, another quincunx *en abyme*, the one formed by the five relations of the first part of the diary. As soon as we reach the third relation, we discover that the pages Mary tore out and threw to the fire shortly before she died (and which contained vital information about John's origins) should be placed, precisely, about the middle part of this third relation. In

---

[37]   Palliser, *Quincunx* 1990, 1030.

addition, chapter 65 symmetrically reflects chapter 61 by containing another blank at the center, which consists of five entries under which Mary wrote nothing but the number of laudanum grains that she took every day.

All in all, the missing pages and blank entries mentioned above definitely undermine the illusion of a center for the whole novel. This inability to locate and, even less, grasp a fixed stable center is what John expresses when, on reaching the Old Hall, he declares that "the pattern of tiles making black and white lozenges [were] like endlessly proliferating and ramifying quincunxes ... whose center changed as I advanced";[38] when he tries to interpret the time-worn countenance of the marble figure brought to the house at Melthorpe from the center of the mausoleum at Hougham Park, he is struck by the fact that, as he tries to grasp its meaning, "the pattern receded endlessly, like the tiles of the broken floor of the Old Hall";[39] and, eventually, this is also what he feels with regard to his attempts to reconstruct a definitely coherent version of the past: "I wondered if I would ever know the truth. Each time I seemed about to grasp it, it receded further."[40] Consequently, the center contains infinite centers and can never be perfectly located, for it changes according to the position of the observer, endlessly multiplying itself in a *mise en abyme ad infinitum*.

II

In the light of all this, the correspondences between Browne's analysis of the quincunxial pattern and my own approach to it in *The Quincunx* definitely appear to unveil a crucial difference. Browne interprets the quincunx as a symbol of stability and intelligibility. He associates the stability of the number five with its spherical character, derived from its ultimate source in the Divinity and embodied in the letters of

---

[38]   Palliser, *Quincunx* 1990, 1133.

[39]   Palliser, *Quincunx* 1990, 1180.

[40]   Palliser, *Quincunx* 1990, 1010.

God's name (each connected with a spherical number). Similarly, the quincunx represents God's infallible intelligence while it also embodies the main "tools" man uses to decipher the universe: mathematics, geometry, and language. The V shape—also considered as a geometric representation of the fold of the hand—is a basic metaphor for human knowledge: just as the hand grasps objects, the forceps-like decussation grasps the world, and the quincunxial structure—with its knots and closed rhombi—captures it within a net. By contrast, Palliser's novel relies on the symbolic associations of the quincunx to unravel a plot and impose a formal structure that evoke not stability but vacillation, not intelligibility but puzzlement. Thus, though *The Quincunx* is based on a figure that can be dated back to Antiquity—or even to the origins of the world, if we follow Browne in his view of the Garden of Eden as the first quincunxial pattern on earth—the connotations that the quincunxial design acquires in Palliser's work present it as something not so "straight" and one-sided as Quintilian and Browne thought it to be. There is a pervading sense of hazard, disorder, chaos, which incorporates its opposite: order, pattern, design. This blending of contraries and, above all, the structure of the novel as such, may bring to mind what some regard as the paramount representation of chaos, but also as a proof that order is at the heart of chaotic systems: fractal figures. Fractals are usually formed by an iterative process that can go on and on ad infinitum in such a way that the resulting image becomes more and more complex by means of a simple operation. Fractals also have in common with the structure of *The Quincunx* the fact that both of them are self-similar, which means that each small portion, when magnified, can reproduce exactly a larger portion. As Katherine Hayles puts it referring to fractal geometry, the same general form (self-similarity) is repeated (iterative formation) across many different length scales introducing an element of predictability, which thus emerges amidst chaos and arbitrariness.[41] These remarks perfectly apply to the structure of the novel we are dealing with (and they may also be extended to other postmodernist novels). However, to analyze possible correspondences and their implications would lead us into the discourse of the New Physics, which would require another article. Be it enough to say here that *The Quincunx* shares with fractals this tug-of-war between simplicity and complexity, order and chaos, pattern and randomness. In the last reading, though, neither fractality nor any other "metaphor" we could graft onto Palliser's book could fill in the gap left by the novel's centerlessness.

The more than complex plot of *The Quincunx* and the striking coincidences that make up John's story constitute a sort of chaotic system out of which a carefully devised pattern emerges. The order imposed by the figure of the quincunx may initially seem absolute and complete. This is, for instance, what the elements of the paratext suggest: Quintilian's sentence (with its intertextual wink at Browne's essay) is intended to praise the pattern of the quincunx as perfect, regular, stable; the titles of each part coincide with the names of the five families; the order in which they appear is the same as the one followed by their respective coats of arms in the heraldic device, etc. However, the randomness underlying such a design is never done away with. One may wonder, for instance, why the five family devices are arranged in this order (first the Huffams, second the Mompessons, third the Clothiers, fourth the Palphramonds, and fifth the Maliphants) and not in a different one. Even if the quincunx of roses comes from the Huffam crest, the quincunx of quincunxes, according to Miss Lydia, might have been devised by her own father, Sir Hugo Mompesson, on the occasion of his wedding to Alice Huffam.[42] If it was a Mompesson who devised it, one may expect that the Mompesson version would be the first, or even the central one.

---

[41] Katherine Hayles, ed. *Chaos and Order: Complex Dynamics in Literature and Science* (Chicago: U of Chicago P, 1991) 10.

[42] Palliser, *Quincunx* 1990, 1014.

On the other hand, the fact that the Huffam crest is the original motif and the family the most ancient one may account for the fact that it occupies the first place, seen in this way as the point of departure.[43] But, for the same reason, it might have occupied the center, since, from an archetypal point of view, the center always represents the origin of everything: the origin of the world, the place where the Creation started, the place occupied by the paradise where God made Adam and Eve, the sacred place par excellence.[44] Yet, and as has been pointed out, the reality about the work's center is not so clear. All arguments seem thus to end up at the same point, as if there were no way to avoid facing the question of the absence/presence of a center for the whole novel: the geometrical center of the work is chapter 63, which has no peculiarity, but if we follow the structure of quincunxes *en abyme* the center corresponds not to chapter 63 but to the missing pages in Mary's diary, that is, an absent center.

This formal centerlessness is supported and enhanced by the uncertainty surrounding the main (central) questions within the mystery plot of the novel: What is John's final decision in as far as his inheritance is concerned? Who killed John's grandfather? Above all, who was John's father? Enough clues are given for the reader to question the fact that John is really the son of his mother's husband, Peter Clothier. These clues point in two directions: John's father may have been Martin Fortisquince, a close friend of John's grandfather, whom John strikingly resembles to the point that, on his first meeting with Miss Lydia, the latter takes him for Martin's son.[45] But there is an even more disturbing possibility, according to which Mary

---

[43] Palliser, *Quincunx* 1990, 1015.

[44] Mircea Eliade, *El mito del eterno retorno*, trans. Ricardo Anaya (1951; Barcelona: Altaya, 1954) 24.

[45] Palliser, *Quincunx* 1990, 959.

Huffam may have had an incestuous relationship with her father, John being the offspring of their unlawful affair.[46]

A center in a labyrinth implies a place of rest, an end to the disorientation experienced by the explorer who treads its convoluted paths, or, at least, a temporary respite from confusion. The center may contain a variety of experiences, perhaps the most common being the adversary (the Minotaur) or the illumination (the temple).[47] In this quincunxial labyrinth of sorts, the goal of John's quest lay perhaps at the center, written on the pages that his mother burnt. The information there might have enlightened John: Unveiling the truth would at least have given sense to his ordeal, even if it forced him to face a hard reality about his origins. Likewise, the center also stands for the interpreter's goal, the meaning buried in the depths of the work. Yet the center may also be, as is in *The Quincunx*, the novel's central deception: Contrary to all appearances and expectations, it intensifies John's and the reader's doubts instead of definitely clarifying them.

By the time s/he reaches the end of the novel, the reader cannot but agree with Pentecost when he tells John that "a pattern ... is always arbitrary or partial in that there could always be a different one or a further elaboration of the same."[48] Almost everything in Palliser's work can be questioned, as any possible interpretation fails to exclude its opposite. Therefore,

---

[46] See Onega, "Mirror Games" 2000, 162. All in all, these puzzling hints regarding John's origins suggest that, though by the end of the novel the protagonist is in the position to claim both the Huffam and the Clothier inheritance, he may not be rightfully entitled to any of them. If John eventually claimed them, his decision would bear witness to the fact that he has not remained untainted by the events that make up his life, and that, since he probaby knows more than he openly states, the reasons for taking what does not actually belong to him are rather dubious, at least from the moral point of view. Yet, as is the case with many other key questions in the novel, the reader never learns about John's final decision about accepting or rejecting his inheritance.

[47] Faris, *Labyrinths* 1988, 4.

[48] Palliser, *Quincunx* 1990, 1152.

one may reach the conclusion that understanding the novel means perceiving and accepting the openness on which it is ultimately based. Thus, *The Quincunx* appears as subscribing and, simultaneously, questioning other forms—be it a formal pattern, numerical symbolism, or many of the conventions at the heart of nineteenth-century literary realism. This writing over and against what has been written constitutes the essence of most postmodernist literature, a literature which is both enjoyable and disquieting, playful and serious and, above all, illustrative of the complex dialectics by which the forms of the past can be turned into wonderful vehicles for expressing the concerns of the present. These forms remain operative as intertexts and, as I have tried to show, they are not limited, in as far as Palliser's novel is concerned, to past literary works. They also include the quincunxial design itself, subverted here both in its iconic and symbolic dimensions. If we agree with Juri Lotman's contention that "the structure of the space of a text becomes a model of the structure of the space of the universe,"[49] we have to conclude that the hesitancy which affects the center of the quincunx in the novel hides a deeper uneasiness regarding the once solid belief that the universe has a center—be it God or human reason—which can explain all and solve all puzzles. It also questions the reliance on a coherent reality (the World) and a unified human subject (the Self). *The Quincunx*, then, is not so much concerned with providing a neat ending that can ultimately fill the void of the world with definite answers. On the contrary, it tries to dramatize that void and, more specifically, it tries to do so through the figure of the quincunx.

In conclusion, Palliser's novel can be said to rely on a symbol that swerves away from unity and closure, and into the ambivalent terrain that characterizes the postmodern ethos. As the symbol swerves, its meaning slides into something different: The quincunx stops being here what it was in

---

[49] In Faris, *Labyrinths* 1988, 167.

Browne—an image of the omnipresence of the creator in His creation, of the closeness of God to man—in order to become an image of the distance of man from any absolute ground of meaning. Palliser's work, then, brings the air of an old melody that lulls us into handsome groves. However, the melody is sung in a different tone to wake us to the fact that, in our time and age, handsome groves can only be the stuff of dreams.

WRITING THE SELF "IN THE LANGUAGE OF THE OTHER": CHINESE MEMOIRS AND THE POLITICS OF ENGLISH[1]

Ruth Y. Hung

ABSTRACT

This paper is a study of Chinese memoirs in English, and it resituates the postcolonial debates on the politics of English under the new global conditions. Since the mid-1980s a substantial number of Chinese nationals started to write discursively about their experience of the Cultural Revolution (1966-1976) across national and linguistic borders; Nien Cheng's *Life and Death in Shanghai* (1986) and Jung Chang's *Wild Swans* (1991) are often considered to be the forerunners of this emergent literary formation. That these Chinese writers have chosen to write in English about their personal traumatic experience compels us to reconsider the global spread of English and its implications. In the postcolonial critique of the politics of English, the global spread of English has often been attributed to the history and practice of British colonialism. Postcolonial writers and critics, however, have yet to explain the continuing spread and domination of English as the de facto international language at the present time. Despite the demise of the British Empire after the Second World War, English has remained to be the most widely used language both within and outside anglophone societies. This paper argues that it is necessary to move beyond the postcolonial theoretical framework in order to adequately understand the empire of English and that the phenomenal success of the Chinese memoirs shows how global capitalism and the demand for linguistic uniformity reinforce each other. In this new phase of "late capitalism," English serves not only as a tool of various sociopolitical projects such as cultural imperialism, nation-building,

---

[1] I am most grateful to Q.S. Tong for his detailed and constructive comments on the various drafts of this paper.

or postcolonial resistance, but also as a commodity, a form of capital and power, whether discursive, social, or economic.

Around the mid-1980s a substantial number of Chinese nationals started to write, beyond the borders of their motherland and against the backdrop of a remembered China, about their traumatic experience of the Cultural Revolution (1966-1976) and have since accumulated a significant repertoire of Chinese writing in English abroad. Nien Cheng's *Life and Death in Shanghai* and Jung Chang's *Wild Swans* are often considered to be the forerunners of these Chinese memoirs in English.[2] For this group of Chinese writers, English is not just a new linguistic medium of expression, but an enabling and empowering force of creativity and freedom. "English allows me to enjoy the absolute freedom of creativity, to write without self-censorship," says Annie Wang, author of *Lili*, in an interview. "In this new language environment, there are no expectations from my old readers, nor cultural or political pressure."[3] Liu Hong speaks with no irony of English thus: "I liked the sound of English, and there were no negative overtones, like colonialism, where I lived ... Chinese language and culture are like the

---

[2]   The term "Chinese memoirs" refers to those memoirs that are set against the background of the Chinese Cultural Revolution and are written mostly by Chinese nationals who moved abroad after the Cultural Revolution. Included among them are: *Son of the Revolution* (1983) by Liang Heng and Judith Shapiro, *Life and Death in Shanghai* (1986) by Nien Cheng, *Wild Swans* (1991) by Jung Chang, *Red Azalea* (1993) by Anchee Min, *A Single Tear* (1993) by Wu Ningkun, *Spider Eaters* (1997) by Rae Yang, *A Leaf in the Bitter Wind* (1997) by Ye Ting-xing, *Thirty Years in a Red House* (1998) by Zhu Xiao-di, *Colours of the Mountain* (1999) by Da Chen, *Daughter of China* (1999) by Xu Meihong and Larry Engelmann, *To the Edge of the Sky* (2000) by Gao Anhua, and *Vermilion Gate* (2000) by Aiping Mu.

[3]   Annie Wang, interview, *South China Morning Post*, [Hong Kong] 20 Oct. 2001.

soil that gave me nutrients, but English is the language that has made me free."[4]

Readers familiar with the postcolonial critique of cultural imperialism may have questions about whether a "foreign" tongue can function as the language of creativity and represent fully the Chinese subject. What is there inside its system that has made English such a language of freedom and creativity? Questions of this kind, although frequently raised in postcolonial debates over the politics of English, do not seem to be a serious concern for Annie Wang or Liu Hong and indeed for many other "exiled" Chinese writers. The phenomenon, that these Chinese memoirists choose to write in English in the postimperial era, poses a challenge and adds a new dimension to the postcolonial critique of the politics of English, for it urges, and indeed requires, us to consider the issue of linguistic imperialism beyond the history of British colonialism and beyond the nation-state framework. As English is no longer under the monopoly of the British, and as the concept of nation-state slowly gives way to the weight of globalization, the debate over the relationship between mother tongue and national identity must be resituated in the new global context, and the phenomenon of the continuing spread of English should be considered in close relation to the constitution of global capitalism that has enabled English to function as the de facto international language.

Beyond the Postcolonial Paradigm

The adoption of English, while not a problem to this group of Chinese writers, has been a serious concern for writers from former colonies and has generated a series of debates among them over the politics and global spread of English. Such debates constitute a discursive part of the postcolonial critique of the cultural practice of colonialism and are often concerned

---

[4] Liu Hong, "These Words of FREEDOM," *South China Morning Post* [Hong Kong] 23 Mar. 2003.

with how the indigenous languages are marginalized, suppressed or even devastated in those former colonies.[5] The debates between Chinua Achebe and Ngũgĩ Wa Thiong'o, which lasted for several years, foreground the difficulties and paradoxes the postcolonial critique of English is faced with.

In his celebrated essay "The African Writer and the English Language," written as an afterword to a collection of papers from "A Conference of African Writers of English Expression," which was held in 1962, Achebe broaches the issue of whether English can serve as a bearer of indigenous culture.[6] Arguing that any attempts to arrive at a tentative definition of "African Literature" are in themselves problematic, Achebe distinguishes "national literature" from "ethnic literature," proposing English as the language of the former (75). He explains that his proposal of English as the language of the national literature of Nigeria and that of some other countries in Africa is a response to "the reality of present-day Africa" (76). And that reality is, Achebe continues, that these new nation-states have been "created in the first place by the intervention of the British" (77). Since English is a "world language which history has forced down our throats," a constructive discussion of the relationship between English and African culture should focus on finding ways to make the best use of English for the present and future (79). Taking into account the shaping influence of history upon human action, therefore, Achebe is in favor of the idea of English as a unifying and liberating force. The essay ends with several working examples of African English, showing how the creative writer, as an artist conscious of his role as a cultural ambassador, is capable of "fashioning out an English which is at once universal and able to carry his peculiar experience" (82).

---

[5]   Robert Phillipson, *Linguistic Imperialism* (Oxford: Oxford U P, 1992) 18.

[6]   Chinua Achebe, "The African Writer and the English Language" in *Morning Yet on Creation Day: Essays* (New York: Anchor, 1975) 74-84.

Ngũgĩ and Obi Wali, whom S. N. Sridhar regards as "ultranationalist critics,"[7] have, however, difficulties sharing Achebe's liberal attitude toward English. In response to Achebe's essay, Ngũgĩ, in "The Language of African Literature," holds that "authentic" cultural identity can only be written in the indigenous language and that a "specific culture" can only be transmitted by the "particularity" of a language that belongs to "a specific community with a specific history."[8]

It is perhaps predictable that debates of this kind, though helpful in improving our understanding of the linguistic situations in these former colonies, will not lead to a consensus over whether or not English should be replaced with an indigenous language as the vehicle of "national literature." That English is historically constituted and most widely used in these colonies is a given and a reality, which, as Achebe suggests, should be perhaps recognized in the first place before investigations into the politics of English could start. The long debates between Achebe and Ngũgĩ reveal the complexities of the politics of English in those former colonies and at the same time perhaps the unproductiveness of this kind of debate if conducted *only* within the critical framework of nation-state and linguistic identity.

What is ironical is that these debates, staged and conducted in English, are enabled by the very object of inquiry that is at the same time a means of inquiry. Perhaps a conference on English should acknowledge in the first place the paradox that the participants have to share a common language before they can decide whether that common language should be used. Jürgen Habermas's notion of "performative contradiction" is useful here for the understanding of the ironic situation created by

---

[7] S. N. Sridhar, "Non-Native English Literatures: Context and Relevance" in *The Other Tongue: English Across Cultures*, ed. Braj B. Kachru (Oxford: Pergamon, 1983) 293.

[8] Ngũgĩ Wa Thiong'o, "The Language of African Literature" in *Decolonising the Mind: the Politics of Language in African Literature* (London: James Currey, 1986) 15.

these African writers' inability to escape from their instrument of engagement—English, which not only has given rise to these debates but also has provided a means through which they can be staged. Habermas writes:

> The totalising self-critique of reason gets caught in a performative contradiction since subject-centered reason can be convicted of being authoritarian in nature only by having recourse to its own tools. The tools of thought, which miss the "dimension of nonidentity" and are imbued with the "metaphysics of presence," are nevertheless the only available means for uncovering their own insufficiency.[9]

Critical studies of "third-world literature" need to make it known that a country with a colonial history is, as Sudipta Kaviraj says, "historically instituted by the nationalist imagination" and by the imperial language that has always already been part of the national and cultural identity of the native land.[10] Despite their critical orientations toward English, we hear those

---

[9] Jürgen Habermas, *The Philosophical Discourse of Modernity: Twelve Lectures*, trans. Frederick Lawrence (Cambridge: MIT P, 1987) 185. Along a similar line of thought, Michel Foucault in The *Archaeology of Knowledge* draws our attention to the processes through which a discourse is formed and to the historical conditions of possibility that give rise to it. Foucault understands language use in terms of the relationship between the language system and its user, that is, in terms of how the user's thought and intellectual make-up are constructed by the language itself, by what Michel Pêcheux refers to as "the ideological meanings and values that fill our linguistic creativity." See Foucault, *The Archaeology of Knowledge*, trans. A. M. Sheridan Smith (New York: Routledge, 1989) 31-36; cf. Pêcheux, *Language, Semantics and Ideology: Stating the Obvious*, trans. Harbans Nagpal (London: Macmillan, 1982) 111.

[10] Sudipta Kaviraj, "The Imaginary Institution of India" in *Subaltern Studies: Writings on South Asian History and Society* 7, eds. Partha Chatterjee and Gyanendra Pandey (New York: Oxford U P, 1993) 1.

postcolonial critics and writers speak English at the conference, even though it was held in Uganda, Africa. We also see African writers preoccupied with language standards and their application to emergent "third-world literature." Decolonization only allows more young scholars and critics to participate in the discursive debates over the use of English, but has failed to get rid of the set of protocols of academic debates defined in English, let alone English itself.

I have no intention to valorize the two polemics presented by Achebe and Ngũgĩ. What I am concerned with here is the *framework* in which the issue of the politics of English has been approached in the postcolonial context. English continues to spread across the globe and consolidate those parts of the world it has conquered *after* the period of active imperialism and colonialism. Notwithstanding the collapse of the British Empire after the Second World War, English has never stopped to be the dominant language. "The biggest spurt in English writing," writes Sridhar not without an ironic undertone, "has come in the years immediately surrounding the demise of the British Empire."[11]

This is perhaps nowhere more manifest than in those places outside the sphere of British colonialism. In China, for example, the spread of English has never stopped, even during the Cultural Revolution, a period in which the country is perceived as radically hostile to anything western. Though the postcolonial critique of the spread of English has no obligation to deal with the case of China in order to legitimize its agenda, the complexities of the politics of English cannot be adequately comprehended without considering its global presence; it is by no coincidence that English is spread to China. Kachru observes that at present there are "many more English-using Chinese [in China] than the total population of the United Kingdom, if we estimate just five percent of the Chinese using

---

[11] Sridhar, "Non-Native English Literatures" 1983, 291.

English."[12] The limitations of the postcolonial critique of the politics of English lie in its reluctance to reach beyond its own paradigm to engage with the problem of English in other political, social, or historical contexts; its limitations, in other words, lie in its tendency to localize the global presence of English, which is not confined only to the historical practice of colonialism or to those former colonies.

In *A Cultural History of the English Language*, Gerry Knowles provides a brief historical account of three different ways in which English spreads over the globe: First, English is transplanted from Britain to its colonies; second, it is introduced as a second language alongside existing national languages; and third, it interacts with native languages.[13] Whereas the exportation of English to and its implementation in colonies take on the first and third paths, English voyages to noncolonial regions through the second. Implicit in Knowles' model is the distinction between the factors contributing to the spread of English as a colonial language and from those that contribute to the spread of English as an international language, without losing, of course, the historical sense that British colonialism has paved the way for the internationalization of English at the present time. The *continual* expansion of English in places like China, a phenomenon predicted by John Adams and referred to by people like Kachru, has yet to be adequately explained.[14] China has never been a colony, and the acceptability and popularity of English there, especially after the Communist

---

[12] Kachru, "World Englishes: Agony and Ecstasy," *Journal of Aesthetic Education* 30, no. 2 (1996): 139.

[13] Gerry Knowles, *A Cultural History of the English Language* (New York: St. Martin's P, 1997) 139-40.

[14] John Adams (1735-1826), cited by Kachru in 1992, predicted that "English will be the most respectable language in the world and the most universally read and spoken in the next century, if not before the close of this one." Kachru, "The Second Diaspora of English," in *English in its Social Contexts: Essays in Historical Socio-Linguistics*, eds. T. W. Machan and C. T. Scott (N.Y.: Oxford U P, 1992) 230.

Party took over power in 1949, necessarily invites us to think if there are other routes by which English expands its territorial influence apart from those mentioned by Knowles.[15] If Britain's first settlement in Botany Bay, Australia, in 1788 marked the beginning of the global journey of English, the end of the colonial era does not conclude that journey with a final destination.

English and Politics of Transgression

Although those Chinese memoirists, as mentioned above, are not burdened with the historical baggage of English,[16] their knowledge of English and their later adoption of English in

---

[15] Alma Rubal-Lopez brings to our attention some "potentially significant variables" that, although ignored in previous studies of the relationship between colonialism and the spread of English, may be affecting the spread of English. He singles out the case of China as a "perfect" yet "difficult" example of a non-colony where English is used as a second language: "China is a perfect example of a polity in which the spread of English has not been extensively studied even though this area of the world is one in which English is currently spreading most rapidly. Little is known about the spread of English in this nation because ... studies of English-language spread are usually conducted on former colonies of the United States or Britain rather than on a nation like China, which, although it had economic ties with both the United Kingdom and the United States, cannot by any means be considered a colony or either of these two world powers." Alma Rubal-Lopez, "A Comparative Analysis of Former Anglo-American Colonies with Non-Colonies" in *Post-Imperial English: Status Change in Former British and American Colonies, 1940-1990*, eds. Joshua A. Fishman, Andrew W. Conrad, and Alma Rubal-Lopez (Berlin: Mouton de Gruyter, 1996) 38-39.

[16] For those exiled Chinese writers, the choice of English is more related to how the act of writing can be performed against a set of pragmatic constraints—from practical concerns about writing materials and readership to their anxieties about career advancement and survival. Coming to the United States in 1987 and now working at Harvard, Zhu Xiao-di, for example, is constantly perturbed and frustrated by his inability to communicate fully in English. The language problem becomes for him a natural barrier to the advancement of his career. See Chow Zhuzhi, *The World Daily News*, 17 June, 2000.

writing are necessarily historically conditioned. Many of them started to acquire some knowledge of English during the Cultural Revolution, especially in its later phase. There is a double irony here: The Cultural Revolution not only provides them with a subject to write about, but also, in most cases, makes it possible for them to acquire a language in which to write about it. While discontents about the political and social chaos during the Cultural Revolution are prominently represented in their memoirs, "exiled" Chinese writers do not always acknowledge the fact that it is during this chaotic period that many of them took "advantage" of the political and social anarchy and started to learn English. The Cultural Revolution, in other words, has created a specific social and political vacuum that allowed individual Chinese to develop an officially illegitimate interest in English.

In those years when a desire for almost anything foreign was considered a "decadent" capitalistic pursuit in China, English, whether as the national language of Britain or its cultural institution, is no exception. "I dared not read English now, or do any kind of study when the Cultural Revolution began," says Gao Anhua, author of *To the Edge of the Sky*.[17] "[T]o speak to [foreigners] without authorization was a criminal offence," Jung Chang, later an English major at Sichuan University, recalls.[18] In times of the Party's internal power struggle, things foreign were ritualistically sacrificed: "Zhou and Deng had been making tentative efforts to open the country up, so Mme Mao launched a fresh attack on foreign culture" (619). As a result, Chang concludes that "there was almost no way to learn [English]". (621)

For some, however, to learn English is an act of resistance and a silent challenge to the authority, and the sense of danger involved in learning English offers a form of excitement and

---

[17] Gao Anhua, *To the Edge of the Sky* (London: Penguin, 2001) 147; hereafter *Edge*.
[18] Jung Chang, *Wild Swans: Three Daughters of China* (London: Flamingo, 1993) 621; hereafter *Swans*.

self-fulfillment amidst the barrenness of intellectual life during the Cultural Revolution. Although it was prohibited to tune in to foreign radio broadcasts at the time, thousands of English-learners in China became loyal listeners of the BBC and the Voice of America. "Those of us who listened surreptitiously never dared to talk about what we heard even before the Cultural Revolution,"[19] for, as Jung Chang makes clear, "[w]e could be put into prison" for doing so.[20] Zhu Xiao-di, author of *Thirty Years in a Red House,* obviously took pleasure from this act of political transgression: "My father found out what I was doing, but he didn't stop me. He just asked me to be very careful, and not to turn the radio too loud."[21] Playing the role of a father who is supposed to represent the state authority at a domestic level, Zhu Qiluan, the author's father, fulfils his duty only by defining more strictly where and when it is possible to talk about the "taboo."[22]

Precisely because of official suppression, learning English was more than just a matter of acquiring linguistic skills and became an act tinged with political and perhaps moral adventurism. Forbidden knowledge is often a source of excitement, and the political suppression of foreign culture during the ten dark years has given a strange prominence to it. Speaking of her experience of "learning English in Mao's wake," Jung Chang remembers, after eighteen years, "the thrill of being given permission once, just once, to look at a copy" of *The Worker* (the paper of the minuscule Maoist Communist Party of Britain), which would otherwise be "locked up in a special

---

[19] Nien Cheng, *Life and Death in Shanghai* (London: Flamingo, 1995) 608; hereafter *Life and Death.*

[20] Chang, *Swans* 1993, 621.

[21] Zhu Xiao-di, *Thirty Years in a Red House: A Memoir of Childhood and Youth in Communist China* (Amherst: U of Massachusetts P, 1998) 133-34; hereafter *Thirty Years.*

[22] "To listen to foreign broadcasts had always been taboo in Communist China" (Cheng, *Life and Death* 1995, 608).

room."[23] Zhu Xiao-di considers it a source of transgressive pleasure to read a few more English books than his classmates. Without being apologetic, he "confesses" that "forbidden fruit always tastes better."[24] Because English was "designated as the evil to be eliminated" during the Cultural Revolution, the desire for it—a desire the society could not and dared not recognize—was kindled and intensified.

Largely because he was a politically "backward element," Wu Ningkun was "left out" from various bustling faculty and student activities and happily found "time to finish reading Tolstoy's *War and Peace* and the Moncrieff translation of Marcel Proust's *Remembrance of Things Past*."[25] With China just about to recover from the Revolution, Zhu Xiao-di gained a year's time for self-studies before he was assigned a job after his graduation from secondary school in the summer of 1975: "I knew I would have some time to myself, and it felt great. I spent most of my time reading foreign literary works that had been translated into Chinese."[26] Exiled to the edge of the Himalayas, Jung Chang began her first serious study of English out of boredom and disillusionment with the Revolution: "[T]here was no fun outside. I longed for something to read. But apart from the four volumes of *The Selected Works of Mao Zedong*, all I discovered in the house was a dictionary."[27] And now con-

---

[23] Chang, *Swans* 1993, 621.

[24] Zhu, *Thirty Years* 1998, 187. "Father told me that he had read [*The Communist Manifesto*] in English when he was young. ... I knew that in his time communist books were forbidden by the government. One could be put in jail or even lose one's head if detected reading them by the police. Of course, if the books were in English, few policemen could tell they were about communism. His story sounded so marvelous that I immediately liked the idea of reading *The Communist Manifesto* in English" (131).

[25] Wu Ningkun, *A Single Tear: a Family's Persecution, Love, and Endurance in Communist China* (Boston: Backbay Books, 1993) 21; hereafter *Tear*.

[26] Zhu, *Thirty Years* 1998, 162.

[27] Chang, *Swans* 1993, 518.

sidering herself "among people who had benefited from the Cultural Revolution," Chang thinks the activity of learning English gives her reason enough to feel "nostalgic" for her years in the countryside and the factory, "when [she] had been left relatively alone" (623). Like Chang, Rae Yang's acquaintance with English results more from the circumstantial than the intentional. A Red Guard herself, Yang was fed up with going to factories and people's communes. Considering those trips "worse than futile" and an "interruption" of studies, Yang detached herself as much as she could from school and concentrated on her studies at home. It was when she "relax[ed] behind closed doors" that she found time for translations of foreign masterpieces. Having given a one-paragraph-long list of the books she has read,[28] Yang concludes that the list not only reflects her taste, but shows what has been available to her during the Revolution.[29]

The secret desire for English and its continuing presence during the Cultural Revolution testify to Foucault's remarkable observation that official repression, even at its worst, is discursively "productive."[30]

---

[28] "Of the foreign books I read in translation, my favourite ones were *La Dame aux camélias*, *Les Misérables*, *Wuthering Heights*, *Jane Eyre*, *A Tale of Two Cities*, *War and Peace*, *The Captain's Daughter*, *The Gadfly*, *How Steel Was Made*, *The Scarlet Letter*, *Life on the Mississippi*, *Twenty Thousand Leagues Under the Sea* and all the rest of Jules Verne's science fiction, plus the detective stories by Arthur Conan Doyle, *The Thousand and One Nights*, the Greek myths, and Shakespeare's tragedies" (Chang, *Swans* 1993, 103).

[29] Rae Yang, *Spider Eaters: A Memoir* (Berkeley: U of California P, 1997) 95-102; hereafter *Spider*.

[30] In his study of sexuality, Foucault observes: "there was a steady proliferation of discourses concerned with sex. ... an institution excitement to speak about it, and to do so more and more; a determination on the part of the agencies of power to hear it spoken about, and to cause it to speak through explicit articulation and endlessly accumulated detail." See *The Will to Knowledge: The History of*

English and Cultural Capital

"[K]nowing English is like possessing the fabled Aladdin's lamp, which permits one to open, as it were, the linguistic gates to international business, science, and travel."[31] Although commenting on the pervasiveness of English in our global experience, Kachru, in equating the "magical" power of English *today* with that of "Aladdin's lamp," seems ready to let go of the implications in the constitution and propagation of English as a desired tongue. And it reveals perhaps a certain political unconscious to take English as a form of cultural capital. For my purpose here, it is important to examine the relationship between English as a language of transnational and transcultural knowledge and English as a formation and discourse of power, to examine the "context of situation" in which the choice and use of English are understood as beneficial and the global spread of English is made possible.

What English can do for this group of Chinese memoirists is already shown in the fact that they have chosen English in the production of their memoirs and more significantly in their view of English as the only effective medium of cross-linguistic representation—a fetishism of language which takes English as commodity and embodiment of success. For Gao Anhua, the only true teaching from Karl Marx is that knowledge of English language is "a weapon in the struggle of life,"[32] and thanks to her excellent English, Gao managed to get a job as a translator in the Electronics Import and Export Corporation of Jiangsu Province at the time she, left as a widow, was in a financial plight (309). Being "the only foreign-language speaker out of a staff of twelve," Gao enjoyed "great face"

Sexuality, vol. 1, trans. Robert Hurley (London: Penguin, 1998) 17-18, 29-30.

[31] Kachru, *The Alchemy of English: The Spread, Functions and Models of Non-native Englishes* (Oxford: Pergamon, 1985) 1.

[32] Gao, *Edge* 2001, 262.

among colleagues (378). But English offers far more than just that. "Through taking a postgraduate course abroad," says Aiping Mu, "I could further improve my educational qualifications and gain an adequate knowledge of English, which would open more options in the future, so that I need not rely on jobs offered by the state."[33]

The myth of English as a "neutral choice" has little to do with the linguistic structure inherent in English, but a lot with class and social divisions in a society which has *accepted* the use of English for different reasons and considerations.[34] In his study of the historical formation of the literary canon, John Guillory examines the politics of language acquisition and provides a useful point of entry into the issue of the relationship between social development and the spread of English.[35] "What

---

[33] Aiping Mu, *Vermilion Gate: A Family Story of Communist China* (London: Little, 2000) 767; hereafter *Gate*.

[34] Kachru claims: "[English] has acquired a neutrality in a linguistic context where native languages, dialects, and styles sometimes have acquired undesirable connotations ... It was originally the foreign (alien) ruler's language, but that drawback is often overshadowed by what it can do for its users. True, English is associated with a small and elite group; but it is in their role that the neutrality of a language becomes vital" (Kachru, *The Alchemy of English* 1985, 8-9).

[35] John Guillory, *Cultural Capital: The Problem of Literary Canon Formation* (Chicago: U of Chicago P, 1993). Although Guillory is primarily concerned with the politics of the formation of the literary canon, his analysis of the unequal distribution of literary language and the effect it has on the reproduction of social relations is useful as it helps to explain the way Chinese understand English as cultural capital. Guillory makes a more general comment on the apparatus of education and the social function it performs: "The system of educational institutions reproduces social relations by distributing, and where necessary, redistributing, knowledges" (56). Pierre Bourdieu examines the function of education in maintaining social order and argues that a person lacking in academic qualification is perceived as intrinsically handicapped. He writes: "The educational system, an institutionalized classifier which is itself an objectified system of classification reproducing the hierarchies of the social world in a transformed form."

one learns to read is always another language," Guillory observes, "and because that language is unequally distributed, it is a form of capital." There is, Guillory argues, an innate relationship between linguistic stratification and social stratification: The former is "constructed upon" the latter and also "reproduces," within a specific institution of reproduction, that is, the school, social relations that are hierarchical in nature (61-62). As a consequence, the unequal distribution of linguistic competences creates an internal social distinction between the literate and the illiterate.

The sense that literacy in English creates social distinction manifests itself pointedly, though in a different manner, in some of the Chinese writers' desire for the ownership of English. While the acquisition of English skills appears to Da Chen's mother to be "too fancy" and "exotic," "nothing sound[s] better than that" to Da Chen himself, author of *Colours of the Mountain*. This is because "crippled by political mumbo-jumbo," Chen would have been "shovelling mud for life and living way below the international poverty line" if he had not had the chance to study English, and subsequently the opportunity to enrol in an institution in Beijing.[36] Immediately after the Cultural Revolution,

> [t]he radio talked about young heroes who had overcome severe difficulties and had made it to prestigious colleges. There was heroism, glamour, money, and cushy jobs awaiting those who crossed the threshold. A college education was money in the bank—getting there was as rare as hitting all six numbers in the lottery.[37]

Bourdieu, *Distinction: A Social Critique of the Judgement of Taste*, trans. Richard Nice (Cambridge: Harvard U P, 1984) 387.

[36] Da Chen, *Colours of the Mountain: A Memoir* (London: Arrow Books, 2000) 227; hereafter *Colours*.

[37] Chen, *Colours* 2000, 285.

Conscious of what English as a form of cultural capital can offer, the Chinese writers not only see the possession of it as a mark of social distinction but also strategically propagate it as an agency ensuring privileges and enabling social mobility. "I had long believed that there were advantages to learning English that were greater than just the ability to speak another language," Zhu Xiao-di confesses. "Now as a teacher, I wanted my students to benefit as well."[38] Nien Cheng offered, during the period of the Cultural Revolution, regular English lessons to a few eager learners. Her students included youngsters who later used English as a travelling ticket to America and others who considered English a stepping stone for personal advancement, economic and social. Teaching English has been considered a desirable profession; being proficient in English allows one to enjoy a wider portfolio of jobs. Two of Nien Cheng's students—a crippled girl and a former Red Guard—strove hard to acquire the qualification required to join the army of middle-school English teachers. Shortly following the death of Mao, the English Department of the Foreign Languages Institute in Shanghai, as those elsewhere across the whole nation, acquired prominence.[39] On their way to recruit qualified teachers, the party secretary of the Institute told Nien Cheng: "There is now a great need to teach our young people foreign languages, especially English."[40]

Literacy in English as a symbolic order of social distinction generates more than just "the money in the bank." Under the sway of the instrumental reason governing the use of English in the global context, these Chinese writers have reasons to choose English in their self-representation, and these reasons

---

[38] Zhu, *Thirty Years* 1998, 209.

[39] "Many changes occurred, beginning in 1979," observes Zhu Xiao-di. "In the cities, small private enterprises could take on second jobs. One booming market was continuing education, and evening classes mushroomed in the large cities. College teachers were in high demand, especially English teachers." Zhu, *Thirty Years* 1998, 211.

[40] Cheng, *Life and Death* 1995, 608.

reveal how the adoption of English actually encourages critical reflections upon the Chinese society from which these writers come and about which they write. For those who have brushed up their English during the Revolution, their experience of English reaches beyond the level of language skills and allows them to think more seriously about the values—cultural, political or symbolic—embedded in and embodied by English.[41] Zhu Xiao-di, later a student of Nanjing Normal University, sums up: "In college, I had learned much more through English than I had learned about English."[42] It may be worth our effort to ponder the difference between what Zhu has learnt "*through*" English and what he has learnt "*about*" English. Knowledge of English produces a more critical consciousness of Chinese society in which English was once banned. "English was a tool that could open our minds for perceiving things we would not otherwise be able to see," Zhu claims (187). And as he read more in English, he "became more critical of our society and the political system." Likewise, Jung Chang, who started to learn English during the Cultural Revolution, has "benefited enormously" from her ability to read English:

> With the help of dictionaries which some professors lent me, I became acquainted with Longfellow, Walt Whitman, and American history. I *memorized* the whole of the Declaration of Independence, and *my heart swelled* at the words "We hold these truths to be self-evident, that all men are equated equal," and those about men's "unalienable Rights," among them "Liberty and the pursuit of Happiness." These concepts were unheard of in China, and opened up a marvellous new world for me. My notebooks, which I kept with me at all times, were full of passages like these, *passionately and tearfully* copied out.[43]

---

[41] Cheng, *Life and Death* 1995, 506, see also 579, 608.

[42] Zhu, *Thirty Years* 1998, 209.

[43] Chang, *Swans* 1991, 631; emphasis added.

In English, Chang experiences "the thrill of challenging Mao openly in [her] mind for the first time."[44] After a decade of internal turmoil, the west and its civilization seem to be "rediscovered" in China and become a source of inspiration for some Chinese.

If indeed the west is the beacon of hope for the Chinese, English language becomes the passport to the land of freedom. Having moved and decided to remain abroad,[45] some Chinese memoirists feel they can write about their past without the fear of censorship. "Abroad, memory becomes an opportunity—however danger ridden—for a new kind of self-becoming that benefits from forcible distance from the mother tongue," asserts Vera Schwarscz.[46] What English has created for them is the opportunity to enter a cultural and political space of freedom. "Speaking for and on behalf of millions of Chinese," Zhu claims that "the best and most realistic hope was to go abroad, either on a short visit or as a permanent immigrant …, that seemed to be the only chance to enjoy modern civilization."[47] This is one of the reasons why he chose to study English.[48] For these Chinese writers who are still entangled in the web of horrible memories, writing in English is an experience of psycho-

---

[44] Chang, *Swans* 1991, 631.

[45] "I had decided already that I would never come back. I would die elsewhere, in some country that would accept me" (Cheng, *Life and Death* 1995, 651).

[46] "No Solace from Lethe: History, Memory, and Cultural Identity in Twentieth-Century China" in *The Living Tree: The Changing Meaning of Being Chinese Today*, ed. Tu Wei-ming (Stanford: Stanford U P, 1994) 65.

[47] Zhu, *Thirty Years* 1998, 212.

[48] "I was interested in many areas, including electronics and English. Finally, for two reasons, [father and I] decided that I should pursue an English major. First, my English was already much better than that of most of my peers, so I had a considerable competitive advantage. Second, with a good command in English, I might have a better chance to study abroad in the future." Zhu, *Thirty Years* 1998, 179.

logical condolence and allows them to reach a readership that
would readily understand and sympathize with them. Nien
Cheng, for example, needs a "new language environment" precisely because she feels "a compulsion to speak out and let
those who have the good fortune to live in freedom know what
[her] life was like in Communist China." As Cheng has suffered unjustly, it would seem better and safer to stage, far away
from her home country and in a foreign language, her recollec-
tions of the traumatic past and her open challenge to China's
inhuman treatment of political dissidents. The psychological
and emotional distance created by writing in English provides a
linguistic buffer in addition to the geographical and the temporal ones, which absorbs Cheng's pain from the past.[49] Once
back in Beijing and detached from the circle of his Western
friends, Wu Ningkun found it "practically impossible to continue working on" his memoir, for his mind "simply declined to
function in a sterile climate."[50]

A person who has not lived through a colonial history perhaps also needs a "tongue for sighing."[51]

Global Production in English

Indeed, it is English that has created these Chinese writers'
identity, has defined them as authors of their narratives about
themselves and about the nation; it is English that has made
them known to us. For sure, their choice of English as the language of transnational self-representation must have been
rooted in their earlier experience of the language either as for-

---

[49] Cheng, *Life and Death* 1995, 656.
[50] Wu, *Tear* 1993, x.
[51] Not without a sense of irony and perhaps humor, Achebe addresses the
social effect of colonialism: "on the whole [colonialism] did bring
together many peoples that had hitherto gone their several ways. And it
gave them a language with which to talk to one another. If it failed to
give them a song, it at least gave them a tongue, for sighing." Achebe,
"The African Writer and the English Language" 1975, 77.

bidden knowledge or as a subject of institutional study in China. The fact that English has allowed this group of writers to achieve wide international visibility shows that English, for them, is a form of empowerment, not just because it gives them a language to articulate but because it catapults them into the global system of circulation. We may wonder where *Wild Swans*, for example, would be published if written in Chinese. Would it still have the good fortune of being translated into twenty-five languages and selling over seven million copies world-wide and reaching number one in the best-seller lists over a dozen of countries?

Crossing not only one but multiple national borders, not only spatial but temporal boundaries, English has established itself as the international language of knowledge production, of the Internet and of international corporations after the demise of the British Empire.[52] Speaking of English in the context of globalization, Joshua A. Fishman writes: "the half century following the collapse of the former British, French, and American Empires has been witness to one of the most vigorous and lasting periods of economic expansion in world history."[53] The rapid growth of transnational corporations and the demand for linguistic uniformity reinforce each other. English has swiftly mastered the changing situations in the second half of the twentieth century: discarding its role as the "mask of conquest" and reinventing itself as the language of multinational enterprises and global capitalism.[54]

---

[52] Ferguson observes: "When the need for global communication came to exceed the limits set by language barriers, the spread of English accelerated, transforming existing patterns of international communication." Ferguson, *The Other Tongue* 1982, ix.

[53] Joshua A. Fishman, "Introduction: Some Empirical and Theoretical Issues" in *Post-Imperial English: Status Change in Former British and American Colonies, 1940-1990*, eds. Joshua A. Fishman, Andrew W. Conrad, and Alma Rubal-Lopez (Berlin: Mouton de Gruyter, 1996) 7.

[54] In *Masks of Conquest*, Gauri Viswanathan elucidates the relationship between the institutionalization of English in India and the exercise of colonial power. English teaching participates in the colonial project by

The success of these Chinese memoirs must be considered, therefore, in close relation not only to what they have to say about their authors and about China, but also to the global conditions under which they become popular readings. It is worth noting that most of the Chinese memoirs are not distributed in mainland China, and all of them are first published abroad, receiving funding from international publishing enterprises: Bantam Books, DoubleDay/Anchor, Flamingo, Indigo, Penguin Books, Vintage, to name just a few. The expansion of international corporations—publishing houses among them—blurs national boundaries, facilitates transnational movements, and puts the memoirs in the global systems of production and circulation. The function and importance of English, just in light of these publishing factors alone, should be so manifest to the Chinese memoirists, who desire to reach the largest possible numbers of readers.

Despite, more often because of, the need to abandon their mother tongue, the "exiled" Chinese writers, who manage to resort to English as an alternative vehicle of expression, enjoy, in most cases, privileged access to the international book market and a reading public larger than one that could possibly be pooled together in their homeland. The impressive sales of the Chinese memoirs written and published in English necessarily contribute to the debates about English as a discourse of power operating in the global market, especially considering the fact that "modern Chinese writing in English translation has not made much impact in English-speaking countries."[55]

---

way of controlling the minds and the practices of the "natives": "In the name of teaching the mechanics of the English language, the British government saw no violation of its own injunction against religious inference by providing religious instruction indirectly." Viswanathan, *Masks of Conquest: Literary Study and British Rule in India* (London: Faber and Faber, 1990) 3, 78.

[55] W. J. F. Jenner, "Insuperable Barriers? Some Thoughts on the Reception of Chinese Writing in English Translation" in *Worlds Apart: Recent Chinese Writing and its Audiences*, ed. Howard Goldblatt (London: M. E. Sharpe, 1990) 177.

English allows these Chinese authors not just to have a sense of fulfilment and to achieve a high degree of international visibility, but to join the international community of English. Entitled "How the book came to be written," the prologue of *A Single Tear* details how the project of recollecting and translating the author's experience is done, and has to be done, in the community of English. *A Single Tear* would never have been written, Wu says, "without the sustained and inspiring support of [his] family and so many dear friends." The "friends" referred to include Bill and Ann Burton, his American hosts, Sam and Marilee Anderson, his American neighbors, Professor Derek Brewer, chairman of the Faculty Board of English and Master of Emmanuel College, Valerie Myer, a distinguished writer based in Cambridge, and Richard Bernstein of the *New York Times*. Apart from the "inspiring support" that Wu receives from his friends, William Robinson and Eldon E. Fahs, president and vice president of Manchester College in Indiana, together have made Wu an "alumnus-in-residence" at their college for the year in which Wu, the "returned-expatriate," while enjoying "life-sustaining humane values," wrote his memoir in English.[56] The prologue is in a way an elaborate acknowledgement of his friends, neighbors, reviewers, colleagues, and publisher in America, who have "made" Wu "promise" to write an autobiographical essay and urged him "to make the fragment part of a whole" (ix-x). In short, it is the very luxury of the Western environment that has, on the one hand, created for Wu a measure of expression, and on the other, compelled him to write in the language of his hosts.

As part of the strategy of recognizing the West that provides the conditions of possibility for writing, almost all notes of acknowledgements in the Chinese memoirs pay special tribute to those who have helped their authors "search for the right word." Tokens of gratitude to Westerners, mostly Americans, who have helped the Chinese authors in the area of language,

---

[56]   Wu, *Tear* 1993, xi.

are unfailingly and lavishly paid. Standard lines like the following abound in the acknowledgements of these memoirs: "Thank you: Michele Smith for helping me with my English since I arrived in the United States,"[57] "I feel fortunate to work with my agent, Peter Robinson of Curtis Brown, and Alan Samson, my editor at Little Brown and Company (U.K.). I treasured their wise advice about my writing."[58]

Liang Heng, co-author of *Son of the Revolution*, is a college graduate majoring in Chinese language and literature. Having no formal training in English, Liang's contribution to the memoir, one can reasonably assume, is restricted to a recounting of his experience as "a good representative of his generation" and has to leave the final representation in writing to his co-author and wife, Judith Shapiro, "whose writing skill and knowledge of what a foreign audience needs to know about China," we are told, "make this book a delight to read."[59] Xu Meihong's "ordeal" was first written by Elizabeth Fernandez of *San Francisco Examiner*, who suggested the possibility of a book. And the experience indeed appeared later in the form of a book, after of course Xu received "enthusiastic" and "constant encouragement and support" from Sandra Dijkstra and substantial help from Larry Engelmann, Xu's American husband and co-author.[60] Co-authorship, or rather a "division of labour," between Chinese as the source of information and their Western partners as the "vehicle" of expression, is already indicative of some of the Chinese memoirists' embarrassment arising from their inability to express fully in English.

---

[57] Anchee Min, "Acknowledgements" in *Red Azalea* (London: Indigo, 1996).

[58] Mu, "Acknowledgements," in *Gate* 2000.

[59] Jerome Alan Cohen, "Foreword" to *Son of the Revolution* by Liang Heng and Judith Shapiro (New York: Vintage, 1984) x.

[60] Xu Meihong and Larry Engelmann, "Acknowledgements" in *Daughter of China: the True Story of Forbidden Love in Modern China* (London: Headline, 1999) vii; hereafter *Daughter*.

Unlike those writers from former colonies, who are inescapable from colonial education in English and are preoccupied with issues of political morality and national identity in language choice, a lot of Chinese writers are burdened *only* by the anxiety over their belated and limited exposure to English and their incompetence in the use of English.[61] They are not so much concerned, as Ngũgĩ would be, with the possible "danger" of English "preying" on peculiarities of the indigenous and national language as with their acceptability to their Western readers in the global market. Zhu Xiao-di's appreciation of the constructive role the editor has played in the production of his memoir might be seen as a special example of the effects of linguistic "intervention." He writes:

> American editors can almost *rewrite* authors' original manuscript. The value of the author lies primarily in providing unique materials that no one else can, and the editor is responsible for polishing and improving the style of writing. American writers themselves are used to, and appreciate, the editorial practice of massively revising and even *reconstructing* their manuscripts, an experience which [I] also share.[62]

Zhu's experience of the editor's active involvement in the production of his memoir unveils a process in which the collaboration between editor and author is more than just a linguistic intervention on the editor's part. The collaboration between Chinese and Western writers provides perhaps an

---

[61] Writers from former colonies are confined to writing in English, to the extent that some feel even more at home in English than in their native tongue. "The majority of African writers," Sridhar points out, "write only in English." Sridhar, "Non-Native English Literatures" 1983, 293.

[62] See Zhu Waiye, "Westerners Understand China through Reading: Zhu Xiao-di Talks about his New Book Thirty Years in a Red House," *Sampan* (December 4, 1998): 44; my translation.

example of what Fredric Jameson calls "late capitalism," in
which there is, for the first time in the history of capitalism, "a
new international division of labor."[63]

Jung Chang's gratitude to Jon Halliday, the editor of *Wild
Swans*, makes one wonder how much of the story originally
conceived by the author has survived the editing:

> Jon Halliday has helped me *create Wild Swans.* Of
> his many contributions, polishing my English was
> only the most obvious. Through our daily dis-
> cussions, he *forced* me into greater clarification of
> both the stories and my thoughts, and helped me
> search the English language for the exact
> expressions. I felt safer under his historian's know-
> ledgeable and *meticulous scrutiny*, and relied on his
> sound judgement.[64]

As the above piece of acknowledgement reads like an apol-
ogy, it tells the reader, before the actual text begins to tell its
own story, how Chang, as a non-native user of English, has
been placed in a "disadvantaged" position unable to perform
fully the task of an author, and how, with the help of her "editor," she is able to claim to the authorship of the book. Chang's
submission to Halliday's forceful editorial inter-vention is perhaps suggestive not only of the author's inability to find "the
exact expressions" and her inability to tell the story or to tell
the story in the right way, but more tellingly, of the Chinese
writer's desire to identify, at least linguistically, with her host
country. For some, like Nien Cheng, the question of English
competences is more related to an anxiety about recognition,
that is, about whether their use of English is acceptable to na-

---

63 Folker Fröber, qtd. in Arif Dirlik, "The Postcolonial Aura: Third World
    Criticism in the Age of Global Capitalism," *Critical Inquiry* 20 (Winter
    1994): 348.
64 Chang, "Acknowledgements" in *Swans* 1991; emphasis added.

tive English users.[65] As assistant to the manager of Shell's Shanghai office responsible for translating and drafting "more important correspondence the company had with the Chinese government agencies," Nien Cheng should not have found the linguistic barrier to be a serious challenge. The most rewarding moment for her in the struggle to write in English is perhaps when Arthur Miller recognizes her narrative power and "her amazing mastery of English."[66]

The case of exiled Chinese writers writing in English illustrates that linguistic hegemony could be developed quietly, as one group of people are compelled to learn the language of another, and as these Chinese memoirists seek identification with their American and British friends, neighbors, editors, and partners. In the collection of more than twenty Chinese memoirs, the imperial history of English is nowhere addressed. There is no sense that these writers are concerned with their identity, linguistic, national, or ethnic, and for them, the act of writing in English does not seem to entail a loss of the self. This striking lack of interest in the political implications of the imperial history and the current global dominance of English can perhaps be explained in terms of these writers' freedom from the experience of British colonialism. Taking for granted the legitimacy of writing in English, therefore, they feel free from the need to defend their language choice, a choice which is made in the recognition and acceptance of English as an in-

---

[65] In an attempt to establish the relation between language as "symbolic capital" and a "recognized power," Pierre Bourdieu writes, "The linguistic relation of power is never defined solely by the relation between the linguistic competences present. And the weight of different agents depends on their symbolic capital, i.e., on the recognition, institutionalized or not that they receive from a group." See "Price Formation and the Anticipation of Profits," in *Language & Symbolic Power*, trans. Gino Raymond and Matthew Adamson, ed. John B. Thompson (Cambridge: Harvard U P, 1991) 72.

[66] Arthur Miller, Review of *Life and Death* 1995, book jacket of *Life and Death*.

stituted language of cross-cultural articulation and representation.

But let us not forget that the Chinese do have a language
choice. Although the most widely studied language in China
today, English is not and has never been, as in the case of Africa, the national language of China.[67] Those postcolonial critics and commentators, who are constantly troubled by the state
of English in the former colonies, have yet to explain the continuing spread and use of English after the demise of the British
Empire, to delineate the path by which English is spread to
non-colonies like China, and to address the phenomenon of the
general trend of "consensual acceptance" by the Chinese writers of the hegemonic dominance of English as the de facto
world language. The debates between Achebe and Ngũgĩ mentioned at the beginning of this paper are significant for my purpose here, not just because the issues and questions raised by
them can help account for Chinese writers' choice of English
against the discursive postcolonial critique of cultural and linguistic imperialism, but more importantly because they direct
our attention to the differences between writers from former
colonies and Chinese writers, in terms of their attitudes toward
English and their preoccupations and concerns with regard to
the spread and politics of English.

---

[67] Foreign languages in China are often studied as additional languages,
and there is little concern about cultural imperialism at the back of them.
In Kachru and Nelson's "circles model" that describes the global
situation of English, China belongs to "the expanding circle," in which
English is "widely studied but for more specific purposes including
reading knowledge for scientific and technical purposes." Kachru & C.
L. Nelson, "World Englishes," in *Analysing English in a Global
Context*, eds. A. Burns and C. Coffin (London: Routledge, 2001) 13; see
also Kachru, "The Second Diaspora of English" 1992, 230-52. English
in China has been regarded as a transnational linguistic system and a
language of modernity rather than the language of certain nations.
Learning English, for most Chinese, is neither a threat to their Chinese
identity nor a reminder of British imperialism.

Said, in his recent memoir *Out of Place*, speaks of his ambivalences and ambiguities in relation to his split linguistic identity as a result of his early colonial education. "More interesting for me as author," Said writes,

> was the sense I had of trying always to translate experiences that I had not only in a remote environment but also in a different language. Everyone lives life in a given language; everyone's experiences therefore are had, absorbed, and recalled in that language. The basic split in my life was the one between Arabic, my native language, and English, the language of my education and subsequent expression as a scholar and teacher, and so trying to produce a narrative of one in the language of the other—to say nothing of the numerous ways in which the languages were mixed up for me and crossed over from one realm to the other—has been a complicated task.[68]

Like Said, the Chinese memoirists produce narratives of the self "in the language of the other" and from "a remote environment," but unlike Said they have shown no awareness of the kind of "split" that Said has experienced. Language "choice"— whether it is Achebe's, Ngũgĩ's, or the Chinese writers'—is not subject only to the history and practice of colonialism, neither is it just a matter of personal preference. For the writers from former colonies, that choice is made for them, and their adoption of English is innately linked to the history of the British Empire. In contrast, English in China is received with relatively less hostility, and most of the time is welcomed as a language

---

[68] Edward Said, *Out of Place: A Memoir* (New York: Vintage, 2000) xi-xii.

of modernity at different stages in the modern history of China.[69]

The situation created by global capitalism, of which English is a discursive part, helps to explain the proliferation and global consumption of the Chinese memoirs.[70] As the English language enters into this new phase of "late capitalism," it serves not only as a tool of various socio-political projects such as cultural imperialism, nation-building, or postcolonial resistance, but also as a commodity, a form of capital and power, whether discursive, social, or economic. In the studies of the politics of English, therefore, before we can return to the historical causes of the spread of English, it is important to recognize in the first place that the power has already fallen into the hands of the privileged. This is not to legitimize the global domination of one language, but on the contrary is to show how

[69] Travelling to China through a route and in a manner less patently imperialistic than the one it took to former nation-states, English has often been received by Chinese with relatively little resistance if not some enthusiasm. English has no doubt occupied a privileged position internally in China, especially prior to 1949 (cf. Phillipson, *Linguistic Imperialism* 1992, 30-31). There is a good amount of research done on the spread of English to China through trade, education, or the implementation of language policy. See, for example, Robert Hall, *Pidgin and Creole Languages* (Ithaca: Cornell U P, 1966); Q. S. Tong, "The Bathos of a Universalism: I. A. Richards and His Basic English" in *Tokens of Exchange: The Problem of Translation in Global Circulation,* ed. Lydia H. Liu (Durham: Duke U P, 1999) 331-54; Zhou Xiaoyi & Q. S. Tong, "English Literary Studies and China's Modernity" in *English in China: Interdisciplinary Perspectives,* Special Issue of *World Englishes* 21, no. 2 (2002): 337-48. Y. F. Dzau's *English in China* (Hong Kong: API, 1990) is perhaps the most comprehensive study of English in China. Despite their differences in orientation and emphasis, scholars all agree that China has been hospitable to English.

[70] Addressing a more general situation of Chinese writing in English, Cheng Chin-Chuan writes, "English is used primarily in international communication, and written English in China appears in publications mainly for international consumption." Cheng Chin-Chuan, "Chinese Varieties of English" in *The Other Tongue* 1983, 126.

the empire of English has reinvented itself after the demise of the British Empire as the language of what Michael Hardt and Antonio Negri call a new global empire,[71] and to remind us of how this fact alone requires a new set of discursive articulations about the politics of English.

---

[71] For Hardt and Negri, "Empire" is a concept that has no geographical or temporal boundaries. See *Empire* (Cambridge: Harvard U P, 2000) especially xiv-xv.

BOOK REVIEWS

**Vanessa Schormann, *Shakespeares Globe.
Repliken, Rekonstruktionen und Bespielbarkeit.*
Heidelberg: Universitätsverlag C. Winter, 2002,
xvii+399 pp.**

Why should theater people in command of palatial venues
equipped with the most efficient stage machinery and with
electronic controls for fabulous light and sound effects suddenly wish to perform on bare platforms? Or, equally strange:
Why should spectators used to climatized interiors and uphol-
stered seats be prepared to endure hard benches and the uncertainties of the weather? The answers are many, some historical,
some literary, some to do with tourism, some with academe,
but they all reflect the desire either to practice, to experience, or
to study long-lost forms of presentation believed to be invested
with unusual power and immediacy. How to perform Shakespeare's plays to the greatest effect has exercised the ingenuity
of actors, directors and designers for centuries. Architects are
relative newcomers to this band. Their rising importance shows
in the increase of Globe replicas during recent years, proof of a
global search for both innovation and authenticity, a wide field
indeed, and one admirably charted and surveyed by Vanessa
Schormann in her Munich dissertation.

The fierce debate raging around the recently re-erected London Globe ("authentic reconstruction" versus "essentially
kitsch—part of the heritage industry", 351) has tended to cloud
the fact that attempts to recreate the shape of Shakespeare's
stage go back almost two hundred years. The beginnings of this
reform movement were in Germany. Friedrich Schinkel, the
great architect of classicist Berlin and builder of the

Königliches Schauspielhaus (1818-1821), was one of the first to expostulate against "excessive decoration." He thought a symbolic indication of the place of action sufficient to stimulate the productive imagination of the audience. Subsequent nineteenth-century reformers rebelled against the tawdry realism of the average set and the grating stylistic dissonances from one set to the next in the same play. They wanted to be able to perform Shakespeare's text in the rhythm demanded by the words and the action onstage rather than the slow motion dictated by the scene-shifters backstage. In pursuit of this aim they reduced the décor and gradually weaned audiences away from expecting every scene to be topographically represented. However, the proscenium arch stages invariably had the effect of "framing" a scene as in a picture and inducing actors to go for tableau-like effects in which the dynamism of Shakespeare's dramaturgy was lost. The only means to overcome such pictorialism lay in the discovery of three-dimensional scenic space in which the experiments with so-called Shakespeare stages played an important part.

Among the early reformers three men stand out. Ludwig Tieck, Shakespeare translator and dramaturg in Dresden from 1825-1842, persuaded Gottfried Semper, famous architect of the Dresden opera house, to draft a plan on the basis of the recently discovered contract (between Phillip Henslowe and his partner Edward Alleyn and the builder Peter Street) for the building of the Fortune theater in 1600. Tieck already pleaded for a stage broad rather than deep to bring actors and audience closer together. Jocza Savits, originator of the Munich Shakespeare Stage (built inside the Munich court theater) which opened in 1889, increased the depth of the three-tiered stage by a rounded thrust and shed much of the décor then regarded as indispensable. William Poel, founder of the Elizabethan Stage Society (1894) and impressed by the Munich experiments, was the first to have a stage erected according to roughly the measurements given in the Fortune contract. It was a mobile construction intended to be fitted into conventional proscenium arch stages, easy to set up and dismantle, the so-called "Fortune fit-up." It must have fulfilled the ideal of a man who confessed himself "content with a balcony, a recess, two doors and the forward platform" (61).

From the early twentieth-century onwards there was also an increase of scholarly interest in the material conditions under which Elizabethan playhouses functioned. Was there an inner stage and, if so, what were its uses and its drawbacks? Was the stage platform rectangular or angled, i.e., narrower at the front? Where exactly were the pillars placed that supported the stage roof? Did the actors include them in their play? How was the balcony reached? How did 3,000 spectators fit into a "wooden O" of less than hundred feet in diameter? These and many other questions needed answering before the operation of an Elizabethan playhouse could be fully understood. But the limited documentary evidence meant that many answers either had to remain inspired circumstantial guesswork or that particular sources, like the famous drawing by the Dutch traveler Johannes de Witt of 1596 giving an inside view of the Swan theater, were analyzed and interpreted over and over again.

It might be supposed that theater people who only wanted some sort of working replica of an Elizabethan playhouse could not be troubled with the minutiae of scholarship. The opposite is the case. They and their architects were usually enthusiasts who had immersed themselves in the relevant research, and if they deviated from received opinion it was not for lack of knowledge. This becomes increasingly clear if one follows Dr. Schormann in her fascinating chronological survey of the nearly two dozen Globe theaters in Europe, North America, and Japan. The survey ranges from "The Earl's Court Globe" in London of 1912 through a number of mostly temporary and subsequently reused structures (called "The Old Globe" and erected at the instigation of a true Shakespeare devotee, the director Thomas Wood Stevens and his company) in Chicago (1933-34), San Diego (1935-36), Dallas (1936), Cleveland (1936), New York (1939); it studies the buildings serving the long-established Shakespeare Festivals in Ashland (Oregon), Cedar City (Utah), and Stratford (Ontario); it includes several German plus one Swiss and one Japanese Globes before moving on to its imperial theme: the London Globe Reconstruction (219–373) in a thoroughgoing investigation of what the stunned reader feels must be all its aspects.

In each case Dr. Schormann gives a brief history of the particular replica, lists the exact measurements, and discusses how far the structure tallies with what is known of the Globe and why it differs. She also includes interviews with present owners or operators of the venues, and with directors and actors about the "usability" of the stage for the performers. This is the core of the term "Bespielbarkeit" in her title. Do stage and auditorium form an ensemble in which Shakespeare's "Raumkonzept," a kind of unifying space, is in operation? Apparently some adaptations of Shakespeare's stage though ideal for the actors' free movement do not support this unifying effect because auditoria slanting away in an arena-type semicircle remove the audience to a distance where the direct interaction between actor and audience as a consequence of the true "Raumkonzept" cannot be achieved. Even in the more compact Globe structures this mutual exchange does not result as a matter of course. It may be hampered by obstructed sight-lines for part of the audience or because scenes on the balcony or in the recess lack in visibility or audibility. The advantages and disadvantages of each individual structure are discussed in necessary detail and the arguments supported by seventy-two ground-plans and photographs. Among the partial replicas the "Swan Theater" in Stratford-upon-Avon gets the best marks for "Bespielbarkeit."

> ... the proximity of actors and spectators and the communication between them here are central. It is a stage which demands movement and tempo ... In contrast to the reconstructed *Globe* in London there is no danger of *The Swan* being misunderstood as a

"museum theater"; on the contrary: the free adaptation of the original Shakespeare stage ... allows a
great deal of free experimentation ... (193).

What emerges from the historical part of this survey is the
complexity of the task confronting the planners of the London
Globe. Whereas previous builders could accept all manner of
compromises for their temporary solutions or, as in the case of
the permanent structures for the Shakespeare Festivals in the
U.S. and Canada, had to take the expectations of the tourist
audiences into account, the London Globe Reconstruction had
to meet more stringent demands; it was, at last, to be "the real
thing." Little wonder that from inception to completion (in
1997) the project took twenty-seven years, and the American
actor Sam Wanamaker, unflagging promoter of the cause, died
before he could see his dream realized. The decision to rebuild
the First Globe (burnt down in 1613) rather than its better
documented sequel, shows the desire to get as close to Shakespeare's actual venue as possible. Authenticity was the prime
concern also in the building materials used (e.g. the filling of
the panels between the oaken beams of the structure made of
"lathe, lyme & haire," as stipulated in the Fortune contract) and
in the techniques employed. Compromises due to modern
safety regulations except the resulting building on the Bankside
some two-hundred yards distant from the original site must be
accounted the nearest possible approximation to the place
Shakespeare worked in.

But is it also the place which conveys the authentic thrill to
modern actors and audiences? Dr. Schormann pursues this
question with critical acumen from the so-called "Prologue
Season" of 1996 onwards and registers both audience responses
and above all actors' experiences. Not surprisingly actors used
to working on proscenium arch stages who suddenly found
themselves hemmed in by audiences on three sides had to learn
how to engage the attention of the groundlings standing at their
feet as well as of spectators sitting in the last row of the third

gallery high above their heads. They soon realized that in spite of the relative closeness of the audience and the good acoustics they needed both to project their voices *and* to act in an expressive, demonstrative manner. Above all, they had to keep moving. No soliloquising, however deep and introspective, while rooted to the spot. The partially obstructed sightlines demanded a kind of acting in motion. "This stage requires the actor's absolute presence to three sides" (369). Even if the companies playing at the London Globe in the past years met this demand with varying success they all acknowledged the challenge exerted by the unusual space and the need to relate to an audience in eager, if sometimes unruly, expectation of contact with those onstage.

Is the London *Globe* a museum or a contemporary stage? Dr Schormann makes her position unmistakably clear. "The fascination of the London *Globe* lies in being both, a theater as well as a museum. But both institutions should remain distinct; form and function must be kept separate" (371). She doubts the validity of historicizing productions and pleads instead for the London *Globe*, in fact for Globes of all kinds, to be used as *contemporary* acting spaces "in which interaction and communication occupy first place" (71). This aim can be reached in replicas as well as faithful reconstructions as long as they contain the Elizabethan basics: a stage with at least two doors and a balcony at the back, two or three tiers of spectators' galleries on three sides of the stage, standing room for the groundlings to surround the stage, and identical lighting for stage and auditorium. Where such conditions obtain the performance "offers the chance for actors and audience to rub shoulders and together to experience the exceptional effect of Shakespeare's dramaturgy in relation to the space it originated in" (372). Dr. Schormann apparently is no purist. Replica and reconstruction are welcome if they serve the purpose of allowing or promoting living theater. A theater enthusiast's conclusion to a comprehensive, painstaking, and highly meritorious investigation.

Wilhelm Hortmann   Duisburg

Kwok-kan Tam, Andrew Parkin, Terry Siu-han Yip (eds.), *Shakespeare Global/Local. The Hong Kong Imaginary in Transcultural Production.* (Anglo-American Studies, vol. 17). Frankfurt am Main: Peter Lang, 2002. vi + 155 pp.

Shakespeare Global/Local is a book title that seems to sum up a core characteristic of Shakespeare's work and reception from the Renaissance to our own day. Expertly geared and adapted to the requirements of the London theaters and their audiences, Shakespeare's plays were clearly situated within a very specific theatrical and cultural context. Yet, what Jerome McGann said of what he saw as the best Romantic poems could also be applied to Shakespeare: "[S]uch works transcend their age and speak to alien cultures because they are so completely true to themselves, because they are time and place specific."[1] It is patently received wisdom that Shakespeare's work has, as it were, an ingrained global dimension. The themes and topographies of his plays covered the whole vista of the world, mythical as well as geographic, known to Europeans at the time, from Britain and its history to the furthest horizon constituted by the antipodes, which are mentioned five times throughout his works as the place with the greatest possible distance on earth.[2] Even during Shakespeare's lifetime, his plays already crossed with ease cultural and national boundaries, spread throughout Europe by strolling players,

---

[1] Jerome J. McGann, *The Romantic Ideology: A Critical Investigation* (Chicago: Chicago U P, 1983) 82.

[2] *3 Henry 6*, I.iv.135; *Richard 2*, III.ii.50; *The Merchant of Venice* V.i.127, *A Midsummer Night's Dream* III.ii.55; *Much Ado* II.i.249.

even travelling to India as early as 1607, as two performances of *Hamlet* are said to have taken place aboard the *Hector* under William Hawkins's command. When national identities started to ossify and cultural border controls were tightened, Shakespeare's works had the good fortune to be adopted as central cultural texts by the one nation which was to have the most widespread colonial impact. Worldwide dispersal of Shakespeare's plays thus profited twice: as cosmopolitan scripts which travelled easily across borders whenever this was possible, and again, as closely-guarded national treasures and thus as primary points of reference when nineteenth-century Britain saw itself on a mission to export such hallmarks of Britishness, "civilizing" and educating the world. Today, in our postcolonial times, it is, once again, the cosmopolitan, culturally open world of Shakespeare's plays which provides their global appeal, but this is further enhanced by the extended reach of the former British Empire where the ground, as it were, seems particularly well prepared for such re-readings of Shakespeare's plays.

Here, precisely, is the position taken up and explored by *Shakespeare Global / Local*, edited by Kwok-kan Tam, Andrew Parkin, and Terry Siu-han Yip, all of whom are professors at universities (CUHK and HK Baptist University) in Hong Kong. As this place of origin already suggests and the subtitle "The Hong Kong Imaginary in Transcultural Production" further indicates, the trajectory of this book takes up the multicultural genius loci of Hong Kong where East and West are said to meet as in few other places in the world. From this very stimulating point of reference the contributors to the volume take a look around at the Asian context, several examinations starting out from the specific situation in Hong Kong and English-language productions there, others exploring the wider crosscultural issues of the Chinese theatrical traditions, and the final two contributions introducing a comparative dimension by looking at the reception of Shakespeare in Japan.

While the setup of the volume thus remains kaleidoscopic rather than progressively structured or in thematic pursuit of an argument, all of these fragments presented in the individual contributions share in the cumulative effect of illustrating what the editors so succinctly maintain in their preface: "The significance of Shakespeare in Hong Kong and China today can be seen in the fact that the playwright has actually become a site of contestation between the global and the local imaginary in transcultural production" (vii). This central point of reference is further elaborated in Kwok-kan Tam's introduction, when he stresses the universal elements in Shakespeare even within the context of the English literary tradition. Concerning the possibilities of Shakespeare's "Asianization," he then shows that such transfer is definitely possible, making the English playwright "an important link in transnational culture" (8). Tam seems to echo McGann's above-quoted phrase when he concludes that "the globalization of Shakespeare lies exactly in its localizability" (8).

Tam then goes on to prove with a vengeance the former point of his introduction regarding Shakespeare's adaptability to Asian transitions by analysing Law Ka Ying's highly successful adaptation of *Macbeth* to Chinese opera as *Yingxiong panguo* (*A Hero Traitor*). This point is taken up by Jessica Yeung and extended to cover further examples of successful translations of Shakespeare texts into *xiqu* (traditional Chinese music drama). Yeung also foregrounds the political dimensions of Shakespearean theater, much against Richard Schechner's claims to see such cultural exchange "above petty politics" (25).

The following contributions by Mike Ingham and David Booth look at productions of Shakespeare in English Hong Kong and further afield in Asia in which they were involved, as actor and director respectively. Ingham's approch is deeply self-reflexive in so far as he realizes that the apparent ease with which Shakespeare can be brought to English-speaking audiences in Hong Kong can be treacherous and actually prevent a clear perception of the need for cultural re-contextualizations. Booth has important observations on the translation of a playtext into a successful performance in general and across cultures, ending on "the truth about what the texts really say" (54). The latter is of course a curiously dated version of understanding a text in general and a literary text in particular, although it can arguable claim to be ahead of its time with truth claims becoming fashionable again in our post-postmodern age.[3]

Returning to the details of cultural translation, Louise Ho then analyses what she calls "cross-references" (61). These are highly instructive even in their commendable modesty of only showing the way to a more comprehensive translation exercise which would acknowledge the fact that Shakespeare's cultural context, while historically dated in European terms, still easily tallies in many most interesting ways with Chinese forms of communication, such as the address of "uncle" or "aunt" to strangers of a certain age, or certain kinds of ritual politeness of decorum which Europeans seem to have got rid of in their fast-food culture, but which are currently alive in Chinese traditions (60).

Dorothy Wong and Daniel S. P. Yang in their respective contributions then provide a sweeping survey of the history of Shakespearean productions in Hong Kong, ranging from first stagings of Shakespeare for the entertainment of the British military stationed in Hong Kong in the nineteenth century to an ever-increasing sophistication and cultural appropriation in recent years with a proportionately growing number of performances in Chinese theaters. This development is confirmed by Michael Mullin, who looks at Shakespeare in Hong Kong from an international perspective.

---

[3] See Terry Eagleton, *After Theory* (London: Allen Lane, 2003) or Ihab Hassan, "Beyond Postmodernism: Toward an Aesthetic of Trust" in Klaus Stierstorfer (ed.), *Beyond Postmodernism* (Berlin: de Gruyter, 2003), 199-212.

It is not quite clear why this assessment of Shakespeare's Asian reception and appropriation is then interrupted by John Gillies's—in itself highly instructive—Australian perspective at Asian practices of staging and adopting Shakespearean texts, as the two following essays by Meng Xianquian and Sun Fuliang continue to chart the progress of Shakespeare's textual reception in China from its earliest instances to the present and, indeed, a look into the future. It will be gratifying to all readers to note that the development covered by Meng and Sun reaches from Lin Zexu's first translation of Shakespeare's name in the context of his rendering into Chinese of a British cyclopedia "in the process of learning foreign knowledge with the aim of resisting the foreign aggression" (116) all the way to the Sixth World Shakespeare Congress in Los Angeles in 1996, where a Chinese delegation of no less than eleven scholars was present and Fang Ping, one of the group, was a elected member of the executive committed of the International Shakespeare Association, thus fully establishing Chinese Shakespeare criticism as a tradition in its own right.

The final two contributions by Masae Suzuki and Koji Takao are most enlightening in so far as they can show parallels in the crosscultural reception of Shakespeare in Japan with those aspects discussed in a Hong Kong and mainland Chinese context. However, readers of this volume will need to pick out these parallels themselves and it is this structural disconnectedness which leaves the Japanese discussions dangling appendix-like at the end of a discussion of Chinese approaches to Shakespeare.

But these are a reviewer's minor nigglings in the face of the impressive achievement presented in this volume. In its crosscultural reach, its multifaceted reflections, its contributors' comprehensive knowledge of both Western and Eastern cultural traditions, and the general enthusiasm for a worldwide reception of Shakespeare's plays this book will remain an important work in Asian as well as global Shakespeare studies for many years. By virtue of its accessible style it can be read with great benefit by Shakespeare scholars and amateurs alike.

Klaus Stierstorfer　　　　　　　　　　　　　　　　　　　Münster

Peter Hulme and Tim Youngs (eds.), *The Cambridge Companion to Travel Writing.* Cambridge: Cambridge UP, 2002. 343 pp.

In recent years, international discourses of travel and their criticism have grown ever more prominent in cultural studies. Many readers have overcome their previous reluctance to take travel seriously as a research subject and have adjusted their tools of literary analysis to take into consideration a large body of writing linked to travel experiences made in different parts of the world over an extended period of time, often in the service of ideological interests defined by social and historical circumstances. This timely collection of essays edited by Peter Hulme (University of Essex) and Tim Youngs (Nottingham Trent University) continues previous attempts at inventorying true and invented accounts of travel, such as F. A. Kirkpatrick's elegantly written entry on the "Literature of Travel, 1700–1900" in volume fourteen of the *Cambridge History of English Literature* (1916) or Edward G. Cox's comprehensive *Reference Guide to the Literature of Travel, including Voyages, Geographical Descriptions, Adventures, Shipwrecks and Expeditions* (1935). It brings together specialists from various disciplines and areas of research including history, anthropology and geography, offering a broad and vibrant introduction to discourses of travel in Great Britain and the English-speaking world between 1500 and the present time in overlapping chapters. The most wide-ranging and substantial collection of its kind, the *Companion to Travel*

Writing features specially commissioned contributions addressing the specific aims and purposes of travel literature, including five essays surveying the respective period's modes of textual representation, a further seven concentrating on geographical areas of particular interest, and three final chapters addressing issues of theoretical and methodological import.

Conceiving their ambitious task, the editors admit to having encountered the serious problem of generic definition. They concede that unlike other, well-defined areas of study, critical discourses of travel have to bring their subject into focus; this is especially difficult since travel writing raises important questions with regard to the fundamental fictionality of all representation, the truth value of individual expression, and the genre's valences with colonial history and geography, not to mention literary concerns with authorial perspective. Due to the much acclaimed versatility and indeterminacy of the genre, Hulme's and Youngs's collection can therefore only provide "a tentative map of a vast, little-explored area" (1). Travel writing, the editors argue, has always been and is still so varied that it is not appropriate to describe it as a single form. In fact, its very heterogeneity and openness to multiple points of view is what appears to make out its specific potential, its particular "chance" as narrative mode consigned to the margins of a generic structure of literary forms. Travel discourse is by definition unhierarchical and decenterd: it provides a meeting ground for widely divergent cultural perceptions and modes of action. Moreover, it serves as a paradigm for testing new and interculturally defined approaches to reality. As Said puts it in *Orientalism*: "Travel books or guidebooks are about as "natural" a kind of text, as logical in their composition and in their use, as any book one can think of, precisely because of this human tendency to fall back on a text when the uncertainties of travel in strange parts seem to threaten one's equanimity."[4] Clearly, the textual organization of a travel narrative is prone to reproducing the haphazard nature of traveling itself; seen in more formal terms, travel books depend on the mediating techniques and strategies of literary fiction. Conversely, it has become a commonplace to argue that modern prose fiction has built its house on the "disputed territory" (6) of travel writing, bringing together the early modern focus on the centrality of the autonomous self, a new concern with empirical and factual detail, and the quest for new representations of otherness enriching and transforming western discourse. Dean MacCannell, in his pathbreaking study of modern tourism, goes a step further: For him, the emergence of travel discourse is a result of the crisis of European culture, an aesthetic response to the modern preoccupation with the growing fragmentariness of western experience.[5] Reacting to the dissolution of society, religion and morality, travelers and explorers invaded the domain of the cultural Other, forging actual differences in outward appearance into a unified design and subsuming the—nomadic, inexpressible, elusive—Other to their own view or perspective. Taking in possession even the remotest parts of the globe, Western travellers preserved and "musealised" everything that appeared to offer the promise of continuity and wholeness—for instance, premodern or "primitive" identities in colonized cultures—thus affording it a major position in western commodity culture.[6] The end of this process, only recently disrupted by the emergence of a postcolonial phenomenology of travel, has not led to more authentic experiences but, on the contrary, to an accumulation of *reflexive* experiences, of "simulacra" that synthesize fiction

---

[4] Edward Said, *Orientalism. Western Conceptions of the Orient* (1978; London: Penguin 1995) 93.

[5] Dean MacCannell, *The Tourist. A New Theory of the Leisure Class* (1976; Berkeley: U of California P, 1999). See also his *Empty Meeting Grounds. The Tourist Papers* (London: Routledge, 1992).

[6] See also Boris Groys, "Unsere Welt auf Reisen" in *DIE ZEIT* 29 (11 July 2002): 35.

and reality into a vast symbolism of touristic signs and signifying practices apparently existing outside concrete history.

The articles collected by Hulme and Youngs partly reflect this criticism. They point towards the important fact that travel is a form of cultural intervention; writing about one's encounter with a remote culture is to create an artificial yet intermediary space that constantly stimulates the traveler's consciousness, moving him to revise judgements passed on members of his own as well as on the other culture. Historically, this intervention has taken the shape of a narrative form seeking at once to overcome irreconcilable contradictions *and* to mystify the historical conditions which demand a powerful discourse of Otherness. Indeed, there is no single travel book that does not exemplify in itself a specific moment of perceptual crisis defined by historical and political circumstances. This is reflected in William Sherman's survey of travel writing produced between 1500 and 1720. He argues that part of the ideological effort taken by travelers in Elizabethan times was to challenge "European perceptions of English inaction and to promote new initiatives by showing that the English had been 'men full of activity, stirrers abroad, and searchers of the remote parts of the world'" (19). In this they were supported by an emerging new caste of merchants who sought to profit from the development of international trade after the defeat of the Spanish Armada, editors, such as Richard Hakluyt who published the first comprehensive collection of travel records in 1589 (*Principal Navigations, Voyages, Traffics, and Discoveries of the English Nation*), and printers for whom the growing number of travel accounts represented a reliable commodity in a profitable new business: In the early seventeenth century, books about travel came to occupy a central place on the bookshelves, with popular accounts of remote cultures emerging as one of the period's most flexible subgenres.

As the pilgrim gave way to the merchant and the merchant to the explorer or mundane philosopher, forms gradually changed (although the story is not quite so neat, as Sherman willingly concedes). A large cast of characters—pirates and ambassadors, captives and castaways—had their say in the shaping of the genre as we know it today. Already at that time, "complex rhetorical strategies" (31) served to secure travel writing's entrenched position between accepted literary genres on the one hand and new or emergent forms of documentation, portrayal and scientific investigation on the other. From the very outset, travel literature as a discursive mode based on an ethnographic impulse was caught in a kind of "aporetic circle," although Sherman fails to emphasize this point: With the old views and certainties threatening to dissolve under the impact of new encounters, different forms of knowledge had to be accommodated in an increasingly complex process of mediation relating patterns of meaning drawn from widely divergent and often conflicting fields of experience. Divorced from their primary cultural affiliations and ways of life, balancing "the known and the unknown" (31), English travelers had to find a place for the unfamiliar and the new in their received repertory of modes of description. The more they struggled to integrate these elements, however, the more they distanced themselves from their original domain of narrative and representative power. As a result, travel discourse was transformed to become a site of cultural exchange involving different perspectival concerns without epistemological correlative outside the text, an empty meeting ground indeed, leaving the writers with "acute problems of authenticity and credibility" (31)—a fact which accounts for the assurances of writers during the centuries that they would report only what their eyes had seen in remote parts of the world.

These truth claims would, in fact, be mocked in the fantastic voyages beginning to proliferate in the eighteenth century. Writings such as More's *Utopia* (1516) inspired both serious and satirical counterworlds from the seventeenth century onwards. The heroic exploits of English explorers were lampooned and parodied in a whole series of writings mixing the inventive mockery of writers like Joseph Hall (1574–1656) with the more solemn descriptions given by travellers such as William Dampier (1652–1715) and John Dunton (1659–1733). As James Buzard remarks in his essay on the *Grand Tour* in Europe between 1660 and 1840, the transition to a new age of travel writing was largely heralded by the new ideal of philosophical empiricism that had gained wide acceptance in Britain by the end of the Restoration. If knowledge is rooted in experience and nothing else, Buzard writes, travel naturally gains in importance and desirability. Thus, new ideas and arguments emerged, some of them devoted to promoting the ideal of travel in the service of self-improvement and education—preparing "young men to assume the leadership positions preordained for them at home" (38)—others to exploring the general *value* of traveling, rather than that of writing and publishing travel accounts. Issues of taste, manners and moral conduct entered the genre, inviting it to become more useful in the cultivation of a trans-European class consciousness. The Grand Tour, its proponents held, could usher the "unformed" young Englishman into that "domain of good manners and educated tastes which transcended single nations" (41). For several decades, Buzard notes, the major obstacle to extensive travels in Spain and Italy was the Catholic Church and the immorality associated with life in southern Europe: The "whore of Babylon" ... "whose corruption had led Christians astray" and under whose influence Rome had withered to a "squalid, impoverished town" (40). As fear and suspicion gradually gave way to a critical foregrounding of the pitiful conditions of life in Italy, the British were prepared to "take up the imperial banner" (40) from their fallen forerunner and to extend their picturesque "rambles" to countries and regions removed from the oversight of the protective middle classes. There was a great deal of optimism at that time that the creation of wealth and social change based on scientific discoveries might all be promoted to the mutual advantage of Britain and overseas areas.

Judging from what I have gathered from these remarkable essays, modern mass tourism and colonization seem to be related phenomena. The "paramount wish" of British subjects to hasten to the Continent once the treaty with France was signed and to pour, "in one vast stream" (46), across the Pas de Calais into the neighboring countries, parallels the growing interest in colonial expansion and the securing of imperial power gradually acquired in previous centuries. The energy greasing the wheels on which travel was heading into the provinces of modern mass tourism seems to have been identical to the force shaping the restless itineraries of a nation devoted to military adventure and to bringing large parts of the world into a position where it could be influenced or directly controlled. Roy Bridges, in his article on exploration outside Europe until the end of the Great War, stresses in particular the relation between travelling and the various kinds of indirect administration termed "informal empire" or "unofficial imperialism" (53). He maintains that changes in the relationship between Britain and the wider world tended to make travel writing more "obviously utilitarian" (53), more explicitly linked to practices of territorial surveillance, appropriation of resources and administrative control. Quite convincingly, he distinguishes between a "non-annexationist" Britain and one more distinctly implicated in the colonial enterprise and the national effort of overseas expansion. Focussing on travel writing's complex relationship with the situations in which it arose, Bridges yanks the rug from under the feet of those who still conceive of travel writing as a predominantly informative and therefore politically innocent form of textual production. Like a few other articles collected in the book, however, his essay suffers from a rather naïve conception of the written text as an outcome of events having taken place in the realm of political history. Here, it would have been more profitable to see the individual work not so much as a simple reflection of accredited social facts registered through participation and observation but as a model of ideological interpellation interwoven with the discursive reality of imperialism. It is not surprising, under theses circumstances, that Bridges leaves out two major examples of travel fiction of the period that strove to undercut the convenient construction of an "imperialism of improvement" propagated by Britain's political elite: both George Henry Borrow's *The Bible in Spain* (1834) and Alexander Kinglake's *Eothen* (1844), already immensely popular in their own time, must be seen as works expressing anxiety about the place of Western culture at a stage in history when commercial and industrial capitalism triumphed and colonial societies were rudely sacrificed to Britain's international interests. Both narratives worked in a literary mode deconstructing the values and attitudes of the high-minded Victorian reading public, featuring enchanting and stylized, antirealistic scenes and episodes calling into question the prevailing expansionist ideology and the culture of civilised rationality that supported it.[7] As Helen Carr points out in her critically more advanced essay "Modernism and Travel," imperialism needs "undoing as a 'coherent object'" (71); late Victorian colonialism, she holds, has been more variable and complex than has been generally acknowledged. In her view, it was during the later stages of modernism and with the almost programmatic dilettantism of travel writers like D. H. Lawrence and Robert Byron that a new consciousness was introduced into travel literature—a consciousness that has changed the outlook of the genre considerably in recent decades. With Carr's lively interpretation of the alienated modern vagabond in mind, what emerges is a revisionist account of travel writing as a dialectic mode of textual production concerned with revealing the interconnections

---

[7] For a detailed account see Ralph Pordzik, "Off the Beaten Track: Victorian Culture and the Refashioning of Late Romantic Travel Writing," *In the Footsteps of Queen Victoria. Wege zum viktorianischen Zeitalter*, ed. Christa Jansohn (Münster: LIT Verlag, 2002) 315-30.

between practical and imaginative discourses and registering the delegitimizing process taking place when different semantic and epistemological zones are negotiated. Looked at from this angle, travel writing is a kind of interstitial space in which different patterns of thought and forms of mediating knowledge can meet to enrich or subvert one another. Helen Carr touches on this important fact when she identifies a "double sphere of reference" (75) in modern travel fiction. In her view, the writing of pretentiously factual travelogues as part of the search for precise and accurate information has been rendered problematic by the very distinctions travelers sought to uphold and perpetuate: Processes of transculturation and modes of social interaction with the Other have slowly undermined their belief in the genre's positive identity and added a practical dimension of contact and exchange entailing its own transformational dynamics. Without openly acknowledging it, writers have required the conflict with the Other in order to demonstrate their narrative power; in the long run, however, this Other has turned against them to subvert and disperse their representational superiority.

The next chapters continue to explore the framework of expectations and assumptions within which colonial and postcolonial travel writing has been produced. On the increasingly beaten track of international travelling, their authors maintain, self-differentiation and rejection of mass tourism became a guiding purpose. Robert Byron and Bruce Chatwin have provided examples for this new type of traveler desiring to put a distance between himself and the burgeoning droves of commercial tourists. Subjected to the twin pressures of feeling both "one of a crowd" and "late on the scene," visitors to Europe, Asia, and the Americas found themselves at pains to find anything new to say about the hallowed sites opened to them. The aims of traveling turned "inward," so to say, and created in every individual mind the honorific sense of being somehow superior to the average tourist, answering a universal call for unaltered romantic landscapes, authenticity and unique experience. But not all writers shared this dismay at the growing democratization of travel. Creeping into their work was the fear that the world was losing its distinctive otherness, and the recognition that the lines of demarcation between Europe and the Other were becoming disturbingly blurred. The complexities of this mental change are worth spelling out, and in her essay on "The Middle East," Billie Melman contests the now common view that English travel to the Orient has been habitually informed by the asymmetry of power relations between Britain and the East. Referring to Edward Said's epochal 1978 study *Orientalism*, she claims that "neither the British experience of travel nor the diverse representations of this experience were homogeneous" (106). Rather than dividing the world into two unequal and "hierarchically positioned" parts, travelers' representations of the East were "inflected by gender, class, and nationality" (107). Quite compellingly, Melman rectifies distorted impressions by rethinking Said's one-sided view of cultural exchange and by going beyond Mary Louise Pratt's claim that western travelers "produced" the rest of the world for Europeans.[8] Her outstanding example is Jonathan Raban's *Arabia Through the Looking Glass* (1979) which marks a journey away from the explorers' construction of Arabia, acknowledging the fact that "modernisation, rather than controlling the Arabs of the Gulf states and ruining them, was controlled by them through acculturation" (118). Melman's revisionist effort is paralleled by the work of Neil Whitehead and Rod Edmond, the former examining how sociopolitical realities have defined the place of the Amazon in the colonial imagination and why this resulted in a "significant continuity in the aesthetics of travel writing" from the sixteenth century onwards (123), the latter showing how the Pacific region was constructed as a suitable space for the erotic desires and fantasies of western explorers. Especially Tahiti, the "Queen of the South Sea Isles," became the gold

---

[8] See Mary Louise Pratt, *Imperial Eyes. Travel Writing and Transcultura-tion* (London: Routledge, 1992) 5.

standard against which other Pacific cultures were measured, a "fixed term" in a whole series of comparisons between "different others" (140) constituted in the western traveler's imagination. Again, it is important to note that the arrival of postcolonialism on the agenda of travel writing seems to have changed much of that: As Rod Edmond shows, the tropes and literary conventions projected on the Pacific have been challenged by a younger generation of writers who so far have avoided falling into the trap of reproducing the clichés about Tahiti fashioned in the era of colonialist expansion. Some of these considerations are taken further by Tim Youngs in his article on African travel writing in which he emphasizes the fact that colonial images of the Congo as the "essence of Africa" (157) have been shaped not so much by observant Victorian travelers but by Joseph Conrad's modern masterpiece *Heart of Darkness*—a novel written in the years after Conrad's 250-mile trek from Matadi to Kinshasa in the service of the Société Anonyme pour le Commerce du Haut-Congo in 1890. Youngs demonstrates how in recent travel writing the notion of mythical Africa has been transformed through intertextual reference, deliberate cutting across previous explorers' accounts and other techniques taken from ethnography and journalism all of which work to create a revised, postcolonial image of the region. The most important individual text to have emerged from this process is Jeffrey Tayler's *Facing the Congo* (2000) in which the writer draws on the fact of Europe's invention of Africa as a "playground" (170) on which to solve its own existential dilemmas. What the various articles brought together in the "Sites" section all have in common is that they demonstrate how nostalgia for a lost Eden, for a "prelapsarian world free of the guilty burdens and prohibitions of Judeo-Christian cultures" (139), served as the main impetus behind many modern itineraries: Most of the writers visiting South America, the Pacific, India, California, Ireland, or Stanley's "Darkest Africa" were motivated by this sense of nostalgia for a taintless, unaltered reality and their propensity to look "elsewhere" for markers of authenticity. The quest for new pleasures, fresh images, simpler lifestyles and, last but not least, relief from the ills of metropolitan culture compelled them to move further and further into what they perceived to be the margins of the world; hence their insatiable desire to appropriate new spaces which for Europeans to control was becoming more and more difficult as the nineteenth century drew to a close. Some of the theoretical implications of this all-consuming desire for surveillance are explored by Mary Baine Campbell in her essay on "Travel Writing and its Theory," in which she dwells on the importance of intercultural and deconstructive readings ideally suited to texts that are "notably suspicious in themselves" (262). Only by drawing on research done in the field of interdisciplinary cultural studies, she argues, can we begin to understand the collectively produced discourse "surrounding and constituting a particular matter of social interest or action" (262). Seen in the light of current issues such as Diaspora, gender, and nomadism they all attend to, the "Site" and "Topics" sections of the *Companion* are therefore the most rewarding, densely packed with historical information and offering challenging views on the constitution of social and geographic locations through the cultural imagination of Western travellers. Many of the articles printed here refrain from providing large selections of authors and book titles without giving further attention to the specifics of the historical contexts wherein the texts were produced and received; only in a very few cases, the reader is left with an off-hand presentation of names and dates that jumps rather unexpectedly from a specific locality to a form of summarizing and generalized abstraction amenable to co-opting the very diversity and difference that gives rise to such complex and versatile writing.

These minor criticisms aside, readers interested in travel literature are well advised to take a close look at these survey essays and topical articles. It will most certainly strengthen their sense that travel writing is a broad and ever-shifting genre, with a complex history that has yet to be properly studied. Providing an extensive list of secondary reading and a detailed five-hundred-year chronology linking important historical events and publication dates, this carefully edited volume can legitimately claim to be of great interest to teachers and students of travel literature. Readers new to the field or looking for a particular information do not have to consult additional reference sources but can focus directly on the essays or the chronology. Indispensable key terms are defined in the introductory sections, while the individual problems of mediating cultures identified by later critics in the wake of deconstructivism and the New Historicism are engaged with in the final section. Especially in regard to issues of cultural transfer, global migration and postcolonial "writing back" (10) against Western modes of representing the encounter with an elusive Other, these interconnections are of inestimable help; above all, the reader is enabled to see formerly isolated problems and issues positioned in relation to corresponding developments and/or lines of argument. Moreover, the history of travel writing is presented not as a linear string of historically or causally related events narrated by western "specialists" but as an interrelated field or "mosaic" in which each text or major event fits into larger units and frames of discussion. The selected bibliography is the most representative one I have come across so far, conveniently divided into subcategories and profiles and listing earlier collections of travel criticism along with journals and specialized studies on individual areas and periods. By including works from different disciplines, the editors show they have taken note of the important fact that some of the most innovative studies in the field have been "hybrid" texts—incorporating and amalgamating various strands of thought and syncretic forms of theoretical approach to accommodate socially and culturally varying perceptions.

All in all, then, the *Companion to Travel Writing* is a book indicating that the topic in question deserves our academic interest. Travel narratives, the volume shows, raise important questions about the relation of self and other as well as the future of political relationships between Western and Eastern cultures; they raise to a new level of understanding the pressing conflict between North and South and call to mind the discontinuities governing processes of cultural exchange in a still largely Western-oriented global economy. In the field of literature, travel writing opens narrative analysis to neighboring disciplines and cultural traditions; it transforms the western reader's interpretive "gaze" by recasting the traditional exegesis of known texts and by bringing to light new, unheard-of ones. Peter Hulme's and Tim Youngs's collection of essays must be seen as an important signpost on the road to a better understanding of the meaning of travel and travel writing in a globalized world; as a fascinating compound of wide-ranging excursions in the field and as a scholarly and editorial effort in itself, this original project deserves our full critical recognition.

Ralph Pordzik   Würzburg

Marian Eide, *Ethical Joyce*. Cambridge: Cambridge UP 2002. x + 199 pp.

Scepticism assails the critic when he receives a study that claims to discuss whatever might be implicit in the phrase "ethical Joyce." Joyce's fictional work is an exceptional case of "the art of making," as Sidney defined "poetry," representing the paralytic social state of Ireland, undermining any settled principles and purposefully subverting the manifold discourses of authority and manipulation. For this reason, its association with the abstract and often normative notions of philosophical ethics appears to be esoteric, at least at first glance. Moreover, ethics has been a contested philosophical branch since classical antiquity. In its most general sense, it is concerned with values that guide human beings in making morally right choices. For this reason ethics is said to be an integral discipline which overarches political, economic, aesthetic and scientific activities. But the choice between alternative values is inevitably linked to the metyphysical problem of what the highest good or standard of valuation really is. In very practical terms, a political ruler may see the world divided into evil and good regimes, authoritatively laying down what good (certainly his own regime) and evil (the other) are. Simon Critchley recently counterbalanced political arbitrariness of this kind, outlining a conception of ethics for the sake of politics called "the justified Said," which "is a political discourse of reflection and interrogation, a language of decision, judgment, and critique that is informed and interrupted by the responsibility of ethical Saying."[9] In ancient times, preceding Plato's cosmic principles, Socrates assigned the right choice among alternatives of the external world to the critical intelligence of the individual. The "father of moral philosophy" praised human self-examination and intellectual inquiry, on which moral judgments should be based. (In *Ulysses*, for Stephen Dedalus, Socrates stands out for having learned "dialectic," not ethical principles, "from Xanthippe"; *U* 9.233-35). Socrates's ideas were refined and amplified by Aristotle, who put particular stress on the social aspects of ethics. Aristotle suggests that the principle of *megalopsychia*, which embraces moral qualities such as reason, sanity, greatness of soul, and moderation, should direct man's conduct and help him to contend with irrational desires.

Since Joyce's appropriation of Aristotle is well known and well documented, one would expect of a book on Joyce's ethics, or ethics in Joyce's fiction, to provide an answer, for instance, to the question of whether the philosopher's

[9] Simon Critchley, *Ethics-Politics-Subjectivity: Essays on Derrida, Levinas and Contemporary French Thought* (London: Verso, 1999) 167.

significance for the writer may be directly derived from the philosopher's pre-Christian "materialism," which differed substantially from the Judeo-Christian ethical ideals publicized in the Old and New Testaments. These ideals were in turn philosophically qualified by Aquinas, another of Joyce's spiritual authorities, who integrated Aristotle's principle of rational thinking into a system of dual valuation which was part of his theological cosmos. The critical elucidation of the "philosophical" prerequisites then might usher in the practical analysis of the fictional manifestation or critique of the ethical Cardinal values and their relationship with Catholic dogma, British colonialism, and Irish nationalism, as represented by Joyce. But neither Aristotle nor Thomas figure in Eide's book.[10]

This omission is metonymically significant. The study is, in fact, not concerned with historical philosophical ethics proper, but rather with a personal ethical construct which Eide derives from Levinas's and Derrida's subsequent notion of the ethical subject as responsible for the other[11] and from mostly French, feminist writings. What Eide calls "literary ethics," "implicit ethical practice," and "performative ethics" (2) are exercises in metaphysics which do not fit in easily (or at all) with Joyce's narratives. Her first thesis tells us that in Joyce's texts "ethics, which etymologically signifies both "character" and "habitat" [but one may add "custom" and "usage": so what?], might best be understood as an interaction between immediate and intimate processes (character) and more external and enduring structures (habitat)" (2). This proposition, however, stands for nothing less than a fundamental principle on which narrative and epic fiction are generally based. There remains no recognizable reason to introduce the concept of "ethics" and specially apply it to Joyce. Eide's second thesis is more

---

[10] Aquinas is not entered into the book's index; but Eco's reference to his esthetics (!) is mentioned in passing (31).

[11] See, for instance, Jacques Derrida, "Violence and Metaphysics: An Essay on the Thought of Emmanuel Levinas" in *Writing and Difference*, trans. A. Bass (Chicago: Chicago U P, 1978) 79-154.

convincing and surprising. She encourages us to consider that "ethics, as I am defining it, is an engagement with radical alterity, or difference, within the context of ultimate responsibility (which encompasses responsiveness) to the other in his or her habitat. The alterities that Joyce addresses in his fictions include the differences between text and reader, text and author, between genders in a marriage, generations in a family, nations in a colonial empire, and races in conflict" (3). Loudly crying "ethics," Eide flings herself into a round of poststructuralist interpreters of Joyce, as she herself admits in annotation six to the 'introduction,' mentioning Jacques Derrida, Margot Norris, Jean-Michel Rabaté, Stephen Heath, and Jacques Aubert, and elsewhere (see 32). In other words, the confusing title and the obsessive ubiquitous use of the word "ethics/ethical" throughout the text paradoxically lead the author to ambitious readings, augmenting and gracing "this ground-breaking approach" (148), which has become forceful and convincing in Joyce studies over the last two or three decades.

Eide's claim to have brought to light "Joyce's ethical theory" (4) amounts to a revelation no Joyce critic has ever made known. All one can say is that Joyce turned his attention to various philosophical and religious questions and that in Joyce criticism, a *functional* application of "ethics" may be occasionally found. Valente, for instance, referred to Joyce's "critique of ... the ethics/politics of identification," emphasizing that the writer's counter-representational stylistics served "ethico-political ends."[12] But to maintain, as Eide does, that Joyce set up an *ethical theory* is plainly sustained on the subjective reflection of the critic's mind. On a more positive note, the construction of "ethics" is the terminological, albeit metaphysical, means by which Eide discusses problems of subjectivity, the interactions between subjects, the exchanges

---

[12] Joseph Valente, *James Joyce and the Problem of Justice* (Cambridge: Cambridge UP, 1995) 191.

between the subject and the external social conditions, the location of the reader in a position between opposing claims and, last but not least, the political resonances embedded in the fictional world. In this context, to invent the argot of the "ethical" is unnecessary, as deconstructive, psychoanalytical, historicist, and juridical analyses of Joyce's work vigorously ascertain. By contrast, Eide ascribes ethical principles to Joyce with the express purpose of neutralizing his radicalism, positioning him in a "situation" which "demands that a subject communicate ethically across incommensurable difference. For Joyce the first ethical consideration is the experience and expression of sympathy within the preservation of difference. In other words, ethical response makes possible a communion that does not obscure necessary separation" (4). The politics of this approach is to bring Joyce under the control of feminist desire, which fashions and legitimizes itself through a Platonic conception of idealizing and idealistic "feminist ethics." Eide's main argument, then, is that "feminist ethics, like Joyce's, regards difference as the point of departure or basic assumption and proceeds interactively, often through models of sympathy or mutuality toward the other who is radically and even incommensurably different from the self who addresses him or her" (13). In this way, Joyce is well-nigh made Saint James' Aloysius, who smiles benignly on the misdemeanours and conflicts of this world and gives everyone his blessing, notably the truly feminist woman. Joyce himself might have noted that Marian Eide is going to "round up in her own escapology this canonisator's day".[13]

The strength of the book becomes perceptible when the reader ignores without further ado the term "ethical" and its implication of transcendental meanings. Chapter one deals with "the elliptical subject" (30), which Joyce defines in his narratives as unstable and decenterd. Eide suggests that the

---

[13] James Joyce, *Finnegans Wake*, rpt. (London: Faber and Faber, 1949) [1939] 428.

figure of the *gnomon*, which Joyce introduces in his story "The Sisters," indicates both the gaps evoking uncertainty and the necessary relationship of the subject to others (including the position of the reader). Further discussing Joyce's undermining of determinate meanings, Eide introduces Derrida's notion of *aporia* in order to unravel the threats of the "rhetoric of aposiopesis" (33); of the "impassable passage" (30) arresting the subject "in (t)his dilemma between doubt and desire, between wondering and wanting" (33); of the ambivalent position of the reader; and of the interpreter's open, contextual struggle with the text. Of particular interest is Eide's reading of Joyce's only play, *Exiles*, as what Joyce himself called a "revolt of women against the idea that they are the mere instruments of men."[14] In a sort of applied Derrida, she shows that Joyce explored this theme by way of "a series of *aporias*" (41). In this way, the crucial focus of the play is neither the dramatic friction between the protagonists nor their contrasting definitions of love but rather "conflict itself, the failure of understanding, the impassable passage, the impossibility of knowing" (47).

In chapter two, Eide examines "knowledge and errant pedagogy" (54), focussing attention on Joyce's representation of authoritarian pedagogy and its effects of either producing subjugation or resistance and protest. Drawing on this supposition, she discusses the first three chapters of *Ulysses*, exploring one of the most fascinating structures of meaning in Joyce's narrative works. Her main thesis is that, for Joyce, knowledge "rests on *making change*" (56). In this way, what happens in the novel is associated with "a time of considerable political *change*" (56) in Ireland between 1904 and 1922. Within the text, the political aspects are reflected through the punning association of "change" with the metaphor of the "coin," of "crowns" with "crown," "sovereigns" with

---

[14] Arthur Power, *Conversations with James Joyce* (New York: Barnes and Noble, 1974) 35 (quoted 41).

"sovereignty." Eide focusses attention on the fact that the narration of the story is dominated by Stephen's teaching methods, which are "heretical" (70) and parallelled on a wider scale by the heresy of his political and religious thinking. In this part of her book, Eide provides an exemplary insight into Joyce's literary method of disrupting "totalizing orthodoxies" (72) and mimicking the "illusory system of metaphorical truths" (73).

Chapter three on "opposition and fluid sensibility" turns to *Finnegans Wake* and in particular to Anna Livia Plurabelle's river language. Eide elucidates Joyce's artistic philosophy of drawing connections, from the "undoing (of) each certainty with the language of extended possibilities" (88) to interpretative acts which tend to "also constitute a public or political intervention" (85). In concrete terms, in the course of ALP's monologue upon her marriage to HCE, Joyce, according to Eide, "allows readers to see difference as not merely structurally oppositional and irresolvable" (102), yet also as "a transition into interdependence" (102). The marriage, thus, becomes a metaphor of the historical rape and colonization of Ireland by foreign masculine powers. The association of the marriage with political history gives voice to a Joycean understanding of history that is free of victim stasis and fundamentalist nationalism, but rather lays stress on the fact that colonization is strongly marked by ambivalence and mutuality. Eide's argumentation decidedly supports the recent trends of a revisionist view of Irish history. Thus, she summarizes that with regard to Revivalist discourses, "Joyce recognizes that ossified, stereotypical readings of history become less true as they become more stable" (105).

In chapter four, Eide engages in a biographical reading of the conspicuous subject of the exchange and interpretation of letters in *Finnegans Wake*. She argues that HCE's disturbing relations with his daughter Issy and her "resultant dissociation and feelings of guilt and culpability" record Joyce's caring "over-identification with Lucia," who suffered from advancing schizophrenia, "a preoccupation bordering on obsession with her disorder, and, most tragically, a fear of his own culpability in producing her schizophrenia" (111). Tracing the composition of Issy in detail, Eide is careful not to succumb to the biographical fallacy of conflating "Issy's multiplicity" with "Lucia's schizophrenia" (113). Yet on the other hand she ostentatiously insists on the correlation between the fictional portrayal of Issy and the writer's personal identification with his daughter. This relapse into the biographical method is evidently prompted by Eide's preoccupation with the ever-present notion of "ethics," which, for her, "defines one's responsibility to an other" (112). "Ethical representation" is, according to Eide's logic, "*partial* identification" (112), registering both the persona's sympathy to and difference from an Other.

This conception triggers a game of abstractions which are certainly legitimate within the realm of spiritual self-absorption: "Representing Lucia in his final work raised ethical questions for Joyce concerning the potential of characterization to usurp another, actual person's voice or self-definition, and also concerning the possible failure of that representation to acknowledge the gap or difference between the writer's concerns and desires and those of his subject" (112). The "ethiquethical fact" (*FW* 109. 21), ethics regarded qua ethics, appears to be nothing more than feminist "etiquette."

This subjugation of Joyce's fictional narratives under the pervasive dominance of a one-sided construct of "ethics" delineates the book's weakness, which, however, is neutralized by the power and vigour of its analytical passages.

Wolfgang Wicht   Potsdam/Krauthausen

Christine van Boheemen-Saaf. *Joyce, Derrida, Lacan, and the Trauma of History: Reading,*

Narrative, and Postcolonialism. **Cambridge UP, 1999. 227 pp.**

"Trauma-studies" is a new but fast growing field. It is for the most part an interdisciplinary venture, situated at the place where literature, philosophy, and psychoanalysis meet. The same site was occupied earlier by the various approaches that were called, in the late seventies and in the eighties, "deconstructionist" or "post-structuralist" and that developed out of the work of Roland Barthes, Jacques Derrida, and Jacques Lacan, first in France, later in the United Kingdom and the United States.

In the English-speaking world a further shift occurred. Under pressure from more "contextualist" recent approaches such as New Historicism, cultural and postcolonial studies, followers of Derrida and Lacan have opened up the strict text-centered and theoretical approach that celebrated unlimited semiosis. Part of this turn towards context was due to developments in Lacanian psychoanalysis when theorists like Julia Kristeva began to write about analytic practice and about the power of literary texts to embody the trauma of the writer on the one hand and to heal the reader by empathy on the other.

Trauma studies represents a successful attempt at interdisciplinary work: It belongs both to the field of mental health and that of human rights, and it addresses "pressing needs in the areas of domestic and communal violence, ethno-political violence and refugee trauma, and disasters of natural and human origin." Human tragedies in Rwanda, Bosnia, and Kosovo and natural disasters are central, as are historical catastrophes such as the holocaust and Vietnam. But trauma studies also looks at victims of domestic or personal violence. The establishment of university degree program, centers, and journals shows that, as the director of one such program puts it, "trauma is here to stay."

Obviously, given the object of study, the emphasis is on the disciplines of law, international politics, psychology, social studies. But central to trauma studies is also the need for victims to tell their stories and this has become the entry-point for literary scholars. They have started on the one hand to use literary techniques to analyze survivors' tales and on the other to study works of literature that have trauma as their overt or covert theme. Christine van Boheemen-Saaf's book *Joyce, Derrida, Lacan, and the Trauma of History* belongs to the latter subdiscipline.

The book's subtitle, "Reading, Narrative and Post-colonialism" signals the author's view that Joyce's "postmodern textuality" is related to the traumatic history of colonialism in Ireland. She suggests not only that Joyce's writing functions as an indirect "witnessing" of a trauma that itself remains unspeakable, but that the loss of a natural relationship to language in his work calls for a new ethical kind of reading: "The practice of reading becomes an act of empathy to what the text cannot express in words." In this way Joyce's texts turn into the "material location for the inner voice of Irish cultural memory." The central concern of the book is developed in a dialogue with literary theorists, philosophers and psychoanalysts (most centrally Žižek, Adorno, Lyotard, Homi Bhabha, Shoshana Felman, Mikkel Borch-Jacobsen) and on the basis of a roughly chronological discussion of Joyce's major works: *A Portrait of the Artist as a Young Man*, *Ulysses*, and *Finnegans Wake*. Finally, the author also offers a postcolonial corrective on the way Joyce's writing had an influence on the development of Lacan's psychoanalysis and of Derrida's thinking.

Such a full program in a book of just over two hundred pages does not make for easy reading and the author is not helped by the kind of sloppy copy-editing that one does not expect from Cambridge University Press. In one sense this book is a corrective to the "post-structuralist Joyce" (the title of a very influential collection of essays published by the same Press). Whereas the essays in that book, edited by Derek Attridge and Daniel Ferrer, celebrated the *jouissance* of radical *écriture*, the writing of a Joyce "who laughingly eludes the split between signifier and signified, and endlessly makes signification its own signified in the act of signifying" (177), Van Boheemen wants to shift her readers' attention to a sense of loss, to Freud's death instinct. Although this movement from freefloating signifiers to the realities of psychic and historical trauma does entail a form of recontextualization, the social, political, and historical contexts of Joyce's work remain strangely absent.

This book takes as its assumption that Joyce's works represent "the death-in-life of Irish experience" in what she calls a "traumatized discursivity." Van Boheemen argues that Joyce's modernist writing "opens up a new, intersubjective realm of communication which may help to make it possible to work out the heritage of the past and transform the ghostly uncanniness of the 'death instinct' into full discourse" (1). This has important implications for literary theory. First the author unsettles the distinction between literature and theory by arguing that literature may be a form of *theoria*. Second it offers a new perspective on the history of poststructuralist theory, especially the work of Derrida and Lacan, "as itself the product of a certain resistance against the trauma of history" and third it argues for a new kind of reading that "emphasizes the reader's responsibility to listen beyond the conventional systems of sign and structure, and claims the ethical obligation to hear the pain which may not have been expressed in so many words" (2). From that perspective this book represents a cross-polination of psychoanalysis and literature, of philosophy and postcolonial history.

But Van Boheemen's is a book of poststructuralist theory that seems to have little to offer to those who do not share its basic assumptions; readers who are not convinced by what Derrida and Lacan and others in their wake have written about language and literature, will find the theoretical arguments developed here extremely esoteric and of limited help in a better understanding of Joyce's work. This is not just true of

Van Boheemen's claims about the development of Lacan and
Derrida's thinking in which she gives a central role to Joyce's
work: She writes that Joyce's texts "made their ideas possible,"
I have elsewhere offered a completely different view.[1] The
author also makes momentous claims for the importance of
Joyce's works that are unfortunately backed up only with the
kind of psychoanalytical theory that outside of literary studies
has almost completely lost its influence. In this context it is
noted that "Joyce's embodied texts offer themselves as the
material locus of the truth of the unconscious of the historical
process" (26); that Joyce's "mimemis of loss" manages to
project "a writerly subjectivity propelled by the historically
traumatic nature of its inscription to self-dialectical repetition
as the only means of working this heritage out" (11, the
author's emphasis); *Finnegans Wake* "is the metonymic
materialization of the dissolution of meaning which history
perpetrated on Irish culture" (163).

Is it possible to argue these ambitious claims *outside* poststructuralist discourse? This does not seem to be the case. First
the central theoretical concepts are either so vague or so
absolute that most of the arguments could lead us anywhere at
all. The author's repeated use of phrases such as "I wish to see
this as ..." or "I propose we ..." or "I want to reclaim" is
revealingly symptomatic of the theorist's will to power. Despite
all the references to the "affective demands" on the reader
made by literature, the dominant impression in this book is the
sense of mastery in the theorist who through sheer will power
can see things as they really are. In her account, Lacan and
Derrida become like Shem and Shaun, characters in Joyce's
last book, and in effect they are psychoanalyzed by Van
Boheemen in the same way as they themselves had analyzed
Joyce. Derrida is blamed for only belatedly discovering that he
is an Algerian Jew and another critic's dedication of a book to
his "personal dead" is seen as symptomatic of his inability to

---

[1]   *The French Joyce* (U of Michigan P, 1990).

safeguard his text "from the infective threat of blurring and indistinction in Joyce" (40).

This is the theorist in the guise of the all-seeing, all-knowing psychoanalyst, who, by some never unexplained miracle, has herself escaped from the logic of transference that enables her to read the truth of others to which they themselves are blind (Freud's famous "sometimes a cigar is just a cigar"). What stops her readers from applying a similar logic to Van Boheemen's study? Should we perhaps find it significant or even symptomatic that the title of Joyce's first novel only appears here in a (sometimes even doubly) castrated form? Or might we find it interesting to point out the curious insistence, in the acknowledgements to a book that gives a central role to Poe's "The Purloined Letter," that the author has been unable to find a particular book in Dutch libraries? Let's hope not.

A second reason why this book's claims about Joyce's central role cannot be argued outside of a poststructuralist context has to do with the absence of a critical scrutiny of Joyce's relationship to his Irish background. Although she refers to critics who have written on the subject such as Joep Leerssen, David Lloyd, Declan Kiberd, and Enda Duffy, there is no awareness of the debates among these critics and in Irish historiography in general about nationalism, revisionism, or the role of the Irish language. Instead we find the assertion that underneath its seeming modernity, Joyce's work "participates in the sense of the traumatic nature of the Irish experience of those who now write in Irish" (13). How can we be certain if we don't read Irish? How do we know that the condition of being born Irish seems to be synonymous with "lacking a natural relationship to language" (50)? Are inhabitants of other nations lucky enough to have such a natural relationship?

References to an Ireland that is a concrete historical reality are scarce and when they do appear they are questionable. In a footnote we are told that the word "otherworld" fuses the material and the spiritual according to "Irish mythology." Which Irish mythology is that? And what is the central trauma of the Irish condition we are told about? The disappearance of the Irish language? Why is it then that there are still people who speak that language and writers who write in it? How can the author accuse another critic of "ignoring the cultural specificity of Joyce's Irish situation," if we are given no specific information about the nature of that situation nor of Joyce's complicated and changing attitudes towards what he refused to consider as his nation? What happened to Joyce when Ireland ceased being a colonial nation in 1922 and why did he refuse to become a member of the Irish academy and why did he retain a British passport? In this book specific historical questions are not even asked.

Paradoxically, this study would have been more coherent if it had entirely remained within the confines of a textualist poststructuralism. As long as the trauma in the title is that of representation and of a Lacanian split subject, there is no problem in maintaining an entirely theoretical and thus unassailable position. But when claims are made about the role of trauma in history and in a sociopolitical context, an author must leave the purely theoretical realm. We can then legitimately ask what the social, political and even ethic relevance is of implicit or overt comparisons between the trauma of representation and real traumatic events.

Van Boheemen has taken on the additional and contradictory burden of arguing on the one hand that the claims she makes for Joyce's writing constitute the writer's own conscious strategies and on the other that these may all be effects of language that he himself was unaware of. Where does she find evidence that *Finnegans Wake* is Joyce's "pedagogic attempt to inscribe racial darkness into Western culture on the eve of World War II"? And how can this be so when that same text "testifies, *beyond its knowing*, to the unspeakable moment of destitution and repression" (12, my italics)? Surely there is a fundamental difference between traumas *in* history and those traumas in the "form of unconscious knowledge or experience which resists memorization and is written in or on the body without our conscious awareness," especially if that knowledge "may translate itself from speaker to listener without articulate entry into language" (61). What a study of recent cases of so-called "repressed memory syndrome" has revealed is that in a world where trauma has become fashionable, the trouble with these kinds of memories is that although the psychic trauma may be real, its causes are fictional (self-induced or suggested by therapists) and do not correspond to anything outside of the sufferer's memory. Maybe this is what is so deeply problematic about theoretical trauma studies: Instead of providing a text-centered poststructuralism with a context, it only succeeds in turning history into a text.

Geert Lernout   Antwerp

Barbara M. Benedict. *Curiosity: A Cultural History of Early Modern Inquiry.* Chicago: U of Chicago P, 2001. 296 pp.

Benedict's exploration of the conception of curiosity in Early Modern England centers on the semiotic polyvalence of the words "curiosity" and "curious." The noun, of course, indicates both a mental inclination to investigate and pry, and a particularly intriguing object of that inclination, while the adjective describes not only the person who exercises curiosity, but also two possible aspects of the object of curiosity, either its oddness or its neatness. A related word, "curio" also plays a role in Benedict's discussion. Three of Benedict's five chapter titles also contain a bit of linguistic fun that subtly bolsters the underlying idea of the book. The titles of chapter one, "Regulating Curiosity," chapter two, "Consuming Curiosity" and chapter five, "Performing Curiosity," with their ambiguous gerunds, all invite the reader to ponder whether curiosity is in the subject or the object. Ultimately, Benedict shows us, early modern curiosity inheres in both subject and objects so powerfully that it is capable of turning the curious person into a veritable curiosity.

After establishing a theoretical framework in which curiosity is defined as "a transgression visually received" (3), " a sign of the rejection of the known as inadequate, incorrect, even uninteresting," "the mark of the peculiarly modern identity of the solitary searcher, the inquiring everyman, the democratic detective" (8), and "the transgressive desire to improve one's place in the world" (20), Benedict proceeds to use curiosity as an organizing principle to hold together divergent cultural phenomenon ranging from science to carnival. Her first chapter uses Restoration satirists' portrayal of "the scientist" (an intentionally anachronistic designation) as a springboard for a discussion of the perception of curiosity as dangerous and needing to be controlled or "regulated." Here she pits the members of the Royal Society against satirists such as Aphra Behn and Samuel Butler, seeing the latter as articulating the voice of conservative moral thought attempting to stave off the corrupting influence of the "social threats represented by the Royal Society"—threats of "a power [i.e., curiosity] unallied to traditional institutional structures" (70).

Chapter two moves forward to the early eighteenth century, when curiosity, as manifested in both empiricism and fashionable consumerism, is rampant, yet still (or even more than ever) perceived as dangerous and morally corrupt: It "still challenged traditional social values, and writers allying themselves to such values sprang to turn curiosity against itself" (71). Satirists such as Pope and Swift now stand in for humanistic values reacting against the objectification and commodification of human relationships implied by fashionable consumerism, attacking this objectifying consumption by portraying such consumers as prurient and ultimately self-consuming. In this rather complicated chapter, Benedict also introduces the genre of the "curious" periodical, publications that gave a "public language" to topics formerly considered off-limits for public discourse (sexual information specifically, in Benedict's discussion). Functioning as a now legitimate form of gossip, periodicals such as *The Spy, The British Apollo,* and *The Spectator* helped to form the modern subject, a subjectivity both fragmented and defined by curiosity.

Collecting curiosities and (female) gossip are tied together in chapter three, which depicts the transformation, during the book's period, of the portrayal of women, from being active perpetrators of curiosity in all its worst forms, to being themselves objects of curiosity (and/or collecting)—"curios." This transformation, Benedict argues, took place at least in part under the pressure of fear of women's increasing prominence and power in public life. The association between curiosity and destabilizing social ambition, a theme Benedict returns to throughout this piece, prompted renewed "indictment" of the evils of a particularly feminine curiosity, one associated with sexual prying and peeping and with impertinence. The power wielded by women thus appears as "a perversion of nature that made women monstrous." The triumph of the novel, with its "commodified" female characters, represents another form of control or usurpation of the feminine traits of curiosity and investigation. In an odd elision of women and sexuality, the chapter slides seamlessly into a discussion of collections of objects, specifically erotic artifacts: "[t]hese connections between investigation, possession, and sexuality worked to make women's curiosity into curiosity about women: the habit of collecting sex" (156-57).

Chapter four continues the motif of the "cabinet of curiosities," applying it now to the concept of (literary) connoisseurship and the professionalization of cultural production and critique. Benedict's discussion here focuses on a "channel[ing] of curiosity into safe forms" (200), specifically, "spectatorship of curiosities" through museum-going, and participation (of the general public) in the literary collecting of cultural elites, who functioned as approved literary guides. The powerfully subversive nature of curiosity nonetheless found outlets even within this neat, controlled schema, Benedict suggests: Gothic fiction "mocked the moral channeling of inquiry into a search for moral principles" and "refigured curiosity as the urge for personal enjoyment through the exploration of forbidden ideas" (201).

Finally, in chapter five, Benedict returns to the perceived dangers of curiosity as a threat to the social order. Fascination with "scientific" spectacles as well as with monsters and freaks, as expressed in the form of circuses and other exhibitions of abnormality are seen as controlled forms of transgression, which both license curiosity and at the same time help to defuse its dangerous power. Yet the power of the curiosity of the public fed into the literary elite's fearful fascination with the "force of unseen political and social power" (244). The ambiguity of Romantic protagonists such as Mary Shelley's monster testify to the frightening power of curiosity as a social force.

As my very rapid summary has perhaps already suggested, Benedict traces a few key themes—curiosity as transgression and its power to transform curious persons into curiosities— engagingly, if loosely, through a broad literary landscape. Benedict's somewhat unsatisfying efforts to fulfill the promise implied by the book's subtitle (*A Cultural History of Early Modern Inquiry*) will surely disappoint readers looking for a more empirically based analysis. Nonetheless, this is an artfully composed and fascinating exploration of a topic that the reader's own curiosity is likely to find irresistible.

Celestina Wroth

Bloomington

Renate Brosch, *Krisen des Sehens. Henry James und die Veränderung der Wahrnehmung im 19. Jahrhundert*. Tübingen: Stauffenburg Verlag, 2000. xiv + 568 pp.

"He and his neighbours are watching the same show, but one seeing more where the other sees less, one seeing black where the other sees white ... The spreading field, the human scene, is the choice of subject; the pierced aperture, either broad or balconied or slit-like and low-browed is the 'literary form'; but they are, singly or together as nothing without the posted presence of the watcher—without, in other words, the consciousness of the artist."[1]

In the foreword of *The Portrait of a Lady*, Henry James used the view through a window in order to render the endless opportunities to perceive reality. At the same time, he emphasized the central position of vision within his conception of perception and reality. In her habilitation thesis, *Krisen des Sehens. Henry James und die Veränderung der Wahrnehmung im 19. Jahrhundert* Renate Brosch employs both, a historicist as well as a contemporary approach. Ascertaining the quality of textual visibility within James' prose, she pursues the ever varying visual culture of the late nineteenth and the early twentieth century.

Brosch's study elaborates upon the "interdependence of visual reorientation and the novel construction of subjects and the world of things" (7). The conception of a subject needed to be redefined in accordance with exterior conditions and was beginning to be on the move. Emphasis is given to a novel evaluation of the visual. Here Brosch works upon the basis of one of the basic assumptions of "post-structuralist and semiotic theory, maintaining that perception is a culturally and historically conditioned act" (8). Perception is understood as a socio-cultural product which is malleable (4-6). James makes use of the gap between those reflections induced within the reader and those that are portrayed in the text itself which are drifting apart. Brosch analyzes a persisting and subversive process,

---

[1] *The Portrait of a Lady,* cf. Brosch, 123f.

sabotaging the works' reception continually. This study bluntly ignores approaches that consider James in psychological terms. "Other than traditional opinion, I do not consider James to be a "psychological realist" revealing the inner life of his figures. Instead, he creates a visual field around those figures, hence creating secondary meanings through associations that are able to influence the figures in a vague manner" (357). Thus, it is no longer the reception by a reader of traditional prose which is required but an open process that renders James our contemporary.

As his central paradigm, James considers visual perception to be a metaphor for any action of consciousness. Here and elsewhere, Brosch sees James as a precursor of James Joyce and Virginia Woolf. In anticipation of Woolf's and Joyce's nonlinear conception of time (371), James makes use of the spectator figure disassociating within a certain image, thus intimating Woolf's later somewhat mystic experiences of transgression. Vision is perceived as a primary means of cognizance, inextricably combining perception and comprehension (527). Brosch distinguishes between a male dominated "gaze" and a female "glance" and shows how the "gaze" was established in the Romantic age, implying a "rapt and worshipping manner of appraisal of nature and the beauty of art" (47). The actively looking, perceiving and realizing subject is defined in male terms and is complemented by the female subject, remaining silent. Brosch then is able to show how the "glance" associates itself in terms of a "saboteur, trickster" with the gaze (48). The male gaze as such is treachery and violent and is being sabotaged through female vision. "The possessive grasp of male vision within James's final novels is characterized in terms of presumption. Vision demanding male propriety and dominance of women are, in *The Princess Casamassima* and *The Golden Bowl* associated with excesses of consumer culture agreeably displaying their products everywhere. James locates these fetish-like glances within the visual onslaught of mass producing capitalism and its concomitant accommodation of perception to the requirements of consumer culture." Hence, James is by implication seen as a highly political author realizing and deconstructing the increasing accommodation of perception to the basic principles of a commodified culture.

Without explicity contributing to feminist cultural discourse, Brosch places her book in the context of feminist literary studies.[2] Brosch also explains how the central perspective and the order of vision between the sexes has become fragile and controversial (256). Michel Foucault has shown how the "aggregate of power increasingly centering on the life of the individual succeeds with an entire ensemble of discourses on sexuality and achieves a fusion of power and knowledge" (260). Brosch gains some profit from Foucault's research that brought considerable progress in theoretical discourse, particularly with regard to sexuality and historically malleable conceptions of the physical. Brosch takes her cue from a striking blank space in Jamesian research by analyzing visual interaction in his works. His epoch produced a subject realizing its pliancy within a process Brosch ascertains as synonymous with the act of vision (127). In her core chapter on the perceiver (3.0), she reads James against the background of Foucault who saw the space represented in Velazquez's "Las Meninas" as a basic sketch of the representational space of Enlightenment.

According to Brosch, James's obsession with the visual basically has two sides. His preference for this primary mode of perception is to be seen between the extremes of desire and renunciation, denial and rejection (154f.). Female vision is seen as distinct from male through an inferior pleasure in seeing as a substitute of participation (155). The possessive "gaze" is renounced owing to an intrinsic lack of interest. Above and beyond gender James elevated the perceiver to a central narrative construction in order to offer the denial of action as a

---

[2] Cf. footnote 100, p. 22.

solution for the perceived conflicts between aesthetics and morals.

Mixing spirituality, commerce, and desire James reveals the onslaught of goods and the ensuing fetishism. Wares and women used to being judged are combined and the affinity of sexuality and the exchange of goods becomes obvious. According to Calder, the proximity of "sex and money [is] often more intimate than that between men and women." The representation of female physicality is perfectly rendered in the "image of a prolific purse" in *The Golden Bowl* (288). In this novel, the "patriarchal gaze is obviously used as a strategy of dominance within capitalist laws of commerce and hierarchy" (287). Renate Brosch is able to show the deconstruction of patriarchy and economic principles of power within James' final finished novel (289).

An astute perception of the scope of Brosch's study is to be gained from the discussion of Henry James's perspicacious and revealing novel *The Ambassadors*. Here Henry James approximates his brother William James' philosophy by supporting the structure of time by metaphors sustaining the "unchronological flux of consciousness" (374). William James saw facts as a complex of various and invariant associations beyond unilateral causality (384). According to him, the individual dissociated into sustaining sentiments. The world was constructed through the subject's mutable impulses (385). In "Sacred Fount," James excessively imports the conjecture that reality only existed within the perceiver's consciousness. The impressionistic novel *The Ambassadors'* void of action is centered on the protagonist's consciousness and perception. "It seems as if James was trying to illustrate his brother's theories about cognizance in literary terms. Strether's interrupted images are spots of recognition within the flow of his experience. William James had emphasized the importance of images for qualifying leaps of thought. Images accompany recognition, whereas words simply awaken the following words: images are halting places in the stream of thought" (404 f.). While Henry admired his older brother, William James considered Henry to be superficial. Strether, as so many Jamesian protagonists, prevails among his challenge through renunciation. The girlish and virginal Strether James employs to maintain a fictitious asexual personal relationship (410). James blurs gender attributes in order to reveal "the conditional codes of perception" (410), making use of art and culture as systems of reference. The elimination of human interaction which is substituted by commodified human interrelations serving as a fetish becomes obvious in this novel. James's dismissal was initially based on his being read as a "eunuch" (213) and a representative of unmanly literature, "i.e. unmanly in terms of a traditional perception of masculinity as a commitment to action, to the dynamic and expansive and to the exterior." Brosch reveals the surrogate aspects of gender and shows how James conception of the visual is able to deconstruct the established order of vision (215). Hence, James is seen as a visionary author discovering the social conditions and arbitrariness of gender, transcending androgynous concepts of the author that were to emerge at a later point in time.

Vision is informed by sexuality and power as the most important relation to the exterior world in James's work. Sexuality and recognition are seen as different forms of dominance (539). Recognition and power are not to be separated and perception is recognized as the key to power as revealed through the "novel construction of the attitudes of the spectator among a commodified culture" (538). Perpetual accommodation is required within an unstable world redefining the interrelation of subject and world. Momentary states of feeling constitute the individual who is dynamic and erratic and is receptacle of increasingly contingent behavior. In contrast to Crary, Brosch does not discern any continuous innovation of vision in the nineteenth Century. "Instead, a complex interactive process of modernization and an obstinate use of traditional visual organization prevailed."[3] In James work, the description of paintings are "almost always informed by traditional perspective and organization, precise outline and statuary figuration as is known from conventional painting" (23). Radical innovation in literature is complemented by both traditional as well as innovative pictorial representation which is easy to consume.

James demanded an audience of "intense perceivers" (132) whose subtle perception he both required and formed. His texts called for a reader with pronounced epistemological rather than empathetic interests.[4] Brosch's insights become precarious when she claims that James not only tackled concepts of realism but also revealed how his representation "of viewers displayed the manner in which the relation of the subject and the object of perception is determined through the structure of power" (138). In his work, the perceiver is implicitly and explicitly elevated. The perceiver is the most important textual element (145) and is negotiated into a position occasionally close to the limits of language (147). "Strether in *The Ambassadors,* Milly in *The Wings of the Dove,* and Maggie in *The Golden Bowl* all have their sudden shock of recognition from a balcony or a similar elevation" (145). The recognition which might eventually occur is "almost always painful but it also leads to a higher level of consciousness" (213). However, Brosch shows that James's representations of literary vision deconstructs the established hierarchy of vision and renders the Surrogate aspects of gender obvious (215). *The Wings of the Dove* is seen as the sum of James's work. This novel comprises all "accounts of literary structures and strategy in terms of vision and perceiver: It contains the experience of transgression of the perceiver, first Susan's, then Milly's" (452).

---

[3] Cf. Jonathan Crary, *Techniken des Betrachters. Sehen und Moderne im 19. Jahrhundert* (Dresden, Basel: Verlag der Kunst, 1996) 17.
[4] Footnote 126, p. 518.

As psychoanalysis directs its "neutral" attention to the slightest and to the violent particles of the unconscious, the text indifferently places the most shocking abyss of human life next to the most banal words in an excess of difference" (455). In his last phase, James pursued the visual concentration of the "representation of power and the desire to dominate and made that the central topic of his work" (461). Literature became the medium of elaborate discourses on perception, consciousness and identity. Henry James shares considerably "in a shift of paradigms which accounted for privileges and hierarchies on the basis of cultural arguments rather than economic" (533). Brosch has shown how literature became a conduit of elaborated discourses on perception and she proves convincingly that James employed both modes of seeing simultaneously as a means of perception and the execution of power. Thus, Henry James is moving on the same level as his culture on the way to a consumer culture whose desire is informed by both, power and sexuality. Eventually, recognition and sexuality are "shown as different forms of dominance" (539). The reader may profit from a variety of inspiring insights in the visual arts from Edweard Muybridge to Edouard Manet and Claude Monet with regard to their preference of the contingent moment. Perhaps he might eventually also understand James's development from initial rejection (23) to enthusiastic endorsement (386f.) of Impressionism. The road to recognition in James's work is precarious and full of unfathomable dangers. Recognition can only be achieved as a particular glimpse of reality. In its totality, truth is not to be ascertained (198). Renate Brosch's book is a contribution to Henry James studies offering art historians as well as literary scholars immeasurable profit.

Wolfgang Werth   Duisburg

LIST OF CONTRIBUTORS

Rüdiger Ahrens has held a chair of English Studies at the University of Würzburg, Germany, since 1980. As a visiting professor he worked at the universities of Cambridge (UK), Beijing, Tokyo, Nanchang, Guangzhou, and Vancouver. He was awarded an honorary professorship by the Jiangxi University of Finance and Economics (P.R. of China) in 1994 and a honorary doctorate by the University of Caen (France) in 1996. From 1990 to 1994 he served as vice-president of the German Association of University Professors. He was also a Fulbright grantee in the U.S. (1978), a grantee of the Volkswagen Foundation (1979-1989), and in 1990 he won an endorsement of the German Research Council to visit several universities in Australia. In 1995, he was granted a government stipend by the Canadian Council to carry out research in Vancouver and Toronto. He is a member of numerous national and international societies such as IAUPE, MLA, German Shakespeare Society, and Goerres Society. In 1995, he was elected a member of the European Academy of Sciences and Arts. Among his books are *Die Essays von Francis Bacon* (1974); *Englische literaturtheoretische Essays* (2 vols., 1975); with E. Wolff, *Englische und amerikanische Literaturtheorie* (1978-79); with H.W. Drescher and K.H. Stoll, *Lexikon der englischen Literatur* (1979); *Amerikanische Bildungswirklichkeit heute* (1980); *W. Shakespeare: Didaktisches Handbuch* (1982); with H. Antor, *Text—Culture—Reception. Crosscultural Aspects of English Studies* (1992); with W.D. Bald and W. Hüllen, *Handbuch Englisch als Fremdsprache* (1995); with L. Volkmann, *Why Literature Matters. Theories and Functions of Literature* (1996). He is editor of three scholarly series:

Anglistische Forschungen (Heidelberg); *Anglo-American Studies* (Bern, Frankfurt, New York), and *Grundlagen der Anglistik und Amerikanistik* (Berlin). From 1998 to 2000 he served as dean of faculty at his university. In 1999 he was granted the Order of Merit of the Federal Republic of Germany. In 2004, he was awarded the Order of the British Empire (OBE) by the English Queen and in 2005 the International Peace Prize by the American Biographical Institute.

Samuel Baker is an assistant professor of English at the University of Texas at Austin, where he specializes in British Romanticism. He is currently at work on a book about British Romantic writers and the sea, in which he argues that the Romantics formulated the idea of universal culture within imaginative horizons given by their experience of maritime empire.

Douglas Bruster is associate professor of English at The University of Texas at Austin. He is the author of several books on Shakespeare, including *Drama and the Market in the Age of Shakespeare*; *Quoting Shakespeare: Form and Culture in Early Modern Drama*; and *Shakespeare and the Question of Culture: Early Modern Literature and the Cultural Turn*.

Liu Dan graduated from the Foreign Studies College of Nanjing University and received her MA degree in English language and literature in 1997. She is a lecturer in the Continuing Education College of Beijing Language and Culture University, teaching various courses on English language and literature. Among her published articles on English literature and English language teaching are "Inner Reality and *To the Light House*" and "Imitation or Plagiarizing—On Thornton Wilder's *The Skin of Our Teeth*." She also co-edited several books, including *Cambridge Young Learners' English (Band Three)* (1999) and *Training on Reading Comprehension for PETS 5* (2000).

Scott Paul Gordon is associate professor of English at Lehigh University. He has published *The Power of the Passive Self in English Literature, 1640-1770* (Cambridge UP, 2002) and has recently completed a study of eighteenth-century female quixotes that explores texts by Mary Wortley Montagu, Charlotte Lennox, Sarah Fielding, Sophia Lee, Ann Radcliffe, and Tabitha Tenney. Gordon has written numerous articles on seventeenth- and eighteenth-century subjects, including "Reading Patriot Art: James Barry's *King Lear*" in *Eighteenth-Century Studies* (2003).

Sandra Gottfreund, born 1974, studied Anglo-American literature and history at Mainz/Germany, Bergen/Norway, and Middlebury/USA. Having completed her Ph.D. in English studies with a dissertation on the applicability of systems theory to an analysis of technologies of feminine subjectivity in modernist texts, she now is holder of a research grant and teaches at the English department of Mainz University. Her current work focuses on the gendering of flânerie into flâneuserie and a literary genealogy of violence from the late eighteenth to the early twentieth century.

Hildegard Hammerschmidt-Hummel has been teaching English literature and culture at the Universities of Marburg and Mainz since 1977. From 1979 to 1982, she served as Consul for Cultural Affairs at the German Consulate General in Toronto. As the long-standing senior research scholar and editor of the research project "The Shakespeare Illustration," funded by the German Research Council (Bonn) and the

Academy of Sciences and Literature (Mainz), she greatly enlarged and edited the Shakespeare Illustration Archive's collection at the University of Mainz (since 1996 at the Mainz Academy of Sciences and Literature), founded by the late Professor Dr. Horst Oppel (Marburg). In 1995, she was able to prove the authenticity of the Darmstadt Shakespeare death mask (Hessian State and University Library, Darmstadt) as well as the Shakespeare portraits "Chandos" (NPG, London) and "Flower" (RSC, Stratford-upon-Avon). Her results were confirmed by further evidence in 1996 and 1997-98. Dr. Hammerschmidt-Hummel has published numerous articles in scholarly periodicals and national newspapers, edited (together with Modris Eksteins) the Toronto Symposium volume *Nineteenth Century Germany* (1983) and has written several books (all published in German, some with summaries in *English and American Studies in German. A Suppl. to 'Anglia,'* 1973, 1981 and 1993): *The Historical Drama in England* (1972); *The Import Commodities of the City of London and their Impact on the Life-Style, Language and Dramatic Literature of Elizabethan England* (1979); *The Shakespeare Illustrations by the Frankfurt Painter Victor Müller in the Städelsches Kunstinstitut* [Frankfurt am Main] (1990); *20th-Century Dream Theories and the Dreams of Shakespeare's Characters* (1992); *Shakespeare's 'Dark Lady'* (1999); *The Hidden Existence of William Shakespeare* (2001); *William Shakespeare: His Time—His Life—His work* (2003); and *Shakespearian Illustrations (1594-2000). Pictorial Representations to the Plays of William Shakespeare: Catalogue, History, Function and Interpretation.* With a Dictionary of Artists, a Classified Bibliography and Indexes. Compiled, authored and edited by H.H.H. 3 vols. With 3100 illustrations in black and white (2003) and *William Shakespeare: The Authentic Images* (under preparation—c. 2005-06).

Ruth Y. Hung is a Ph.D. candidate in Oriental Studies at Oxford University and is currently working on a project on radical intellectuals and their ambiguous relationships with the political and social establishment in China.

María Jesús Martínez Alfaro is lecturer at the Department of English of the University of Zaragoza (Spain), where she teaches English language and literature. She is the author of *Text and Intertexts in Charles Palliser's* The Quincunx (Ann Arbor, U of Michigan P, 1996) and coeditor of a collection of articles entitled *Beyond Borders: Re-defining Generic and Ontological Boundaries* (Heidelberg, C. Winter, 2002). She has also published numerous articles on postmodernist literature, focusing on such issues as metafiction, parody, and intertextuality, as well as on the work of writers like John Fowles, Peter Ackroyd, Toni Morrison, and Charles Palliser, among others. Her research so far has developed within the wider projects of several research teams working on postmodernist fiction and ideology.

Nic Panagopoulos is assistant professor of English at Southeastern College, The American University of Athens. His research has mostly focused on the philosophical presuppositions of Conrad's fiction, and he has published two books on this subject: *The Fiction of Joseph Conrad: The Influence of Schopenhauer and Nietzsche* (1998) and *Heart of Darkness and The Birth of Tragedy: A Comparative Study* (2002). He is also interested in the aesthetics of the stage and has written essays on Conrad's theatrical adaptations of his own novels.

Karl Ludwig Pfeiffer is professor of English and comparative literature, University of Siegen (Germany). He has been a visiting and distinguished visiting professor in several

American, Japanese and Brazilian universities, a visiting fellow
at Harvard and a fellow of the Humanities Research Institute of
the University of California, Irvine, as well as of the Japanese
Society for the Promotion of Science (twice). His teaching and
research, while based on literature, have gradually also moved
into the domains of comparative media and cultural studies.
His most recent books are *Das Mediale und das Imaginäre.
Dimensionen kulturanthropologischer Medientheorie* (Frankfurt am Main: Suhrkamp, 1999) and *The Protoliterary. Steps
toward an Anthropology of Culture* (Stanford: Stanford UP,
2002). He has written more than 100 articles and edited/
coedited books on, among other topics, style, materialities of
communication, paradoxes and cognitive dissonance, writing
and the history and cultural role of the humanities and of
theory.

Ralph Pordzik has taught English and American literature at
the Universities of Bayreuth, Essen, Munich and Freiburg. He
is author of several books and has published widely in various
journals in and outside Germany. Publications include:
*Signaturen der Postmoderne: Lyrik als Paradigma post-
moderner Literatur* (1996), *Die moderne englischsprachige
Lyrik in Südafrika 1950-1980* (2000), *The Quest for
Postcolonial Utopia. A Comparative Introduction to the
Utopian Novel in the New English Literatures* (2001) and *Der
englische Roman im neunzehnten Jahrhundert* (2001). He has
edited, together with Hans Ulrich Seeber, *Utopie und Dystopie
in den neuen englischen Literaturen* (2002) and is currently
working on a book on the American short story.

Ian Simpson Ross is professor emeritus of English, The University of British Columbia, and Fellow of the Royal Society of
Canada; author of *Lord Kames and the Scotland of His Day*
(1972), *William Dunbar* (1981), and *The Life of Adam Smith*

(1995); coeditor with Ernest C. Mossner of *The Correspondence of Adam Smith* (1987), and editor of *Contemporary Responses to Adam Smith: On the Wealth of Nations* (1998). He has written and lectured extensively on Scottish literature and thought and is now preparing a second edition of the Smith biography.

Klaus Stierstorfer is professor of English at the University of Münster, Germany. He studied English language and literature and theology at the Universities of Regensburg and Oxford. In 1993 he received his Ph.D. at the University of Oxford and moved, after a teacher training program for secondary education in Bavaria, to work as assistant professor at the University of Wuerzburg, whence he moved on to Duesseldorf in 2001. His publications include *John Oxenford (1812-1877) as Farceur and Critic of Comedy* (Frankfurt: Lang, 1996); with Heinz Antor (eds), *English Literatures in International Contexts* (Heidelberg: Heidelberg UP, 2000); (ed., intro., annot.), *London Assurance and Other Victorian Comedies.* Oxford World's Classics (Oxford: Oxford UP, 2001); *Konstruktion literarischer Vergangenheit: Die englische Literaturgeschichtsschreibung von Warton bis Courthope und Ward* (Heidelberg: C. Winter, 2001), also forthcoming, in an extended and revised version, with OUP in 2005; and several other books and book contributions and articles on a variety of issues in the study of literature in English.

Robert Weimann is professor of drama at the School of Arts, University of California (Irvine) and honorary professor at the Humboldt University (Berlin). From 1985 to 1993 he was president of the *Deutsche Shakespeare Gesellschaft* in Weimar. Two of his most important publications are *Shakespeare und die Macht der Mimesis* (1988) and *Authority and Representation in Early Modern Discourse* (1996).

Wolfgang Wicht was, until his early retirement, professor of English literature at the University of Potsdam. His publications include *Woolf, Joyce, Eliot: Kunstkonzeptionen und Künstlergestalten* (1981), *Utopianism in James Joyce's "Ulysses"* (2000) and a number of recent articles on various aspects of Joyce's works. He has published papers on Shakespeare, Woolf, Eliot, Yeats, Wilson Harris, and the representation of the Caribbean locus, Heaney and others.

STYLE SHEET FOR *SYMBOLISM*

Contributors are requested to observe the following rules when preparing their MSS:

The text should be single-spaced, footnotes single-spaced as well. Footnotes should be placed at the bottom of the page and numbered consecutively through the whole MS.

1. Italics are used for foreign words in the English text, for titles of books, plays, poems, etc. Articles in periodicals or books are enclosed in double quotation marks (no italics), titles of periodicals etc. are given in italics.

2. Double quotation marks are used for all quotations not separated from the context. Quotations of more than two lines should be separated from the context and indented on the left and right margin (0.5 cm) without quotation marks.

3. Bibliographical references are given in the footnotes in full at first occurrence and then in shortened form (see examples). A bibliography should thus not be added.

4. Please supply a copy of your MS on an Windows-compatible computer disk.

6. Please enclose an abstract of your essay (10 to 15 lines) and a short biographical note referring to your special field of interest and to your major publications (up to 10 lines). Both will be printed in the respective volume.

Sample bibliographical references:

Northrop Frye, *Anatomy of Criticism: Four Essays*
(Princeton: Princeton UP, 1957) 85.
Subsequent references: Frye, *Anatomy* 1957, 85.

James L. Rosier, "Design for Treachery: The Unferth
Intrigue," *PMLA* 77 (1962): 1-7, 6.
Subsequent references: Rosier, Unferth Intrigue
1962, 6.

Beowulf: A Student Edition, ed. George Jack (Oxford:
Clarendon, 1994) 15.
Subsequent references: Jack, *Beowulf* 1994, 15.

Isabell Allende, "Toad's Mouth," trans. Margaret Sayers
Peden, *A Hammock beneath the Mangoes: Stories from
Latin America*, ed. Thomas Colchie (New York: Plume,
1992) 83.
Subsequent references: Allende, Toad's Mouth 1992,
83.

Other bibliographical references should observe the
conventions set out in *the MLA Handbook for Writers of
Research Papers* (Sixth Edition).

VERY IMPORTANT:

- Please always send a hard copy (print out) of your
  article/review with your disk.

- Make sure that printed and disk versions are identical. If
  there is a difference then please state clearly which version
  should be regarded as final.

- Label your disk properly giving exact details regarding software and operating system used.

- Label your disk with your address.

- Always retain a backup copy of your disk.

- Do not hyphenate words at the end of a line. Use only one hyphen for compound words.

- Do not use Hard Returns except when absolutely necessary, such as at the end of paragraphs, headings.

INDEX

Due to technical difficulties that arose during production, the Index for this volume has regretfully been omitted. A complete Index for Volume 6 will appear in Volume 7 of Symbolism.